Śrī Caitanya-caritāmṛta

BOOKS by
His Divine Grace A.C. Bhaktivedanta Swami Prabhupāda

Bhagavad-gītā As It Is
Śrīmad-Bhāgavatam, Cantos 1-5 (15 Vols.)
Śrī Caitanya-caritāmṛta (17 Vols.)
Teachings of Lord Caitanya
The Nectar of Devotion
Śrī Īśopaniṣad
Easy Journey to Other Planets
Kṛṣṇa Consciousness: The Topmost Yoga System
Kṛṣṇa, The Supreme Personality of Godhead (3 Vols.)
Transcendental Teachings of Prahlād Mahārāja
Kṛṣṇa, the Reservoir of Pleasure
The Perfection of Yoga
Beyond Birth and Death
On the Way to Kṛṣṇa
Rāja-vidyā: The King of Knowledge
Elevation to Kṛṣṇa Consciousness
Kṛṣṇa Consciousness: The Matchless Gift
Back to Godhead Magazine (Founder)

A complete catalogue is available upon request

International Society for Krishna Consciousness
3764 Watseka Avenue
Los Angeles, California 90034

All Glory to Śrī Guru and Gaurāṅga

ŚRĪ CAITANYA-CARITĀMṚTA

of Kṛṣṇadāsa Kavirāja Gosvāmī

Antya-līlā
Volume Five

"The Confidential Pastimes of Śrī Caitanya Mahāprabhu"

with the original Bengali text, Roman transliterations, synonyms, translation and elaborate purports

by

HIS DIVINE GRACE
A.C. Bhaktivedanta Swami Prabhupāda
Founder-Ācārya of the International Society for Krishna Consciousness

THE BHAKTIVEDANTA BOOK TRUST
New York · Los Angeles · London · Bombay

Readers interested in the subject matter of this book
are invited by the International Society for Krishna Consciousness
to correspond with its Secretary.

International Society for Krishna Consciousness
3764 Watseka Avenue
Los Angeles, California 90034

Library of Congress Catalogue Card Number: 73-93206
International Standard Book Number: 0-912776-77-3

First printing, 1975: 20,000 copies

Printed in the United States of America

Contents

Introduction

Śrī Caitanya-caritāmṛta is the principal work on the life and teachings of Śrī Kṛṣṇa Caitanya. Śrī Caitanya is the pioneer of a great social and religious movement which began in India a little less than five hundred years ago and which has directly and indirectly influenced the subsequent course of religious and philosophical thinking not only in India but in the recent West as well.

Caitanya Mahāprabhu is regarded as a figure of great historical significance. However, our conventional method of historical analysis—that of seeing a man as a product of his times—fails here. Śrī Caitanya is a personality who transcends the limited scope of historical settings.

At a time when, in the West, man was directing his explorative spirit toward studying the structure of the physical universe and circumnavigating the world in search of new oceans and continents, Śrī Kṛṣṇa Caitanya, in the East, was inaugurating and masterminding a revolution directed inward, toward a scientific understanding of the highest knowledge of man's spiritual nature.

The chief historical sources for the life of Śrī Kṛṣṇa Caitanya are the *kaḍacās* (diaries) kept by Murāri Gupta and Svarūpa Dāmodara Gosvāmī. Murāri Gupta, a physician and close associate of Śrī Caitanya's, recorded extensive notes on the first twenty-four years of Śrī Caitanya's life, culminating in his initiation into the renounced order, *sannyāsa*. The events of the rest of Caitanya Mahāprabhu's forty-eight years are recorded in the diary of Svarūpa Dāmodora Gosvāmī, another of Caitanya Mahāprabhu's intimate associates.

Śrī Caitanya-caritāmṛta is divided into three sections called *līlās,* which literally means "pastimes"—*Ādi-līlā* (the early period), *Madhya-līlā* (the middle period) and *Antya-līlā* (the final period). The notes of Murāri Gupta form the basis of the *Ādi-līlā,* and Svarūpa Dāmodara's diary provides the details for the *Madhya-* and *Antya-līlās.*

The first twelve of the seventeen chapters of *Ādi-līlā* constitute the preface for the entire work. By referring to Vedic scriptural evidence, this preface establishes Śrī Caitanya as the *avatāra* (incarnation) of Kṛṣṇa (God) for the age of Kali—the current epoch, beginning five thousand years ago and characterized by materialism, hypocrisy and dissension. In these descriptions, Caitanya Mahāprabhu, who is identical with Lord Kṛṣṇa, descends to liberally grant pure love of God to the fallen souls of this degraded age by propagating *saṅkīrtana*—literally, "congregational glorification of God"—especially by organizing massive public chanting of the *mahā-mantra* (Great Chant for Deliverance). The esoteric purpose of Lord Caitanya's appearance in the world is revealed, his co-*avatāras* and principal devotees are described and his teachings are summarized. The remaining portion of *Ādi-līlā,* chapters thirteen through seventeen, briefly recounts his divine birth and his life until he accepted the renounced order. This includes his childhood miracles, schooling, marriage and early philosophical confrontations, as well as his organization of a widespread *saṅkīrtana* movement and his civil disobedience against the repression of the Mohammedan government.

The subject of *Madhya-līlā,* the longest of the three divisions, is a detailed narration of Lord Caitanya's extensive and eventful travels throughout India as a renounced mendicant, teacher, philosopher, spiritual preceptor and mystic. During this period of six years, Śrī Caitanya transmits his teachings to his principal disciples. He debates and converts many of the most renowned philosophers and theologians of his time, including Śaṅkarites, Buddhists and Muslims, and incorporates their many thousands of followers and disciples into his own burgeoning numbers. A dramatic account of Caitanya Mahāprabhu's miraculous activities at the giant Jagannātha Cart Festival in Orissa is also included in this section.

Antya-līlā concerns the last eighteen years of Śrī Caitanya's manifest presence, spent in semiseclusion near the famous Jagannātha temple at Jagannātha Purī in Orissa. During these final years, Śrī Caitanya drifted deeper and deeper into trances of spiritual ecstasy unparalleled in all of religious and literary history, Eastern or Western. Śrī Caitanya's perpetual and ever-increasing religious beatitude, graphically described in the eyewitness accounts of Svarūpa Dāmodara Gosvāmī, his constant companion during this period, clearly defy the investigative and descriptive abilities of modern psychologists and phenomenologists of religious experience.

The author of this great classic, Kṛṣṇadāsa Kavirāja Gosvāmī, born in the year 1507, was a disciple of Raghunātha dāsa Gosvāmī, a confidential follower of Caitanya Mahāprabhu. Raghunātha dāsa, a renowned ascetic saint, heard and memorized all the activities of Caitanya Mahāprabhu told to him by Svarūpa Dāmodara. After the passing away of Śrī Caitanya and Svarūpa Dāmodara, Raghunātha dāsa, unable to bear the pain of separation from these objects of his complete devotion, traveled to Vṛndāvana, intending to commit suicide by jumping from Govardhana Hill. In Vṛndāvana, however, he encountered Rūpa Gosvāmī and Sanātana Gosvāmī, the most confidential disciples of Caitanya Mahāprabhu. They convinced him to give up his plan of suicide and impelled him to reveal to them the spiritually inspiring events of Lord Caitanya's later life. Kṛṣṇadāsa Kavirāja Gosvāmī was also residing in Vṛndāvana at this time, and Raghunātha dāsa Gosvāmī endowed him with a full comprehension of the transcendental life of Śrī Caitanya.

By this time, several biographical works had already been written on the life of Śrī Caitanya by contemporary and near-contemporary scholars and devotees. These included *Śrī Caitanya-carita* by Murāri Gupta, *Caitanya-maṅgala* by Locana dāsa Ṭhākura and *Caitanya-bhāgavata.* This latter text, a work by Vṛndāvana dāsa Ṭhākura, who was then considered the principal authority on Śrī Caitanya's life, was highly revered. While composing his important work, Vṛndāvana dāsa, fearing that it would become too voluminous, avoided elaborately describing many of the events of Śrī Caitanya's life, particulary the later ones. Anxious to hear of these later pastimes, the devotees of Vṛndāvana requested Kṛṣṇadāsa Kavirāja Gosvāmī, whom they respected as a great saint, to compose a book to narrate these episodes in detail. Upon this request, and with the permission and blessings of the Madana-mohana Deity of Vṛndāvana, he began compiling *Śrī Caitanya-caritāmṛta,* which, due to its biographical excellence and thorough exposition of Lord Caitanya's profound philosophy and teachings, is regarded as the most significant of biographical works on Śrī Caitanya.

He commenced work on the text while in his late nineties and in failing health, as he vividly describes in the text itself: "I have now become too old and disturbed in invalidity. While writing, my hands tremble. I cannot remember anything, nor can I see or hear properly. Still I write, and this is a great wonder." That he nevertheless completed, under such debilitating conditions, the greatest literary gem of medieval India is surely one of the wonders of literary history.

This English translation and commentary is the work of His Divine Grace A. C. Bhaktivedanta Swami Prabhupāda, the world's most distinguished teacher of Indian religious and philosophical thought. His commentary is based upon two Bengali commentaries, one by his teacher Śrīla Bhaktisiddhānta Sarasvatī Gosvāmī, the eminent Vedic scholar who predicted, "The time will come when the people of the world will learn Bengali to read *Śrī Caitanya-caritāmṛta,"* and the other by Śrīla Bhaktisiddhānta's father, Bhaktivinoda Ṭhākura.

His Divine Grace A. C. Bhaktivedanta Swami Prabhupāda is himself a disciplic descendant of Śrī Caitanya Mahāprabhu, and he is the first scholar to execute systematic English translations of the major works of Śrī Caitanya's followers. His consummate Bengali and Sanskrit scholarship and intimate familiarity with the precepts of Śrī Kṛṣṇa Caitanya are a fitting combination that eminently qualifies him to present this important classic to the English-speaking world. The ease and clarity with which he expounds upon difficult philosophical concepts lures even a reader totally unfamiliar with Indian religious tradition into a genuine understanding and appreciation of this profound and monumental work.

The entire text, with commentary, presented in seventeen lavishly illustrated volumes by the Bhaktivedanta Book Trust, represents a contribution of major importance to the intellectual, cultural and spiritual life of contemporary man.

—The Publishers

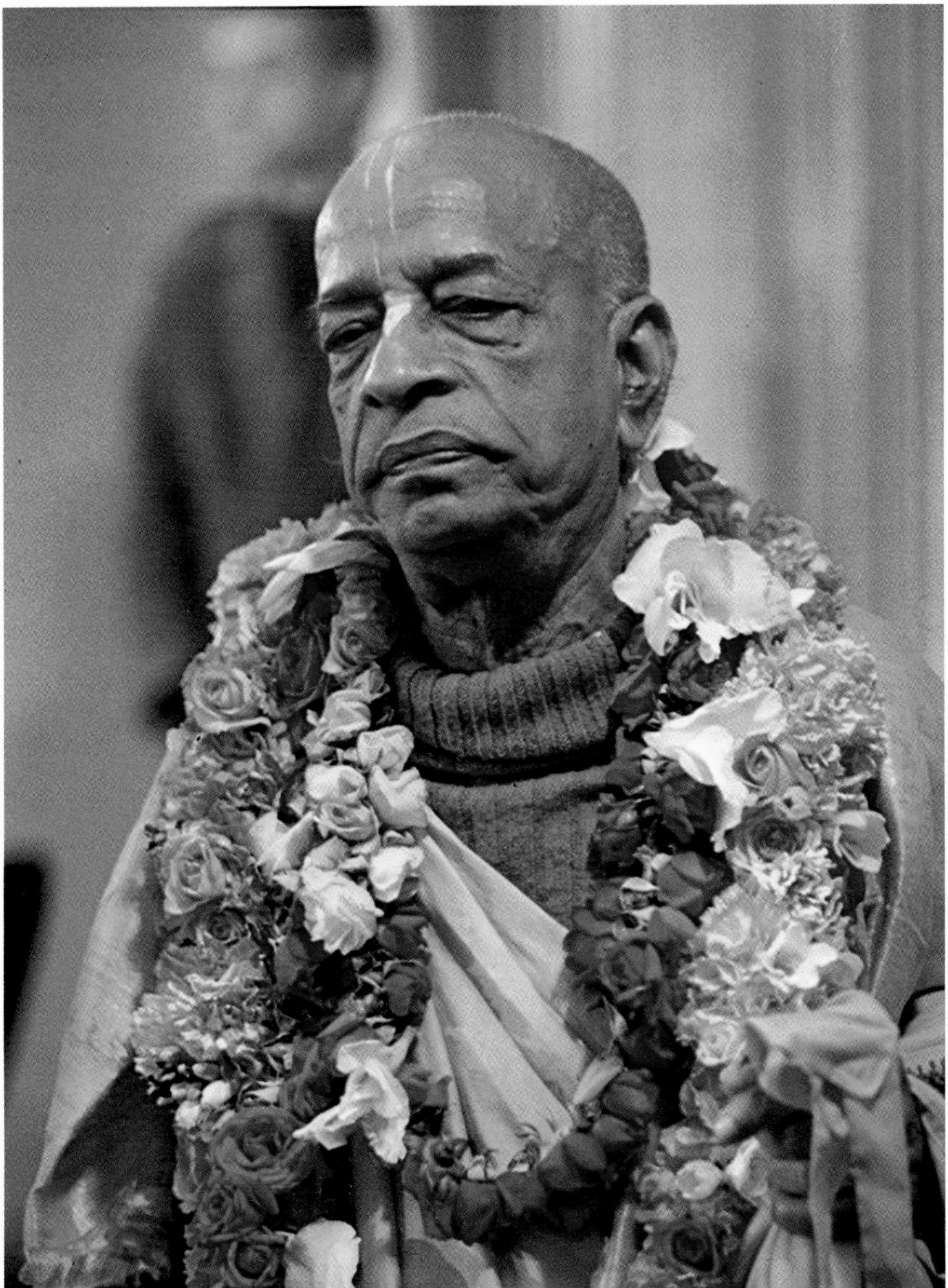

His Divine Grace
A. C. Bhaktivedanta Swami Prabhupāda
Founder-Ācārya of the International Society for Krishna Consciousness

Śrī Puruṣottama-kṣetra (Jagannātha Purī), the sacred site where Śrī Caitanya Mahāprabhu taught and exhibited the highest principles of devotional service to the Lord.

The temple of Lord Nṛsiṁhadeva in Purī. Śrī Caitanya Mahāprabhu would personally cleanse this temple along with the Guṇḍicā temple every year before the Ratha-yātrā festival.

The house of Kāśī Miśra in Purī, where Śrī Caitanya Mahāprabhu resided during the last eighteen years of His manifest presence. It was here that the Lord, overwhelmed with pure love of Godhead, experienced various inconceivable transcendental ecstasies.

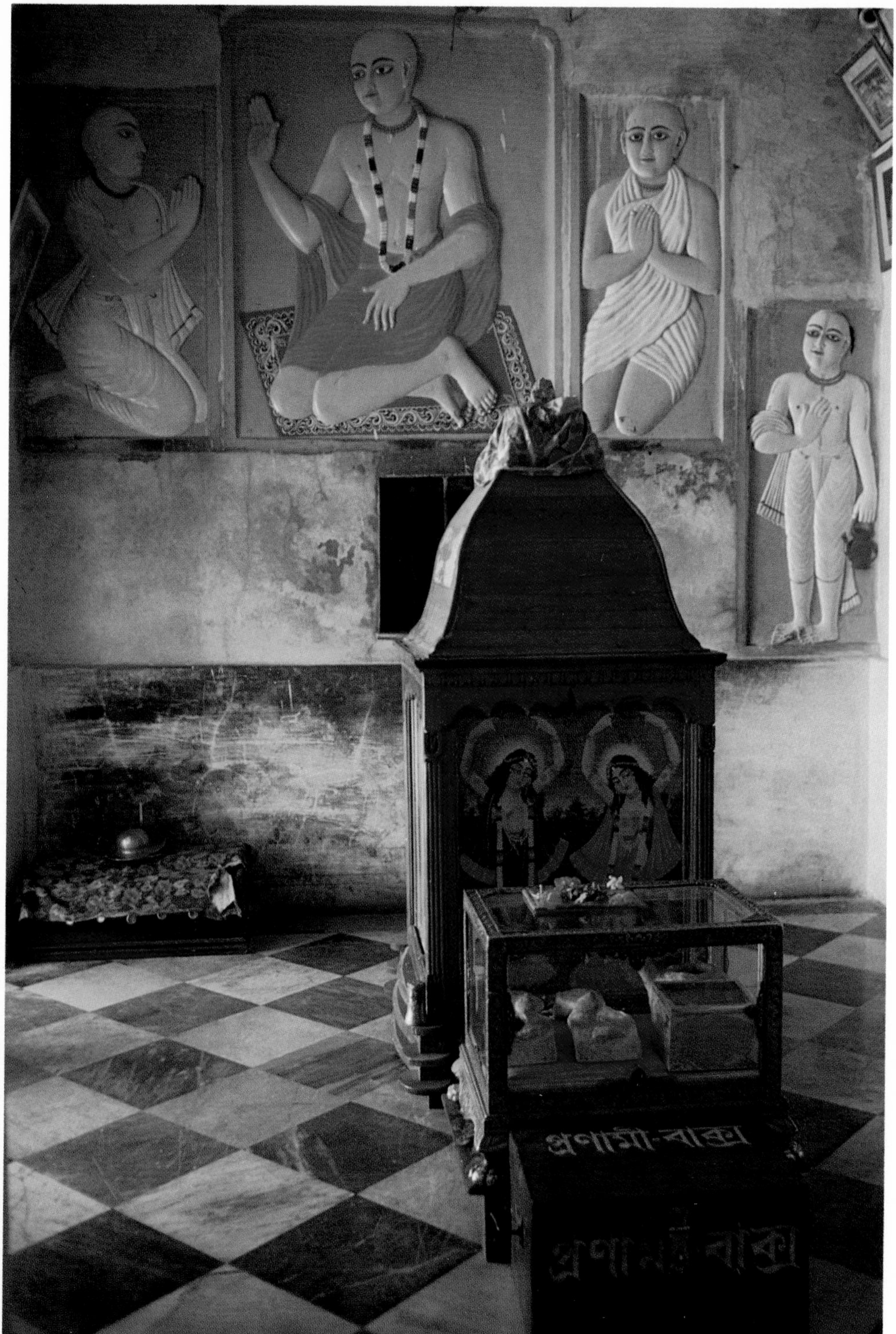

The Gambhīrā, the actual room where Śrī Caitanya Mahāprabhu lived. The Lord's shoes and water pot are preserved in the glass case (foreground).

LEFT: The *bhajana-kuṭira* (place of worship) of Śrīla Jīva Gosvāmī at Rādhā-kuṇḍa in Vṛndāvana. Śrīla Jīva Gosvāmī is known as the greatest philosopher of all time, and he compiled 400,000 verses in all his books about the transcendental love of Kṛṣṇa. After the disappearance of Śrīla Rūpa and Sanātana Gosvāmīs, Śrīla Jīva Gosvāmī became the *ācārya* of all the Vaiṣṇavas in the world.
RIGHT: The *samādhi* (tomb) of Śrīla Jīva Gosvāmī at the Rādhā-Dāmodara temple in Vṛndāvana.

The temple of Śrī Śrī Rādhā-Dāmodara, established in Vṛndāvana by Śrīla Jīva Gosvāmī. While living very humbly at this sacred place, His Divine Grace A. C. Bhaktivedanta Swami Prabhupāda wrote the first three volumes of his life's masterpiece—the eighteen thousand verse *Śrīmad-Bhāgavatam*. Thereafter, in 1965, His Divine Grace Śrīla Prabhupāda traveled to the United States to fulfill the great mission of his spiritual master—to teach the message of Lord Caitanya and deliver the Western countries from voidism and impersonalism.

PLATE ONE

"I offer my respectful obeisances unto You, Lord Nṛsiṁhadeva. You are the giver of pleasure to Mahārāja Prahlāda, and Your nails cut the chest of Hiraṇyakaśipu like a chisel cutting stone. Lord Nṛsiṁhadeva is here, and He is also there on the opposite side. Wherever I go, there I see Lord Nṛsiṁhadeva. He is outside and within my heart. Therefore I take shelter of Lord Nṛsiṁhadeva, the original Supreme Personality of Godhead." (*pp.28-29*)

PLATE TWO

"One day when Śrī Caitanya Mahāprabhu went to visit the temple of Lord Jagannātha, the gatekeeper at Siṁha-dvāra approached Him and offered respectful obeisances. The Lord asked him, 'Where is Kṛṣṇa, My life and soul? Please show Me Kṛṣṇa.' Saying this, He caught the doorkeeper's hand. The doorkeeper replied, 'The son of Mahārāja Nanda is here; please come along with me, and I shall show You.' Lord Caitanya said to the doorman, 'You are My friend. Please show Me where the Lord of My heart is.' After the Lord said this, they both went to the place known as Jagamohana, where everyone views Lord Jagannātha. 'Just see!' the doorkeeper said. 'Here is the best of the Personalities of Godhead. From here You may see the Lord to the full satisfaction of Your eyes.' Śrī Caitanya Mahāprabhu stayed behind the huge column called the Garuḍa-stambha and looked upon Lord Jagannātha, but as He looked He saw that Lord Jagannātha had become Lord Kṛṣṇa, with His flute to His mouth." (*pp.40-42*)

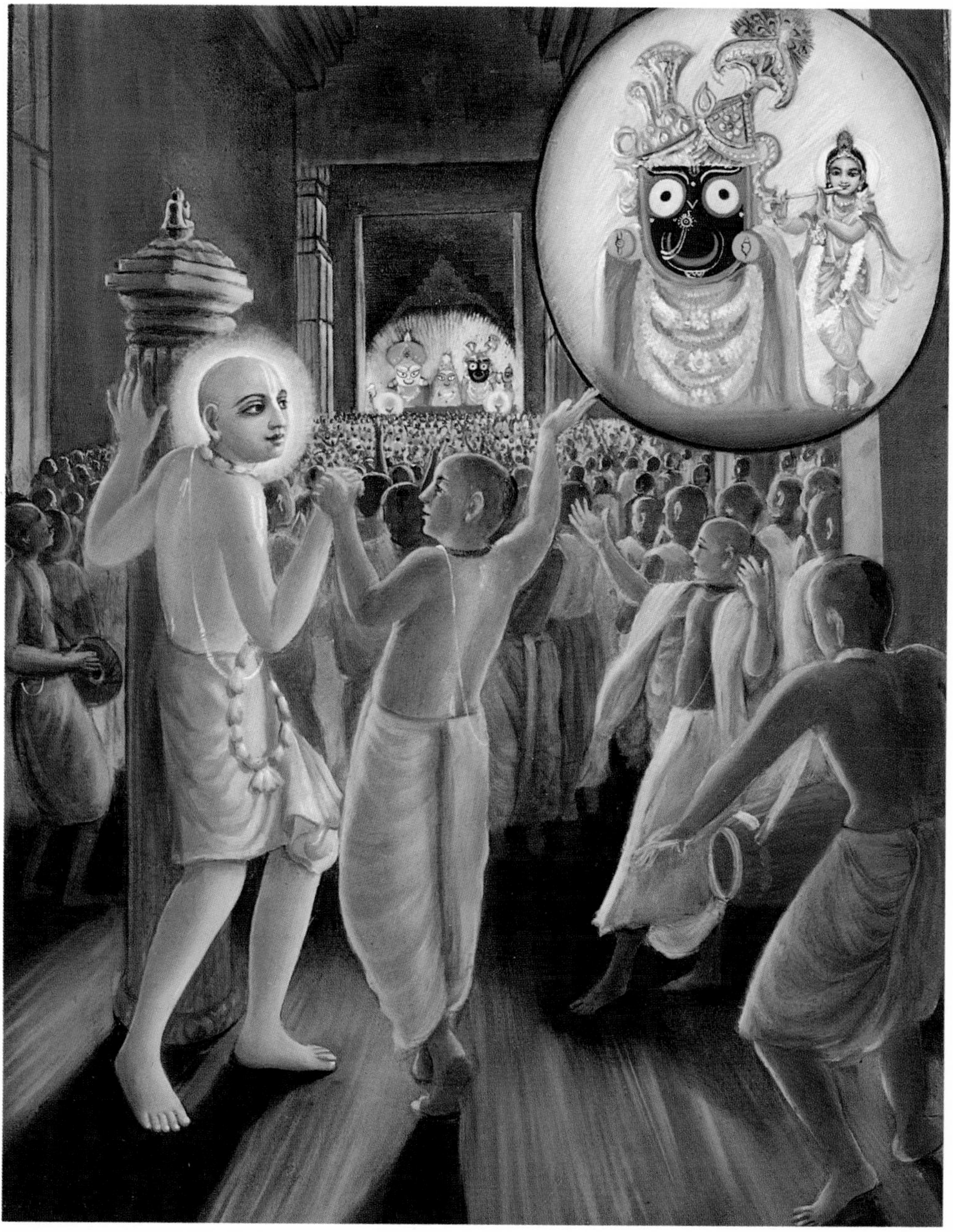

PLATE THREE

"Śrī Caitanya Mahāprabhu stood up, and then sat down again. Looking here and there, He inquired from Svarūpa Dāmodara, 'Where have you brought Me? After hearing the vibration of a flute, I went to Vṛndāvana, and there I saw that Kṛṣṇa, the son of Mahārāja Nanda, was playing on His flute in the pasturing grounds. He brought Śrīmatī Rādhārāṇī to a bower by signalling with His flute. Then He entered that bower to perform pastimes with Her. I entered the bower just behind Kṛṣṇa, My ears captivated by the sound of His ornaments. I saw Kṛṣṇa and the *gopīs* enjoying all kinds of pastimes while laughing and joking together. Hearing their vocal expressions enhanced the joy of My ears. Just then, all of you made a tumultuous sound and brought Me back here by force. Because you brought Me back here, I could no longer hear the nectarean voices of Kṛṣṇa and the *gopīs,* nor could I hear the sounds of their ornaments or the flute.'" (*pp.88-91*)

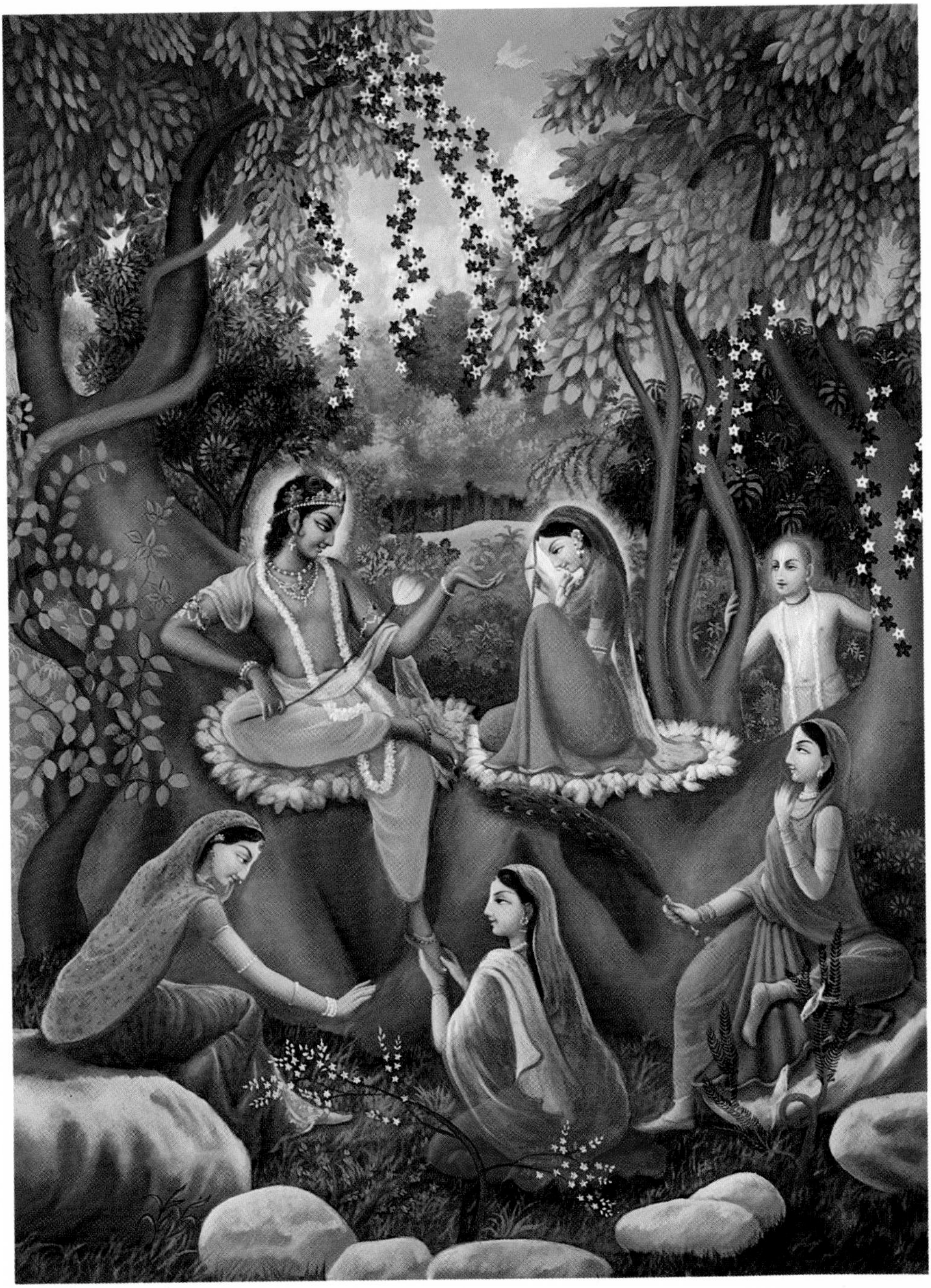

PLATE FOUR

"Passing along the beach, the devotees saw a fisherman approaching with his net over his shoulder. Laughing, crying, dancing and singing, he kept repeating the holy name, 'Hari, Hari.' Seeing the activities of the fisherman, everyone was astonished. Svarūpa Dāmodara Gosvāmī, therefore, asked him for information. 'My dear fisherman,' he said, 'why are you behaving like this? Have you seen someone hereabouts? What is the cause of your behavior? Please tell us.' The fisherman replied, 'I have not seen a single person here, but while casting my net in the water, I captured a dead body. I lifted it with great care, thinking it a big fish, but as soon as I saw that it was a corpse, great fear arose in my mind. As I tried to release the net I touched the body, and as soon as I touched it, a ghost entered my heart. I shivered in fear and shed tears. My voice faltered, and all the hairs on my person stood up. . . ' Svarūpa Dāmodara said to the fisherman, 'My dear sir, the person whom you are thinking a ghost is actually not a ghost but the Supreme Personality of Godhead, Śrī Kṛṣṇa Caitanya Mahāprabhu. Because of ecstatic love, the Lord fell into the sea, and you have caught Him in your net and rescued Him.' " (*pp.138-147*)

PLATE FIVE

"In His half-external consciousness, Śrī Caitanya Mahāprabhu talked like a madman. The devotees could distinctly hear Him speaking to the sky. 'Seeing the River Yamunā,' He said, 'I went to Vṛndāvana. There I saw the son of Nanda Mahārāja performing His sporting pastimes in the water. Lord Kṛṣṇa was in the water of the Yamunā in the company of the *gopīs,* headed by Śrīmatī Rādhārāṇī. They were performing pastimes in a great sporting manner. I saw the pastimes as I stood on the bank of the Yamunā in the company of the *gopīs.* One *gopī* was showing some other *gopīs* the pastimes of Rādhā and Kṛṣṇa in the water. All the *gopīs* entrusted their silken garments and ornaments to the care of their friends and then put on fine white cloth. Taking His beloved *gopīs* with Him, Lord Kṛṣṇa bathed and performed very nice pastimes in the water. Kṛṣṇa's restless palms resemble lotus flowers. He is just like a chief of mad elephants, and the *gopīs* who accompany Him are like she-elephants. The sporting pastimes in the water began, and everyone started splashing water back and forth. In the tumultuous showers of water, no one could be certain which party was winning and which was losing. This sporting water fight increased unlimitedly.' " (*pp.153-156*)

PLATE SIX

"Śrī Caitanya Mahāprabhu continued to describe His pastimes with Lord Kṛṣṇa in Vṛndāvana: 'In Vṛndāvana, the trees and creepers are wonderful because throughout the entire year they produce all kinds of fruits and flowers. The *gopīs* and maidservants in the bowers of Vṛndāvana pick these fruits and flowers and bring them before Rādhā and Kṛṣṇa. The *gopīs* peeled all the fruits and placed them together on large plates on a platform in the jeweled cottage. They arranged the fruit in orderly rows for eating, and in front of it they made a place to sit. Among the fruits were many varieties of coconut and mango, bananas, berries, jackfruits, dates, tangerines, oranges, blackberries, *santarās,* grapes, almonds and all kinds of dried fruit. There were cantaloupes, *kṣirikās,* palmfruits, *keśuras,* water fruits, lotus fruits, bael, *pīlu,* pomegranate and many others. Some of them are variously known in different places, but in Vṛndāvana they are always available in so many thousands of varieties that no one can fully describe them. At home Śrīmatī Rādhārāṇī had made various types of sweetmeats from milk and sugar, such as *gaṅgājala, amṛtakeli, pīyūṣagranthi, karpūrakeli, sarapūrī, amṛti, padmacini* and *kaṇḍa-kṣīrisāra-vṛkṣa.* She had then brought them all for Kṛṣṇa. When Kṛṣṇa saw the very nice arrangement of food, He happily sat down and had a forest picnic.' " (*pp.167-170*)

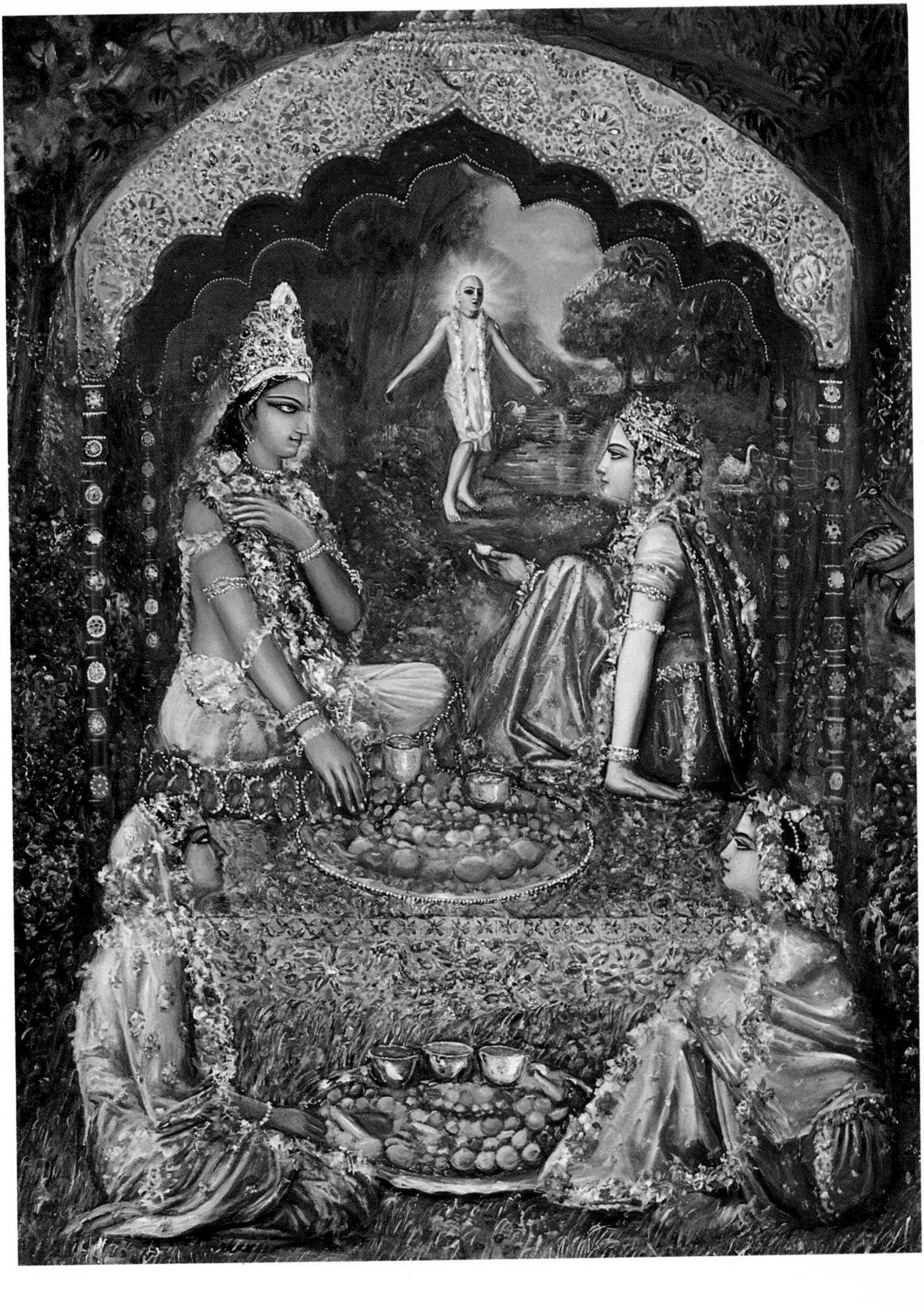

PLATE SEVEN

"As His feelings of separation in the ecstasy of Śrīmatī Rādhārāṇī increased at every moment, Lord Caitanya's activities, both day and night, were now wild, insane performances. Suddenly there awoke within Śrī Caitanya Mahāprabhu the scene of Lord Kṛṣṇa's departure to Mathurā, and He began exhibiting the symptom of ecstatic madness known as *udghūrṇā*. Śrī Caitanya Mahāprabhu spoke like a madman, holding Rāmānanda Rāya by the neck, and He questioned Svarūpa Dāmodara, thinking him to be His *gopī* friend. Just as Śrīmatī Rādhārāṇī inquired from Her personal friend Viśākhā, Śrī Caitanya Mahāprabhu began speaking like a madman." (*pp.193-194*)

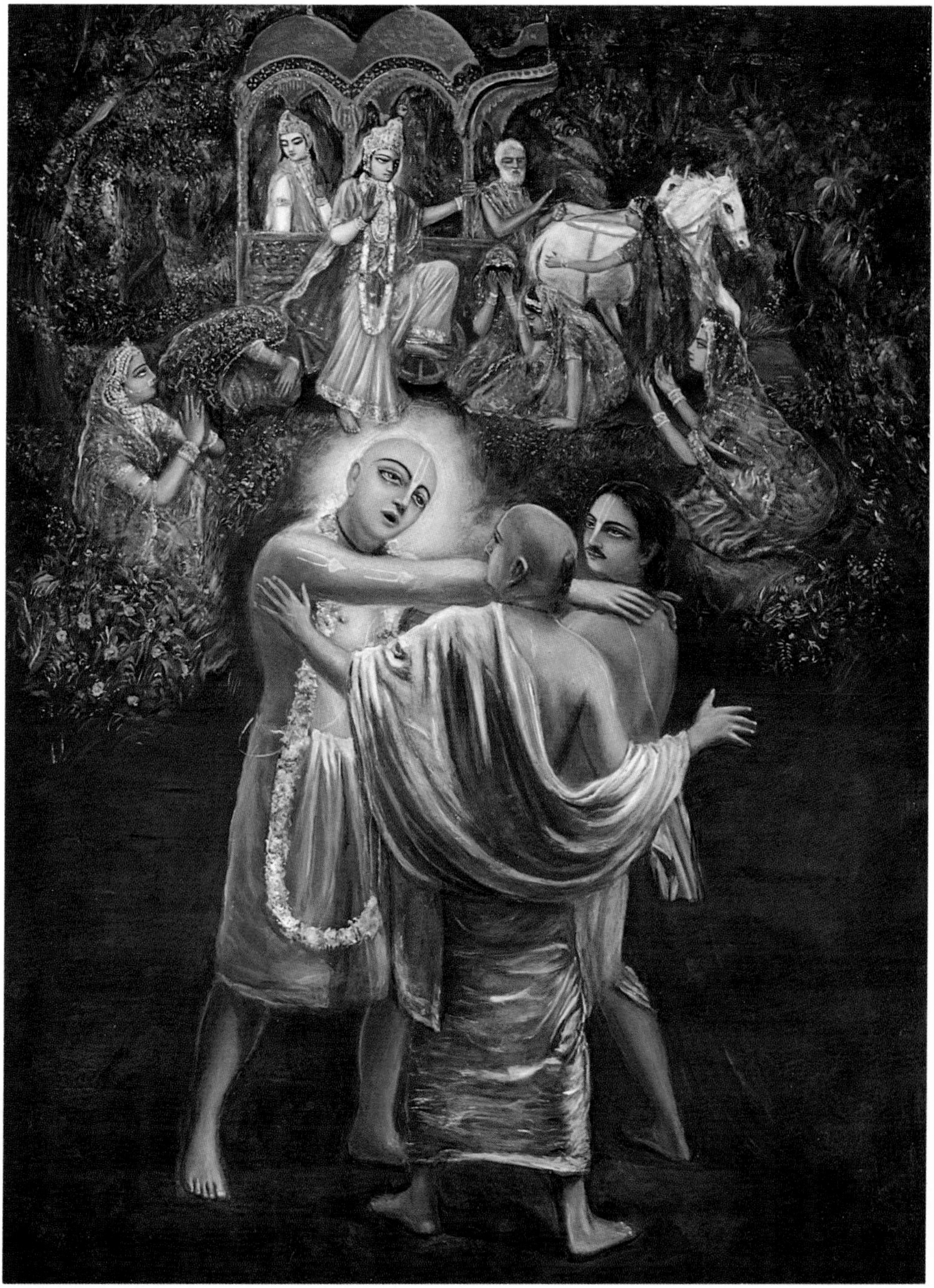

PLATE EIGHT

"One full-moon night in the month of Vaiśākha (April and May), Śrī Caitanya Mahāprabhu went to a garden. The Lord, along with His devotees, entered one of the nicest gardens, called Jagannātha-vallabha. In the garden were fully blossomed trees and creepers exactly like those in Vṛndāvana. Bumblebees and birds like the *śuka, śārī* and *pika* talked with one another. A mild breeze was blowing, carrying the fragrance of aromatic flowers. The breeze had become a *guru* and was teaching all the trees and creepers how to dance. Brightly illuminated by the full moon, the trees and creepers glittered in the light. The six seasons, especially spring, seemed present there. Seeing the garden, Śrī Caitanya Mahāprabhu, the Supreme Personality of Godhead, was very happy. In this atmosphere, the Lord had His associates sing a verse from the Gīta-govinda, as He danced and wandered about with them. As He thus wandered around every tree and creeper, He came beneath an *aśoka* tree and suddenly saw Lord Kṛṣṇa. When He saw Kṛṣṇa, Śrī Caitanya Mahāprabhu began running very swiftly, but Kṛṣṇa smiled and disappeared." (*pp.218-221*)

CHAPTER 16

Lord Śrī Caitanya Mahāprabhu Tastes Nectar from the Lips of Lord Śrī Kṛṣṇa

The Sixteenth Chapter is summarized by Śrīla Bhaktivinoda Ṭhākura in his *Amṛta-pravāha-bhāṣya.* When the Bengali devotees of the Lord returned to Jagannātha Purī, a gentleman named Kālidāsa who was an uncle of Raghunātha dāsa Gosvāmī went with them to see Śrī Caitanya Mahāprabhu. Kālidāsa had tasted the remnants of food of all the Vaiṣṇavas in Bengal, even Jhaḍu Ṭhākura. Because of this, he received the shelter of Śrī Caitanya Mahāprabhu at Jagannātha Purī.

When Kavi-karṇapūra was only seven years old, he was initiated by Śrī Caitanya Mahāprabhu into the Hare Kṛṣṇa *mahā-mantra.* He later became the greatest poet among the Vaiṣṇava *ācāryas.*

When Śrī Caitanya Mahāprabhu ate the remnants of food known as *vallabha-bhoga,* He described the glories of such remnants of the Lord's food and then fed all the devotees the *prasāda.* Thus they all tasted *adharāmṛta,* the nectar from the lips of Lord Śrī Kṛṣṇa.

TEXT 1

বন্দে শ্রীকৃষ্ণচৈতন্যং কৃষ্ণভাবামৃতং হি যঃ ।
আস্বাদ্যাস্বাদয়ন্ ভক্তান্ প্রেমদীক্ষামশিক্ষয়ৎ ॥ ১ ॥

vande śrī-kṛṣṇa-caitanyaṁ
kṛṣṇa-bhāvāmṛtaṁ hi yaḥ
āsvādyāsvādayan bhaktān
prema-dīkṣām aśikṣayat

SYNONYMS

vande—I offer my respectful obeisances; *śrī-kṛṣṇa-caitanyam*—unto Lord Śrī Caitanya Mahāprabhu; *kṛṣṇa-bhāva-amṛtam*—the nectar of ecstatic love of Kṛṣṇa; *hi*—certainly; *yaḥ*—He who; *āsvādya*—tasting; *āsvādayan*—causing to taste; *bhaktān*—the devotees; *prema*—in love of Kṛṣṇa; *dīkṣām*—initiation; *aśikṣayat*—instructed.

TRANSLATION

Let me offer my respectful obeisances unto Śrī Caitanya Mahāprabhu, who personally tasted the nectar of ecstatic love for Kṛṣṇa and then instructed His devotees how to taste it. Thus He enlightened them about ecstatic love of Kṛṣṇa to initiate them into transcendental knowledge.

TEXT 2

জয় জয় শ্রীচৈতন্য জয় নিত্যানন্দ ।
জয়াদ্বৈতচন্দ্র জয় গৌরভক্তবৃন্দ ॥ ২ ॥

jaya jaya śrī-caitanya jaya nityānanda
jayādvaita-candra jaya gaura-bhakta-vṛnda

SYNONYMS

jaya jaya—all glories; *śrī-caitanya*—to Lord Śrī Kṛṣṇa Caitanya Mahāprabhu; *jaya*—all glories; *nityānanda*—to Nityānanda Prabhu; *jaya*—all glories; *advaita-candra*—to Advaita Ācārya; *jaya*—all glories; *gaura-bhakta-vṛnda*—to all the devotees of Lord Caitanya Mahāprabhu.

TRANSLATION

All glories to Śrī Caitanya Mahāprabhu! All glories to Lord Nityānanda! All glories to Advaita Ācārya! And all glories to all the devotees of the Lord!

TEXT 3

এইমত মহাপ্রভু রহেন নীলাচলে ।
ভক্তগণ-সঙ্গে সদা প্রেম-বিহ্বলে ॥ ৩ ॥

ei-mata mahāprabhu rahena nīlācale
bhakta-gaṇa-saṅge sadā prema-vihvale

SYNONYMS

ei-mata—in this way; *mahāprabhu*—Śrī Caitanya Mahāprabhu; *rahena*—stays; *nīlācale*—in Jagannātha Purī; *bhakta-gaṇa-saṅge*—in the association of devotees; *sadā*—always; *prema-vihvale*—merged in ecstatic love.

TRANSLATION

Śrī Caitanya Mahāprabhu thus stayed at Jagannātha Purī in the association of His devotees, always merged in ecstatic devotional love.

TEXT 4

বর্ষান্তরে আইলা সব গৌড়ের ভক্তগণ ।
পূর্ব্ববৎ আসি' কৈল প্রভুর মিলন ॥ ৪ ॥

varṣāntare āilā saba gauḍera bhakta-gaṇa
pūrvavat āsi' kaila prabhura milana

SYNONYMS

varṣa-antare—the next year; *āilā*—came; *saba*—all; *gauḍera*—of Bengal; *bhakta-gaṇa*—the devotees; *pūrva-vat*—as previously; *āsi'*—coming; *kaila*—did; *prabhura milana*—meeting with Śrī Caitanya Mahāprabhu.

TRANSLATION

The next year, as usual, all the devotees from Bengal went to Jagannātha Purī, and, as in previous years, there was a meeting between Śrī Caitanya Mahāprabhu and the devotees.

TEXT 5

তাঁ-সবার সঙ্গে আইল কালিদাস নাম ।
কৃষ্ণনাম বিনা তেঁহো নাহি কহে আন ॥ ৫ ॥

tāṅ-sabāra saṅge āila kālidāsa nāma
kṛṣṇa-nāma vinā teṅho nāhi kahe āna

SYNONYMS

tāṅ-sabāra saṅge—with all of them; *āila*—came; *kāli-dāsa nāma*—a man named Kālidāsa; *kṛṣṇa-nāma*—the holy name of Kṛṣṇa; *vinā*—besides; *teṅho*—he; *nāhi*—does not; *kahe*—say; *āna*—anything else.

TRANSLATION

Along with the devotees from Bengal came a gentleman named Kālidāsa. He never uttered anything but the holy name of Kṛṣṇa.

TEXT 6

মহাভাগবত তেঁহো সরল উদার ।
কৃষ্ণনাম-'সঙ্কেতে' চালায় ব্যবহার ॥ ৬ ॥

mahā-bhāgavata teṅho sarala udāra
kṛṣṇa-nāma-'saṅkete' cālāya vyavahāra

SYNONYMS

mahā-bhāgavata—a highly advanced devotee; *teṅho*—he; *sarala udāra*—very simple and liberal; *kṛṣṇa-nāma-saṅkete*—with chanting of the holy name of Kṛṣṇa; *cālāya*—performs; *vyavahāra*—ordinary dealings.

TRANSLATION

Kālidāsa was a very advanced devotee, yet he was simple and liberal. He would chant the holy name of Kṛṣṇa while performing all his ordinary dealings.

TEXT 7

কৌতুকেতে তেঁহো যদি পাশক খেলায় ।
'হরে কৃষ্ণ' 'কৃষ্ণ' করি' পাশক চালায় ॥ ৭ ॥

kautukete teṅho yadi pāśaka khelāya
'hare kṛṣṇa' 'kṛṣṇa' kari' pāśaka cālāya

SYNONYMS

kautukete—in jest; *teṅho*—he; *yadi*—when; *pāśaka khelāya*—plays with dice; *hare kṛṣṇa*—the holy name of the Lord; *kṛṣṇa*—Kṛṣṇa; *kari'*—chanting; *pāśaka cālāya*—throws the dice.

TRANSLATION

When he used to throw dice in jest, he would throw the dice while chanting Hare Kṛṣṇa.

PURPORT

In this connection Śrīla Bhaktisiddhānta Sarasvatī Ṭhākura warns the men of this age not to imitate the jesting of a *mahā-bhāgavata* like Kālidāsa. If someone imitates him by playing with dice or gambling while chanting the Hare Kṛṣṇa *mahā-mantra,* he will certainly become a victim of offenses unto the holy name. As it is said, *hari-nāma-bale pāpe pravṛtti:* one must not commit sinful activities on the strength of chanting the Hare Kṛṣṇa *mantra.* Playing with dice is certainly gambling, but it is clearly said here that Kālidāsa did this only in jest. A *mahā-bhāgavata* can do anything, but he never forgets the basic principles. Therefore it is said, *vaiṣṇavera kriyā-mudrā vijñeha nā bujhaya:* "No one can understand the activities of a pure devotee." We should not imitate Kālidāsa.

TEXT 8

রঘুনাথ-দাসের তেঁহো হয় জ্ঞাতি-খুড়া ।
বৈষ্ণবের উচ্ছিষ্ট খাইতে তেঁহো হৈল বুড়া ॥ ৮ ॥

raghunātha-dāsera teṅho haya jñāti-khuḍā
vaiṣṇavera ucchiṣṭa khāite teṅho haila buḍā

SYNONYMS

raghunātha-dāsera—of Raghunātha dāsa Gosvāmī; *teṅho*—he (Kālidāsa); *haya*—is; *jñāti*—relative; *khuḍā*—uncle; *vaiṣṇavera*—of the Vaiṣṇavas; *ucchiṣṭa*—remnants of food; *khāite*—eating; *teṅho*—he; *haila*—became; *buḍā*—aged.

TRANSLATION

Kālidāsa was an uncle of Raghunātha dāsa Gosvāmī. Throughout his entire life, even in his old age, he tried to eat the remnants of food left by Vaiṣṇavas.

TEXT 9

গৌড়দেশে হয় যত বৈষ্ণবের গণ ।
সবার উচ্ছিষ্ট তেঁহো করিল ভোজন ॥ ৯ ॥

gauḍa-deśe haya yata vaiṣṇavera gaṇa
sabāra ucchiṣṭa teṅho karila bhojana

SYNONYMS

gauḍa-deśe—in Bengal; *haya*—are; *yata*—as many; *vaiṣṇavera gaṇa*—Vaiṣṇavas; *sabāra*—of all; *ucchiṣṭa*—remnants of food; *teṅho*—he; *karila bhojana*—ate.

TRANSLATION

Kālidāsa ate the remnants of food of as many Vaiṣṇavas as there were in Bengal.

TEXT 10

ব্রাহ্মণ-বৈষ্ণব যত – ছোট, বড় হয় ।
উত্তম-বস্তু ভেট লঞা তাঁর ঠাঞি যায় ॥ ১০ ॥

brāhmaṇa-vaiṣṇava yata——choṭa, baḍa haya
uttama-vastu bheṭa lañā tāṅra ṭhāñi yāya

SYNONYMS

brāhmaṇa-vaiṣṇava—Vaiṣṇavas coming from *brāhmaṇa* families; *yata*—all; *choṭa*—neophyte; *baḍa*—highly advanced; *haya*—are; *uttama-vastu*—first-class eatables; *bheṭa lañā*—taking as gifts; *tāṅra ṭhāñi*—to them; *yāya*—goes.

TRANSLATION

He would go to all the Vaiṣṇavas born in brāhmaṇa families, be they neophyte or advanced devotees, and present them gifts of first-class eatables.

TEXT 11

তাঁর ঠাঞি শেষ-পাত্র লয়েন মাগিয়া ।
কাহাঁ না পায়, তবে রহে লুকাঞা ॥ ১১ ॥

tāṅra ṭhāñi śeṣa-pātra layena māgiyā
kāhāṅ nā pāya, tabe rahe lukāñā

SYNONYMS

tāṅra ṭhāñi—from them; *śeṣa-pātra*—plates of remnants; *layena*—takes; *māgiyā*—begging; *kāhāṅ*—where; *nā pāya*—does not get; *tabe*—then; *rahe*—remains; *lukāñā*—hiding.

TRANSLATION

He would beg remnants of food from such Vaiṣṇavas, and if he did not receive any, he would hide.

TEXT 12

ভোজন করিলে পাত্র ফেলাঞা যায় ।
লুকাঞা সেই পাত্র আনি' চাটি' খায় ॥ ১২ ॥

bhojana karile pātra phelāñā yāya
lukāñā sei pātra āni' cāṭi' khāya

SYNONYMS

bhojana karile—after eating; *pātra*—the plate; *phelāñā yāya*—is thrown away; *lukāñā*—hiding; *sei pātra*—that plate; *āni'*—bringing; *cāṭi' khāya*—he licks up.

TRANSLATION

After the Vaiṣṇavas finished eating, they would throw away their dishes or leaves, and Kālidāsa would come out of hiding, take the leaves and lick up the remnants.

TEXT 13

শূদ্র-বৈষ্ণবের ঘরে যায় ভেট লঞা ।
এইমত তাঁর উচ্ছিষ্ট খায় লুকাঞা ॥ ১৩ ॥

śūdra-vaiṣṇavera ghare yāya bheṭa lañā
ei-mata tāṅra ucchiṣṭa khāya lukāñā

SYNONYMS

śūdra-vaiṣṇavera—of Vaiṣṇavas born in *śūdra* families; *ghare*—at the homes; *yāya*—goes; *bheṭa lañā*—taking gifts; *ei-mata*—in this way; *tāṅra*—their; *ucchiṣṭa*—remnants of food; *khāya*—eats; *lukāñā*—hiding.

TRANSLATION

He would also take gifts to the homes of Vaiṣṇavas born in śūdra families. Then he would hide and eat the remnants of food they threw away in this manner.

TEXT 14

ভুঁইমালি-জাতি, 'বৈষ্ণব'—'ঝড়ু' তাঁর নাম ।
আম্রফল লঞা তেঁহো গেলা তাঁর স্থান ॥ ১৪ ॥

bhūṅimāli-jāti, 'vaiṣṇava'——'jhaḍu' tāṅra nāma
āmra-phala lañā teṅho gelā tāṅra sthāna

SYNONYMS

bhūṅimāli-jāti—belonging to the *bhūṅimāli* caste; *vaiṣṇava*—a great devotee; *jhaḍu*—Jhaḍu; *tāṅra*—his; *nāma*—name; *āmra-phala*—mango fruits; *lañā*—taking; *teṅho*—he; *gelā*—went; *tāṅra sthāna*—to his place.

TRANSLATION

There was a great Vaiṣṇava named Jhaḍu Ṭhākura, who belonged to the bhūṅimāli caste. Kālidāsa went to his home, taking mangoes with him.

PURPORT

Śrīla Bhaktisiddhānta Sarasvatī Ṭhākura remarks that both Kālidāsa and Jhaḍu Ṭhākura are worshiped at a place called Śrīpāṭabāṭī, in the village known as Bhedo or Bhaduyā. This village is situated about three miles south of the village of Kṛṣṇapura, the birthplace of Raghunātha dāsa Gosvāmī, which is about one mile west of the Byāṇḍel junction of the Burdwan line. A post office there is named

Devānanda-pura. Jhaḍu Ṭhākura used to worship the Deity of Śrī Madana-gopāla. The Deity is still worshiped by one Rāmaprasāda dāsa, who belongs to the *rāmāyet* community. It is said that the Deity worshiped by Kālidāsa had been worshiped until now in the village of Śaṅkhya on the bank of the Sarasvatī River, but the Deity has been taken away by a gentleman named Matilāla Caṭṭopādhyāya from the village of Triveṇī. The Deity is now being worshiped at his place.

TEXT 15

আম্র ভেট দিয়া তাঁর চরণ বন্দিলা ।
তাঁর পত্নীরে তবে নমস্কার কৈলা ॥ ১৫ ॥

āmra bheṭa diyā tāṅra caraṇa vandilā
tāṅra patnīre tabe namaskāra kailā

SYNONYMS

āmra—mangoes; *bheṭa*—gift; *diyā*—presenting; *tāṅra*—his; *caraṇa*—feet; *vandilā*—offered respects to; *tāṅra patnīre*—to his wife; *tabe*—thereafter; *namaskāra kailā*—offered respectful obeisances.

TRANSLATION

Kālidāsa presented the mangoes to Jhaḍu Ṭhākura and offered him respectful obeisances. Then he also offered respectful obeisances to the Ṭhākura's wife.

TEXT 16

পত্নী-সহিত তেঁহো আছেন বসিয়া ।
বহু সম্মান কৈলা কালিদাসেরে দেখিয়া ॥ ১৬ ॥

patnī-sahita teṅho āchena vasiyā
bahu sammāna kailā kālidāsere dekhiyā

SYNONYMS

patnī-sahita—with his wife; *teṅho*—he (Jhaḍu Ṭhākura); *āchena vasiyā*—was sitting; *bahu*—much; *sammāna*—respect; *kailā*—offered; *kālidāsere dekhiyā*—seeing Kālidāsa.

TRANSLATION

When Kālidāsa went to Jhaḍu Ṭhākura, he saw that saintly person sitting with his wife. As soon as Jhaḍu Ṭhākura saw Kālidāsa, he likewise offered his respectful obeisances unto him.

TEXT 17

ইষ্টগোষ্ঠী কতক্ষণ করি' তাঁর সনে ।
ঝড়ু-ঠাকুর কহে তাঁরে মধুর বচনে ॥ ১৭ ॥

iṣṭagoṣṭhī kata-kṣaṇa kari' tāṅra sane
jhaḍu-ṭhākura kahe tāṅre madhura vacane

SYNONYMS

iṣṭa-goṣṭhī—discussion; *kata-kṣaṇa*—for some time; *kari'*—performing; *tāṅra sane*—with him; *jhaḍu-ṭhākura*—Jhaḍu Ṭhākura; *kahe*—says; *tāṅre*—unto him (Kālidāsa); *madhura vacane*—in sweet words.

TRANSLATION

After a discussion for some time with Kālidāsa, Jhaḍu Ṭhākura said something to him in sweet words.

TEXT 18

"আমি—নীচজাতি, তুমি,—অতিথি সর্বোত্তম ।
কোন্ প্রকারে করিমু আমি তোমার সেবন ? ১৮ ॥

"āmi——nīca-jāti, tumi,——atithi sarvottama
kon prakāre karimu āmi tomāra sevana?

SYNONYMS

āmi—I; *nīca-jāti*—belong to a low caste; *tumi*—you; *atithi*—guest; *sarva-uttama*—very respectable; *kon prakāre*—how; *karimu*—shall perform; *āmi*—I; *tomāra sevana*—your service.

TRANSLATION

"I belong to a low caste, and you are a very respectable guest. How shall I serve you?

TEXT 19

আজ্ঞা দেহ',—ব্রাহ্মণ-ঘরে অন্ন লঞা দিয়ে ।
তাহাঁ তুমি প্রসাদ পাও, তবে আমি জীয়ে ॥"১৯॥

ājñā deha',——brāhmaṇa-ghare anna lañā diye
tāhāṅ tumi prasāda pāo, tabe āmi jīye"

SYNONYMS

ājñā deha'—permit me; *brāhmaṇa-ghare*—to the house of a *brāhmaṇa; anna*—food; *lañā diye*—I shall offer; *tāhāṅ*—there; *tumi*—you; *prasāda pāo*—take *prasāda; tabe*—then; *āmi*—I; *jīye*—shall live.

TRANSLATION

"If you will permit me, I shall send some food to a brāhmaṇa's house, and there you may take prasāda. If you do so, I shall then live very comfortably."

TEXT 20

কালিদাস কহে,—"ঠাকুর, কৃপা কর মোরে।
তোমার দর্শনে আইনু মুই পতিত পামরে ॥ ২০ ॥

kālidāsa kahe,——"ṭhākura, kṛpā kara more
tomāra darśane āinu mui patita pāmare

SYNONYMS

kālidāsa kahe—Kālidāsa replied; *ṭhākura*—my dear saintly person; *kṛpā kara*—bestow your mercy; *more*—upon me; *tomāra darśane*—to see you; *āinu*—have come; *mui*—I; *patita pāmare*—very fallen and sinful.

TRANSLATION

Kālidāsa replied, "My dear sir, please bestow your mercy upon me. I have come to see you, although I am very fallen and sinful.

TEXT 21

পবিত্র হইনু মুই পাইনু দরশন।
কৃতার্থ হইনু, মোর সফল জীবন ॥ ২১ ॥

pavitra ha-inu mui pāinu daraśana
kṛtārtha ha-inu, mora saphala jīvana

SYNONYMS

pavitra ha-inu—have become purified; *mui*—I; *pāinu daraśana*—have gotten your interview; *kṛta-artha*—obliged; *ha-inu*—I have become; *mora*—my; *saphala*—successful; *jīvana*—life.

TRANSLATION

"Simply by seeing you, I have become purified. I am very obligated to you, for my life is now successful.

TEXT 22

এক বাঞ্ছা হয়,—যদি কৃপা করি' কর ।
পাদরজ দেহ', পাদ মোর মাথে ধর ॥"২২ ॥

eka vāñchā haya,——yadi kṛpā kari' kara
pāda-raja deha', pāda mora māthe dhara"

SYNONYMS

eka vāñchā—one desire; *haya*—there is; *yadi*—if; *kṛpā kari'*—being merciful; *kara*—you do; *pāda-raja*—the dust of your feet; *deha'*—give; *pāda*—feet; *mora*—my; *māthe*—on the head; *dhara*—please place.

TRANSLATION

"My dear sir, I have one desire. Please be merciful to me by kindly placing your feet upon my head so that the dust on your feet may touch it."

TEXT 23

ঠাকুর কহে,—"ঐছে বাত্ কহিতে না যুয়ায় ।
আমি—নীচজাতি, তুমি—সুসজ্জন রায় ॥"২৩ ॥

ṭhākura kahe,——"aiche vāt kahite nā yuyāya
āmi——nīca-jāti, tumi——susajjana rāya"

SYNONYMS

ṭhākura kahe—Jhaḍu Ṭhākura said; *aiche vāt*—such a request; *kahite nā yuyāya*—should not be spoken; *āmi*—I; *nīca-jāti*—coming from a family of a very low caste; *tumi*—you; *su-sat-jana rāya*—very respectable and rich gentleman.

TRANSLATION

Jhaḍu Ṭhākura replied, "It does not befit you to ask this of me. I belong to a very low-caste family, whereas you are a respectable rich gentleman."

TEXT 24

তবে কালিদাস শ্লোক পড়ি' শুনাইল ।
শুনি' ঝড়ু-ঠাকুরের বড় সুখ হইল ॥ ২৪ ॥

tabe kālidāsa śloka paḍi' śunāila
śuni' jhaḍu-ṭhākurera baḍa sukha ha-ila

SYNONYMS

tabe—thereafter; *kālidāsa*—Kālidāsa; *śloka*—verses; *paḍi'*—reciting; *śunāila*—caused to hear; *śuni'*—hearing; *jhaḍu-ṭhākurera*—of Jhaḍu Ṭhākura; *baḍa*—very great; *sukha*—happiness; *ha-ila*—there was.

TRANSLATION

Kālidāsa then recited some verses, which Jhaḍu Ṭhākura was very happy to hear.

TEXT 25

ন মেঽভক্তশ্চতুর্বেদী মদ্ভক্তঃ শ্বপচঃ প্রিয়ঃ ।
তস্মৈ দেয়ং ততো গ্রাহ্যং স চ পূজ্যো যথা হ্যহম্ ॥ ২৫ ॥

na me 'bhaktaś catur-vedī
mad-bhaktaḥ śva-pacaḥ priyaḥ
tasmai deyaṁ tato grāhyaṁ
sa ca pūjyo yathā hy aham

SYNONYMS

no—not; *me*—My; *abhaktaḥ*—devoid of pure devotional service; *catuḥ-vedī*—a scholar of the four *Vedas; mat-bhaktaḥ*—My devotee; *śva-pacaḥ*—even from a family of dog-eaters; *priyaḥ*—very dear; *tasmai*—to him (the pure devotee); *deyam*—should be given; *tataḥ*—from him; *grāhyam*—should be accepted (remnants of food); *saḥ*—that person; *ca*—also; *pūjyaḥ*—is worshipable; *yathā*—as much as; *hi*—certainly; *aham*—I.

TRANSLATION

" 'Even though one is a very learned scholar in Sanskrit literature, if he is not engaged in pure devotional service, he is not accepted as My devotee. But if someone born in a family of dog-eaters is a pure devotee with no motives for enjoyment through fruitive activity or mental speculation, he is very dear to Me. All respect should be given to him, and whatever he offers should be accepted, for such devotees are indeed as worshipable as I am.'

PURPORT

This verse spoken by the Supreme Personality of Godhead is found in *Hari-bhakti-vilāsa.*

TEXT 26

বিপ্রাদ্দ্বিষড়্ গুণযুতাদরবিন্দনাভ-
পাদারবিন্দবিমুখাৎ শ্বপচং বরিষ্ঠম্ ।
মন্যে তদর্পিতমনোবচনেহিতার্থ-
প্রাণং পুনাতি স কুলং ন তু ভূরিমানঃ ॥ ২৬ ॥

viprād dvi-ṣaḍ-guṇa-yutād aravinda-nābha-
pādāravinda-vimukhāt śva-pacaṁ variṣṭham
manye tad-arpita-mano-vacanehitārtha-
prāṇaṁ punāti sa kulaṁ na tu bhūri-mānaḥ

SYNONYMS

viprāt—than a *brāhmaṇa; dvi-ṣaṭ-guṇa-yutāt*—who is qualified with twelve brahminical qualifications; *aravinda-nābha*—of Lord Viṣṇu, who has a lotuslike navel; *pāda-aravinda*—unto the lotus feet; *vimukhāt*—than a person bereft of devotion; *śva-pacam*—a *caṇḍāla,* or person accustomed to eating dogs; *variṣṭham*—more glorified; *manye*—I think; *tat-arpita*—dedicated unto Him; *manaḥ*—mind; *vacana*—words; *īhita*—activities; *artha*—wealth; *prāṇam*—life; *punāti*—purifies; *saḥ*—he; *kulam*—his family; *na tu*—but not; *bhūri-mānaḥ*—a *brāhmaṇa* proud of possessing such qualities.

TRANSLATION

" 'A person may be born in a brāhmaṇa family and have all twelve brahminical qualities, but if in spite of being qualified he is not devoted to the lotus feet of Lord Kṛṣṇa, who has a navel shaped like a lotus, he is not as good as a caṇḍāla who has dedicated his mind, words, activities, wealth and life to the service of the Lord. Simply to take birth in a brāhmaṇa family or to have brahminical qualities is not sufficient. One must become a pure devotee of the Lord. If a śva-paca or caṇḍāla is a devotee, he delivers not only himself but his whole family, whereas a brāhmaṇa who is not a devotee but simply has brahminical qualifications cannot even purify himself, not to speak of his family.'

PURPORT

This and the following verse are quoted from *Śrīmad-Bhāgavatam* (7.9.10 and 3.33.7).

TEXT 27

অহো বত শ্বপচোঽতো গরীয়ান্
যজ্জিহ্বাগ্রে বর্ততে নাম তুভ্যম্ ।

তেপুস্তপস্তে জুহুবুঃ সস্নুরার্যা
ব্রহ্মানূচুর্নাম গৃণন্তি যে তে ॥ ২৭ ॥

aho bata śva-paco 'to garīyān
yaj-jihvāgre vartate nāma tubhyam
tepus tapas te juhuvuḥ sasnur āryā
brahmānūcur nāma gṛṇanti ye te

SYNONYMS

aho bata—how wonderful it is; *śva-pacaḥ*—a dog-eater; *ataḥ*—than the initiated *brāhmaṇa; garīyān*—more glorious; *yat*—of whom; *jihvā-agre*—on the tip of the tongue; *vartate*—remains; *nāma*—the holy name; *tubhyam*—of You, my Lord; *tepuḥ*—have performed; *tapaḥ*—austerity; *te*—they; *juhuvuḥ*—have performed sacrifices; *sasnuḥ*—have bathed in all holy places; *āryāḥ*—actually belonging to the Āryan race; *brahma*—all the *Vedas; anūcuḥ*—have studied; *nāma*—the holy name; *gṛṇanti*—chant; *ye*—who; *te*—they.

TRANSLATION

" 'My dear Lord, anyone who always keeps Your holy name on his tongue is greater than an initiated brāhmaṇa. Although he may be born in a family of dog-eaters and therefore, by material calculations, be the lowest of men, he is glorious nevertheless. That is the wonderful power of chanting the holy name of the Lord. One who chants the holy name is understood to have performed all kinds of austerities. He has studied all the Vedas, he has performed all the great sacrifices mentioned in the Vedas, he has already taken his bath in all the holy places of pilgrimage, and it is he who is factually the Āryan.' "

TEXT 28

শুনি' ঠাকুর কহে,—"শাস্ত্র এই সত্য কয়।
সেই শ্রেষ্ঠ, ঐছে যাঁতে কৃষ্ণভক্তি হয় ॥ ২৮ ॥

śuni' ṭhākura kahe,—"śāstra ei satya kaya
sei śreṣṭha, aiche yāṅte kṛṣṇa-bhakti haya

SYNONYMS

śuni'—hearing; *ṭhākura kahe*—Jhaḍu Ṭhākura said; *śāstra*—revealed scripture; *ei*—this; *satya*—truth; *kaya*—says; *sei*—he; *śreṣṭha*—best; *aiche*—in such a way; *yāṅte*—in whom; *kṛṣṇa-bhakti*—devotion to Kṛṣṇa; *haya*—there is.

TRANSLATION

Hearing these quotations from the revealed scripture Śrīmad-Bhāgavatam, Jhaḍu Ṭhākura replied, "Yes, this is true, for it is the version of śāstra. It is true, however, for one who is genuinely advanced in devotion to Kṛṣṇa.

TEXT 29

আমি—নীচজাতি, আমার নাহি কৃষ্ণভক্তি ।
অন্য ঐছে হয়, আমায় নাহি ঐছে শক্তি ॥" ২৯ ॥

āmi——nīca-jāti, āmāra nāhi kṛṣṇa-bhakti
anya aiche haya, āmāya nāhi aiche śakti"

SYNONYMS

āmi—I; *nīca-jāti*—belonging to a lower caste; *āmāra*—my; *nāhi*—there is not; *kṛṣṇa-bhakti*—devotion to Kṛṣṇa; *anya*—others; *aiche haya*—may be such; *āmāya*—unto me; *nāhi*—there is not; *aiche śakti*—such power.

TRANSLATION

"Such a position may befit others, but I do not possess such spiritual power. I belong to a lower class and have not even a pinch of devotion to Kṛṣṇa."

PURPORT

In his statement, Jhaḍu Ṭhākura presents himself as being born in a low-caste family and not having the qualifications of a bona fide devotee of Lord Kṛṣṇa. He accepts the statements declaring a lowborn person highly exalted if he is a Vaiṣṇava. However, he feels that these descriptions from *Śrīmad-Bhāgavatam* appropriately describe others, but not himself. Jhaḍu Ṭhākura's attitude is quite befitting a real Vaiṣṇava, for a Vaiṣṇava never considers himself exalted, even if he factually is. He is always meek and humble and never thinks that he is an advanced devotee. He assigns himself to a lower position, but that does not mean that he is indeed low. Sanātana Gosvāmī once said that he belonged to a low-caste family, for although he was born in a *brāhmaṇa* family, he had associated with *mlecchas* and *yavanas* in his service as a government minister. Similarly, Jhaḍu Ṭhākura presented himself as someone who belonged to a low caste, but he was actually elevated above many persons born in *brāhmaṇa* families. Not only is there evidence for this in *Śrīmad-Bhāgavatam,* as quoted by Kālidāsa in verses 26 and 27; there is also considerable evidence for this conclusion in other *śāstras.* For example, in the *Mahābhārata, Vana-parva,* Chapter 180, it is stated:

śūdre tu yad bhavel lakṣma
dvije tac ca na vidyate
na vai śūdro bhavec chūdro
brāhmaṇo na ca brāhmaṇaḥ

"If the characteristics of a *brāhmaṇa* are found in a *śūdra* and not in a *brāhmaṇa,* that *śūdra* should not be known as a *śūdra,* and that *brāhmaṇa* should not be known as a *brāhmaṇa.*"

Similarly, in the *Vana-parva,* Chapter 211, it is said:

śūdra-yonau hi jātasya
sad-guṇānupatiṣṭhataḥ
ārjave vartamānasya
brāhmaṇyam abhijāyate

"If a person born in a *śūdra* family has developed the qualities of a *brāhmaṇa,* such as *satya* [truthfulness], *śama* [peacefulness], *dama* [self-control] and *ārjava* [simplicity], he attains the exalted position of a *brāhmaṇa.*"

In the *Anuśāsana-parva,* Chapter 163, it is said:

sthito brāhmaṇa-dharmeṇa
brāhmaṇyam upajīvati
kṣatriyo vātha vaiśyo vā
brahma-bhūyaḥ sa gacchati

ebhis tu karmabhir devi
śubhair ācaritais tathā
śūdro brāhmaṇatāṁ yāti
vaiśyaḥ kṣatriyatāṁ vrajet

na yonir nāpi saṁskāro
na śrutaṁ na ca santatiḥ
kāraṇāni dvijatvasya
vṛttam eva tu kāraṇam

"If one is factually situated in the occupation of a *brāhmaṇa,* he must be considered a *brāhmaṇa,* even if born of a *kṣatriya* or *vaiśya* family.

"O Devī, if even a *śūdra* is actually engaged in the occupation and pure behavior of a *brāhmaṇa,* he becomes a *brāhmaṇa.* Moreover, a *vaiśya* can become a *kṣatriya.*

"Therefore, neither the source of one's birth, nor his reformation, nor his education is the criterion of a *brāhmaṇa.* The *vṛtta,* or occupation, is the real standard by which one is known as a *brāhmaṇa.*"

We have seen that a person who is not the son of a doctor and has not attended a medical college is sometimes able to practice medicine. By practical knowledge of how to perform a surgical operation, how to mix medicine and how to give certain medicines for certain diseases, a person can receive a certificate and be registered as a medical practitioner in the practical field. He can do a medical man's work and be known as a doctor. Although qualified medical men may consider him a quack, the government will recognize his work. Especially in India, there are many such doctors who perform their medical services perfectly. They are accepted even by the government. Similarly, if one is engaged in brahminical service or occupational duties, he must be considered a *brāhmaṇa* despite the family in which he is born. That is the verdict of all the *śāstras.*

In the *Śrīmad-Bhāgavatam,* (7.11.35), it is said:

yasya yal lakṣaṇaṁ proktaṁ
puṁso varṇābhivyañjakam
yad anyatrāpi dṛśyeta
tat tenaiva vinirdiśet

This is a statement by Nārada Muni to Mahārāja Yudhiṣṭhira, wherein Nārada says that the symptoms of a *brāhmaṇa, kṣatriya* and *vaiśya* are all described in *śāstra.* Therefore, if one is found exhibiting the symptoms and qualities of a *brāhmaṇa* and serving in a brahminical occupation, even if he is not born a *brāhmaṇa* or *kṣatriya,* he should be considered according to his qualifications and occupation.

Similarly, in the *Padma Purāṇa* it is said:

na śūdrā bhagavad-bhaktās
te tu bhāgavatā matāḥ
sarva-varṇeṣu te śūdrā
ye na bhaktā janārdane

"A devotee should never be considered a *śūdra.* All the devotees of the Supreme Personality of Godhead should be recognized as *bhāgavatas.* If one is not a devotee of Lord Kṛṣṇa, however, even if born of a *brāhmaṇa, kṣatriya* or *vaiśya* family, he should be considered a *śūdra.*"

In the *Padma Purāṇa* it is also said:

śva-pākam iva nekṣeta
loke vipram avaiṣṇavam
vaiṣṇavo varṇo-bāhyo 'pi
punāti bhuvana-trayam

"If a person born in a *brāhmaṇa* family is an *avaiṣṇava,* a nondevotee, one should not see his face, exactly as one should not look upon the face of a *caṇḍāla,* or dog-eater. However, a *vaiṣṇava* found in *varṇas* other than *brāhmaṇa* can purify all the three worlds."

The *Padma Purāṇa* further says:

śūdraṁ vā bhagavad-bhaktaṁ
niṣādaṁ śva-pacaṁ tathā
vīkṣate jāti-sāmānyāt
sa yāti narakaṁ dhruvam

"One who considers a devotee of the Supreme Personality of Godhead who was born in a family of *śūdras, niṣādas* or *caṇḍālas* to belong to that particular caste certainly goes to hell."

A *brāhmaṇa* must be a Vaiṣṇava and a learned scholar. Therefore in India it is customary to address a *brāhmaṇa* as *paṇḍita*. Without knowledge of Brahman, one cannot understand the Supreme Personality of Godhead. Therefore a Vaiṣṇava is already a *brāhmaṇa,* whereas a *brāhmaṇa* may become a Vaiṣṇava. In the *Garuḍa Purāṇa* it is said:

bhaktir aṣṭa-vidhā hy eṣā
yasmin mlecche 'pi vartate
sa viprendro muni-śreṣṭhaḥ
sa jñānī sa ca paṇḍitaḥ

"If even a *mleccha* becomes a devotee, he is to be considered the best of the *brāhmaṇas* and a learned *paṇḍita*."

Similarly, *Tattva-sāgara* says:

yathā kāñcanatāṁ yāti
kāṁsyaṁ rasa-vidhānataḥ
tathā dīkṣā-vidhānena
dvijatvaṁ jāyate nṛṇām

"As bell metal is turned to gold when mixed with mercury in an alchemical process, so one who is properly trained and initiated by a bona fide spiritual master becomes a *brāhmaṇa* immediately." All this evidence found in the revealed scriptures proves that according to the Vedic version, a Vaiṣṇava is never to be considered an *abrāhmaṇa,* or non-*brāhmaṇa.* A Vaiṣṇava should not be thought to belong to a lower caste even if born in a *mleccha* or *yavana* family. Because he has become a devotee of Lord Kṛṣṇa, he has become purified and has attained the stage of *brāhmaṇa* (*dvijatvaṁ jāyate nṛṇām*).

TEXT 30

তারে নমস্করি' কালিদাস বিদায় মাগিলা ।
ঝড়ু-ঠাকুর তবে তাঁর অনুব্রজি' আইলা ॥ ৩০ ॥

tāre namaskari' kālidāsa vidāya māgilā
jhaḍu-ṭhākura tabe tāṅra anuvraji' āilā

SYNONYMS

tāre—unto him (Jhaḍu Ṭhākura); *namaskari'*—offering obeisances; *kālidāsa*—Kālidāsa; *vidāya māgilā*—asked permission to go; *jhaḍu-ṭhākura*—Jhaḍu Ṭhākura; *tabe*—at that time; *tāṅra*—him; *anuvraji'*—following; *āilā*—went.

TRANSLATION

Kālidāsa again offered his obeisances to Jhaḍu Ṭhākura and asked his permission to go. The saint Jhaḍu Ṭhākura followed him as he left.

TEXT 31

তাঁরে বিদায় দিয়া ঠাকুর যদি ঘরে আইল ।
তাঁর চরণ-চিহ্ন যেই ঠাঞি পড়িল ॥ ৩১ ॥

tāṅre vidāya diyā ṭhākura yadi ghare āila
tāṅra caraṇa-cihna yei ṭhāñi paḍila

SYNONYMS

tāṅre—unto him (Kālidāsa); *vidāya diyā*—bidding farewell; *ṭhākura*—Jhaḍu Ṭhākura; *yadi*—when; *ghare āila*—returned to his home; *tāṅra caraṇa-cihna*—the mark of his feet; *yei ṭhāñi*—wherever; *paḍila*—fell.

TRANSLATION

After bidding farewell to Kālidāsa, Jhaḍu Ṭhākura returned to his home, leaving the marks of his feet plainly visible in many places.

TEXT 32

সেই ধূলি লঞা কালিদাস সর্বাঙ্গে লেপিলা ।
তাঁর নিকট একস্থানে লুকাঞা রহিলা ॥ ৩২ ॥

sei dhūli lañā kālidāsa sarvāṅge lepilā
tāṅra nikaṭa eka-sthāne lukāñā rahilā

SYNONYMS

sei dhūli—that dust; *lañā*—taking; *kālidāsa*—Kālidāsa; *sarva-aṅge*—all over his body; *lepilā*—smeared; *tāṅra nikaṭa*—near his place; *eka-sthāne*—in one place; *lukāñā rahilā*—remained hidden.

TRANSLATION

Kālidāsa smeared the dust from those footprints all over his body. Then he hid in a place near Jhaḍu Ṭhākura's home.

TEXT 33

ঝড়ু-ঠাকুর ঘর যাই' দেখি' আম্রফল ।
মানসেই কৃষ্ণচন্দ্রে অর্পিলা সকল ॥ ৩৩ ॥

jhaḍu-ṭhākura ghara yāi' dekhi' āmra-phala
mānasei kṛṣṇa-candre arpilā sakala

SYNONYMS

jhaḍu-ṭhākura—Jhaḍu Ṭhākura; *ghara yāi'*—returning home; *dekhi' āmra-phala*—seeing the mangoes; *mānasei*—within his mind; *kṛṣṇa-candre*—unto Kṛṣṇa; *arpilā*—offered; *sakala*—all.

TRANSLATION

Upon returning home, Jhaḍu Ṭhākura saw the mangoes Kālidāsa had presented. Within his mind he offered them to Kṛṣṇa-candra.

TEXT 34

কলার পাটুয়া-খোলা হৈতে আম্র নিকাশিয়া ।
তাঁর পত্নী তাঁরে দেন, খায়েন চূষিয়া ॥ ৩৪ ॥

kalāra pāṭuyā-kholā haite āmra nikāśiyā
tāṅra patnī tāṅre dena, khāyena cūṣiyā

SYNONYMS

kalāra—of the banana tree; *pāṭuyā-kholā*—leaves and bark; *haite*—from within; *āmra*—mangoes; *nikāśiyā*—taking out; *tāṅra patnī*—his wife; *tāṅre*—to him; *dena*—gives; *khāyena*—eats; *cūṣiyā*—sucking.

TRANSLATION

Jhaḍu Ṭhākura's wife then took the mangoes from their covering of banana tree leaves and bark and offered them to Jhaḍu Ṭhākura, who began to suck and eat them.

TEXT 35

চুষি' চুষি' চোষা আঁঠি ফেলিলা পাটুয়াতে ।
তারে খাওয়াঞা তাঁর পত্নী খায় পশ্চাতে ॥ ৩৫ ॥

cūṣi' cūṣi' coṣā āṅṭhi phelilā pāṭuyāte
tāre khāoyāñā tāṅra patnī khāya paścāte

SYNONYMS

cūṣi' cūṣi'—sucking and sucking; *coṣā*—sucked; *āṅṭhi*—the seeds; *phelilā*—left; *pāṭuyāte*—on the plantain leaf; *tāre*—him; *khāoyāñā*—after feeding; *tāṅra patnī*—his wife; *khāya*—eats; *paścāte*—afterwards.

TRANSLATION

When he finished eating, he left the seeds on the banana leaf, and his wife, after feeding her husband, later began to eat.

TEXT 36

আঁঠি-চোষা সেই পাটুয়া-খোলাতে ভরিয়া ।
বাহিরে উচ্ছিষ্ট-গর্তে ফেলাইলা লঞা ॥ ৩৬ ॥

āṅṭhi-coṣā sei pāṭuyā-kholāte bhariyā
bāhire ucchiṣṭa-garte phelāilā lañā

SYNONYMS

āṅṭhi—the seeds; *coṣā*—that had been sucked; *sei*—that; *pāṭuyā-kholāte*—banana leaf and bark; *bhariyā*—filling; *bāhire*—outside; *ucchiṣṭa-garte*—in the ditch where refuse was thrown; *phelāilā lañā*—picked up and threw.

TRANSLATION

After she finished eating, she filled the banana leaves and bark with the seeds, picked them up and threw them in the ditch where all the refuse was thrown.

TEXT 37

সেই খোলা, আঁঠি, চোকলা চূষে কালিদাস ।
চূষিতে চূষিতে হয় প্রেমেতে উল্লাস ॥ ৩৭ ॥

sei kholā, āṅṭhi, cokalā cūṣe kālidāsa
cūṣite cūṣite haya premete ullāsa

SYNONYMS

sei—that; *kholā*—bark of the banana tree; *āṅṭhi*—seeds of the mango; *cokalā*—skin of the mango; *cūṣe*—licks up; *kālidāsa*—Kālidāsa; *cūṣite cūṣite*—while licking up; *haya*—there was; *premete ullāsa*—great jubilation in ecstatic love.

TRANSLATION

Kālidāsa licked the banana bark and the mango seeds and skins, and while licking them he was overwhelmed in jubilation by ecstatic love.

TEXT 38

এইমত যত বৈষ্ণব বৈসে গৌড়দেশে ।
কালিদাস ঐছে সবার নিলা অবশেষে ॥ ৩৮ ॥

ei-mata yata vaiṣṇava vaise gauḍa-deśe
kālidāsa aiche sabāra nilā avaśeṣe

SYNONYMS

ei-mata—in this way; *yata*—as many as; *vaiṣṇava*—Vaiṣṇavas; *vaise*—reside; *gauḍa-deśe*—in Bengal; *kālidāsa*—Kālidāsa; *aiche*—in that way; *sabāra*—of all of them; *nilā*—took; *avaśeṣe*—the remnants.

TRANSLATION

In this way Kālidāsa ate the remnants of food left by all the Vaiṣṇavas residing in Bengal.

TEXT 39

সেই কালিদাস যবে নীলাচলে আইলা ।
মহাপ্রভু তাঁর উপর মহাকৃপা কৈলা ॥ ৩৯ ॥

sei kālidāsa yabe nīlācale āilā
mahāprabhu tāṅra upara mahā-kṛpā kailā

SYNONYMS

sei kālidāsa—that Kālidāsa; *yabe*—when; *nīlācale āilā*—came to Jagannātha Purī; *mahāprabhu*—Śrī Caitanya Mahāprabhu; *tāṅra upara*—upon him; *mahā-kṛpā*—great mercy; *kailā*—bestowed.

TRANSLATION

When Kālidāsa visited Jagannātha Purī, Nīlācala, Śrī Caitanya Mahāprabhu bestowed great mercy upon him.

TEXT 40

প্রতিদিন প্রভু যদি যা'ন দরশনে ।
জল-করঙ্গ লঞা গোবিন্দ যায় প্রভু-সনে ॥ ৪০ ॥

prati-dina prabhu yadi yā'na daraśane
jala-karaṅga lañā govinda yāya prabhu-sane

SYNONYMS

prati-dina—every day; *prabhu*—Śrī Caitanya Mahāprabhu; *yadi*—when; *yā'na*—goes; *daraśane*—to see Lord Jagannātha; *jala-karaṅga*—a waterpot; *lañā*—taking; *govinda*—the personal servant of the Lord (Govinda); *yāya*—goes; *prabhu-sane*—with Śrī Caitanya Mahāprabhu.

TRANSLATION

Śrī Caitanya Mahāprabhu had been regularly visiting the temple of Jagannātha every day, and at that time Govinda, His personal servant, used to carry His waterpot and go with Him.

TEXT 41

সিংহদ্বারের উত্তরদিকে কপাটের আড়ে ।
বাইশ 'পাহাচ'-তলে আছে এক নিম্ন গাড়ে ॥ ৪১ ॥

siṁha-dvārera uttara-dike kapāṭera āḍe
bāiśa 'pāhāca'-tale āche eka nimna gāḍe

SYNONYMS

siṁha-dvārera—of the Siṁha-dvāra; *uttara-dike*—on the northern side; *kapāṭera āḍe*—behind the door; *bāiśa 'pāhāca'*—of the twenty-two steps; *tale*—at the bottom; *āche*—there is; *eka*—one; *nimna*—low; *gāḍe*—ditch.

TRANSLATION

On the northern side of the Siṁha-dvāra, behind the door, there are twenty-two steps leading to the temple, and at the bottom of those steps is a ditch.

TEXT 42

সেই গাড়ে করেন প্রভু পাদ-প্রক্ষালনে ।
তবে করিবারে যায় ঈশ্বর-দরশনে ॥ ৪২ ॥

sei gāḍe karena prabhu pāda-prakṣālane
tabe karibāre yāya īśvara-daraśane

SYNONYMS

sei gāḍe—in that ditch; *karena*—does; *prabhu*—Śrī Caitanya Mahāprabhu; *pāda-prakṣālane*—washing the feet; *tabe*—thereafter; *karibāre*—to do; *yāya*—He goes; *īśvara-daraśane*—to visit Lord Jagannātha.

TRANSLATION

Śrī Caitanya Mahāprabhu would wash His feet in this ditch, and then He would enter the temple to see Lord Jagannātha.

TEXT 43

গোবিন্দেরে মহাপ্রভু কৈরাছে নিয়ম ।
'মোর পাদজল যেন না লয় কোন জন' ॥ ৪৩ ॥

govindere mahāprabhu kairāche niyama
'mora pāda-jala yena nā laya kona jana'

SYNONYMS

govindere—unto Govinda; *mahāprabhu*—Śrī Caitanya Mahāprabhu; *kairāche*—has given; *niyama*—a regulative principle; *mora*—My; *pāda-jala*—water from washing the feet; *yena*—that; *nā laya*—does not take; *kona jana*—anyone.

TRANSLATION

Śrī Caitanya Mahāprabhu ordered His personal servant Govinda that no one should take the water that had washed His feet.

TEXT 44

প্রাণিমাত্র লইতে না পায় সেই জল।
অন্তরঙ্গ ভক্ত লয় করি' কোন ছল ॥ ৪৪ ॥

prāṇi-mātra la-ite nā pāya sei jala
antaraṅga bhakta laya kari' kona chala

SYNONYMS

prāṇi-mātra—all living beings; *la-ite*—to take; *nā pāya*—do not get; *sei jala*—that water; *antaraṅga*—very intimate; *bhakta*—devotees; *laya*—take; *kari'*—doing; *kona chala*—some trick.

TRANSLATION

Because of the Lord's strict order, no living being could take the water. Some of His intimate devotees, however, would take it by some trick.

TEXT 45

একদিন প্রভু তাঁহা পাদ প্রক্ষালিতে।
কালিদাস আসি' তাহাঁ পাতিলেন হাতে ॥ ৪৫ ॥

eka-dina prabhu tāṅhā pāda prakṣālite
kālidāsa āsi' tāhāṅ pātilena hāte

SYNONYMS

eka-dina—one day; *prabhu*—Śrī Caitanya Mahāprabhu; *tāṅhā*—there; *pāda prakṣālite*—washing His feet; *kālidāsa*—Kālidāsa; *āsi'*—coming; *tāhāṅ*—there; *pātilena*—spread; *hāte*—his palm.

TRANSLATION

One day as Śrī Caitanya Mahāprabhu was washing His feet in that place, Kālidāsa came and extended his palm to take the water.

TEXT 46

এক অঞ্জলি, দুই অঞ্জলি, তিন অঞ্জলি পিলা।
তবে মহাপ্রভু তাঁরে নিষেধ করিলা ॥ ৪৬ ॥

eka añjali, dui añjali, tina añjali pilā
tabe mahāprabhu tāṅre niṣedha karilā

SYNONYMS

eka añjali—one palmful; *dui añjali*—two palmfuls; *tina añjali*—three palmfuls; *pilā*—he drank; *tabe*—at that time; *mahāprabhu*—Śrī Caitanya Mahāprabhu; *tāṅre*—him; *niṣedha karilā*—forbade.

TRANSLATION

Kālidāsa drank one palmful and then a second and a third. Then Śrī Caitanya Mahāprabhu forbade him to drink more.

TEXT 47

"অতঃপর আর না করিহ পুনর্বার ।
এতাবতা বাঞ্ছা-পূরণ করিলুঁ তোমার ॥" ৪৭ ॥

"ataḥpara āra nā kariha punar-bāra
etāvatā vāñchā-pūraṇa kariluṅ tomāra"

SYNONYMS

ataḥpara—hereafter; *āra*—any more; *nā kariha*—do not do; *punaḥ-bāra*—again; *etāvatā*—so far; *vāñchā-pūraṇa*—fulfilling the desire; *kariluṅ*—I have done; *tomāra*—of you.

TRANSLATION

"Do not act in this way any more. I have fulfilled your desire as far as possible."

TEXT 48

সর্বজ্ঞ-শিরোমণি চৈতন্য ঈশ্বর ।
বৈষ্ণবে তাঁহার বিশ্বাস, জানেন অন্তর ॥ ৪৮ ॥

sarvajña-śiromaṇi caitanya īśvara
vaiṣṇave tāṅhāra viśvāsa, jānena antara

SYNONYMS

sarva-jña—omniscient; *śiromaṇi*—topmost; *caitanya*—Lord Śrī Caitanya Mahāprabhu; *īśvara*—the Supreme Personality of Godhead; *vaiṣṇave*—unto the Vaiṣṇavas; *tāṅhāra viśvāsa*—his faith; *jānena*—He knows; *antara*—the heart.

TRANSLATION

Śrī Caitanya Mahāprabhu is the most exalted, omniscient Supreme Personality of Godhead, and therefore He knew that Kālidāsa, in the core of his heart, had full faith in Vaiṣṇavas.

TEXT 49

সেইগুণ লঞা প্রভু তাঁরে তুষ্ট হইলা ।
অন্যের দুর্লভ প্রসাদ তাঁহারে করিলা ॥ ৪৯ ॥

sei-guṇa lañā prabhu tāṅre tuṣṭa ha-ilā
anyera durlabha prasāda tāṅhāre karilā

SYNONYMS

sei-guṇa—that quality; *lañā*—accepting; *prabhu*—Śrī Caitanya Mahāprabhu; *tāṅre*—him; *tuṣṭa ha-ilā*—satisfied; *anyera*—for others; *durlabha*—not attainable; *prasāda*—mercy; *tāṅhāre*—unto him; *karilā*—showed.

TRANSLATION

Because of this quality, Śrī Caitanya Mahāprabhu satisfied him with mercy not attainable by anyone else.

TEXT 50

বাইশ 'পাহাচ'-পাছে উপর দক্ষিণ-দিকে ।
এক নৃসিংহ-মূর্তি আছেন উঠিতে বামভাগে ॥ ৫০ ॥

bāiśa 'pāhāca'-pāche upara dakṣiṇa-dike
eka nṛsiṁha-mūrti āchena uṭhite vāma-bhāge

SYNONYMS

bāiśa pāhāca—of the twenty-two steps; *pāche*—toward the back; *upara*—above; *dakṣiṇa-dike*—on the southern side; *eka*—one; *nṛsiṁha-mūrti*—Deity of Lord Nṛsiṁha; *āchena*—there is; *uṭhite*—while stepping upward; *vāma-bhāge*—on the left side.

TRANSLATION

On the southern side, behind and above the twenty-two steps, is a Deity of Lord Nṛsiṁhadeva. It is on the left as one goes up the steps toward the temple.

TEXT 51

প্রতিদিন তাঁরে প্রভু করেন নমস্কার ।
নমস্করি' এই শ্লোক পড়ে বারবার ॥ ৫১ ॥

prati-dina tāṅre prabhu karena namaskāra
namaskari' ei śloka paḍe bāra-bāra

SYNONYMS

prati-dina—every day; *tāṅre*—unto the Deity of Lord Nṛsiṁhadeva; *prabhu*—Śrī Caitanya Mahāprabhu; *karena*—does; *namaskāra*—obeisances; *namaskari'*—offering obeisances; *ei śloka*—these verses; *paḍe*—recites; *bāra-bāra*—again and again.

TRANSLATION

Śrī Caitanya Mahāprabhu, His left side toward the Deity, offered obeisances to Lord Nṛsiṁha as He proceeded toward the temple. He recited the following verses again and again while offering obeisances.

TEXT 52

নমস্তে নরসিংহায় প্রহ্লাদাহ্লাদদায়িনে ।
হিরণ্যকশিপোর্বক্ষঃশিলাটঙ্ক-নখালয়ে ॥ ৫২ ॥

namas te nara-siṁhāya
prahlādāhlāda-dāyine
hiraṇyakaśipor vakṣaḥ-
śilā-ṭaṅka-nakhālaye

SYNONYMS

namaḥ—I offer my respectful obeisances; *te*—unto You; *nara-siṁhāya*—Lord Nṛsiṁhadeva; *prahlāda*—to Mahārāja Prahlāda; *āhlāda*—of pleasure; *dāyine*—giver; *hiraṇya-kaśipoḥ*—of Hiraṇyakaśipu; *vakṣaḥ*—chest; *śilā*—like stone; *ṭaṅka*—like the chisel; *nakha-ālaye*—whose fingernails.

TRANSLATION

"I offer my respectful obeisances unto You, Lord Nṛsiṁhadeva. You are the giver of pleasure to Mahārāja Prahlāda, and Your nails cut the chest of Hiraṇyakaśipu like a chisel cutting stone.

PURPORT

This and the following verse are quoted from the *Nṛsiṁha Purāṇa.*

TEXT 53

ইতো নৃসিংহঃ পরতো নৃসিংহো
যতো যতো যামি ততো নৃসিংহঃ ।
বহির্নৃসিংহো হৃদয়ে নৃসিংহো
নৃসিংহমাদিং শরণং প্রপদ্যে ॥ ৫৩ ॥

ito nṛsiṁhaḥ parato nṛsiṁho
yato yato yāmi tato nṛsiṁhaḥ
bahir nṛsiṁho hṛdaye nṛsiṁho
nṛsiṁham ādiṁ śaraṇaṁ prapadye

SYNONYMS

itaḥ—here; *nṛsiṁhaḥ*—Lord Nṛsiṁha; *parataḥ*—on the opposite side; *nṛsiṁhaḥ*—Lord Nṛsiṁha; *yataḥ yataḥ*—wherever; *yāmi*—I go; *tataḥ*—there; *nṛsiṁhaḥ*—Lord Nṛsiṁha; *bahiḥ*—outside; *nṛsiṁhaḥ*—Lord Nṛsiṁha; *hṛdaye*—in my heart; *nṛsiṁhaḥ*—Lord Nṛsiṁha; *nṛsiṁham*—Lord Nṛsiṁha; *ādim*—the original Supreme Personality; *śaraṇam prapadye*—I take shelter of.

TRANSLATION

"Lord Nṛsiṁhadeva is here, and He is also there on the opposite side. Wherever I go, there I see Lord Nṛsiṁhadeva. He is outside and within My heart. Therefore I take shelter of Lord Nṛsiṁhadeva, the original Supreme Personality of Godhead."

TEXT 54

তবে প্রভু করিলা জগন্নাথ দরশন।
ঘরে আসি' মধ্যাহ্ন করি' করিল ভোজন ॥ ৫৪ ॥

tabe prabhu karilā jagannātha daraśana
ghare āsi' madhyāhna kari' karila bhojana

SYNONYMS

tabe—after this; *prabhu*—Śrī Caitanya Mahāprabhu; *karilā*—did; *jagannātha daraśana*—visiting Lord Jagannātha; *ghare āsi'*—after returning home; *madhyāhna kari'*—after performing His noon activities; *karila bhojana*—took lunch.

TRANSLATION

Having offered obeisances to Lord Nṛsiṁhadeva, Śrī Caitanya Mahāprabhu visited the temple of Lord Jagannātha. Then He returned to His residence, finished His noon duties and took His lunch.

TEXT 55

বহির্দ্বারে আছে কালিদাস প্রত্যাশা করিয়া।
গোবিন্দেরে ঠারে প্রভু কহেন জানিয়া ॥ ৫৫ ॥

bahir-dvāre āche kālidāsa pratyāśā kariyā
govindere ṭhāre prabhu kahena jāniyā

SYNONYMS

bahiḥ-dvāre—outside the door; *āche*—there was; *kālidāsa*—Kālidāsa; *pratyāśā kariyā*—expecting; *govindere*—unto Govinda; *ṭhāre*—by indications; *prabhu*—Śrī Caitanya Mahāprabhu; *kahena*—speaks; *jāniyā*—knowing.

TRANSLATION

Kālidāsa was standing outside the door, expecting the remnants of food from Śrī Caitanya Mahāprabhu. Knowing this, Mahāprabhu gave an indication to Govinda.

TEXT 56

মহাপ্রভুর ইঙ্গিত গোবিন্দ সব জানে ।
কালিদাসেরে দিল প্রভুর শেষপাত্র-দানে ॥ ৫৬ ॥

mahāprabhura iṅgita govinda saba jāne
kālidāsere dila prabhura śeṣa-pātra-dāne

SYNONYMS

mahāprabhura—of Śrī Caitanya Mahāprabhu; *iṅgita*—indications; *govinda*—His personal servant; *saba*—all; *jāne*—knows; *kālidāsere*—unto Kālidāsa; *dila*—delivered; *prabhura*—of Śrī Caitanya Mahāprabhu; *śeṣa-pātra*—the remnants of food; *dāne*—presentation.

TRANSLATION

Govinda understood all the indications of Śrī Caitanya Mahāprabhu. Therefore he immediately delivered the remnants of Śrī Caitanya Mahāprabhu's food to Kālidāsa.

TEXT 57

বৈষ্ণবের শেষ-ভক্ষণের এতেক মহিমা ।
কালিদাসে পাওয়াইল প্রভুর কৃপা-সীমা ॥ ৫৭ ॥

vaiṣṇavera śeṣa-bhakṣaṇera eteka mahimā
kālidāse pāoyāila prabhura kṛpā-sīmā

SYNONYMS

vaiṣṇavera—of Vaiṣṇavas; *śeṣa-bhakṣaṇera*—of eating the remnants of food; *eteka mahimā*—so much value; *kālidāse*—Kālidāsa; *pāoyāila*—caused to get; *prabhura*—of Śrī Caitanya Mahāprabhu; *kṛpā-sīmā*—the supreme mercy.

TRANSLATION

Taking the remnants of the food of Vaiṣṇavas is so valuable that it induced Śrī Caitanya Mahāprabhu to offer Kālidāsa His supreme mercy.

TEXT 58

তাতে 'বৈষ্ণবের ঝুটা' খাও ছাড়ি' ঘৃণা-লাজ ।
যাহা হৈতে পাইবা নিজ বাঞ্ছিত সব কাজ ॥ ৫৮ ॥

tāte 'vaiṣṇavera jhuṭā' khāo chāḍi' ghṛṇā-lāja
yāhā haite pāibā nija vāñchita saba kāja

SYNONYMS

tāte—therefore; *vaiṣṇavera jhuṭā*—remnants of the food of Vaiṣṇavas; *khāo*—eat; *chāḍi'*—giving up; *ghṛṇā-lāja*—hate and hesitation; *yāhā haite*—by which; *pāibā*—you will get; *nija*—your own; *vāñchita*—desired; *saba*—all; *kāja*—success.

TRANSLATION

Therefore, giving up hatred and hesitation, try to eat the remnants of the food of Vaiṣṇavas, for you will thus be able to achieve your desired goal of life.

TEXT 59

কৃষ্ণের উচ্ছিষ্ট হয় 'মহাপ্রসাদ' নাম ।
'ভক্তশেষ' হৈলে 'মহা-মহাপ্রসাদাখ্যান' ॥ ৫৯ ॥

kṛṣṇera ucchiṣṭa haya 'mahā-prasāda' nāma
'bhakta-śeṣa' haile 'mahā-mahā-prasādākhyāna'

SYNONYMS

kṛṣṇera ucchiṣṭa—remnants of the food of Kṛṣṇa; *haya*—are; *mahā-prasāda nāma*—called *mahā-prasāda; bhakta-śeṣa*—the remnants of a devotee; *haile*—when it becomes; *mahā-mahā-prasāda*—great *mahā-prasāda; ākhyāna*—named.

TRANSLATION

The remnants of food offered to Lord Kṛṣṇa are called mahā-prasāda. After this same mahā-prasāda has been taken by a devotee, the remnants are elevated to mahā-mahā-prasāda.

TEXT 60

ভক্তপদধূলি আর ভক্তপদ-জল ।
ভক্তভুক্ত-অবশেষ,—তিন মহাবল ॥ ৬০ ॥

bhakta-pada-dhūli āra bhakta-pada-jala
bhakta-bhukta-avaśeṣa,——tina mahā-bala

SYNONYMS

bhakta-pada-dhūli—the dust of the lotus feet of a devotee; *āra*—and; *bhakta-pada-jala*—the water that washed the feet of a devotee; *bhakta-bhukta-avaśeṣa*—and the remnants of food eaten by a devotee; *tina*—three; *mahā-bala*—very powerful.

TRANSLATION

The dust of the feet of a devotee, the water that has washed the feet of a devotee, and the remnants of food left by a devotee are three very powerful substances.

TEXT 61

এই তিন-সেবা হৈতে কৃষ্ণপ্রেমা হয় ।
পুনঃ পুনঃ সর্বশাস্ত্রে ফুকারিয়া কয় ॥ ৬১ ॥

ei tina-sevā haite kṛṣṇa-premā haya
punaḥ punaḥ sarva-śāstre phukāriyā kaya

SYNONYMS

ei tina-sevā—rendering service to these three; *haite*—from; *kṛṣṇa-premā*—ecstatic love for Kṛṣṇa; *haya*—there is; *punaḥ punaḥ*—again and again; *sarva-śāstre*—all the revealed scriptures; *phu-kāriyā kaya*—declare loudly.

TRANSLATION

By rendering service to these three, one attains the supreme goal of ecstatic love for Kṛṣṇa. In all the revealed scriptures this is loudly declared again and again.

TEXT 62

তাতে বার বার কহি,—শুন ভক্তগণ ।
বিশ্বাস করিয়া কর এ-তিন সেবন ॥ ৬২ ॥

tāte bāra bāra kahi,—śuna bhakta-gaṇa
viśvāsa kariyā kara e-tina sevana

SYNONYMS

tāte—therefore; *bāra bāra*—again and again; *kahi*—I say; *śuna*—hear; *bhakta-gaṇa*—devotees; *viśvāsa kariyā*—keeping faith; *kara*—do; *e-tina sevana*—rendering service to these three.

TRANSLATION

Therefore, my dear devotees, please hear from me, for I insist again and again: please keep faith in these three and render service to them without hesitation.

TEXT 63

তিন হৈতে কৃষ্ণনাম-প্রেমের উল্লাস ।
কৃষ্ণের প্রসাদ, তাতে 'সাক্ষী' কালিদাস ॥ ৬৩ ॥

tina haite kṛṣṇa-nāma-premera ullāsa
kṛṣṇera prasāda, tāte 'sākṣī' kālidāsa

SYNONYMS

tina haite—from these three; *kṛṣṇa-nāma*—of the holy name of Lord Kṛṣṇa; *premera ullāsa*—awakening of ecstatic love; *kṛṣṇera prasāda*—the mercy of Lord Kṛṣṇa; *tāte*—in that; *sākṣī*—evidence; *kālidāsa*—Kālidāsa.

TRANSLATION

From these three one achieves the highest goal of life—ecstatic love of Kṛṣṇa. This is the greatest mercy of Lord Kṛṣṇa. The evidence is Kālidāsa himself.

TEXT 64

নীলাচলে মহাপ্রভু রহে এইমতে ।
কালিদাসে মহাকৃপা কৈলা অলক্ষিতে ॥ ৬৪ ॥

nīlācale mahāprabhu rahe ei-mate
kālidāse mahā-kṛpā kailā alakṣite

SYNONYMS

nīlācale—at Jagannātha Purī; *mahāprabhu*—Śrī Caitanya Mahāprabhu; *rahe*—remains; *ei-mate*—in this way; *kālidāse*—unto Kālidāsa; *mahā-kṛpā*—great favor; *kailā*—bestowed; *alakṣite*—invisibly.

TRANSLATION

In this way Śrī Caitanya Mahāprabhu remained at Jagannātha Purī, Nīlācala, and He invisibly bestowed great mercy upon Kālidāsa.

TEXT 65

সে বৎসর শিবানন্দ পত্নী লঞা আইলা।
'পুরীদাস'-ছোটপুত্রে সঙ্গেতে আনিলা ॥ ৬৫ ॥

se vatsara śivānanda patnī lañā āilā
'purīdāsa'-choṭa-putre saṅgete ānilā

SYNONYMS

se vatsara—that year; *śivānanda*—Śivānanda Sena; *patnī*—the wife; *lañā*—bringing; *āilā*—came; *purī-dāsa*—Purīdāsa; *choṭa-putre*—the youngest son; *saṅgete ānilā*—he brought with him.

TRANSLATION

That year, Śivānanda Sena brought with him his wife and youngest son, Purīdāsa.

TEXT 66

পুত্র সঙ্গে লঞা তেঁহো আইলা প্রভু-স্থানে।
পুত্রেরে করাইলা প্রভুর চরণ বন্দনে ॥ ৬৬ ॥

putra saṅge lañā teṅho āilā prabhu-sthāne
putrere karāilā prabhura caraṇa vandane

SYNONYMS

putra—the son; *saṅge*—along; *lañā*—taking; *teṅho*—he; *āilā*—came; *prabhu-sthāne*—to the place of Śrī Caitanya Mahāprabhu; *putrere*—his son; *karāilā*—made to do; *prabhura*—of Śrī Caitanya Mahāprabhu; *caraṇa vandane*—worshiping the lotus feet.

TRANSLATION

Taking his son, Śivānanda Sena went to see Śrī Caitanya Mahāprabhu at His residence. He made his son offer respectful obeisances at the lotus feet of the Lord.

TEXT 67

'কৃষ্ণ কহ' বলি' প্রভু বলেন বার বার।
তবু কৃষ্ণনাম বালক না করে উচ্চার ॥ ৬৭ ॥

'kṛṣṇa kaha' bali' prabhu balena bāra bāra
tabu kṛṣṇa-nāma bālaka nā kare uccāra

SYNONYMS

kṛṣṇa kaha—say Kṛṣṇa; *bali'*—saying; *prabhu*—Śrī Caitanya Mahāprabhu; *balena*—said; *bāra bāra*—again and again; *tabu*—still; *kṛṣṇa-nāma*—the holy name of Kṛṣṇa; *bālaka*—the boy; *nā kare uccāra*—did not utter.

TRANSLATION

Śrī Caitanya Mahāprabhu asked the boy again and again to chant the name of Kṛṣṇa, but the boy would not utter the holy name.

TEXT 68

শিবানন্দ বালকেরে বহু যত্ন করিলা।
তবু সেই বালক কৃষ্ণনাম না কহিলা ॥ ॥ ৬৮ ॥

śivānanda bālakere bahu yatna karilā
tabu sei bālaka kṛṣṇa-nāma nā kahilā

SYNONYMS

śivānanda—Śivānanda Sena; *bālakere*—unto the boy; *bahu*—much; *yatna*—endeavor; *karilā*—did; *tabu*—still; *sei bālaka*—that boy; *kṛṣṇa-nāma*—the name of Kṛṣṇa; *nā kahilā*—did not utter.

TRANSLATION

Although Śivānanda Sena tried with much endeavor to get his boy to speak Kṛṣṇa's holy name, the boy would not utter it.

TEXT 69

প্রভু কহে,—"আমি নাম জগতে লওয়াইলুঁ।
স্থাবরে পর্যন্ত কৃষ্ণনাম কহাইলুঁ ॥ ৬৯ ॥

prabhu kahe,—"āmi nāma jagate laoyāiluṅ
sthāvare paryanta kṛṣṇa-nāma kahāiluṅ

SYNONYMS

prabhu kahe—Śrī Caitanya Mahāprabhu said; *āmi*—I; *nāma*—the holy name; *jagate*—throughout the whole world; *laoyāiluṅ*—induced to take; *sthāvare*—the unmovable; *paryanta*—up to; *kṛṣṇa-nāma*—the holy name of Kṛṣṇa; *kahāiluṅ*—I induced to chant.

TRANSLATION

Śrī Caitanya Mahāprabhu said, "I have induced the whole world to take to the holy name of Kṛṣṇa. I have induced even the trees and immovable plants to chant the holy name.

TEXT 70

ইহারে নারিলুঁ কৃষ্ণনাম কহাইতে !"
শুনিয়া স্বরূপগোসাঞি লাগিলা কহিতে ॥ ৭০ ॥

ihāre nāriluṅ kṛṣṇa-nāma kahāite!"
śuniyā svarūpa-gosāñi lāgilā kahite

SYNONYMS

ihāre—this boy; *nāriluṅ*—I could not; *kṛṣṇa-nāma*—the holy name of Kṛṣṇa; *kahāite*—cause to speak; *śuniyā*—hearing; *svarūpa-gosāñi*—Svarūpa Dāmodara Gosāñi; *lāgilā*—began; *kahite*—to say.

TRANSLATION

"But I could not induce this boy to chant the holy name of Kṛṣṇa." Hearing this, Svarūpa Dāmodara Gosvāmī began to speak.

TEXT 71

"তুমি কৃষ্ণনাম-মন্ত্র কৈলা উপদেশে ।
মন্ত্র পাঞা কা'র আগে না করে প্রকাশে ॥ ৭১ ॥

"tumi kṛṣṇa-nāma-mantra kailā upadeśe
mantra pāñā kā'ra āge nā kare prakāśe

SYNONYMS

tumi—You; *kṛṣṇa-nāma*—the holy name of Kṛṣṇa; *mantra*—this hymn; *kailā upadeśe*—have instructed; *mantra pāñā*—getting the hymn; *kā'ra āge*—in front of everyone; *nā kare prakāśe*—he does not express.

TRANSLATION

"My Lord," he said, "You have given him initiation into the name of Kṛṣṇa, but after receiving the mantra he will not express it in front of everyone.

TEXT 72

মনে মনে জপে, মুখে না করে আখ্যান ।
এই ইহার মনঃকথা—করি অনুমান ॥" ৭২ ॥

mane mane jape, mukhe nā kare ākhyāna
ei ihāra manaḥ-kathā——kari anumāna"

SYNONYMS

mane mane—within the mind; *jape*—chants; *mukhe*—in the mouth; *nā kare ākhyāna*—does not express; *ei*—this; *ihāra*—his; *manaḥ-kathā*—intention; *kari anumāna*—I guess.

TRANSLATION

"This boy chants the mantra within his mind, but does not say it aloud. That is his intention, as far as I can guess."

TEXT 73

আর দিন কহেন প্রভু,—'পড়, পুরীদাস ।'
এই শ্লোক করি' তেঁহো করিলা প্রকাশ ॥ ৭৩ ॥

āra dina kahena prabhu,——'paḍa, purīdāsa'
ei śloka kari' teṅho karilā prakāśa

SYNONYMS

āra dina—another day; *kahena prabhu*—Śrī Caitanya Mahāprabhu said; *paḍa*—recite; *purīdāsa*—Purīdāsa; *ei*—this; *śloka*—verse; *kari'*—making; *teṅho*—he; *karilā prakāśa*—manifested.

TRANSLATION

Another day, when Śrī Caitanya Mahāprabhu said to the boy, "Recite, My dear Purīdāsa," the boy composed the following verse and expressed it before everyone.

TEXT 74

শ্রবসোঃ কুবলয়মক্ষ্ণোরঞ্জনমুরসো মহেন্দ্রমণিদাম ।
বৃন্দাবনরমণীনাং মণ্ডনমখিলং হরির্জয়তি ॥ ৭৪ ॥

śravasoḥ kuvalayam akṣṇor añjanam
uraso mahendra-maṇi-dāma
vṛndāvana-ramaṇīnāṁ maṇḍanam
akhilaṁ harir jayati

SYNONYMS

śravasoḥ—of the two ears; *kuvalayam*—blue lotus flowers; *akṣṇoḥ*—of the two eyes; *añjanam*—ointment; *urasaḥ*—of the chest; *mahendra-maṇi-dāma*—a necklace of *indranīla* gems; *vṛndāvana-ramaṇīnām*—of the damsels of Vṛndāvana; *maṇḍanam*—ornaments; *akhilam*—all; *hariḥ jayati*—all glories to Lord Śrī Kṛṣṇa.

TRANSLATION

"Lord Śrī Kṛṣṇa is just like a bluish lotus flower for the ears; He is ointment for the eyes, a necklace of indranīla gems for the chest, and universal ornaments for the gopī damsels of Vṛndāvana. Let that Lord Śrī Hari, Kṛṣṇa, be glorified."

TEXT 75

সাত বৎসরের শিশু, নাহি অধ্যয়ন।
ঐছে শ্লোক করে,—লোকের চমৎকার মন ॥ ৭৫ ॥

sāta vatsarera śiśu, nāhi adhyayana
aiche śloka kare,——lokera camatkāra mana

SYNONYMS

sāta vatsarera—seven years old; *śiśu*—the boy; *nāhi adhyayana*—without education; *aiche*—such; *śloka*—verse; *kare*—composes; *lokera*—of all the people; *camatkāra*—struck with wonder; *mana*—mind.

TRANSLATION

Although the boy was only seven years old and still had no education, he composed such a nice verse. Everyone was struck with wonder.

TEXT 76

চৈতন্যপ্রভুর এই কৃপার মহিমা।
ব্রহ্মাদি দেব যার নাহি পায় সীমা ॥ ৭৬ ॥

caitanya-prabhura ei kṛpāra mahimā
brahmādi deva yāra nāhi pāya sīmā

SYNONYMS

caitanya-prabhura—of Lord Śrī Caitanya Mahāprabhu; *ei*—this; *kṛpāra mahimā*—the glory of the mercy; *brahmā-ādi*—headed by Lord Brahmā; *deva*—the demigods; *yāra*—of which; *nāhi pāya*—do not reach; *sīmā*—the limit.

TRANSLATION

This is the glory of Śrī Caitanya Mahāprabhu's causeless mercy, which even the demigods, headed by Lord Brahmā, cannot estimate.

TEXT 77

ভক্তগণ প্রভু-সঙ্গে রহে চারিমাসে ।
প্রভু আজ্ঞা দিলা সবে গেলা গৌড়দেশে ॥ ৭৭ ॥

bhakta-gaṇa prabhu-saṅge rahe cāri-māse
prabhu ājñā dilā sabe gelā gauḍa-deśe

SYNONYMS

bhakta-gaṇa—all the devotees; *prabhu-saṅge*—with Śrī Caitanya Mahāprabhu; *rahe*—remained; *cāri-māse*—for four months; *prabhu*—Lord Śrī Caitanya Mahāprabhu; *ājñā dilā*—gave the order; *sabe*—unto everyone; *gelā*—returned; *gauḍa-deśe*—to Bengal.

TRANSLATION

All the devotees remained with Śrī Caitanya Mahāprabhu continuously for four months. Then the Lord ordered them back to Bengal, and therefore they returned.

TEXT 78

তাঁ-সবার সঙ্গে প্রভুর ছিল বাহ্যজ্ঞান ।
তাঁরা গেলে পুনঃ হৈলা উন্মাদ প্রধান ॥ ৭৮ ॥

tāṅ-sabāra saṅge prabhura chila bāhya-jñāna
tāṅrā gele punaḥ hailā unmāda pradhāna

SYNONYMS

tāṅ-sabāra—all of them; *saṅge*—with; *prabhura*—of Śrī Caitanya Mahāprabhu; *chila*—there was; *bāhya-jñāna*—external consciousness; *tāṅrā gele*—when they departed; *punaḥ*—again; *hailā*—there was; *unmāda*—madness; *pradhāna*—the chief business.

TRANSLATION

As long as the devotees were in Nīlācala, Jagannātha Purī, Śrī Caitanya Mahāprabhu maintained His external consciousness, but after their departure His chief engagement was again the madness of ecstatic love for Kṛṣṇa.

TEXT 79

রাত্রি-দিনে স্ফুরে কৃষ্ণের রূপ-গন্ধ-রস।
সাক্ষাদনুভবে,—যেন কৃষ্ণ-উপস্পর্শ ॥ ৭৯ ॥

rātri-dine sphure kṛṣṇera rūpa-gandha-rasa
sākṣād-anubhave,——yena kṛṣṇa-upasparśa

SYNONYMS

rātri-dine—night and day; *sphure*—appears; *kṛṣṇera*—of Lord Kṛṣṇa; *rūpa*—the beauty; *gandha*—fragrance; *rasa*—mellow; *sākṣāt-anubhave*—directly experienced; *yena*—as if; *kṛṣṇa-upasparśa*—touching Kṛṣṇa.

TRANSLATION

Throughout the entire day and night, Śrī Caitanya Mahāprabhu directly relished Kṛṣṇa's beauty, fragrance and mellow as if He were touching Kṛṣṇa hand to hand.

TEXT 80

একদিন প্রভু গেলা জগন্নাথ-দরশনে।
সিংহদ্বারে দলই আসি' করিল বন্দনে ॥ ৮০ ॥

eka-dina prabhu gelā jagannātha-daraśane
siṁha-dvāre dala-i āsi' karila vandane

SYNONYMS

eka-dina—one day; *prabhu*—Śrī Caitanya Mahāprabhu; *gelā*—went; *jagannātha-daraśane*—to see Lord Jagannātha; *siṁha-dvāre*—at the gate known as Siṁha-dvāra; *dala-i*—the gatekeeper; *āsi'*—coming; *karila vandane*—offered respectful obeisances.

TRANSLATION

One day, when Śrī Caitanya Mahāprabhu went to visit the temple of Lord Jagannātha, the gatekeeper at Siṁha-dvāra approached Him and offered respectful obeisances.

TEXT 81

তারে বলে,—'কোথা কৃষ্ণ, মোর প্রাণনাথ ?
মোরে কৃষ্ণ দেখাও' বলি' ধরে তার হাত ॥ ৮১ ॥

tāre bale,——'kothā kṛṣṇa, mora prāṇa-nātha?
more kṛṣṇa dekhāo' bali' dhare tāra hāta

SYNONYMS

tāre—to him; *bale*—said; *kothā kṛṣṇa*—where is Kṛṣṇa; *mora*—My; *prāṇa-nātha*—Lord of life; *more*—to Me; *kṛṣṇa dekhāo*—please show Kṛṣṇa; *bali'*—saying; *dhare*—catches; *tāra*—his; *hāta*—hand.

TRANSLATION

The Lord asked him, "Where is Kṛṣṇa, My life and soul? Please show Me Kṛṣṇa." Saying this, He caught the doorkeeper's hand.

TEXT 82

সেহ কহে,—'ইঁহা হয় ব্রজেন্দ্রনন্দন ।
আইস তুমি মোর সঙ্গে, করাঙ দরশন ॥' ৮২ ॥

seha kahe,——'iṅhā haya vrajendra-nandana
āisa tumi mora saṅge, karāṅa daraśana'

SYNONYMS

seha kahe—he said; *iṅhā*—here; *haya*—is; *vrajendra-nandana*—the son of Nanda Mahārāja; *āisa*—come; *tumi*—You; *mora saṅge*—with me; *karāṅa daraśana*—I shall show.

TRANSLATION

The doorkeeper replied, "The son of Mahārāja Nanda is here; please come along with me, and I shall show You."

TEXT 83

'তুমি মোর সখা, দেখাহ,—কাহাঁ প্রাণনাথ ?'
এত বলি' জগমোহন গেলা ধরি' তার হাত ॥ ৮৩ ॥

'tumi mora sakhā, dekhāha——kāhāṅ prāṇa-nātha?'
eta bali' jagamohana gelā dhari' tāra hāta

SYNONYMS

tumi—you; *mora sakhā*—My friend; *dekhāha*—please show; *kāhāṅ*—where; *prāṇa-nātha*—the Lord of My heart; *eta bali'*—saying this; *jagamohana*—to Jagamohana; *gelā*—went; *dhari'*—catching; *tāra*—his; *hāta*—hand.

TRANSLATION

Lord Caitanya said to the doorman, "You are My friend. Please show Me where the Lord of My heart is." After the Lord said this, they both went to the place known as Jagamohana, where everyone views Lord Jagannātha.

TEXT 84

সেহ বলে,—'এই দেখ শ্রীপুরুষোত্তম ।
নেত্র ভরিয়া তুমি করহ দরশন ॥' ৮৪ ॥

seha bale,——'ei dekha śrī-puruṣottama
netra bhariyā tumi karaha daraśana'

SYNONYMS

seha bale—he also said; *ei*—this; *dekha*—just see; *śrī-puruṣa-uttama*—Lord Kṛṣṇa, the best of all Personalities of Godhead; *netra bhariyā*—to the full satisfaction of Your eyes; *tumi*—You; *karaha daraśana*—see.

TRANSLATION

"Just see!" the doorkeeper said. "Here is the best of the Personalities of Godhead. From here You may see the Lord to the full satisfaction of Your eyes."

TEXT 85

গরুড়ের পাছে রহি' করেন দরশন ।
দেখেন,—জগন্নাথ হয় মুরলীবদন ॥ ৮৫ ॥

garuḍera pāche rahi' karena daraśana
dekhena,——jagannātha haya muralī-vadana

SYNONYMS

garuḍera pāche—behind the Garuḍa column; *rahi'*—staying; *karena daraśana*—He was seeing; *dekhena*—He saw; *jagannātha*—Lord Jagannātha; *haya*—was; *muralī-vadana*—Lord Kṛṣṇa with His flute to the mouth.

TRANSLATION

Śrī Caitanya Mahāprabhu stayed behind the huge column called the Garuḍa-stambha and looked upon Lord Jagannātha, but as He looked He saw that Lord Jagannātha had become Lord Kṛṣṇa, with His flute to His mouth.

TEXT 86

এই লীলা নিজ-গ্রন্থে রঘুনাথ-দাস।
'গৌরাঙ্গস্তব-কল্পবৃক্ষে' করিয়াছেন প্রকাশ ॥ ৮৬ ॥

ei līlā nija-granthe raghunātha-dāsa
'gaurāṅga-stava-kalpavṛkṣe' kariyāchena prakāśa

SYNONYMS

ei līlā—this pastime; *nija-granthe*—in his own book; *raghunātha-dāsa*—Raghunātha dāsa Gosvāmī; *gaurāṅga-stava-kalpa-vṛkṣe*—*Gaurāṅga-stava-kalpavṛkṣa; kariyāchena prakāśa*—has described.

TRANSLATION

In his book known as Gaurāṅga-stava-kalpavṛkṣa, Raghunātha dāsa Gosvāmī has described this incident very nicely.

TEXT 87

ক্ব মে কান্তঃ কৃষ্ণস্ত্বরিতমিহ তং লোকয় সখে
ত্বমেবেতি দ্বারাধিপমভিবদন্নুন্মদ ইব।
দ্রুতং গচ্ছ দ্রষ্টুং প্রিয়মিতি তদুক্তেন ধৃত-তদ্-
ভুজান্তর্গৌরাঙ্গো হৃদয় উদয়ন্মাং মদয়তি ॥ ৮৭ ॥

kva me kāntaḥ kṛṣṇas tvaritam iha taṁ lokaya sakhe
tvam eveti dvārādhipam abhivadann unmada iva
drutaṁ gaccha draṣṭuṁ priyam iti tad-uktena dhṛta-tad-
bhujāntar gaurāṅgo hṛdaya udayan māṁ madayati

SYNONYMS

kva—where; *me*—My; *kāntaḥ*—beloved; *kṛṣṇaḥ*—Lord Kṛṣṇa; *tvaritam*—quickly; *iha*—here; *tam*—Him; *lokaya*—show; *sakhe*—O friend; *tvam*—you; *eva*—certainly; *iti*—thus; *dvāra-adhipam*—the doorkeeper; *abhivadan*—requesting; *unmadaḥ*—a madman; *iva*—like; *drutam*—very quickly; *gaccha*—come; *draṣṭum*—to see; *priyam*—beloved; *iti*—thus; *tat*—of him; *uktena*—with the words; *dhṛta*—caught; *tat*—His; *bhuja-antaḥ*—end of the arm; *gaurāṅgaḥ*—Lord Śrī Caitanya Mahāprabhu; *hṛdaye*—in my heart; *udayan*—rising; *mām*—me; *madayati*—maddens.

TRANSLATION

" 'My dear friend the doorkeeper, where is Kṛṣṇa, the Lord of My heart? Kindly show Him to Me quickly.' With these words, Lord Śrī Caitanya Mahāprabhu addressed the doorkeeper like a madman. The doorkeeper grasped His hand and replied very hastily, 'Come, see Your beloved!' May that Lord Śrī Caitanya Mahāprabhu rise within my heart and thus make me mad also."

TEXT 88

হেনকালে 'গোপাল-বল্লভ'-ভোগ লাগাইল ।
শঙ্খ-ঘণ্টা-আদি সহ আরতি বাজিল ॥ ৮৮ ॥

hena-kāle 'gopāla-vallabha'-bhoga lāgāila
śaṅkha-ghaṇṭā-ādi saha ārati bājila

SYNONYMS

hena-kāle—at this time; *gopāla-vallabha-bhoga*—the food offered early in the morning; *lāgāila*—was offered; *śaṅkha*—conch; *ghaṇṭā-ādi*—bells and so on; *saha*—with; *ārati*—*ārati; bājila*—sounded.

TRANSLATION

The offering of food known as gopāla-vallabha-bhoga was then given to Lord Jagannātha, and ārati was performed with the sound of the conch and the ringing of bells.

TEXT 89

ভোগ সরিলে জগন্নাথের সেবকগণ ।
প্রসাদ লঞা প্রভু-ঠাঞি কৈল আগমন ॥ ৮৯ ॥

bhoga sarile jagannāthera sevaka-gaṇa
prasāda lañā prabhu-ṭhāñi kaila āgamana

SYNONYMS

bhoga sarile—when the food was taken away; *jagannāthera*—of Lord Jagannātha; *sevaka-gaṇa*—the servants; *prasāda lañā*—taking the *prasāda; prabhu-ṭhāñi*—unto Lord Śrī Caitanya Mahāprabhu; *kaila āgamana*—came.

TRANSLATION

When the ārati finished, the prasāda was taken out, and the servants of Lord Jagannātha came to offer some to Śrī Caitanya Mahāprabhu.

TEXT 90

মালা পরাঞা প্রসাদ দিল প্রভুর হাতে।
আস্বাদ দূরে রহু, যার গন্ধে মন মাতে ॥ ৯০ ॥

mālā parāñā prasāda dila prabhura hāte
āsvāda dūre rahu, yāra gandhe mana māte

SYNONYMS

mālā parāñā—after garlanding; *prasāda*—the remnants of Lord Jagannātha's food; *dila*—delivered; *prabhura hāte*—in the hand of Śrī Caitanya Mahāprabhu; *āsvāda*—tasting; *dūre rahu*—what to speak of; *yāra*—of which; *gandhe*—by the aroma; *mana*—mind; *māte*—becomes maddened.

TRANSLATION

The servants of Lord Jagannātha first garlanded Śrī Caitanya Mahāprabhu and then offered Him Lord Jagannātha's prasāda. The prasāda was so nice that its aroma alone, to say nothing of its taste, would drive the mind mad.

TEXT 91

বহুমূল্য প্রসাদ সেই বস্তু সর্বোত্তম।
তার অল্প খাওয়াইতে সেবক করিল যতন ॥ ৯১ ॥

bahu-mūlya prasāda sei vastu sarvottama
tāra alpa khāoyāite sevaka karila yatana

SYNONYMS

bahu-mūlya—very valuable; *prasāda*—remnants of food; *sei*—that; *vastu*—ingredients; *sarva-uttama*—first class; *tāra*—of that; *alpa*—very little; *khāoyāite*—to feed; *sevaka*—the servant; *karila yatana*—made some endeavor.

TRANSLATION

The prasāda was made of very valuable ingredients. Therefore the servant wanted to feed Śrī Caitanya Mahāprabhu a portion of it.

TEXT 92

তার অল্প লঞা প্রভু জিহ্বাতে যদি দিলা।
আর সব গোবিন্দের আঁচলে বান্ধিলা ॥ ৯২ ॥

tāra alpa lañā prabhu jihvāte yadi dilā
āra saba govindera āṅcale bāndhilā

SYNONYMS

tāra—of that; *alpa*—very little; *lañā*—taking; *prabhu*—Śrī Caitanya Mahāprabhu; *jihvāte*—on the tongue; *yadi*—when; *dilā*—put; *āra saba*—all the balance; *govindera*—of Govinda; *āṅcale*—at the end of the wrapper; *bāndhilā*—bound.

TRANSLATION

Śrī Caitanya Mahāprabhu tasted a portion of the prasāda. Govinda took the rest and bound it in the end of his wrapper.

TEXT 93

কোটি-অমৃত-স্বাদ পাঞা প্রভুর চমৎকার ।
সর্বাঙ্গে পুলক, নেত্রে বহে অশ্রুধার ॥ ৯৩ ॥

koṭi-amṛta-svāda pāñā prabhura camatkāra
sarvāṅge pulaka, netre vahe aśru-dhāra

SYNONYMS

koṭi—millions upon millions; *amṛta*—nectar; *svāda*—taste; *pāñā*—getting; *prabhura*—of Śrī Caitanya Mahāprabhu; *camatkāra*—great satisfaction; *sarva-aṅge*—all over the body; *pulaka*—standing of the hair; *netre*—from the eyes; *vahe*—flows; *aśru-dhāra*—a stream of tears.

TRANSLATION

To Śrī Caitanya Mahāprabhu the prasāda tasted millions upon millions of times better than nectar, and thus He was fully satisfied. The hair all over His body stood on end, and incessant tears flowed from His eyes.

TEXT 94

'এই দ্রব্যে এত স্বাদ কাহাঁ হৈতে আইল ?
কৃষ্ণের অধরামৃত ইথে সঞ্চারিল ॥' ৯৪ ॥

'ei dravye eta svāda kāhāṅ haite āila?
kṛṣṇera adharāmṛta ithe sañcārila'

SYNONYMS

ei dravye—in these ingredients; *eta*—so much; *svāda*—taste; *kāhāṅ*—where; *haite*—from; *āila*—has come; *kṛṣṇera*—of Lord Kṛṣṇa; *adhara-amṛta*—nectar from the lips; *ithe*—in this; *sañcārila*—has spread.

TRANSLATION

Śrī Caitanya Mahāprabhu considered, "Where has such a taste in this prasāda come from? Certainly it is due to its having been touched by the nectar of Kṛṣṇa's lips."

TEXT 95

এই বুদ্ধ্যে মহাপ্রভুর প্রেমাবেশ হৈল ।
জগন্নাথের সেবক দেখি' সম্বরণ কৈল ॥ ৯৫ ॥

ei buddhye mahāprabhura premāveśa haila
jagannāthera sevaka dekhi' saṁvaraṇa kaila

SYNONYMS

ei buddhye—by this understanding; *mahāprabhura*—of Śrī Caitanya Mahāprabhu; *prema-āveśa*—ecstatic emotion; *haila*—there was; *jagannāthera*—of Lord Jagannātha; *sevaka*—servants; *dekhi'*—seeing; *saṁvaraṇa kaila*—restrained Himself.

TRANSLATION

Understanding this, Śrī Caitanya Mahāprabhu felt an emotion of ecstatic love for Kṛṣṇa, but upon seeing the servants of Lord Jagannātha, He restrained Himself.

TEXT 96

'সুকৃতি-লভ্য ফেলা-লব'—বলেন বারবার ।
ঈশ্বর-সেবক পুছে,—'কি অর্থ ইহার' ? ৯৬ ॥

'sukṛti-labhya phelā-lava'——balena bāra-bāra
īśvara-sevaka puche,——'ki artha ihāra'?

SYNONYMS

sukṛti—by great fortune; *labhya*—obtainable; *phelā-lava*—a particle of the remnants; *balena*—says; *bāra-bāra*—again and again; *īśvara-sevaka*—the servants of Jagannātha; *puche*—inquire; *ki*—what; *artha*—the meaning; *ihāra*—of this.

TRANSLATION

The Lord said again and again, "Only by great fortune may one come by a particle of the remnants of food offered to the Lord." The servants of the Jagannātha temple inquired, "What is the meaning of this?"

PURPORT

The remnants of Kṛṣṇa's food are mixed with His saliva. In the *Mahābhārata* and the *Skanda Purāṇa* it is stated:

mahā-prasāde govinde
nāma-brahmaṇi vaiṣṇave
svalpa-puṇyavatāṁ rājan
viśvāso naiva jāyate

"Persons who are not very highly elevated in pious activities cannot believe in the remnants of food [*prasāda*] of the Supreme Personality of Godhead, nor in Govinda, the holy name of the Lord, nor in the Vaiṣṇavas."

TEXT 97

প্রভু কহে,—"এই যে দিলা কৃষ্ণাধরামৃত।
ব্রহ্মাদি-দুর্লভ এই নিন্দয়ে 'অমৃত' ॥ ৯৭ ॥

prabhu kahe,—"ei ye dilā kṛṣṇādharāmṛta
brahmādi-durlabha ei nindaye 'amṛta'

SYNONYMS

prabhu kahe—Śrī Caitanya Mahāprabhu said; *ei*—this; *ye*—which; *dilā*—you have given; *kṛṣṇa*—of Lord Kṛṣṇa; *adhara-amṛta*—nectar from the lips; *brahmā-ādi*—by the demigods, headed by Lord Brahmā; *durlabha*—difficult to obtain; *ei*—this; *nindaye*—defeats; *amṛta*—nectar.

TRANSLATION

Śrī Caitanya Mahāprabhu replied, "These are remnants of food that Kṛṣṇa has eaten and thus turned to nectar with His lips. It surpasses heavenly nectar, and even such demigods as Lord Brahmā find it difficult to obtain.

TEXT 98

কৃষ্ণের যে ভুক্ত-শেষ, তার 'ফেলা'-নাম।
তার এক 'লব' যে পায়, সেই ভাগ্যবান্ ॥ ৯৮ ॥

kṛṣṇera ye bhukta-śeṣa, tāra 'phelā'-nāma
tāra eka 'lava' ye pāya, sei bhāgyavān

SYNONYMS

kṛṣṇera—of Lord Kṛṣṇa; *ye*—whatever; *bhukta-śeṣa*—remnants of food; *tāra*—of that; *phelā-nāma*—the name is *phelā; tāra*—of that; *eka*—one; *lava*—fragment; *ye*—one who; *pāya*—gets; *sei*—he; *bhāgyavān*—fortunate.

TRANSLATION

"Remnants left by Kṛṣṇa are called phelā. Anyone who obtains even a small portion must be considered very fortunate.

TEXT 99

সামান্য ভাগ্য হৈতে তার প্রাপ্তি নাহি হয়।
কৃষ্ণের যাঁতে পূর্ণকৃপা, সেই তাহা পায় ॥ ৯৯ ॥

sāmānya bhāgya haite tāra prāpti nāhi haya
kṛṣṇera yāṅte pūrṇa-kṛpā, sei tāhā pāya

SYNONYMS

sāmānya—ordinary; *bhāgya*—fortune; *haite*—from; *tāra*—of that; *prāpti*—attainment; *nāhi*—not; *haya*—there is; *kṛṣṇera*—of Lord Kṛṣṇa; *yāṅte*—unto whom; *pūrṇa-kṛpā*—full mercy; *sei*—he; *tāhā*—that; *pāya*—can get.

TRANSLATION

"One who is only ordinarily fortunate cannot obtain such mercy. Only persons who have the full mercy of Kṛṣṇa can receive such remnants.

TEXT 100

'সুকৃতি'-শব্দে কহে 'কৃষ্ণকৃপা-হেতু পুণ্য'।
সেই যাঁর হয়, 'ফেলা' পায় সেই ধন্য ॥" ১০০ ॥

'sukṛti'-śabde kahe 'kṛṣṇa-kṛpā-hetu puṇya'
sei yāṅra haya, 'phelā' pāya sei dhanya"

SYNONYMS

sukṛti—*sukṛti* (pious activities); *śabde*—the word; *kahe*—is to be understood; *kṛṣṇa-kṛpā*—the mercy of Kṛṣṇa; *hetu*—because of; *puṇya*—pious activities; *sei*—he; *yāṅra*—of whom; *haya*—there is; *phelā*—the remnants of food; *pāya*—gets; *sei*—he; *dhanya*—very glorious.

TRANSLATION

"The word 'sukṛti' refers to pious activities performed by the mercy of Kṛṣṇa. One who is fortunate enough to obtain such mercy receives the remnants of the Lord's food and thus becomes glorious."

TEXT 101

এত বলি' প্রভু তা-সবারে বিদায় দিলা।
উপল-ভোগ দেখিয়া প্রভু নিজ-বাসা আইলা ॥১০১॥

eta bali' prabhu tā-sabāre vidāya dilā
upala-bhoga dekhiyā prabhu nija-vāsā āilā

SYNONYMS

eta bali'—saying this; *prabhu*—Śrī Caitanya Mahāprabhu; *tā-sabāre*—unto all of them; *vidāya dilā*—bade farewell; *upala-bhoga*—the next offering of food; *dekhiyā*—seeing; *prabhu*—Śrī Caitanya Mahāprabhu; *nija-vāsā*—to His place; *āilā*—returned.

TRANSLATION

After saying this, Śrī Caitanya Mahāprabhu bade farewell to all the servants. After seeing the next offering of food to Lord Jagannātha, a function known as upala-bhoga, He returned to His own quarters.

TEXT 102

মধ্যাহ্ন করিয়া কৈলা ভিক্ষা নির্বাহণ ।
কৃষ্ণাধরামৃত সদা অন্তরে স্মরণ ॥ ১০২ ॥

madhyāhna kariyā kailā bhikṣā nirvāhaṇa
kṛṣṇādharāmṛta sadā antare smaraṇa

SYNONYMS

madhyāhna kariyā—after finishing His noon duties; *kailā bhikṣā nirvāhaṇa*—completed His lunch; *kṛṣṇa-adhara-amṛta*—the nectar from the lips of Kṛṣṇa; *sadā*—always; *antare*—within Himself; *smaraṇa*—remembering.

TRANSLATION

After finishing His noon duties, Śrī Caitanya Mahāprabhu ate His lunch, but He constantly remembered the remnants of Kṛṣṇa's food.

TEXT 103

বাহ্য-কৃত্য করেন, প্রেমে গরগর মন ।
কষ্টে সম্বরণ করেন, আবেশ সঘন ॥ ১০৩ ॥

bāhya-kṛtya karena, preme garagara mana
kaṣṭe samvaraṇa karena, āveśa saghana

SYNONYMS

bāhya-kṛtya—external activities; *karena*—performs; *preme*—in ecstatic love; *garagara*—filled; *mana*—mind; *kaṣṭe*—with great difficulty; *samvaraṇa karena*—restricts; *āveśa*—ecstasy; *saghana*—very deep.

TRANSLATION

Śrī Caitanya Mahāprabhu performed His external activities, but His mind was filled with ecstatic love. With great difficulty He tried to restrain His mind, but it would always be overwhelmed by very deep ecstasy.

TEXT 104

সন্ধ্যা-কৃত্য করি' পুনঃ নিজগণ-সঙ্গে ।
নিভৃতে বসিলা নানা-কৃষ্ণকথা-রঙ্গে ॥ ১০৪ ॥

sandhyā-kṛtya kari' punaḥ nija-gaṇa-saṅge
nibhṛte vasilā nānā-kṛṣṇa-kathā-raṅge

SYNONYMS

sandhyā-kṛtya—the evening duties; *kari'*—after performing; *punaḥ*—again; *nija-gaṇa-saṅge*—along with His personal associates; *nibhṛte*—in a solitary place; *vasilā*—sat down; *nānā*—various; *kṛṣṇa-kathā*—of topics of Kṛṣṇa; *raṅge*—in the jubilation.

TRANSLATION

After finishing His evening duties, Śrī Caitanya Mahāprabhu sat down with His personal associates in a secluded place and discussed the pastimes of Kṛṣṇa in great jubilation.

TEXT 105

প্রভুর ইঙ্গিতে গোবিন্দ প্রসাদ আনিলা ।
পুরী-ভারতীরে প্রভু কিছু পাঠাইলা ॥ ১০৫ ॥

prabhura iṅgite govinda prasāda ānilā
purī-bhāratīre prabhu kichu pāṭhāila

SYNONYMS

prabhura iṅgite—by the indication of Śrī Caitanya Mahāprabhu; *govinda*—Govinda; *prasāda ānilā*—brought the remnants of the food of Lord Jagannātha; *purī*—to Paramānanda Purī; *bhāratīre*—to Brahmānanda Bhāratī; *prabhu*—Lord Śrī Caitanya Mahāprabhu; *kichu*—some; *pāṭhāilā*—sent.

TRANSLATION

Following the indications of Śrī Caitanya Mahāprabhu, Govinda brought the prasāda of Lord Jagannātha. The Lord sent some to Paramānanda Purī and Brahmānanda Bhāratī.

TEXT 106

রামানন্দ-সার্বভৌম-স্বরূপাদি-গণে ।
সবারে প্রসাদ দিল করিয়া বণ্টনে ॥ ১০৬ ॥

rāmānanda-sārvabhauma-svarūpādi-gaṇe
sabāre prasāda dila kariyā baṇṭane

SYNONYMS

rāmānanda—Rāmānanda Rāya; *sārvabhauma*—Sārvabhauma Bhaṭṭācārya; *svarūpa*—Svarūpa Dāmodara Gosvāmī; *ādi*—headed by; *gaṇe*—unto them; *sabāre*—unto all of them; *prasāda*—the remnants of the food of Lord Jagannātha; *dila*—delivered; *kariyā baṇṭane*—making shares.

TRANSLATION

Śrī Caitanya Mahāprabhu then gave shares of the prasāda to Rāmānanda Rāya, Sārvabhauma Bhaṭṭācārya, Svarūpa Dāmodara Gosvāmī and all the other devotees.

TEXT 107

প্রসাদের সৌরভ্য-মাধুর্য করি' আস্বাদন ।
অলৌকিক আস্বাদে সবার বিস্মিত হৈল মন ॥১০৭॥

prasādera saurabhya-mādhurya kari' āsvādana
alaukika āsvāde sabāra vismita haila mana

SYNONYMS

prasādera—of the *prasāda; saurabhya-mādhurya*—the sweetness and fragrance; *kari' āsvādana*—tasting; *alaukika*—uncommon; *āsvāde*—by the taste; *sabāra*—of everyone; *vismita*—struck with wonder; *haila*—became; *mana*—the mind.

TRANSLATION

As they tasted the uncommon sweetness and fragrance of the prasāda, everyone's mind was struck with wonder.

TEXTS 108-109

প্রভু কহে,—"এই সব হয় 'প্রাকৃত' দ্রব্য ।
ঐক্ষব, কর্পূর, মরিচ, এলাইচ, লবঙ্গ, গব্য ॥ ১০৮ ॥
রসবাস, গুড়ত্বক-আদি যত সব ।
'প্রাকৃত' বস্তুর স্বাদ সবার অনুভব ॥ ১০৯ ॥

prabhu kahe,——"ei saba haya 'prākṛta' dravya
aikṣava, karpūra, marica, elāica, lavaṅga, gavya

rasavāsa, guḍatvaka-ādi yata saba
'prākṛta' vastura svāda sabāra anubhava

SYNONYMS

prabhu kahe—Śrī Caitanya Mahāprabhu said; *ei*—these; *saba*—all; *haya*—are; *prākṛta*—material; *dravya*—ingredients; *aikṣava*—sugar; *karpūra*—camphor; *marica*—black pepper; *elāica*—cardamom; *lavaṅga*—cloves; *gavya*—butter; *rasavāsa*—spices; *guḍatvaka*—licorice; *ādi*—and so on; *yata saba*—each and every one of them; *prākṛta*—material; *vastura*—of ingredients; *svāda*—taste; *sabāra*—everyone's; *anubhava*—experience.

TRANSLATION

Śrī Caitanya Mahāprabhu said, "These ingredients, such as sugar, camphor, black pepper, cardamom, cloves, butter, spices and licorice, are all material. Everyone has tasted these material substances before.

PURPORT

The word *prākṛta* refers to things tasted for the sense gratification of the conditioned soul. Such things are limited by the material laws. Śrī Caitanya Mahāprabhu wanted to make the point that material things have already been experienced by materially absorbed persons who are interested only in sense gratification.

TEXT 110

সেই দ্রব্যে এত আস্বাদ, গন্ধ লোকাতীত।
আস্বাদ করিয়া দেখ,—সবার প্রতীত ॥ ১১০ ॥

sei dravye eta āsvāda, gandha lokātīta
āsvāda kariyā dekha, ——sabāra pratīta

SYNONYMS

sei dravye—in such material things; *eta*—so much; *āsvāda*—pleasing taste; *gandha*—fragrance; *loka-atīta*—never experienced by any common man; *āsvāda kariyā*—tasting; *dekha*—see; *sabāra*—of everyone; *pratīta*—experience.

TRANSLATION

"However," the Lord continued, "in these ingredients there are extraordinary tastes and uncommon fragrances. Just taste them and see the difference in the experience.

TEXT 111

আস্বাদ দূরে রহু, যার গন্ধে মাতে মন।
আপনা বিনা অন্য মাধুর্য করায় বিস্মরণ ॥ ১১১ ॥

āsvāda dūre rahu, yāra gandhe māte mana
āpanā vinā anya mādhurya karāya vismaraṇa

SYNONYMS

āsvāda—the taste; *dūre rahu*—leave aside; *yāra*—of which; *gandhe*—by the fragrance; *māte*—becomes pleased; *mana*—the mind; *āpanā vinā*—besides itself; *anya*—different; *mādhurya*—sweetness; *karāya vismaraṇa*—causes to forget.

TRANSLATION

"Apart from the taste, even the fragrance pleases the mind and makes one forget any other sweetness besides its own.

TEXT 112

তাতে এই দ্রব্যে কৃষ্ণাধর-স্পর্শ হৈল।
অধরের গুণ সব ইহাতে সঞ্চারিল ॥ ১১২ ॥

tāte ei dravye kṛṣṇādhara-sparśa haila
adharera guṇa saba ihāte sañcārila

SYNONYMS

tāte—therefore; *ei dravye*—in these ingredients; *kṛṣṇa-adhara*—of the lips of Kṛṣṇa; *sparśa*—touch; *haila*—there was; *adharera*—of the lips; *guṇa*—attributes; *saba*—all; *ihāte*—in these ingredients; *sañcārila*—have become transferred.

TRANSLATION

"Therefore, it is to be understood that the spiritual nectar of Kṛṣṇa's lips has touched these ordinary ingredients and transferred to them all their spiritual qualities.

PURPORT

Since everyone had previously tasted these ingredients, why had they become extraordinary and spiritually tasteful? This was proof that food, *prasāda,* becomes uncommonly flavorful and tasteful by touching Kṛṣṇa's lips.

TEXT 113

অলৌকিক-গন্ধ-স্বাদ, অন্য-বিস্মারণ ।
মহা-মাদক হয় এই কৃষ্ণাধরের গুণ ॥ ১১৩ ॥

alaukika-gandha-svāda, anya-vismāraṇa
mahā-mādaka haya ei kṛṣṇādharera guṇa

SYNONYMS

alaukika—uncommon; *gandha*—fragrance; *svāda*—taste; *anya-vismāraṇa*—forgetting all others; *mahā-mādaka*—highly enchanting; *haya*—are; *ei*—these; *kṛṣṇa-adharera*—of the lips of Kṛṣṇa; *guṇa*—attributes.

TRANSLATION

"An uncommon, greatly enchanting fragrance and taste that make one forget all other experiences are attributes of Kṛṣṇa's lips.

TEXT 114

অনেক 'সুকৃতে' ইহা হঞাছে সম্প্রাপ্তি ।
সবে এই আস্বাদ কর করি' মহাভক্তি ॥" ১১৪ ॥

aneka 'sukṛte' ihā hañāche samprāpti
sabe ei āsvāda kara kari' mahā-bhakti"

SYNONYMS

aneka—many; *sukṛte*—by pious activities; *ihā*—this; *hañāche samprāpti*—has become available; *sabe*—all of you; *ei*—this *prasāda; āsvāda kara*—taste; *kari' mahā-bhakti*—with great devotion.

TRANSLATION

"This prasāda has been made available only as a result of many pious activities. Now taste it with great faith and devotion."

TEXT 115

হরিধ্বনি করি' সবে কৈলা আস্বাদন ।
আস্বাদিতে প্রেমে মত্ত হইল সবার মন ॥ ১১৫ ॥

hari-dhvani kari' sabe kailā āsvādana
āsvādite preme matta ha-ila sabāra mana

SYNONYMS

hari-dhvani kari'—loudly resounding the holy name of Hari; *sabe*—all of them; *kailā āsvādana*—tasted; *āsvādite*—as soon as they tasted; *preme*—in ecstatic love; *matta*—maddened; *ha-ila*—became; *sabāra mana*—the minds of all.

TRANSLATION

Loudly chanting the holy name of Hari, all of them tasted the prasāda. As they tasted it, their minds became mad in the ecstasy of love.

TEXT 116

প্রেমাবেশে মহাপ্রভু যবে আজ্ঞা দিলা ।
রামানন্দ-রায় শ্লোক পড়িতে লাগিলা ॥ ১১৬ ॥

premāveśe mahāprabhu yabe ājñā dilā
rāmānanda-rāya śloka paḍite lāgilā

SYNONYMS

prema-āveśe—in ecstatic love; *mahāprabhu*—Śrī Caitanya Mahāprabhu; *yabe*—when; *ājñā dilā*—ordered; *rāmānanda-rāya*—Rāmānanda Rāya; *śloka*—verses; *paḍite lāgilā*—began to recite.

TRANSLATION

In ecstatic love, Śrī Caitanya Mahāprabhu ordered Rāmānanda Rāya to recite some verses. Thus Rāmānanda Rāya spoke as follows.

TEXT 117

স্থরতবর্ধনং শোকনাশনং, স্বরিতবেণুনা স্থষ্ঠু চুম্বিতম্ ।
ইতররাগবিস্মারণং নৃণাং, বিতর বীর নস্তেঽধরামৃতম্ ॥১১৭॥

surata-vardhanaṁ śoka-nāśanaṁ
svarita-veṇunā suṣṭhu-cumbitam
itara-rāga-vismāraṇaṁ nṛṇāṁ
vitara vīra nas te 'dharāmṛtam

SYNONYMS

surata-vardhanam—which increases the lusty desire for enjoyment; *śoka-nāśanam*—which vanquishes all lamentation; *svarita-veṇunā*—by the vibrating flute; *suṣṭhu*—nicely; *cumbitam*—touched; *itara-rāga-vismāraṇam*—which causes forgetfulness of all other attachment; *nṛṇām*—of the human beings; *vitara*—please deliver; *vīra*—O hero of charity; *naḥ*—unto us; *te*—Your; *adhara-amṛtam*—the nectar of the lips.

TRANSLATION

"O hero of charity, please deliver unto us the nectar of Your lips. That nectar increases lusty desires for enjoyment and diminishes lamentation in the material world. Kindly give us the nectar of Your lips, which are touched by Your transcendentally vibrating flute, for that nectar makes all human beings forget all other attachments."

PURPORT

This is a quotation from *Śrīmad-Bhāgavatam* (10.31.14).

TEXT 118

শ্লোক শুনি' মহাপ্রভু মহাতুষ্ট হৈলা ।
রাধার উৎকণ্ঠা-শ্লোক পড়িতে লাগিলা ॥ ১১৮ ॥

śloka śuni' mahāprabhu mahā-tuṣṭa hailā
rādhāra utkaṇṭhā-śloka paḍite lāgilā

SYNONYMS

śloka śuni'—hearing the verse; *mahāprabhu*—Śrī Caitanya Mahāprabhu; *mahā-tuṣṭa*—very satisfied; *hailā*—became; *rādhāra*—of Śrīmatī Rādhārāṇī; *utkaṇṭhā-śloka*—a verse pertaining to the anxiety; *paḍite lāgilā*—began to recite.

TRANSLATION

Upon hearing Rāmānanda Rāya quote this verse, Śrī Caitanya Mahāprabhu was very satisfied. Then He recited the following verse, which had been spoken by Śrīmatī Rādhārāṇī in great anxiety.

TEXT 119

ব্রজাতুলকুলাঙ্গনেতর-রসালিতৃষ্ণাহর-
প্রদীব্যদধরামৃতঃ সুকৃতিলভ্য-ফেলা-লবঃ ।
সুধাজিদহিবল্লিকা-সুদলবীটিকা-চর্বিতঃ
স মে মদনমোহনঃ সখি তনোতি জিহ্বা-স্পৃহাম ॥ ১১৯ ॥

vrajātula-kulāṅganetara-rasāli-tṛṣṇā-hara-
pradīvyad-adharāmṛtaḥ sukṛti-labhya-phelā-lavaḥ
sudhā-jid-ahivallikā-sudala-vīṭikā-carvitaḥ
sa me madana-mohanaḥ sakhi tanoti jihvā-spṛhām

SYNONYMS

vraja—of Vṛndāvana; *atula*—incomparable; *kulāṅgana*—of the *gopīs; itara*—other; *rasa-āli*—for tastes or mellows; *tṛṣṇā*—desire; *hara*—vanquishing; *pradīvyat*—all-surpassing; *adhara-amṛtaḥ*—whose nectar emanating from the lips; *sukṛti*—after many pious activities; *labhya*—obtainable; *phelā*—of the nectar of whose lips; *lavaḥ*—a small portion; *sudhā-jit*—conquering the nectar; *ahivallikā*—of the betel plant; *su-dala*—made from selected leaves; *vīṭikā*—pan; *carvitaḥ*—chewing; *saḥ*—He; *me*—My; *madana-mohanaḥ*—Madana-mohana; *sakhi*—My dear friend; *tanoti*—increases; *jihvā*—of the tongue; *spṛhām*—desire.

TRANSLATION

"My dear friend, the all-surpassing nectar from the lips of the Supreme Personality of Godhead, Kṛṣṇa, can be obtained only after many, many pious activities. For the beautiful gopīs of Vṛndāvana, that nectar vanquishes the desire for all other tastes. Madana-mohana always chews pan that surpasses the nectar of heaven. He is certainly increasing the desires of My tongue."

PURPORT

This verse is found in the *Govinda-līlāmṛta* (8.8).

TEXT 120

এত কহি' গৌরপ্রভু ভাবাবিষ্ট হঞা ।
দুই শ্লোকের অর্থ করে প্রলাপ করিয়া ॥ ১২০ ॥

eta kahi' gaura-prabhu bhāvāviṣṭa hañā
dui ślokera artha kare pralāpa kariyā

SYNONYMS

eta kahi'—saying this; *gaura-prabhu*—Śrī Caitanya Mahāprabhu; *bhāva-āviṣṭa*—overwhelmed by ecstatic loving emotions; *hañā*—becoming; *dui ślokera*—of the two verses; *artha*—meaning; *kare*—makes; *pralāpa kariyā*—talking like a madman.

TRANSLATION

After saying this, Śrī Caitanya Mahāprabhu was overwhelmed by ecstatic loving emotions. Talking like a madman, He began to explain the meaning of the two verses.

TEXTS 121-122

তনু-মন করায় ক্ষোভ, বাড়ায় সুরত-লোভ,
হর্ষ-শোকাদি-ভার বিনাশয় ।
পাসরায় অন্য রস, জগৎ করে আত্মবশ,
লজ্জা, ধর্ম, ধৈর্য করে ক্ষয় ॥ ১২১ ॥
নাগর, শুন তোমার অধর-চরিত ।
মাতায় নারীর মন, জিহ্বা করে আকর্ষণ,
বিচারিতে সব বিপরীত ॥১২২॥ ধ্রু ॥

tanu-mana karāya kṣobha, bāḍāya surata-lobha,
harṣa-śokādi-bhāra vināśaya
pāsarāya anya rasa, jagat kare ātma-vaśa,
lajjā, dharma, dhairya kare kṣaya

nāgara, śuna tomāra adhara-carita
mātāya nārīra mana, jihvā kare ākarṣaṇa,
vicārite saba viparīta

SYNONYMS

tanu—body; *mana*—mind; *karāya*—cause; *kṣobha*—agitation; *bāḍāya*—increase; *surata-lobha*—lusty desires for enjoyment; *harṣa*—of jubilation; *śoka*—lamentation; *ādi*—and so on; *bhāra*—burden; *vināśaya*—destroy; *pāsarāya*—cause to forget; *anya rasa*—other tastes; *jagat*—the whole world; *kare*—make; *ātma-vaśa*—under their control; *lajjā*—shame; *dharma*—religion; *dhairya*—patience; *kare kṣaya*—vanquish; *nāgara*—O lover; *śuna*—hear; *tomāra*—Your; *adhara*—of lips; *carita*—the characteristics; *mātāya*—madden; *nārīra*—of women; *mana*—mind; *jihvā*—tongue; *kare ākarṣaṇa*—attract; *vicārite*—considering; *saba*—all; *viparīta*—opposite.

TRANSLATION

"My dear lover," He said, "let Me describe some of the characteristics of Your transcendental lips. They agitate the mind and body of everyone, they increase lusty desires for enjoyment, they destroy the burden of material happiness and lamentation, and they make one forget all material tastes. The whole world falls under their control. They vanquish shame, religion and patience, especially in women. Indeed, they inspire madness in the minds of all women. Your lips increase the greed of the tongue and thus attract it. Considering all this, we see that the activities of Your transcendental lips are always perplexing.

TEXT 123

আছুক নারীর কায, কহিতে বাসিয়ে লাজ,
তোমার অধর বড় ধৃষ্ট-রায় ।
পুরুষে করে আকর্ষণ, আপনা পিয়াইতে মন,
অন্যরস সব পাসরায় ॥ ১২৩ ॥

āchuka nārīra kāya, kahite vāsiye lāja,
tomāra adhara baḍa dhṛṣṭa-rāya
puruṣe kare ākarṣaṇa, āpanā piyāite mana,
anya-rasa saba pāsarāya

SYNONYMS

āchuka—let it be; *nārīra*—of women; *kāya*—the bodies; *kahite*—to speak; *vāsiye*—I feel; *lāja*—shame; *tomāra*—Your; *adhara*—lips; *baḍa*—very much; *dhṛṣṭa-rāya*—impudent; *puruṣe*—the male; *kare ākarṣaṇa*—they attract; *āpanā*—themselves; *piyāite*—causing to drink; *mana*—mind; *anya-rasa*—other tastes; *saba*—all; *pāsarāya*—cause to forget.

TRANSLATION

"My dear Kṛṣṇa, since You are a male, it is not very extraordinary that the attraction of Your lips can disturb the minds of women. I am ashamed to say this, but Your lips sometimes attract even Your flute, which is also considered a male. It likes to drink the nectar of Your lips, and thus it also forgets all other tastes.

TEXT 124

সচেতন রহু দূরে, অচেতন সচেতন করে,
তোমার অধর—বড় বাজিকর ।

তোমার বেণু শুষ্কেন্ধন, তার জন্মায় ইন্দ্রিয়-মন,
তারে আপনা পিয়ায় নিরন্তর ॥ ১২৪ ॥

sacetana rahu dūre, acetana sacetana kare,
tomāra adhara——baḍa vājikara
tomāra veṇu śuṣkendhana, tāra janmāya indriya-mana,
tāre āpanā piyāya nirantara

SYNONYMS

sa-cetana—conscious living beings; *rahu dūre*—leave aside; *acetana*—unconscious; *sa-cetana*—conscious; *kare*—make; *tomāra*—Your; *adhara*—lips; *baḍa*—very great; *vājikara*—magicians; *tomāra*—Your; *veṇu*—flute; *śuṣka-indhana*—dry wood; *tāra*—of that; *janmāya*—creates; *indriya-mana*—the senses and mind; *tāre*—the flute; *āpanā*—themselves; *piyāya*—cause to drink; *nirantara*—constantly.

TRANSLATION

"Aside from conscious living beings, even unconscious matter is sometimes made conscious by Your lips. Therefore, Your lips are great magicians. Paradoxically, although Your flute is nothing but dry wood, Your lips make it drink their nectar. They create a mind and senses in the dry wooden flute and give it transcendental bliss.

TEXT 125

বেণু ধৃষ্ট-পুরুষ হঞা, পুরুষাধর পিয়া পিয়া,
গোপীগণে জানায় নিজ-পান।
'অহো শুন, গোপীগণ, বলে পিঙো তোমার ধন,
তোমার যদি থাকে অভিমান ॥ ১২৫ ॥

veṇu dhṛṣṭa-puruṣa hañā, puruṣādhara piyā piyā,
gopī-gaṇe jānāya nija-pāna
'aho śuna, gopī-gaṇa, bale piṅo tomāra dhana,
tomāra yadi thāke abhimāna

SYNONYMS

veṇu—the flute; *dhṛṣṭa-puruṣa*—a cunning male; *hañā*—being; *puruṣa-adhara*—the lips of the male; *piyā piyā*—drinking and drinking; *gopī-gaṇe*—unto the *gopīs; jānāya*—informs; *nija-pāna*—own drinking; *aho*—oh; *śuna*—hear; *gopī-gaṇa*—*gopīs; bale*—says; *piṅo*—drink; *tomāra*—your; *dhana*—property; *tomāra*—your; *yadi*—if; *thāke*—there is; *abhimāna*—pride.

TRANSLATION

"That flute is a very cunning male who drinks again and again the taste of another male's lips. It advertises its qualities and says to the gopīs, 'O gopīs, if you are so proud of being women, come forward and enjoy your property—the nectar of the lips of the Supreme Personality of Godhead.'

TEXT 126

তবে মোরে ক্রোধ করি', লজ্জা ভয়, ধর্ম, ছাড়ি',
ছাড়ি' দিমু, কর আসি' পান ।
নহে পিমু নিরন্তর, তোমায় মোর নাহিক ডর,
অন্যে দেখোঁ তৃণের সমান ॥ ১২৬ ॥

tabe more krodha kari', lajjā bhaya, dharma, chāḍi',
chāḍi' dimu, kara āsi' pāna
nahe pimu nirantara, tomāya mora nāhika ḍara,
anye dekhoṅ tṛṇera samāna

SYNONYMS

tabe—thereupon; *more*—at Me; *krodha kari'*—becoming angry; *lajjā*—shame; *bhaya*—fear; *dharma*—religion; *chāḍi'*—giving up; *chāḍi'*—giving up; *dimu*—I shall give; *kara āsi' pāna*—come drink; *nahe*—not; *pimu*—I shall drink; *nirantara*—continuously; *tomāya*—of You; *mora*—my; *nāhika*—there is not; *ḍara*—fear; *anye*—others; *dekhoṅ*—I see; *tṛṇera samāna*—equal to straw.

TRANSLATION

"Thereupon, the flute said angrily to Me, 'Give up Your shame, fear and religion and come drink the lips of Kṛṣṇa. On that condition, I shall give up my attachment for them. If You do not give up Your shame and fear, however, I shall continuously drink the nectar of Kṛṣṇa's lips. I am slightly fearful because You also have the right to drink that nectar, but as for the others, I consider them like straw.'

TEXT 127

অধরামৃত নিজ-স্বরে, সঞ্চারিয়া সেই বলে,
আকর্ষয় ত্রিজগৎ-জন ।
আমরা ধর্ম-ভয় করি', রহি' যদি ধৈর্য ধরি',
তবে আমায় করে বিড়ম্বন ॥ ১২৭ ॥

adharāmṛta nija-svare, sañcāriyā sei bale,
ākarṣaya trijagat-jana
āmarā dharma-bhaya kari', rahi' yadi dhairya dhari',
tabe āmāya kare viḍambana

SYNONYMS

adhara-amṛta—the nectar of the lips; *nija-svare*—with the vibration of the flute; *sañcāriyā*—combining; *sei*—that; *bale*—by strength; *ākarṣaya*—attract; *tri-jagat-jana*—the people of the three worlds; *āmarā*—we; *dharma*—religion; *bhaya*—fear; *kari'*—because of; *rahi'*—remaining; *yadi*—if; *dhairya dhari'*—keeping patient; *tabe*—then; *āmāya*—us; *kare viḍambana*—criticizes.

TRANSLATION

"The nectar of Kṛṣṇa's lips, combined with the vibration of His flute, attracts all the people of the three worlds. However, if we gopīs remain patient out of respect for religious principles, the flute then criticizes us.

TEXT 128

নীবি খসায় গুরু-আগে, লজ্জা-ধর্ম করায় ত্যাগে,
কেশে ধরি' যেন লঞা যায় ।
আনি' করায় তোমার দাসী, শুনি' লোক করে হাসি',
এইমত নারীরে নাচায় ॥ ১২৮ ॥

nīvi khasāya guru-āge, lajjā-dharma karāya tyāge,
keśe dhari' yena lañā yāya
āni' karāya tomāra dāsī, śuni' loka kare hāsi',
ei-mata nārīre nācāya

SYNONYMS

nīvi—the belts; *khasāya*—cause to loosen; *guru-āge*—before superiors; *lajjā-dharma*—shame and religion; *karāya*—induce; *tyāge*—to give up; *keśe dhari'*—catching by the hair; *yena*—as if; *lañā yāya*—takes us away; *āni'*—bringing; *karāya*—induce to become; *tomāra*—Your; *dāsī*—maidservants; *śuni'*—hearing; *loka*—people; *kare hāsi'*—laugh; *ei-mata*—in this way; *nārīre*—women; *nācāya*—cause to dance.

TRANSLATION

"The nectar of Your lips and vibration of Your flute join together to loosen our belts and induce us to give up shame and religion, even before our

superiors. As if catching us by our hair, they forcibly take us away and surrender us unto You to become Your maidservants. Hearing of these incidents, people laugh at us. We have thus become completely subordinate to the flute.

TEXT 129

শুষ্ক বাঁশের লাঠিখান, এত করে অপমান,
এই দশা করিল, গোসাঞি।
না সহি' কি করিতে পারি, তাহে রহি মৌন ধরি',
চোরার মাকে ডাকি' কান্দিতে নাই ॥১২৯॥

śuṣka bāṅśera lāṭhikhāna, eta kare apamāna,
ei daśā karila, gosāñi
nā sahi' ki karite pāri, tāhe rahi mauna dhari',
corāra māke ḍāki' kāndite nāi

SYNONYMS

śuṣka—dry; *bāṅśera*—of bamboo; *lāṭhi-khāna*—a stick; *eta*—this; *kare apamāna*—insults; *ei*—this; *daśā*—condition; *karila*—made; *gosāñi*—the master; *nā sahi'*—not tolerating; *ki*—what; *karite pāri*—can we do; *tāhe*—at that time; *rahi*—we remain; *mauna dhari'*—keeping silent; *corāra*—of a thief; *māke*—for the mother; *ḍāki'*—calling; *kāndite*—to cry; *nāi*—is not possible.

TRANSLATION

"This flute is nothing but a dry stick of bamboo, but it becomes our master and insults us in so many ways that it forces us into a predicament. What can we do but tolerate it? The mother of a thief cannot cry loudly for justice when the thief is punished. Therefore we simply remain silent.

TEXT 130

অধরের এই রীতি, আর শুন কুনীতি,
সে অধর-সনে যার মেলা।
সেই ভক্ষ্য-ভোজ্য-পান, হয় অমৃত-সমান,
নাম তার হয় 'কৃষ্ণ-ফেলা' ॥ ১৩০ ॥

adharera ei rīti, āra śuna kunīti,
se adhara-sane yāra melā
sei bhakṣya-bhojya-pāna, haya amṛta-samāna,
nāma tāra haya 'kṛṣṇa-phelā'

SYNONYMS

adharera—of the lips; *ei*—this; *rīti*—policy; *āra*—other; *śuna*—hear; *kunīti*—injustices; *se*—those; *adhara*—lips; *sane*—with; *yāra*—of which; *melā*—meeting; *sei*—those; *bhakṣya*—eatables; *bhojya*—foods; *pāna*—drink or betel; *haya*—become; *amṛta-samāna*—like nectar; *nāma*—the name; *tāra*—of those; *haya*—becomes; *kṛṣṇa-phelā*—the remnants of Kṛṣṇa.

TRANSLATION

"That is the policy of these lips. Just consider the other injustices. Everything that touches those lips—including food, drink or betel—becomes just like nectar. It is then called kṛṣṇa-phelā, or remnants left by Kṛṣṇa.

TEXT 131

সে ফেলার এক লব, না পায় দেবতা সব,
এ দম্ভে কেবা পাতিয়ায় ?
বহুজন্ম পুণ্য করে, তবে 'সুকৃতি' নাম ধরে,
সে 'সুকৃতে' তার লব পায় ॥ ১৩১ ॥

se phelāra eka lava, nā pāya devatā saba,
e dambhe kebā pātiyāya?
bahu-janma puṇya kare, tabe 'sukṛti' nāma dhare,
se 'sukṛte' tāra lava pāya

SYNONYMS

se phelāra—of those remnants; *eka*—one; *lava*—small particle; *nā pāya*—do not get; *devatā*—the demigods; *saba*—all; *e dambhe*—this pride; *kebā*—who; *pātiyāya*—can believe; *bahu-janma*—for many births; *puṇya kare*—acts piously; *tabe*—then; *sukṛti*—one who performs pious activities; *nāma*—the name; *dhare*—bears; *se*—those; *sukṛte*—by pious activities; *tāra*—of that; *lava*—a fraction; *pāya*—one can get.

TRANSLATION

"Even after much prayer, the demigods themselves cannot obtain even a small portion of the remnants of such food. Just imagine the pride of those remnants! Only a person who has acted piously for many, many births and has thus become a devotee can obtain the remnants of such food.

TEXT 132

কৃষ্ণ যে খায় তাম্বূল, কহে তার নাহি মূল,
তাহে আর দম্ভ-পরিপাটী ।

তার যেবা উদ্গার, তারে কয় 'অমৃতসার',
গোপীর মুখ করে 'আলবাটী' ॥ ১৩২ ॥

kṛṣṇa ye khāya tāmbūla, kahe tāra nāhi mūla,
tāhe āra dambha-paripāṭī
tāra yebā udgāra, tāre kaya 'amṛta-sāra',
gopīra mukha kare 'ālabāṭī'

SYNONYMS

kṛṣṇa—Lord Kṛṣṇa; *ye*—what; *khāya*—chews; *tāmbūla*—the betel; *kahe*—it is said; *tāra*—of it; *nāhi*—there is not; *mūla*—price; *tāhe*—over and above that; *āra*—also; *dambha-paripāṭī*—complete pride; *tāra*—of that; *yebā*—whatever; *udgāra*—coming out; *tāre*—that; *kaya*—is called; *amṛta-sāra*—the essence of the nectar; *gopīra*—of the *gopīs; mukha*—the mouth; *kare*—makes; *ālabāṭī*—spittoon.

TRANSLATION

"The betel chewed by Kṛṣṇa is priceless, and the remnants of such chewed betel from His mouth are said to be the essence of nectar. When the gopīs accept these remnants, their mouths become like His spittoons.

TEXT 133

এসব—তোমার কুটিনাটি, ছাড় এই পরিপাটী,
বেণুদ্বারে কাঁহে হর' প্রাণ ।
আপনার হাসি লাগি', নহ নারীর বধভাগী,
দেহ' নিজাধরামৃত-দান ॥" ১৩৩ ॥

e-saba——tomāra kuṭināṭi, chāḍa ei paripāṭī,
veṇu-dvāre kāṅhe hara' prāṇa
āpanāra hāsi lāgi', naha nārīra vadha-bhāgī,
deha' nijādharāmṛta-dāna"

SYNONYMS

e-saba—all these; *tomāra*—Your; *kuṭināṭi*—tricks; *chāḍa*—give up; *ei*—these; *paripāṭī*—very expert activities; *veṇu-dvāre*—by the flute; *kāṅhe*—why; *hara*—You take away; *prāṇa*—life; *āpanāra*—Your own; *hāsi*—laughing; *lāgi'*—for the matter of; *naha*—do not be; *nārīra*—of women; *vadha-bhāgī*—responsible for killing; *deha'*—kindly give; *nija-adhara-amṛta*—the nectar of Your lips; *dāna*—charity.

TRANSLATION

"Therefore, My dear Kṛṣṇa, please give up all the tricks You have set up so expertly. Do not try to kill the life of the gopīs with the vibration of Your flute. Because of Your joking and laughing, You are becoming responsible for the killing of women. It would be better for You to satisfy us by giving us the charity of the nectar of Your lips."

TEXT 134

কহিতে কহিতে প্রভুর মন ফিরি' গেল ।
ক্রোধ-অংশ শান্ত হৈল, উৎকণ্ঠা বাড়িল ॥ ১৩৪ ॥

kahite kahite prabhura mana phiri' gela
krodha-aṁśa śānta haila, utkaṇṭhā bāḍila

SYNONYMS

kahite kahite—talking and talking; *prabhura*—of Śrī Caitanya Mahāprabhu; *mana*—mind; *phiri' gela*—became changed; *krodha-aṁśa*—the part of anger; *śānta haila*—became pacified; *utkaṇṭhā*—agitation of the mind; *bāḍila*—increased.

TRANSLATION

While Śrī Caitanya Mahāprabhu was talking like this, His mind changed. His anger subsided, but His mental agitation increased.

TEXT 135

পরম দুর্লভ এই কৃষ্ণাধরামৃত ।
তাহা যেই পায়, তার সফল জীবিত ॥ ১৩৫ ॥

parama durlabha ei kṛṣṇādharāmṛta
tāhā yei pāya, tāra saphala jīvita

SYNONYMS

parama—supremely; *durlabha*—difficult to obtain; *ei*—this; *kṛṣṇa*—of Kṛṣṇa; *adhara-amṛta*—the nectar from the lips; *tāhā*—that; *yei*—one who; *pāya*—gets; *tāra*—his; *sa-phala*—successful; *jīvita*—life.

TRANSLATION

Śrī Caitanya Mahāprabhu continued, "This nectar from Kṛṣṇa's lips is supremely difficult to obtain, but if one gets some, his life becomes successful.

TEXT 136

যোগ্য হঞা কেহ করিতে না পায় পান ।
তথাপি সে নির্লজ্জ, বৃথা ধরে প্রাণ ॥ ১৩৬ ॥

yogya hañā keha karite nā pāya pāna
tathāpi se nirlajja, vṛthā dhare prāṇa

SYNONYMS

yogya—competent; *hañā*—being; *keha*—anyone; *karite*—to do; *nā pāya*—does not get; *pāna*—drinking; *tathāpi*—still; *se*—that person; *nirlajja*—shameless; *vṛthā*—uselessly; *dhare prāṇa*—continues life.

TRANSLATION

"When a person competent to drink that nectar does not do so, that shameless person continues his life uselessly.

TEXT 137

অযোগ্য হঞা তাহা কেহ সদা পান করে ।
যোগ্য জন নাহি পায়, লোভে মাত্র মরে ॥ ১৩৭ ॥

ayogya hañā tāhā keha sadā pāna kare
yogya jana nāhi pāya, lobhe mātra mare

SYNONYMS

ayogya—unfit; *hañā*—being; *tāhā*—that; *keha*—someone; *sadā*—always; *pāna kare*—drinks; *yogya jana*—the competent person; *nāhi pāya*—does not get; *lobhe*—out of greed; *mātra*—simply; *mare*—dies.

TRANSLATION

"There are persons who are unfit to drink that nectar but who nevertheless drink it continuously, whereas some who are suitable never get it and thus die of greed.

TEXT 138

তাতে জানি,—কোন তপস্যার আছে বল ।
অযোগ্যেরে দেওয়ায় কৃষ্ণাধরামৃত-ফল ॥ ১৩৮ ॥

tāte jāni,——kona tapasyāra āche bala
ayogyere deoyāya kṛṣṇādharāmṛta-phala

SYNONYMS

tāte—therefore; *jāni*—I can understand; *kona*—some; *tapasyāra*—of austerity; *āche*—there is; *bala*—strength; *ayogyere*—unto the unfit; *deoyāya*—delivers; *kṛṣṇa-adhara-amṛta*—the nectar of Kṛṣṇa's lips; *phala*—the result.

TRANSLATION

"It is therefore to be understood that such an unfit person must have obtained the nectar of Kṛṣṇa's lips on the strength of some austerity."

TEXT 139

'কহ রাম-রায়, কিছু শুনিতে হয় মন'।
ভাব জানি' পড়ে রায় গোপীর বচন ॥ ১৩৯ ॥

'kaha rāma-rāya, kichu śunite haya mana'
bhāva jāni' paḍe rāya gopīra vacana

SYNONYMS

kaha—speak; *rāma-rāya*—Rāmānanda Rāya; *kichu*—something; *śunite*—to hear; *haya mana*—I wish; *bhāva*—the situation; *jāni'*—understanding; *paḍe rāya*—Rāmānanda Rāya cites; *gopīra vacana*—the words of the *gopīs.*

TRANSLATION

Again Śrī Caitanya Mahāprabhu said to Rāmānanda Rāya, "Please say something. I want to hear." Understanding the situation, Rāmānanda Rāya recited the following words of the gopīs.

TEXT 140

গোপ্যঃ কিমাচরদয়ং কুশলং স্ম বেণু-
র্দামোদরাধরসুধামপি গোপিকানাম্।
ভুঙ্‌ক্তে স্বয়ং যদবশিষ্টরসং হ্রদিন্যো
হৃষ্যত্ত্বচোঽশ্রু মুমুচুস্তরবো যথার্যাঃ ॥১৪০॥

gopyaḥ kim ācarad ayaṁ kuśalaṁ sma veṇur
dāmodarādhara-sudhām api gopikānām
bhuṅkte svayaṁ yad avaśiṣṭa-rasaṁ hradinyo
hṛṣyat-tvaco 'śru mumucus taravo yathāryāḥ

SYNONYMS

gopyaḥ—O *gopīs; kim*—what; *ācarat*—performed; *ayam*—this; *kuśalam*—auspicious activities; *sma*—certainly; *veṇuḥ*—flute; *dāmodara*—of Kṛṣṇa; *adhara-sudhām*—the nectar of the lips; *api*—even; *gopikānām*—which is owed to the *gopīs; bhuṅkte*—enjoys; *svayam*—independently; *yat*—from which; *avaśiṣṭa*—remaining; *rasam*—the taste only; *hradinyaḥ*—the rivers; *hṛṣyat*—feeling jubilant; *tvacaḥ*—whose bodies; *aśru*—tears; *mumucuḥ*—shed; *taravaḥ*—the trees; *yathā*—exactly like; *āryāḥ*—old forefathers.

TRANSLATION

"My dear gopīs, what auspicious activities must the flute have performed to enjoy the nectar of Kṛṣṇa's lips independently and leave only a taste for the gopīs for whom that nectar is actually meant. The forefathers of the flute, the bamboo trees, shed tears of pleasure. His mother, the river, on whose bank the bamboo was born, feels jubilation, and therefore her blooming lotus flowers are standing like hair on her body."

PURPORT

This is a verse quoted from *Śrīmad-Bhāgavatam* (10.21.9) regarding a discussion the *gopīs* had among themselves. As the autumn season began in Vṛndāvana, Lord Kṛṣṇa was tending the cows and blowing on His flute. The *gopīs* then began to praise Kṛṣṇa and discuss the fortunate position of His flute.

TEXT 141

এই শ্লোক শুনি' প্রভু ভাবাবিষ্ট হঞা ।
উৎকণ্ঠাতে অর্থ করে প্রলাপ করিয়া ॥ ১৪১ ॥

ei śloka śuni' prabhu bhāvāviṣṭa hañā
utkaṇṭhāte artha kare pralāpa kariyā

SYNONYMS

ei śloka—this verse; *śuni'*—hearing; *prabhu*—Śrī Caitanya Mahāprabhu; *bhāva-āviṣṭa*—absorbed in ecstatic love; *hañā*—becoming; *utkaṇṭhāte*—in agitation of the mind; *artha kare*—makes the meaning; *pralāpa kariyā*—talking like a madman.

TRANSLATION

Upon hearing the recitation of this verse, Śrī Caitanya Mahāprabhu became absorbed in ecstatic love, and with a greatly agitated mind He began to explain its meaning like a madman.

TEXT 142

এহো ব্রজেন্দ্রনন্দন, ব্রজের কোন কন্যাগণ,
অবশ্য করিব পরিণয় ।
সে-সম্বন্ধে গোপীগণ, যারে মানে নিজধন,
সে সুধা অন্যের লভ্য নয় ॥ ১৪২ ॥

eho vrajendra-nandana, vrajera kona kanyā-gaṇa,
avaśya kariba pariṇaya
se-sambandhe gopī-gaṇa, yāre māne nija-dhana,
se sudhā anyera labhya naya

SYNONYMS

eho—this; *vrajendra-nandana*—the son of Nanda Mahārāja; *vrajera*—of Vṛndāvana; *kona*—any; *kanyā-gaṇa*—*gopīs;* *avaśya*—certainly; *kariba pariṇaya*—will marry; *se-sambandhe*—in that connection; *gopī-gaṇa*—the *gopīs;* *yāre*—which; *māne*—consider; *nija-dhana*—the personal property; *se sudhā*—that nectar; *anyera*—by others; *labhya naya*—is not obtainable.

TRANSLATION

"Some gopīs said to other gopīs, 'Just see the astonishing pastimes of Kṛṣṇa, the son of Vrajendra! He will certainly marry all the gopīs of Vṛndāvana. Therefore, the gopīs know for certain that the nectar of Kṛṣṇa's lips is their own property and cannot be enjoyed by anyone else.'

TEXT 143

গোপীগণ, কহ সব করিয়া বিচারে ।
কোন্ তীর্থ, কোন্ তপ, কোন্ সিদ্ধমন্ত্র-জপ,
এই বেণু কৈল জন্মান্তরে ? ১৪৩ ॥ ধ্রু ॥

gopī-gaṇa, kaha saba kariyā vicāre
kon tīrtha, kon tapa, kon siddha-mantra-japa,
ei veṇu kaila janmāntare?

SYNONYMS

gopī-gaṇa—O *gopīs;* *kaha*—say; *saba*—all; *kariyā vicāre*—after full consideration; *kon*—what; *tīrtha*—holy places; *kon*—what; *tapa*—austerities; *kon*—what; *siddha-mantra-japa*—chanting of a perfect *mantra;* *ei*—this; *veṇu*—flute; *kaila*—did; *janma-antare*—in his past life.

TRANSLATION

" 'My dear gopīs, fully consider how many pious activities this flute performed in his past life. We do not know what places of pilgrimage he visited, what austerities he performed or what perfect mantra he chanted.

TEXT 144

হেন কৃষ্ণাধর-সুধা, যে কৈল অমৃত মুধা,
যার আশায় গোপী ধরে প্রাণ।
এই বেণু অযোগ্য অতি, স্থাবর 'পুরুষজাতি',
সেই সুধা সদা করে পান ॥ ১৪৪ ॥

hena kṛṣṇādhara-sudhā, ye kaila amṛta mudhā,
yāra āśāya gopī dhare prāṇa
ei veṇu ayogya ati, sthāvara 'puruṣa-jāti',
sei sudhā sadā kare pāna

SYNONYMS

hena—such; *kṛṣṇa-adhara*—of Kṛṣṇa's lips; *sudhā*—nectar; *ye*—which; *kaila*—made; *amṛta*—nectar; *mudhā*—surpassed; *yāra āśāya*—by hoping for which; *gopī*—the *gopīs; dhare prāṇa*—continue to live; *ei veṇu*—this flute; *ayogya*—unfit; *ati*—completely; *sthāvara*—dead; *puruṣa-jāti*—belonging to the male class; *sei sudhā*—that nectar; *sadā*—always; *kare pāna*—drinks.

TRANSLATION

" 'This flute is utterly unfit because it is merely a dead bamboo stick. Moreover, it belongs to the male sex. Yet this flute is always drinking the nectar of Kṛṣṇa's lips, which surpasses nectarean sweetness of every description. Only in hope of that nectar do the gopīs continue to live.

TEXT 145

যার ধন, না কহে তারে, পান করে বলাৎকারে,
পিতে তারে ডাকিয়া জানায়।
তার তপস্যার ফল, দেখ ইহার ভাগ্য-বল,
ইহার উচ্ছিষ্ট মহাজনে খায় ॥ ১৪৫ ॥

yāra dhana, nā kahe tāre, pāna kare balātkāre,
pite tāre ḍākiyā jānāya
tāra tapasyāra phala, dekha ihāra bhāgya-bala,
ihāra ucchiṣṭa mahā-jane khāya

SYNONYMS

yāra—of whom; *dhana*—the property; *nā kahe*—does not speak; *tāre*—to them; *pāna kare*—drinks; *balātkāre*—by force; *pite*—while drinking; *tāre*—unto them; *ḍākiyā*—calling loudly; *jānāya*—informs; *tāra*—its; *tapasyāra*—of austerities; *phala*—result; *dekha*—see; *ihāra*—its; *bhāgya-bala*—strength of fortune; *ihāra*—its; *ucchiṣṭa*—remnants; *mahā-jane*—great personalities; *khāya*—drink.

TRANSLATION

" 'Although the nectar of Kṛṣṇa's lips is the absolute property of the gopīs, the flute, which is just an insignificant stick, is forcibly drinking that nectar and loudly inviting the gopīs to come drink it also. Just imagine the strength of the flute's austerities and good fortune. Even great devotees drink the nectar of Kṛṣṇa's lips after the flute has done so.

TEXT 146

মানসগঙ্গা, কালিন্দী, ভুবন-পাবনী নদী,
কৃষ্ণ যদি তাতে করে স্নান।
বেণুর ঝুটাধর-রস, হঞা লোভে পরবশ,
সেই কালে হর্ষে করে পান ॥ ১৪৬ ॥

mānasa-gaṅgā, kālindī, bhuvana-pāvanī nadī,
kṛṣṇa yadi tāte kare snāna
veṇura jhuṭādhara-rasa, hañā lobhe paravaśa,
sei kāle harṣe kare pāna

SYNONYMS

mānasa-gaṅgā—the Ganges of the celestial world; *kālindī*—the Yamunā; *bhuvana*—the world; *pāvanī*—purifying; *nadī*—rivers; *kṛṣṇa*—Lord Kṛṣṇa; *yadi*—if; *tāte*—in those; *kare snāna*—takes a bath; *veṇura*—of the flute; *jhuṭa-adhara-rasa*—remnants of the juice of the lips; *hañā*—being; *lobhe*—by greed; *paravaśa*—controlled; *sei kāle*—at that time; *harṣe*—in jubilation; *kare pāna*—drink.

TRANSLATION

" 'When Kṛṣṇa takes His bath in universally purifying rivers like the Yamunā and the Ganges of the celestial world, the great personalities of those rivers greedily and jubilantly drink the remnants of the nectarean juice from His lips.

TEXT 147

এ-ত নারী রহু দূরে, বৃক্ষ সব তার তীরে,
তপ করে পর-উপকারী ।
নদীর শেষ-রস পাঞা, মূলদ্বারে আকর্ষিয়া,
কেনে পিয়ে, বুঝিতে না পারি ॥ ১৪৭ ॥

e-ta nārī rahu dūre, vṛkṣa saba tāra tīre,
tapa kare para-upakārī
nadīra śeṣa-rasa pāñā, mūla-dvāre ākarṣiyā,
kene piye, bujhite nā pāri

SYNONYMS

e-ta nārī—these women; *rahu dūre*—leaving aside; *vṛkṣa*—the trees; *saba*—all; *tāra tīre*—on their banks; *tapa kare*—perform austerities; *para-upakārī*—benefactors of all other living entities; *nadīra*—of the rivers; *śeṣa-rasa*—the remnants of the nectarean juice; *pāñā*—getting; *mūla-dvāre*—by the roots; *ākarṣiyā*—drawing; *kene*—why; *piye*—drink; *bujhite nā pāri*—we cannot understand.

TRANSLATION

" 'Aside from the rivers, the trees standing on the banks like great ascetics and engaging in welfare activities for all living entities drink the nectar of Kṛṣṇa's lips by drawing water from the river with their roots. We cannot understand why they drink like that.

TEXT 148

নিজাঙ্কুরে পুলকিত, পুষ্পে হাস্য বিকসিত,
মধু-মিষে বহে অশ্রুধার ।
বেণুরে মানি' নিজ-জাতি, আর্যের যেন পুত্র-নাতি,
'বৈষ্ণব' হৈলে আনন্দ-বিকার ॥ ১৪৮ ॥

nijāṅkure pulakita, puṣpe hāsya vikasita,
madhu-miṣe vahe aśru-dhāra
veṇure māni' nija-jāti, āryera yena putra-nāti,
'vaiṣṇava' haile ānanda-vikāra

SYNONYMS

nija-aṅkure—by their buds; *pulakita*—jubilant; *puṣpe*—by flowers; *hāsya*—smiling; *vikasita*—exhibited; *madhu-miṣe*—by the oozing of honey; *vahe*—

flows; *aśru-dhāra*—showers of tears; *veṇure*—the flute; *māni'*—accepting; *nija-jāti*—as belonging to the same family; *āryera*—of forefathers; *yena*—as if; *putra-nāti*—son or grandson; *vaiṣṇava*—a Vaiṣṇava; *haile*—when becomes; *ānanda-vikāra*—transformation of transcendental bliss.

TRANSLATION

" 'The trees on the bank of the Yamunā and Ganges are always jubilant. They appear to be smiling with their flowers and shedding tears in the form of flowing honey. Just as the forefathers of a Vaiṣṇava son or grandson feel transcendental bliss, the trees feel blissful because the flute is a member of their family.'

TEXT 149

বেণুর তপ জানি যবে, সেই তপ করি তবে,
এ—অযোগ্য, আমরা—যোগ্যা নারী।
যা না পাঞা দুঃখে মরি,অযোগ্য পিয়ে সহিতে নারি,
তাহা লাগি' তপস্যা বিচারি ॥ ১৪৯ ॥

veṇura tapa jāni yabe, sei tapa kari tabe,
e——ayogya, āmarā——yogyā nārī
yā nā pāñā duḥkhe mari, ayogya piye sahite nāri,
tāhā lāgi' tapasyā vicāri

SYNONYMS

veṇura—of the flute; *tapa*—austerities; *jāni*—knowing; *yabe*—when; *sei*—those; *tapa*—austerities; *kari*—we perform; *tabe*—at that time; *e*—this (flute); *ayogya*—unfit; *āmarā*—we; *yogyā nārī*—fit women; *yā*—which; *nā pāñā*—not getting; *duḥkhe*—in unhappiness; *mari*—we die; *ayogya*—the most unfit; *piye*—drinks; *sahite nāri*—we cannot tolerate; *tāhā lāgi'*—for that reason; *tapasyā*—austerities; *vicāri*—we are considering.

TRANSLATION

"The gopīs considered, 'The flute is completely unfit for his position. We want to know what kind of austerities the flute executed, so that we may also perform the same austerities. Although the flute is unfit, he is drinking the nectar of Kṛṣṇa's lips. Seeing this, we qualified gopīs are dying of unhappiness. Therefore, we must consider the austerities the flute underwent in his past life.' "

TEXT 150

এতেক প্রলাপ করি', প্রেমাবেশে গৌরহরি,
সঙ্গে লঞা স্বরূপ-রামরায় ।
কভু নাচে, কভু গায়, ভাবাবেশে মূর্চ্ছা যায়,
এইরূপে রাত্রি-দিন যায় ॥ ১৫০ ॥

eteka pralāpa kari', premāveśe gaurahari,
saṅge lañā svarūpa-rāma-rāya
kabhu nāce, kabhu gāya, bhāvāveśe mūrcchā yāya,
ei-rūpe rātri-dina yāya

SYNONYMS

eteka—so much; *pralāpa kari'*—talking like a crazy man; *prema-āveśe*—in ecstatic love; *gaurahari*—Śrī Caitanya Mahāprabhu; *saṅge lañā*—taking with Him; *svarūpa-rāma-rāya*—Svarūpa Dāmodara Gosvāmī and Rāmānanda Rāya; *kabhu nāce*—sometimes dances; *kabhu gāya*—sometimes sings; *bhāva-āveśe*—in ecstatic love; *mūrcchā yāya*—becomes unconscious; *ei-rūpe*—in this way; *rātri-dina*—the whole night and day; *yāya*—passes.

TRANSLATION

While thus speaking like a madman, Śrī Caitanya Mahāprabhu became full of ecstatic emotion. In the company of His two friends, Svarūpa Dāmodara Gosvāmī and Rāmānanda Rāya, He sometimes danced, sometimes sang and sometimes became unconscious in ecstatic love. Śrī Caitanya Mahāprabhu passed His days and nights in this way.

TEXT 151

স্বরূপ, রূপ, সনাতন, রঘুনাথের শ্রীচরণ,
শিরে ধরি' করি যার আশ ।
চৈতন্যচরিতামৃত, অমৃত হৈতে পরামৃত,
গায় দীনহীন কৃষ্ণদাস ॥ ১৫১ ॥

svarūpa, rūpa, sanātana, raghunāthera śrī-caraṇa,
śire dhari' kari yāra āśa
caitanya-caritāmṛta, amṛta haite parāmṛta,
gāya dīna-hīna kṛṣṇadāsa

SYNONYMS

svarūpa—Svarūpa Dāmodara Gosvāmī; *rūpa*—Śrīla Rūpa Gosvāmī; *sanātana*—Sanātana Gosvāmī; *raghunāthera*—of Raghunātha dāsa Gosvāmī; *śrī-caraṇa*—the lotus feet; *śire*—on the head; *dhari'*—taking; *kari yāra āśa*—hoping for their mercy; *caitanya-caritāmṛta*—the book named *Caitanya-caritāmṛta; amṛta haite*—than nectar; *para-amṛta*—more nectarean; *gāya*—chants; *dīna-hīna*—the most wretched; *kṛṣṇadāsa*—Kṛṣṇadāsa Kavirāja Gosvāmī.

TRANSLATION

Expecting the mercy of Svarūpa, Rūpa, Sanātana and Raghunātha dāsa, and taking their lotus feet on my head, I, the most fallen Kṛṣṇadāsa, continue chanting the epic Śrī Caitanya-caritāmṛta, which is sweeter than the nectar of transcendental bliss.

Thus end the Bhaktivedanta purports to the Śrī Caitanya-caritāmṛta, Antya-līlā, *Sixteenth Chapter, describing the nectar flowing from Śrī Kṛṣṇa's lotus lips.*

CHAPTER 17

The Bodily Transformations of Lord Śrī Caitanya Mahāprabhu

Śrīla Bhaktivinoda Ṭhākura gives the following summary of this Seventeenth Chapter in his *Amṛta-pravāha-bhāṣya.* Absorbed in transcendental ecstasy, Śrī Caitanya Mahāprabhu went out one night without opening the doors to His room. After crossing over three walls, He fell down among some cows belonging to the district of Tailaṅga. There He remained unconscious, assuming the aspect of a tortoise.

TEXT 1

লিখ্যতে শ্রীল-গৌরেন্দোরত্যদ্ভুতমলৌকিকম্ ।
যৈর্দৃষ্টং তন্মুখাচ্ছ্রুত্বা দিব্যোন্মাদ-বিচেষ্টিতম্ ॥ ১ ॥

likhyate śrīla-gaurendor
atyadbhutam alaukikam
yair dṛṣṭaṁ tan-mukhāc chrutvā
divyonmāda-viceṣṭitam

SYNONYMS

likhyate—they are being written; *śrīla*—most opulent; *gaura*—of Śrī Caitanya Mahāprabhu; *indoḥ*—moonlike; *ati*—very; *adbhutam*—wonderful; *alaukikam*—uncommon; *yaiḥ*—by whom; *dṛṣṭam*—personally seen; *tat-mukhāt*—from their mouths; *śrutvā*—after hearing; *divya-unmāda*—in transcendental madness; *viceṣṭitam*—activities.

TRANSLATION

I am simply trying to write about Lord Gauracandra's transcendental activities and spiritual madness, which are very wonderful and uncommon. I dare to write of them only because I have heard from the mouths of those who have personally seen the Lord's activities.

TEXT 2

জয় জয় শ্রীচৈতন্য জয় নিত্যানন্দ ।
জয়াদ্বৈতচন্দ্র জয় গৌরভক্তবৃন্দ ॥ ২ ॥

jaya jaya śrī-caitanya jaya nityānanda
jayādvaita-candra jaya gaura-bhakta-vṛnda

SYNONYMS

jaya jaya—all glories; *śrī-caitanya*—to Lord Caitanya Mahāprabhu; *jaya*—all glories; *nityānanda*—to Lord Nityānanda; *jaya*—all glories; *advaita-candra*—to Advaita Ācārya; *jaya*—all glories; *gaura-bhakta-vṛnda*—to the devotees of Śrī Caitanya Mahāprabhu.

TRANSLATION

All glories to Śrī Caitanya Mahāprabhu! All glories to Lord Nityānanda! All glories to Advaitacandra! All glories to all the devotees of the Lord!

TEXT 3

এইমত মহাপ্রভু রাত্রি-দিবসে ।
উন্মাদের চেষ্টা, প্রলাপ করে প্রেমাবেশে ॥ ৩ ॥

ei-mata mahāprabhu rātri-divase
unmādera ceṣṭā, pralāpa kare premāveśe

SYNONYMS

ei-mata—in this way; *mahāprabhu*—Śrī Caitanya Mahāprabhu; *rātri-divase*—night and day; *unmādera*—of a madman; *ceṣṭā*—activities; *pralāpa kare*—talks insanely; *prema-āveśe*—in ecstatic love.

TRANSLATION

Absorbed in ecstasy, Śrī Caitanya Mahāprabhu acted and talked like a madman day and night.

TEXT 4

একদিন প্রভু স্বরূপ-রামানন্দ-সঙ্গে ।
অর্ধরাত্রি গোঙাইলা কৃষ্ণকথা-রঙ্গে ॥ ৪ ॥

eka-dina prabhu svarūpa-rāmānanda-saṅge
ardha-rātri goṅāilā kṛṣṇa-kathā-raṅge

SYNONYMS

eka-dina—one day; *prabhu*—Śrī Caitanya Mahāprabhu; *svarūpa-rāmānanda-saṅge*—with Svarūpa Dāmodara Gosvāmī and Rāmānanda Rāya; *ardha-rātri*—half the night; *goṅāilā*—passed; *kṛṣṇa-kathā*—of discussing Kṛṣṇa's pastimes; *raṅge*—in the matter.

TRANSLATION

In the company of Svarūpa Dāmodara Gosvāmī and Rāmānanda Rāya, Śrī Caitanya Mahāprabhu once passed half the night talking about the pastimes of Lord Kṛṣṇa.

TEXT 5

যবে যেই ভাব প্রভুর করয়ে উদয়।
ভাবানুরূপ গীত গায় স্বরূপ-মহাশয়॥ ৫॥

yabe yei bhāva prabhura karaye udaya
bhāvānurūpa gīta gāya svarūpa-mahāśaya

SYNONYMS

yabe—whenever; *yei*—whatever; *bhāva*—ecstasy; *prabhura*—of Śrī Caitanya Mahāprabhu; *karaye udaya*—rises; *bhāva-anurūpa*—befitting the emotion; *gīta*—song; *gāya*—sings; *svarūpa*—Svarūpa Dāmodara; *mahāśaya*—the great personality.

TRANSLATION

As they talked of Kṛṣṇa, Svarūpa Dāmodara Gosvāmī would sing songs exactly suitable for Śrī Caitanya Mahāprabhu's transcendental emotions.

TEXT 6

বিদ্যাপতি, চণ্ডীদাস, শ্রীগীতগোবিন্দ।
ভাবানুরূপ শ্লোক পড়েন রায়-রামানন্দ॥ ৬॥

vidyāpati, caṇḍīdāsa, śrī-gīta-govinda
bhāvānurūpa śloka paḍena rāya-rāmānanda

SYNONYMS

vidyāpati—the author Vidyāpati; *caṇḍīdāsa*—the author Caṇḍīdāsa; *śrī-gīta-govinda*—the famous book by Jayadeva Gosvāmī; *bhāva-anurūpa*—according to the ecstatic emotion; *śloka*—verses; *paḍena*—recites; *rāya-rāmānanda*—Rāmānanda Rāya.

TRANSLATION

Rāmānanda Rāya would quote verses from the books of Vidyāpati and Caṇḍīdāsa, and especially from the Gīta-govinda by Jayadeva Gosvāmī, to complement the ecstasy of Śrī Caitanya Mahāprabhu.

TEXT 7

মধ্যে মধ্যে আপনে প্রভু শ্লোক পড়িয়া।
শ্লোকের অর্থ করেন প্রভু বিলাপ করিয়া॥ ৭॥

madhye madhye āpane prabhu śloka paḍiyā
ślokera artha karena prabhu vilāpa kariyā

SYNONYMS

madhye madhye—at intervals; *āpane*—personally; *prabhu*—Śrī Caitanya Mahāprabhu; *śloka*—a verse; *paḍiyā*—reciting; *ślokera*—of the verse; *artha*—meaning; *karena*—gives; *prabhu*—Śrī Caitanya Mahāprabhu; *vilāpa kariyā*—lamenting.

TRANSLATION

At intervals, Śrī Caitanya Mahāprabhu would also recite a verse. Then, in great lamentation, He would explain it.

TEXT 8

এইমতে নানাভাবে অর্ধরাত্রি হৈল।
গোসাঞিরে শয়ন করাই' দুঁহে ঘরে গেল॥ ৮॥

ei-mate nānā-bhāve ardha-rātri haila
gosāñire śayana karāi' duṅhe ghare gela

SYNONYMS

ei-mate—in this way; *nānā-bhāve*—in varieties of emotions; *ardha-rātri*—half the night; *haila*—passed; *gosāñire*—Śrī Caitanya Mahāprabhu; *śayana karāi'*—making Him lie down; *duṅhe*—both; *ghare gela*—went home.

TRANSLATION

Śrī Caitanya Mahāprabhu passed half the night experiencing varieties of emotions. Finally, after making the Lord lie down on His bed, both Svarūpa Dāmodara and Rāmānanda Rāya returned to their homes.

TEXT 9

গম্ভীরার দ্বারে গোবিন্দ করিলা শয়ন।
সবরাত্রি প্রভু করেন উচ্চসঙ্কীর্তন॥ ৯॥

gambhīrāra dvāre govinda karilā śayana
saba-rātri prabhu karena ucca-saṅkīrtana

SYNONYMS

gambhīrāra—of Śrī Caitanya Mahāprabhu's room; *dvāre*—at the door; *govinda*—His personal servant; *karilā śayana*—lay down; *saba-rātri*—all night; *prabhu*—Śrī Caitanya Mahāprabhu; *karena*—performs; *ucca-saṅkīrtana*—loud chanting.

TRANSLATION

Śrī Caitanya Mahāprabhu's personal servant, Govinda, lay down at the door of His room, and the Lord very loudly chanted the Hare Kṛṣṇa mahā-mantra all night.

TEXT 10

আচম্বিতে শুনেন প্রভু কৃষ্ণবেণু-গান ।
ভাবাবেশে প্রভু তাহাঁ করিলা প্রয়াণ ॥ ১০ ॥

ācambite śunena prabhu kṛṣṇa-veṇu-gāna
bhāvāveśe prabhu tāhāṅ karilā prayāṇa

SYNONYMS

ācambite—suddenly; *śunena*—hears; *prabhu*—Śrī Caitanya Mahāprabhu; *kṛṣṇa-veṇu*—of Kṛṣṇa's flute; *gāna*—the vibration; *bhāva-āveśe*—in ecstatic emotion; *prabhu*—Śrī Caitanya Mahāprabhu; *tāhāṅ*—there; *karilā prayāṇa*—departed.

TRANSLATION

Suddenly, Śrī Caitanya Mahāprabhu heard the vibration of Kṛṣṇa's flute. Then, in ecstasy, He began to depart to see Lord Kṛṣṇa.

TEXT 11

তিনদ্বারে কপাট ঐছে আছে ত' লাগিয়া ।
ভাবাবেশে প্রভু গেলা বাহির হঞা ॥ ১১ ॥

tina-dvāre kapāṭa aiche āche ta' lāgiyā
bhāvāveśe prabhu gelā bāhira hañā

SYNONYMS

tina-dvāre—in three doorways; *kapāṭa*—the doors; *aiche*—as previously; *āche*—are; *ta' lāgiyā*—being closed; *bhāva-āveśe*—in ecstatic emotion; *prabhu*—Śrī Caitanya Mahāprabhu; *gelā*—went; *bāhira*—out; *hañā*—being.

TRANSLATION

All three doors were fastened as usual, but Śrī Caitanya Mahāprabhu, in great ecstasy, nevertheless got out of the room and left the house.

TEXT 12

সিংহদ্বার-দক্ষিণে আছে তৈলঙ্গী-গাভীগণ ।
তাহাঁ যাই' পড়িলা প্রভু হঞা অচেতন ॥ ১২ ॥

siṁha-dvāra-dakṣiṇe āche tailaṅgī-gābhī-gaṇa
tāhāṅ yāi' paḍilā prabhu hañā acetana

SYNONYMS

siṁha-dvāra—of the gate named Siṁha-dvāra; *dakṣiṇe*—on the southern side; *āche*—there are; *tailaṅgī-gābhī-gaṇa*—cows belonging to the Tailaṅga district; *tāhāṅ*—there; *yāi'*—going; *paḍilā*—fell down; *prabhu*—Lord Śrī Caitanya Mahāprabhu; *hañā acetana*—becoming unconscious.

TRANSLATION

He went to a cow shed on the southern side of the Siṁha-dvāra. There the Lord fell down unconscious among cows from the district of Tailaṅga.

TEXT 13

এথা গোবিন্দ মহাপ্রভুর শব্দ না পাঞা ।
স্বরূপেরে বোলাইল কপাট খুলিয়া ॥ ১৩ ॥

ethā govinda mahāprabhura śabda nā pāñā
svarūpere bolāila kapāṭa khuliyā

SYNONYMS

ethā—here; *govinda*—Govinda; *mahāprabhura*—of Śrī Caitanya Mahāprabhu; *śabda*—sound; *nā pāñā*—not getting; *svarūpere*—Svarūpa Dāmodara Gosvāmī; *bolāila*—called for; *kapāṭa*—the doors; *khuliyā*—opening.

TRANSLATION

Meanwhile, not hearing any sounds from Śrī Caitanya Mahāprabhu, Govinda immediately sent for Svarūpa Dāmodara and opened the doors.

TEXT 14

তবে স্বরূপ-গোসাঞি সঙ্গে লঞা ভক্তগণ ।
দেউটি জ্বালিয়া করেন প্রভুর অন্বেষণ ॥ ১৪ ॥

tabe svarūpa-gosāñi saṅge lañā bhakta-gaṇa
deuṭi jvāliyā karena prabhura anveṣaṇa

SYNONYMS

tabe—thereafter; *svarūpa-gosāñi*—Svarūpa Dāmodara Gosvāmī; *saṅge*—with him; *lañā*—taking; *bhakta-gaṇa*—the devotees; *deuṭi*—lamp; *jvāliyā*—burning; *karena*—does; *prabhura*—for Śrī Caitanya Mahāprabhu; *anveṣaṇa*—searching.

TRANSLATION

Then Svarūpa Dāmodara Gosvāmī lit a torch, and went out with all the devotees to search for Śrī Caitanya Mahāprabhu.

TEXT 15

ইতি-উতি অন্বেষিয়া সিংহদ্বারে গেলা ।
গাভীগণ-মধ্যে যাই' প্রভুরে পাইলা ॥ ১৫ ॥

iti-uti anveṣiyā siṁha-dvāre gelā
gābhī-gaṇa-madhye yāi' prabhure pāilā

SYNONYMS

iti-uti—here and there; *anveṣiyā*—searching; *siṁha-dvāre*—to the gate named Siṁha-dvāra; *gelā*—went; *gābhī-gaṇa-madhye*—among the cows; *yāi'*—going; *prabhure pāilā*—found Śrī Caitanya Mahāprabhu.

TRANSLATION

After searching here and there, they finally came to the cow shed near the Siṁha-dvāra. There they saw Śrī Caitanya Mahāprabhu lying unconscious among the cows.

TEXT 16

পেটের ভিতর হস্ত-পদ—কূর্মের আকার ।
মুখে ফেন, পুলকাঙ্গ, নেত্রে অশ্রুধার ॥ ১৬ ॥

peṭera bhitara hasta-pada——kūrmera ākāra
mukhe phena, pulakāṅga, netre aśru-dhāra

SYNONYMS

peṭera—the abdomen; *bhitara*—within; *hasta-pada*—the arms and legs; *kūrmera ākāra*—just like a tortoise; *mukhe*—in the mouth; *phena*—foam; *pulaka-aṅga*—eruptions on the body; *netre*—in the eyes; *aśru-dhāra*—a flow of tears.

TRANSLATION

His arms and legs had entered the trunk of His body, exactly like those of a tortoise. His mouth was foaming, there were eruptions on His body, and tears flowed from His eyes.

TEXT 17

অচেতন পড়িয়াছেন,—যেন কুষ্মাণ্ড-ফল ।
বাহিরে জড়িমা, অন্তরে আনন্দ-বিহ্বল ॥ ১৭ ॥

acetana paḍiyāchena,——yena kuṣmāṇḍa-phala
bāhire jaḍimā, antare ānanda-vihvala

SYNONYMS

acetana—unconscious; *paḍiyāchena*—was lying down; *yena*—as if; *kuṣmāṇḍa-phala*—a pumpkin; *bāhire*—externally; *jaḍimā*—complete inertia; *antare*—within; *ānanda-vihvala*—overwhelmed with transcendental bliss.

TRANSLATION

As the Lord lay there unconscious, His body resembled a large pumpkin. Externally He was completely inert, but within He felt overwhelming transcendental bliss.

TEXT 18

গাভী সব চৌদিকে শুঁকে প্রভুর শ্রীঅঙ্গ ।
দূর কৈলে নাহি ছাড়ে প্রভুর শ্রীঅঙ্গ-সঙ্গ ॥ ১৮ ॥

gābhī saba caudike śuṅke prabhura śrī-aṅga
dūra kaile nāhi chāḍe prabhura śrī-aṅga-saṅga

SYNONYMS

gābhī—cows; *saba*—all; *cau-dike*—around; *śuṅke*—sniff; *prabhura*—of Śrī Caitanya Mahāprabhu; *śrī-aṅga*—the transcendental body; *dūra kaile*—if they are taken away; *nāhi chāḍe*—they do not give up; *prabhura*—of Śrī Caitanya Mahāprabhu; *śrī-aṅga-saṅga*—association with the transcendental body.

TRANSLATION

All the cows around the Lord were sniffing His transcendental body. When the devotees tried to check them, they refused to give up their association with the transcendental body of Śrī Caitanya Mahāprabhu.

TEXT 19

অনেক করিলা যত্ন, না হয় চেতন ।
প্রভুরে উঠাঞা ঘরে আনিলা ভক্তগণ ॥ ১৯ ॥

aneka karilā yatna, nā haya cetana
prabhure uṭhāñā ghare ānilā bhakta-gaṇa

SYNONYMS

aneka—many; *karilā*—made; *yatna*—endeavors; *nā haya*—there was not; *cetana*—consciousness; *prabhure*—Śrī Caitanya Mahāprabhu; *uṭhāñā*—lifting; *ghare*—home; *ānilā*—brought; *bhakta-gaṇa*—the devotees.

TRANSLATION

The devotees tried to rouse the Lord by various means, but His consciousness did not return. Therefore they all lifted Him and brought Him back home.

TEXT 20

উচ্চ করি' শ্রবণে করে নামসঙ্কীর্তন ।
অনেকক্ষণে মহাপ্রভু পাইলা চেতন ॥ ২০ ॥

ucca kari' śravaṇe kare nāma-saṅkīrtana
aneka-kṣaṇe mahāprabhu pāilā cetana

SYNONYMS

ucca kari'—very loudly; *śravaṇe*—in the ears; *kare*—perform; *nāma-saṅkīrtana*—chanting of the holy name; *aneka-kṣaṇe*—after a considerable time; *mahāprabhu*—Śrī Caitanya Mahāprabhu; *pāilā cetana*—returned to consciousness.

TRANSLATION

All the devotees began to chant the Hare Kṛṣṇa mantra very loudly, and after a considerable time, Śrī Caitanya Mahāprabhu regained consciousness.

TEXT 21

চেতন হইলে হস্ত-পাদ বাহিরে আইল।
পূর্ব্ববৎ যথাযোগ্য শরীর হইল ॥ ২১ ॥

cetana ha-ile hasta-pāda bāhire āila
pūrvavat yathā-yogya śarīra ha-ila

SYNONYMS

cetana ha-ile—when there was consciousness; *hasta-pāda*—the arms and legs; *bāhire*—outside; *āila*—came; *pūrvavat*—as before; *yathā-yogya*—in complete order; *śarīra*—the body; *ha-ila*—was.

TRANSLATION

When He regained consciousness, His arms and legs came out of His body, and His whole body returned to normal.

TEXT 22

উঠিয়া বসিলেন প্রভু, চাহেন ইতি-উতি।
স্বরূপে কহেন,—"তুমি আমা আনিলা কতি ? ২২ ॥

uṭhiyā vasilena prabhu, cāhena iti-uti
svarūpe kahena,—"tumi āmā ānilā kati?

SYNONYMS

uṭhiyā—getting up; *vasilena*—sat down; *prabhu*—Śrī Caitanya Mahāprabhu; *cāhena*—looks; *iti-uti*—here and there; *svarūpe*—to Svarūpa Dāmodara; *kahena*—says; *tumi*—you; *āmā*—Me; *ānilā*—have brought; *kati*—where.

TRANSLATION

Śrī Caitanya Mahāprabhu stood up, and then sat down again. Looking here and there, He inquired from Svarūpa Dāmodara, "Where have you brought Me?

TEXT 23

বেণু-শব্দ শুনি' আমি গেলাঙ বৃন্দাবন।
দেখি,—গোষ্ঠে বেণু বাজায় ব্রজেন্দ্রনন্দন ॥ ২৩ ॥

veṇu-śabda śuni' āmi gelāṅa vṛndāvana
dekhi,—goṣṭhe veṇu bājāya vrajendra-nandana

SYNONYMS

veṇu-śabda—the vibration of the flute; *śuni'*—after hearing; *āmi*—I; *gelāṅa*—went; *vṛndāvana*—to Vṛndāvana; *dekhi*—I saw; *goṣṭhe*—in the pasturing field; *veṇu*—the flute; *bājāya*—played; *vrajendra-nandana*—Kṛṣṇa, the son of Nanda Mahārāja.

TRANSLATION

"After hearing the vibration of a flute, I went to Vṛndāvana, and there I saw that Kṛṣṇa, the son of Mahārāja Nanda, was playing on His flute in the pasturing grounds.

TEXT 24

সঙ্কেত-বেণু-নাদে রাধা আনি' কুঞ্জঘরে।
কুঞ্জেরে চলিলা কৃষ্ণ ক্রীড়া করিবারে ॥ ২৪ ॥

saṅketa-veṇu-nāde rādhā āni' kuñja-ghare
kuñjere calilā kṛṣṇa krīḍā karibāre

SYNONYMS

saṅketa-veṇu-nāde—by the signal of the vibration of the flute; *rādhā*—Śrīmatī Rādhārāṇī; *āni'*—bringing; *kuñja-ghare*—to a bower; *kuñjere*—within the bower; *calilā*—went; *kṛṣṇa*—Lord Kṛṣṇa; *krīḍā karibāre*—to perform pastimes.

TRANSLATION

"He brought Śrīmatī Rādhārāṇī to a bower by signaling with His flute. Then He entered within that bower to perform pastimes with Her.

TEXT 25

তাঁর পাছে পাছে আমি করিনু গমন।
তাঁর ভূষা-ধ্বনিতে আমার হরিল শ্রবণ ॥ ২৫ ॥

tāṅra pāche pāche āmi karinu gamana
tāṅra bhūṣā-dhvanite āmāra harila śravaṇa

SYNONYMS

tāṅra pāche pāche—just behind Him; *āmi*—I; *karinu gamana*—went; *tāṅra*—His; *bhūṣā-dhvanite*—by the sound of ornaments; *āmāra*—My; *harila*—became captivated; *śravaṇa*—ears.

TRANSLATION

"I entered the bower just behind Kṛṣṇa, My ears captivated by the sound of His ornaments.

TEXT 26

গোপীগণ-সহ বিহার, হাস, পরিহাস।
কণ্ঠধ্বনি-উক্তি শুনি' মোর কর্ণোল্লাস ॥ ২৬ ॥

gopī-gaṇa-saha vihāra, hāsa, parihāsa
kaṇṭha-dhvani-ukti śuni' mora karṇollāsa

SYNONYMS

gopī-gaṇa-saha—with the *gopīs; vihāra*—pastimes; *hāsa*—laughing; *parihāsa*—joking; *kaṇṭha-dhvani-ukti*—vocal expressions; *śuni'*—hearing; *mora*—My; *karṇa-ullāsa*—jubilation of the ears.

TRANSLATION

"I saw Kṛṣṇa and the gopīs enjoying all kinds of pastimes while laughing and joking together. Hearing their vocal expressions enhanced the joy of My ears.

TEXT 27

হেনকালে তুমি-সব কোলাহল করি'।
আমা ইঁহা লঞা আইলা বলাৎকার করি' ॥ ২৭ ॥

hena-kāle tumi-saba kolāhala kari'
āmā iṅhā lañā āilā balātkāra kari'

SYNONYMS

hena-kāle—at this time; *tumi-saba*—all of you; *kolāhala kari'*—making a tumultuous sound; *āmā*—Me; *iṅhā*—here; *lañā āilā*—brought back; *balātkāra kari'*—by force.

TRANSLATION

"Just then, all of you made a tumultuous sound and brought Me back here by force.

TEXT 28

শুনিতে না পাইনু সেই অমৃতসম বাণী।
শুনিতে না পাইনু ভূষণ-মুরলীর ধ্বনি ॥" ২৮ ॥

śunite nā pāinu sei amṛta-sama vāṇī
śunite nā pāinu bhūṣaṇa-muralīra dhvani"

SYNONYMS

śunite nā pāinu—I could not hear; *sei*—those; *amṛta-sama*—exactly like nectar; *vāṇī*—voices; *śunite nā pāinu*—I could not hear; *bhūṣaṇa*—of ornaments; *muralīra*—of the flute; *dhvani*—vibration.

TRANSLATION

"Because you brought Me back here, I could no longer hear the nectarean voices of Kṛṣṇa and the gopīs, nor could I hear the sounds of their ornaments or the flute."

TEXT 29

ভাবাবেশে স্বরূপে কহেন গদ্গদ-বাণী ।
'কর্ণ তৃষ্ণায় মরে, পড় রসায়ন, শুনি ॥' ২৯ ॥

bhāvāveśe svarūpe kahena gadgada-vāṇī
'karṇa tṛṣṇāya mare, paḍa rasāyana, śuni'

SYNONYMS

bhāva-āveśe—in great ecstasy; *svarūpe*—to Svarūpa Dāmodara; *kahena*—says; *gadgada-vāṇī*—in a faltering voice; *karṇa*—the ears; *tṛṣṇāya*—because of thirst; *mare*—dies; *paḍa*—recite; *rasa-āyana*—something relishable; *śuni'*—let Me hear.

TRANSLATION

In great ecstasy, Śrī Caitanya Mahāprabhu said to Svarūpa Dāmodara in a faltering voice, "My ears are dying of thirst. Please recite something to quench this thirst. Let me hear it."

TEXT 30

স্বরূপ-গোসাঞি প্রভুর ভাব জানিয়া ।
ভাগবতের শ্লোক পড়ে মধুর করিয়া ॥ ৩০ ॥

svarūpa-gosāñi prabhura bhāva jāniyā
bhāgavatera śloka paḍe madhura kariyā

SYNONYMS

svarūpa-gosāñi—Svarūpa Dāmodara Gosāñi; *prabhura*—of Śrī Caitanya Mahāprabhu; *bhāva*—the emotion; *jāniyā*—understanding; *bhāgavatera*—of *Śrīmad-Bhāgavatam; śloka*—a verse; *paḍe*—recites; *madhura kariyā*—in a sweet voice.

TRANSLATION

Understanding the ecstatic emotions of Śrī Caitanya Mahāprabhu, Svarūpa Dāmodara, in a sweet voice, recited the following verse from Śrīmad-Bhāgavatam.

TEXT 31

কাস্ত্র্যঙ্গ তে কলপদামৃতবেণুগীত-
সম্মোহিতার্যচরিতান্ন চলেৎ ত্রিলোক্যাম্ ।
ত্রৈলোক্য-সৌভগমিদঞ্চ নিরীক্ষ্য রূপং
যদ্গোদ্বিজদ্রুমমৃগাঃ পুলকান্যবিভ্রন্ ॥ ৩১ ॥

kā stry aṅga te kala-padāmṛta-veṇu-gīta-
sammohitārya-caritān na calet trilokyām
trailokya-saubhagam idaṁ ca nirīkṣya rūpaṁ
yad go-dvija-druma-mṛgāḥ pulakāny abibhran

SYNONYMS

kā—what; *strī*—woman; *aṅga*—O Kṛṣṇa; *te*—of You; *kala-pada*—by the rhythms; *amṛta-veṇu-gīta*—of the sweet songs of the flute; *sammohitā*—being captivated; *ārya-caritāt*—from the path of chastity according to Vedic civilization; *na*—not; *calet*—would wander; *tri-lokyām*—in the three worlds; *trai-lokya-saubhagam*—which is the fortune of the three worlds; *idam*—this; *ca*—and; *nirīkṣya*—by observing; *rūpam*—beauty; *yat*—which; *go*—the cows; *dvija*—birds; *druma*—trees; *mṛgāḥ*—forest animals like the deer; *pulakāni*—transcendental jubilation; *abibhran*—manifested.

TRANSLATION

" 'My dear Lord Kṛṣṇa, where is that woman within the three worlds who cannot be captivated by the rhythms of the sweet songs coming from Your wonderful flute? Who cannot fall down from the path of chastity in this way? Your beauty is the most sublime within the three worlds. Upon seeing Your beauty, even cows, birds, animals and trees in the forest are stunned in jubilation.'

PURPORT

This verse is from *Śrīmad-Bhāgavatam* (10.29.40).

TEXT 32

শুনি' প্রভু গোপীভাবে আবিষ্ট হইলা ।
ভাগবতের শ্লোকের অর্থ করিতে লাগিলা ॥ ৩২ ॥

śuni' prabhu gopī-bhāve āviṣṭa ha-ilā
bhāgavatera ślokera artha karite lāgilā

SYNONYMS

śuni'—hearing; *prabhu*—Śrī Caitanya Mahāprabhu; *gopī-bhāve*—in the emotion of the *gopīs; āviṣṭa ha-ilā*—became overwhelmed; *bhāgavatera*—of *Śrīmad-Bhāgavatam; ślokera*—of the verse; *artha*—the meaning; *karite lāgilā*—began to explain.

TRANSLATION

Upon hearing this verse, Śrī Caitanya Mahāprabhu, overwhelmed with the ecstasy of the gopīs, began to explain it.

TEXT 33

হৈল গোপী-ভাবাবেশ, কৈল রাসে পরবেশ,
কৃষ্ণের শুনি' উপেক্ষা-বচন।
কৃষ্ণের মুখ-হাস্য-বাণী, ত্যাগে তাহা সত্য মানি',
রোষে কৃষ্ণে দেন ওলাহন ॥ ৩৩ ॥

haila gopī-bhāvāveśa, kaila rāse paraveśa,
kṛṣṇera śuni' upekṣā-vacana
kṛṣṇera mukha-hāsya-vāṇī, tyāge tāhā satya māni',
roṣe kṛṣṇe dena olāhana

SYNONYMS

haila—there was; *gopī*—of the *gopīs; bhāva-āveśa*—ecstatic emotion; *kaila*—did; *rāse*—in the *rāsa* dance; *paraveśa*—entrance; *kṛṣṇera*—of Lord Kṛṣṇa; *śuni'*—hearing; *upekṣā-vacana*—the words of negligence; *kṛṣṇera*—of Lord Kṛṣṇa; *mukha*—face; *hāsya*—smiling; *vāṇī*—talking; *tyāge*—renounce; *tāhā*—that; *satya māni'*—taking as a fact; *roṣe*—in anger; *kṛṣṇe*—to Lord Kṛṣṇa; *dena*—give; *olāhana*—chastisement.

TRANSLATION

Śrī Caitanya Mahāprabhu said, "The gopīs entered the arena of the rāsa dance in ecstasy, but after hearing Kṛṣṇa's words of negligence and detachment, they understood that He was going to renounce them. Thus they began to chastise Him in anger.

TEXT 34

"নাগর, কহ, তুমি করিয়া নিশ্চয়।
এই ত্রিজগৎ ভরি', আছে যত যোগ্যা নারী,
তোমার বেণু কাহাঁ না আকর্ষয়? ৩৪ ॥ ধ্রু ॥

"nāgara, kaha, tumi kariyā niścaya
ei trijagat bhari', āche yata yogyā nārī,
tomāra veṇu kāhāṅ nā ākarṣaya?

SYNONYMS

nāgara—O lover; *kaha*—say; *tumi*—You; *kariyā*—making; *niścaya*—certain; *ei*—these; *tri-jagat*—three worlds; *bhari'*—filling; *āche*—there are; *yata*—as many; *yogyā*—suitable; *nārī*—women; *tomāra*—Your; *veṇu*—flute; *kāhāṅ*—where; *nā*—not; *ākarṣaya*—attracts.

TRANSLATION

" 'O dear lover,' " they said, " 'please answer just one question. Who among all the youthful women within this universe is not attracted by the sound of Your flute?

TEXT 35

কৈলা জগতে বেণুধ্বনি, সিদ্ধমন্ত্রা যোগিনী,
দূতী হঞা মোহে নারী-মন।
মহোৎকণ্ঠা বাড়াঞা, আর্যপথ ছাড়াঞা,
আনি' তোমায় করে সমর্পণ ॥ ৩৫ ॥

kailā jagate veṇu-dhvani, siddha-mantrā yoginī,
dūtī hañā mohe nārī-mana
mahotkaṇṭhā bāḍāñā, ārya-patha chāḍāñā,
āni' tomāya kare samarpaṇa

SYNONYMS

kailā—You have made; *jagate*—in the world; *veṇu-dhvani*—the vibration of the flute; *siddha-mantrā*—perfected in chanting *mantras; yoginī*—a female mystic; *dūtī*—a messenger; *hañā*—being; *mohe*—enchants; *nārī-mana*—the minds of women; *mahā-utkaṇṭhā*—great anxiety; *bāḍāñā*—increasing; *ārya-patha*—the regulative principles; *chāḍāñā*—inducing to give up; *āni'*—bringing; *tomāya*—to You; *kare samarpaṇa*—delivers.

TRANSLATION

" 'When You play Your flute, it acts like a messenger in the form of a yoginī perfect in the art of chanting mantras. This messenger enchants all the women in the universe and attracts them to You. Then she increases their great anxiety and induces them to give up the regulative principle of obeying superiors. Finally, she forcibly brings them to You to surrender in amorous love.

TEXT 36

ধর্ম ছাড়ায় বেণুদ্বারে, হানে কটাক্ষ-কামশরে,
লজ্জা, ভয়, সকল ছাড়ায়।
এবে আমায় করি' রোষ, কহি' পতিত্যাগে 'দোষ',
ধার্মিক হঞা ধর্ম শিখায়! ৩৬॥

dharma chāḍāya veṇu-dvāre, hāne kaṭākṣa-kāma-śare,
lajjā, bhaya, sakala chāḍāya
ebe āmāya kari' roṣa, kahi' pati-tyāge 'doṣa',
dhārmika hañā dharma śikhāya!

SYNONYMS

dharma—religious principles; *chāḍāya*—induces to reject; *veṇu-dvāre*—through the flute; *hāne*—pierces; *kaṭākṣa*—glancing; *kāma-śare*—by the arrows of lust; *lajjā*—shame; *bhaya*—fear; *sakala*—all; *chāḍāya*—induces to give up; *ebe*—now; *āmāya*—at us; *kari' roṣa*—becoming angry; *kahi'*—saying; *pati-tyāge*—to give up one's husband; *doṣa*—fault; *dhārmika*—very religious; *hañā*—becoming; *dharma*—religious principles; *śikhāya*—You teach.

TRANSLATION

" 'The vibration of Your flute, accompanied by Your glance, which pierces us forcibly with the arrows of lust, induces us to ignore the regulative principles of religious life. Thus we become excited by lusty desires and come to You, giving up all shame and fear. But now You are angry with us. You are finding fault with our violating religious principles and leaving our homes and husbands. And as You instruct us about religious principles, we become helpless.

TEXT 37

অন্যকথা, অন্যমন, বাহিরে অন্য আচরণ,
এই সব শঠ-পরিপাটী।
তুমি জান পরিহাস, হয় নারীর সর্বনাশ,
ছাড় এই সব কুটীনাটী॥ ৩৭॥

anya-kathā, anya-mana, bāhire anya ācaraṇa,
ei saba śaṭha-paripāṭī
tumi jāna parihāsa, haya nārīra sarva-nāśa,
chāḍa ei saba kuṭīnāṭī

SYNONYMS

anya—different; *kathā*—words; *anya*—different; *mana*—mind; *bāhire*—externally; *anya*—different; *ācaraṇa*—behavior; *ei*—these; *saba*—all; *śaṭha-paripāṭī*—well-planned cheating behavior; *tumi*—You; *jāna*—know; *parihāsa*—joking; *haya*—there is; *nārīra*—of women; *sarva-nāśa*—total annihilation; *chāḍa*—please give up; *ei*—these; *saba*—all; *kuṭīnāṭī*—clever tricks.

TRANSLATION

" 'We know that this is all a well-planned trick. You know how to make jokes that cause the complete annihilation of women, but we can understand that Your real mind, words and behavior are different. Therefore please give up all these clever tricks.

TEXT 38

বেণুনাদ অমৃত-ঘোলে, অমৃত-সমান মিঠা বোলে,
অমৃত-সমান ভূষণ-শিঞ্জিত।
তিন অমৃতে হরে কাণ, হরে মন, হরে প্রাণ,
কেমনে নারী ধরিবেক চিত ?" ৩৮ ॥

veṇu-nāda amṛta-ghole, amṛta-samāna miṭhā bole,
amṛta-samāna bhūṣaṇa-śiñjita
tina amṛte hare kāṇa, hare mana, hare prāṇa,
kemane nārī dharibeka cita?"

SYNONYMS

veṇu-nāda—the vibration of the flute; *amṛta-ghole*—like nectarean buttermilk; *amṛta-samāna*—equal to nectar; *miṭhā bole*—sweet talking; *amṛta-samāna*—exactly like nectar; *bhūṣaṇa-śiñjita*—the vibration of ornaments; *tina*—three; *amṛte*—nectars; *hare*—attract; *kāṇa*—the ear; *hare*—attract; *mana*—the mind; *hare*—attract; *prāṇa*—the life; *kemane*—how; *nārī*—women; *dharibeka*—will keep; *cita*—patience or consciousness.

TRANSLATION

" 'The nectarean buttermilk of Your flute's vibration, the nectar of Your sweet words and the nectarean sound of Your ornaments mix together to attract our ears, minds and lives. In this way You are killing us.' "

TEXT 39

এত কহি' ক্রোধাবেশে, ভাবের তরঙ্গে ভাসে,
উৎকণ্ঠা-সাগরে ডুবে মন।
রাধার উৎকণ্ঠা-বাণী, পড়ি' আপনে বাখানি,
কৃষ্ণমাধুর্য করে আস্বাদন ॥ ৩৯ ॥

eta kahi' krodhāveśe, bhāvera taraṅge bhāse,
utkaṇṭhā-sāgare ḍube mana
rādhāra utkaṇṭhā-vāṇī, paḍi' āpane vākhāni,
kṛṣṇa-mādhurya kare āsvādana

SYNONYMS

eta kahi'—saying this; *krodha-āveśe*—in the mood of anger; *bhāvera taraṅge*—in the waves of ecstatic love; *bhāse*—floats; *utkaṇṭhā*—of anxieties; *sāgare*—in the ocean; *ḍube mana*—merges the mind; *rādhāra*—of Śrīmatī Rādhārāṇī; *utkaṇṭhā-vāṇī*—words of anxiety; *paḍi'*—reciting; *āpane*—personally; *vākhāni*—explaining; *kṛṣṇa-mādhurya*—the sweetness of Kṛṣṇa; *kare āsvādana*—tastes.

TRANSLATION

Śrī Caitanya Mahāprabhu spoke these words in a mood of anger as He floated on waves of ecstatic love. Merged in an ocean of anxiety, He recited a verse spoken by Śrīmatī Rādhārāṇī expressing the same emotion. Then He personally explained the verse and thus tasted the sweetness of Kṛṣṇa.

TEXT 40

নদজ্জলদনিস্বনঃ শ্রবণকর্ষিসচ্ছিঞ্জিতঃ
সনর্মরসসূচকাক্ষরপদার্থভঙ্গ্যুক্তিকঃ।
রমাদিক-বরাঙ্গনা-হৃদয়হারি-বংশীকলঃ
স মে মদনমোহনঃ সখি তনোতি কর্ণস্পৃহাম্ ॥ ৪০ ॥

nadaj-jalada-nisvanaḥ śravaṇa-karṣi-sac-chiñjitaḥ
sanarma-rasa-sūcakākṣara-padārtha-bhaṅgy-uktikaḥ
ramādika-varāṅganā-hṛdaya-hāri-vaṁśī-kalaḥ
sa me madana-mohanaḥ sakhi tanoti karṇa-spṛhām

SYNONYMS

nadat—resounding; *jalada*—the cloud; *nisvanaḥ*—whose voice; *śravaṇa*—the ears; *karṣi*—attracting; *sat-śiñjitaḥ*—the tinkling of whose ornaments; *sa-narma*—

with deep meaning; *rasa-sūcaka*—joking; *akṣara*—letters; *pada-artha*—meanings; *bhaṅgi*—indications; *uktikaḥ*—whose talk; *ramā-ādika*—beginning with the goddess of fortune; *vara-aṅganā*—of beautiful women; *hṛdaya-hāri*—attracting the hearts; *vaṁśī-kalaḥ*—the sound of whose flute; *saḥ*—that; *me*—My; *madana-mohanaḥ*—Madana-mohana; *sakhi*—My dear friend; *tanoti*—expands; *karṇa-spṛhām*—the desire of the ears.

TRANSLATION

Śrī Caitanya Mahāprabhu continued, " 'My dear friend, the Supreme Personality of Godhead, Kṛṣṇa, has a voice as deep as a cloud resounding in the sky. With the tinkling of His ornaments, He attracts the ears of the gopīs, and with the sound of His flute He attracts even the goddess of fortune and other beautiful women. That Personality of Godhead, known as Madana-mohana, whose joking words carry many indications and deep meanings, is increasing the lusty desires of My ears.'

PURPORT

This verse is found in the *Govinda-līlāmṛta* (8.5).

TEXT 41

“কণ্ঠের গম্ভীর ধ্বনি, নবঘন-ধ্বনি জিনি’,
যার গুণে কোকিল লাজায় ।
তার এক শ্রুতি-কণে, ডুবায় জগতের কাণে,
পুনঃ কাণ বাহুড়ি’ না আয় ॥ ৪১ ॥

"kaṇṭhera gambhīra dhvani, navaghana-dhvani jini',
yāra guṇe kokila lājāya
tāra eka śruti-kaṇe, ḍubāya jagatera kāṇe,
punaḥ kāṇa bāhuḍi' nā āya

SYNONYMS

kaṇṭhera—of the throat; *gambhīra*—deep; *dhvani*—sound; *nava-ghana*—of new clouds; *dhvani*—the resounding; *jini'*—conquering; *yāra*—of which; *guṇe*—the attributes; *kokila*—the cuckoo; *lājāya*—put to shame; *tāra*—of that; *eka*—one; *śruti-kaṇe*—particle of sound; *ḍubāya*—inundates; *jagatera*—of the whole world; *kāṇe*—the ear; *punaḥ*—again; *kāṇa*—the ear; *bāhuḍi'*—getting out; *nā āya*—cannot come.

TRANSLATION

"Kṛṣṇa's deep voice is more resonant than newly arrived clouds, and His sweet song defeats even the sweet voice of the cuckoo. Indeed, His song is so

sweet that even one particle of its sound can inundate the entire world. If such a particle enters one's ear, one is immediately bereft of all other types of hearing.

TEXT 42

কহ, সখি, কি করি উপায় ?
কৃষ্ণের সে শব্দ-গুণে, হরিলে আমার কাণে,
এবে না পায়, তৃষ্ণায় মরি' যায় ॥ ৪২ ॥ ধ্রু ॥

kaha, sakhi, ki kari upāya?
kṛṣṇera se śabda-guṇe, harile āmāra kāṇe,
ebe nā pāya, tṛṣṇāya mari' yāya

SYNONYMS

kaha—please say; *sakhi*—My dear friend; *ki*—what; *kari*—can I do; *upāya*—means; *kṛṣṇera*—of Kṛṣṇa; *se*—that; *śabda*—of the sound; *guṇe*—the qualities; *harile*—having attracted; *āmāra*—My; *kāṇe*—ears; *ebe*—now; *nā pāya*—do not get; *tṛṣṇāya*—from thirst; *mari' yāya*—I am dying.

TRANSLATION

"My dear friend, please tell me what to do. My ears have been plundered by the qualities of Kṛṣṇa's sound. Now, however, I cannot hear His transcendental sound, and I am almost dead for want of it.

TEXT 43

নূপুর-কিঙ্কিণী-ধ্বনি, হংস-সারস জিনি',
কঙ্কণ-ধ্বনি চটকে লাজায় ।
একবার যেই শুনে, ব্যাপি রহে' তার কাণে,
অন্য শব্দ সে-কাণে না যায় ॥ ৪৩ ॥

nūpura-kiṅkinī-dhvani, haṁsa-sārasa jini',
kaṅkaṇa-dhvani caṭake lājāya
eka-bāra yei śune, vyāpi rahe' tāra kāṇe,
anya śabda se-kāṇe nā yāya

SYNONYMS

nūpura—of the ankle bells; *kiṅkinī*—tinkling; *dhvani*—the sound; *haṁsa*—swans; *sārasa*—cranes; *jini'*—conquering; *kaṅkaṇa-dhvani*—the sound of bangles; *caṭake*—the *caṭaka* bird; *lājāya*—puts to shame; *eka-bāra*—once; *yei*—one who; *śune*—hears; *vyāpi*—expanding; *rahe'*—remains; *tāra kāṇe*—in his ear; *anya*—other; *śabda*—sound; *se-kāṇe*—in that ear; *nā yāya*—does not go.

TRANSLATION

"The tinkling of Kṛṣṇa's ankle bells surpasses the songs of even the swan and crane, and the sound of His bangles puts the singing of the caṭaka bird to shame. Having allowed these sounds to enter the ears even once, one cannot tolerate hearing anything else.

TEXT 44

সে শ্রীমুখ-ভাষিত, অমৃত হৈতে পরামৃত,
স্মিত-কর্পূর তাহাতে মিশ্রিত।
শব্দ, অর্থ,—দুইশক্তি, নানা-রস করে ব্যক্তি,
প্রত্যক্ষর—নর্ম-বিভূষিত ॥ ৪৪ ॥

se śrī-mukha-bhāṣita, amṛta haite parāmṛta,
smita-karpūra tāhāte miśrita
śabda, artha,——dui-śakti, nānā-rasa kare vyakti,
pratyakṣara——narma-vibhūṣita

SYNONYMS

se—that; *śrī*—beautiful; *mukha*—by the mouth; *bhāṣita*—spoken; *amṛta*—nectar; *haite*—than; *para-amṛta*—more nectarean; *smita*—smiling; *karpūra*—camphor; *tāhāte*—in that; *miśrita*—mixed; *śabda*—sound; *artha*—meaning; *dui-śakti*—two energies; *nānā*—various; *rasa*—mellows; *kare vyakti*—express; *prati-akṣara*—every word; *narma-vibhūṣita*—full of meaning.

TRANSLATION

"Kṛṣṇa's speech is far sweeter than nectar. Each of His jubilant words is full of meaning, and when His speech mixes with His smile, which is like camphor, the resultant sound and the deep meaning of Kṛṣṇa's words create various transcendental mellows.

TEXT 45

সে অমৃতের এক-কণ, কর্ণ-চকোর-জীবন,
কর্ণ-চকোর জীয়ে সেই আশে।
ভাগ্যবশে কভু পায়, অভাগ্যে কভু না পায়,
না পাইলে মরয়ে পিয়াসে ॥ ৪৫ ॥

se amṛtera eka-kaṇa, karṇa-cakora-jīvana,
karṇa-cakora jīye sei āśe
bhāgya-vaśe kabhu pāya, abhāgye kabhu nā pāya,
nā pāile maraye piyāse

SYNONYMS

se amṛtera—of that nectar; *eka-kaṇa*—one particle; *karṇa-cakora*—of the ear, which is like a *cakora* bird; *jīvana*—the life; *karṇa*—the ear; *cakora*—the *cakora* bird; *jīye*—lives; *sei āśe*—with that hope; *bhāgya-vaśe*—by good fortune; *kabhu*—sometimes; *pāya*—gets; *abhāgye*—by misfortune; *kabhu*—sometimes; *nā pāya*—does not get; *nā pāile*—if does not get; *maraye*—dies; *piyāse*—from thirst.

TRANSLATION

"One particle of that transcendental, blissful nectar is the life and soul of the ear, which is like a cakora bird that lives in hope of tasting that nectar. Sometimes, by good fortune, the bird can taste it, but at other times he unfortunately cannot and therefore almost dies of thirst.

TEXT 46

যেবা বেণু-কলধ্বনি, একবার তাহা শুনি',
জগন্নারী-চিত্ত আউলায় ।
নীবি-বন্ধ পড়ে খসি', বিনা-মূলে হয় দাসী,
বাউলী হঞা কৃষ্ণ-পাশে ধায় ॥ ৪৬ ॥

yebā veṇu-kala-dhvani, eka-bāra tāhā śuni',
jagan-nārī-citta āulāya
nīvi-bandha paḍe khasi', vinā-mūle haya dāsī,
bāulī hañā kṛṣṇa-pāśe dhāya

SYNONYMS

yebā—whoever; *veṇu*—of the flute; *kala-dhvani*—the sweet vibration; *eka-bāra*—once; *tāhā*—that; *śuni'*—hearing; *jagat*—of the universe; *nārī*—of the women; *citta*—hearts; *āulāya*—become disturbed; *nīvi-bandha*—the fastened belts; *paḍe*—fall; *khasi'*—becoming loosened; *vinā-mūle*—without a price; *haya*—they become; *dāsī*—maidservants; *bāulī*—mad; *hañā*—becoming; *kṛṣṇa-pāśe*—after Kṛṣṇa; *dhāya*—run.

TRANSLATION

"The transcendental vibration of Kṛṣṇa's flute disturbs the hearts of women all over the world, even if they hear it only once. Thus their fastened belts

become loose, and these women become the unpaid maidservants of Kṛṣṇa. Indeed, they run toward Kṛṣṇa exactly like madwomen.

TEXT 47

যেবা লক্ষ্মী-ঠাকুরাণী, তেঁহো যে কাকলী শুনি',
কৃষ্ণ-পাশ আইসে প্রত্যাশায় ।
না পায় কৃষ্ণের সঙ্গ, বাড়ে তৃষ্ণা-তরঙ্গ,
তপ করে, তবু নাহি পায় ॥ ৪৭ ॥

yebā lakṣmī-ṭhākurāṇī, teṅho ye kākalī śuni',
kṛṣṇa-pāśa āise pratyāśāya
nā pāya kṛṣṇera saṅga, bāḍe tṛṣṇā-taraṅga,
tapa kare, tabu nāhi pāya

SYNONYMS

yebā—even; *lakṣmī-ṭhākurāṇī*—the goddess of fortune; *teṅho*—she; *ye*—which; *kākalī*—vibration of the flute; *śuni'*—hearing; *kṛṣṇa-pāśa*—to Lord Kṛṣṇa; *āise*—comes; *pratyāśāya*—with great hope; *nā pāya*—does not get; *kṛṣṇera saṅga*—association with Kṛṣṇa; *bāḍe*—increase; *tṛṣṇā*—of thirst; *taraṅga*—the waves; *tapa kare*—undergoes austerity; *tabu*—still; *nāhi pāya*—does not get.

TRANSLATION

"When she hears the vibration of Kṛṣṇa's flute, even the goddess of fortune comes to Him, greatly hoping for His association, but nevertheless she does not get it. When the waves of thirst for His association increase, she performs austerities, but still she cannot meet Him.

TEXT 48

এই শব্দামৃত চারি, যার হয় ভাগ্য ভারি,
সেই কর্ণে ইহা করে পান ।
ইহা যেই নাহি শুনে, সে কাণ জন্মিল কেনে,
কাণাকড়ি-সম সেই কাণ ॥" ৪৮ ॥

ei śabdāmṛta cāri, yāra haya bhāgya bhāri,
sei karṇe ihā kare pāna
ihā yei nāhi śune, se kāṇa janmila kene,
kāṇākaḍi-sama sei kāṇa"

SYNONYMS

ei—these; *śabda-amṛta*—nectarean sound vibrations; *cāri*—four; *yāra*—of whom; *haya*—there is; *bhāgya bhāri*—great fortune; *sei*—such a person; *karṇe*—by the ears; *ihā*—these sounds; *kare pāna*—drinks; *ihā*—these sounds; *yei*—anyone who; *nāhi śune*—does not hear; *se*—those; *kāṇa*—ears; *janmila*—took birth; *kene*—why; *kāṇākaḍi*—a hole in a small conchshell; *sama*—just like; *sei kāṇa*—those ears.

TRANSLATION

"Only the most fortunate can hear these four nectarean sounds—Kṛṣṇa's words, the tinkling of His ankle bells and bangles, His voice and the vibration of His flute. If one does not hear these sounds, his ears are as useless as small conchshells with holes."

TEXT 49

করিতে ঐছে বিলাপ, উঠিল উদ্বেগ, ভাব,
মনে কাহো নাহি আলম্বন ।
উদ্বেগ, বিষাদ, মতি, ঔৎসুক্য, ত্রাস, ধৃতি, স্মৃতি,
নানা-ভাবের হইল মিলন ॥ ৪৯ ॥

karite aiche vilāpa, uṭhila udvega, bhāva,
mane kāho nāhi ālambana
udvega, viṣāda, mati, autsukya, trāsa, dhṛti, smṛti,
nānā-bhāvera ha-ila milana

SYNONYMS

karite—doing; *aiche*—such; *vilāpa*—lamentation; *uṭhila*—there arose; *udvega*—agitation; *bhāva*—ecstasy; *mane*—in the mind; *kāho*—anywhere; *nāhi*—there is not; *ālambana*—shelter; *udvega*—anxiety; *viṣāda*—lamentation; *mati*—attention; *autsukya*—eagerness; *trāsa*—fear; *dhṛti*—determination; *smṛti*—remembrance; *nānā-bhāvera*—of various ecstasies; *ha-ila*—there was; *milana*—combining.

TRANSLATION

While Śrī Caitanya Mahāprabhu lamented in this way, agitation and ecstasy awoke in His mind, and He became very restless. Many transcendental ecstasies combined in Him, including anxiety, lamentation, attention, eagerness, fear, determination and remembrance.

TEXT 50

ভাবশাবল্যে রাধার উক্তি, লীলাশুকে হৈল স্ফূর্তি,
সেই ভাবে পড়ে এক শ্লোক।
উন্মাদের সামর্থ্যে, সেই শ্লোকের করে অর্থে,
যেই অর্থ নাহি জানে লোক ॥ ৫০ ॥

bhāva-śābalye rādhāra ukti, līlā-śuke haila sphūrti,
sei bhāve paḍe eka śloka
unmādera sāmarthye, sei ślokera kare arthe,
yei artha nāhi jāne loka

SYNONYMS

bhāva-śābalye—in the aggregate of all ecstasies; *rādhāra*—of Śrīmatī Rādhārāṇī; *ukti*—statement; *līlā-śuke*—in Bilvamaṅgala Ṭhākura; *haila*—there was; *sphūrti*—awakening; *sei bhāve*—in that ecstasy; *paḍe*—recites; *eka*—one; *śloka*—verse; *unmādera*—of madness; *sāmarthye*—in the capacity; *sei ślokera*—of that verse; *kare arthe*—describes the meaning; *yei artha*—which meaning; *nāhi*—do not; *jāne*—know; *loka*—people.

TRANSLATION

The aggregate of all these ecstasies awoke a statement by Śrīmatī Rādhārāṇī in the mind of Bilvamaṅgala Ṭhākura [Līlā-śuka]. In the same ecstatic mood, Śrī Caitanya Mahāprabhu now recited that verse, and on the strength of madness, He described its meaning, which is unknown to people in general.

TEXT 51

কিমিহ কৃণুমঃ কস্য ব্রূমঃ কৃতং কৃতমাশয়া
কথয়ত কথামন্যাং ধন্যামহো হৃদয়েশয়ঃ।
মধুরমধুরস্মেরাকারে মনোনয়নোৎসবে
কৃপণকৃপণা কৃষ্ণে তৃষ্ণা চিরং বত লম্বতে ॥ ৫১ ॥

kim iha kṛṇumaḥ kasya brūmaḥ kṛtaṁ kṛtam āśayā
kathayata kathām anyāṁ dhanyām aho hṛdaye śayaḥ
madhura-madhura-smerākāre mano-nayanotsave
kṛpaṇa-kṛpaṇā kṛṣṇe tṛṣṇā ciraṁ bata lambate

SYNONYMS

kim—what; *iha*—here; *kṛṇumaḥ*—shall I do; *kasya*—to whom; *brūmaḥ*—shall I speak; *kṛtam*—what is done; *kṛtam*—done; *āśayā*—in the hope; *kathayata*—

please speak; *kathām*—words; *anyām*—other; *dhanyām*—auspicious; *aho*—alas; *hṛdaye*—within My heart; *śayaḥ*—lying; *madhura-madhura*—sweeter than sweetness; *smera*—smiling; *ākāre*—whose form; *manaḥ-nayana*—to the mind and eyes; *utsave*—who gives pleasure; *kṛpaṇa-kṛpaṇā*—the best of misers; *kṛṣṇe*—for Kṛṣṇa; *tṛṣṇā*—thirst; *ciram*—at every moment; *bata*—alas; *lambate*—is increasing.

TRANSLATION

Śrī Caitanya Mahāprabhu said, " 'Alas, what shall I do? To whom shall I speak? Let whatever I have done in hopes of meeting Kṛṣṇa be finished now. Please say something auspicious, but do not speak about Kṛṣṇa. Alas, Kṛṣṇa is lying within My heart like Cupid; therefore how can I possibly give up talking of Him? I cannot forget Kṛṣṇa, whose smile is sweeter than sweetness itself and who gives pleasure to My mind and eyes. Alas, My great thirst for Kṛṣṇa is increasing moment by moment!'

PURPORT

This statement by Śrīmatī Rādhārāṇī is quoted from *Kṛṣṇa-karṇāmṛta* (42).

TEXT 52

"এই কৃষ্ণের বিরহে, উদ্বেগে মন স্থির নহে,
প্রাপ্ত্যুপায়-চিন্তন না যায়।
যেবা তুমি সখীগণ, বিষাদে বাউল মন,
কারে পুছোঁ, কে কহে উপায় ? ৫২ ॥

"ei kṛṣṇera virahe, udvege mana sthira nahe,
prāpty-upāya-cintana nā yāya
yebā tumi sakhī-gaṇa, viṣāde bāula mana,
kāre puchoṅ, ke kahe upāya?

SYNONYMS

ei—this; *kṛṣṇera*—of Kṛṣṇa; *virahe*—in separation; *udvege*—in anxiety; *mana*—mind; *sthira*—patient; *nahe*—is not; *prāpti-upāya*—the means for obtaining; *cintana nā yāya*—I cannot think of; *yebā*—all; *tumi*—you; *sakhī-gaṇa*—friends; *viṣāde*—in lamentation; *bāula*—maddened; *mana*—minds; *kāre*—whom; *puchoṅ*—shall I ask; *ke*—who; *kahe*—will speak; *upāya*—the means.

TRANSLATION

"The anxiety caused by separation from Kṛṣṇa has made Me impatient, and I can think of no way to meet Him. O My friends, you are also deranged by lamentation. Who, therefore, will tell Me how to find Him?

TEXT 53

হাহা সখি, কি করি উপায় !
কাঁহা করোঁ, কাহাঁ যাঙ, কাহাঁ গেলে কৃষ্ণ পাঙ,
কৃষ্ণ বিনা প্রাণ মোর যায় ॥" ৫৩ ॥ ধ্রু ॥

hā hā sakhi, ki kari upāya!
kāṅhā karoṅ, kāhāṅ yāṅa, kāhāṅ gele kṛṣṇa pāṅa,
kṛṣṇa vinā prāṇa mora yāya"

SYNONYMS

hā hā—O; *sakhi*—friends; *ki*—what; *kari*—shall I do; *upāya*—means; *kāṅhā karoṅ*—what shall I do?; *kāhāṅ yāṅa*—where shall I go; *kāhāṅ gele*—where going; *kṛṣṇa pāṅa*—I can get Kṛṣṇa; *kṛṣṇa vinā*—without Kṛṣṇa; *prāṇa*—life; *mora*—My; *yāya*—is leaving.

TRANSLATION

"O My dear friends, how shall I find Kṛṣṇa? What shall I do? Where shall I go? Where can I meet Him? Because I cannot find Kṛṣṇa, My life is leaving Me."

TEXT 54

ক্ষণে মন স্থির হয়, তবে মনে বিচারয়,
বলিতে হইল ভাবোদ্গম ।
পিঙ্গলার বচন-স্মৃতি, করাইল ভাব-মতি,
তাতে করে অর্থ-নির্ধারণ ॥ ৫৪ ॥

kṣaṇe mana sthira haya, tabe mane vicāraya,
balite ha-ila bhāvodgama
piṅgalāra vacana-smṛti, karāila bhāva-mati,
tāte kare artha-nirdhāraṇa

SYNONYMS

kṣaṇe—in a moment; *mana*—the mind; *sthira haya*—becomes patient; *tabe*—at that time; *mane*—within the mind; *vicāraya*—He considers; *balite*—to speak; *ha-ila*—there was; *bhāva-udgama*—awakening of ecstasy; *piṅgalāra*—of Piṅgalā; *vacana-smṛti*—remembering the words; *karāila*—caused; *bhāva-mati*—ecstatic mind; *tāte*—in that; *kare*—does; *artha-nirdhāraṇa*—ascertaining the meaning.

TRANSLATION

Suddenly, Śrī Caitanya Mahāprabhu became calm and considered His state of mind. He remembered the words of Piṅgalā, and this aroused an ecstasy that moved Him to speak. Thus He explained the meaning of the verse.

PURPORT

Piṅgalā was a prostitute who said, "To hope against hope produces only misery. Utter hopelessness is the greatest happiness." Remembering this statement, Śrī Caitanya Mahāprabhu became ecstatic. The story of Piṅgalā is found in *Śrīmad-Bhāgavatam,* Eleventh Canto, Eighth Chapter, verses 22-44, as well as in *Mahābhārata, Śānti-parva,* Chapter 174.

TEXT 55

"দেখি এই উপায়ে, কৃষ্ণ-আশা ছাড়ি' দিয়ে,
আশা ছাড়িলে সুখী হয় মন।
ছাড়' কৃষ্ণকথা অধন্য, কহ অন্যকথা ধন্য,
যাতে হয় কৃষ্ণ-বিস্মরণ ॥" ৫৫ ॥

"dekhi ei upāye, kṛṣṇa-āśā chāḍi' diye,
āśā chāḍile sukhī haya mana
chāḍa' kṛṣṇa-kathā adhanya, kaha anya-kathā dhanya,
yāte haya kṛṣṇa-vismaraṇa"

SYNONYMS

dekhi—I see; *ei upāye*—this means; *kṛṣṇa-āśā*—hope for Kṛṣṇa; *chāḍi' diye*—I give up; *āśā*—hope; *chāḍile*—if I give up; *sukhī*—happy; *haya*—becomes; *mana*—the mind; *chāḍa'*—give up; *kṛṣṇa-kathā*—talks of Kṛṣṇa; *adhanya*—most inglorious; *kaha*—speak; *anya-kathā*—other topics; *dhanya*—glorious; *yāte*—by which; *haya*—there is; *kṛṣṇa-vismaraṇa*—forgetfulness of Kṛṣṇa.

TRANSLATION

Śrī Caitanya Mahāprabhu said, " 'If I give up hope of meeting Kṛṣṇa, I shall then be happy. Therefore, let us stop this most inglorious discussion of Kṛṣṇa. It would be better for us to talk of glorious topics and forget Him.'

TEXT 56

কহিতেই হইল স্মৃতি, চিত্তে হৈল কৃষ্ণস্ফূর্তি,
সখীরে কহে হঞা বিস্মিতে।

"যারে চাহি ছাড়িতে, সেই শুঞা আছে চিত্তে,
কোন রীতে না পারি ছাড়িতে ॥" ৫৬ ॥

kahitei ha-ila smṛti, citte haila kṛṣṇa-sphūrti,
sakhīre kahe hañā vismite
"yāre cāhi chāḍite, sei śuñā āche citte,
kona rīte nā pāri chāḍite"

SYNONYMS

kahitei—while speaking; *ha-ila*—there was; *smṛti*—remembrance; *citte*—in the heart; *haila*—there was; *kṛṣṇa-sphūrti*—the appearance of Kṛṣṇa; *sakhīre*—to the friends; *kahe*—said; *hañā vismite*—being very astonished; *yāre*—He whom; *cāhi chāḍite*—I want to give up; *sei*—that person; *śuñā āche*—is lying; *citte*—in the heart; *kona rīte*—by any process; *nā pāri*—I am not able; *chāḍite*—to give up.

TRANSLATION

"While speaking in this way, Śrīmatī Rādhārāṇī suddenly remembered Kṛṣṇa. Indeed, He appeared within Her heart. Greatly astonished, She told Her friends, 'The person I want to forget is lying in My heart.'

TEXT 57

রাধাভাবের স্বভাব আন, কৃষ্ণে করায় 'কাম'-জ্ঞান,
কাম-জ্ঞানে ত্রাস হৈল চিত্তে ।
কহে—"যে জগৎ মারে, সে পশিল অন্তরে,
এই বৈরী না দেয় পাসরিতে ॥" ৫৭ ॥

rādhā-bhāvera svabhāva āna, kṛṣṇe karāya 'kāma'-jñāna,
kāma-jñāne trāsa haila citte
kahe—"ye jagat māre, se paśila antare,
ei vairī nā deya pāsarite"

SYNONYMS

rādhā-bhāvera—of the ecstasy of Śrīmatī Rādhārāṇī; *sva-bhāva*—characteristic; *āna*—another; *kṛṣṇe*—to Kṛṣṇa; *karāya*—causes Her to do; *kāma-jñāna*—understanding as Cupid; *kāma*—as Cupid; *jñāne*—in the understanding; *trāsa*—fear; *haila*—was; *citte*—in the mind; *kahe*—She says; *ye*—the person who; *jagat*—the whole world; *māre*—conquers; *se*—that person; *paśila*—entered; *antare*—within My heart; *ei vairī*—this enemy; *nā deya*—does not allow; *pāsarite*—to forget.

TRANSLATION

"Śrīmatī Rādhārāṇī's ecstasy also made Her think of Kṛṣṇa as Cupid, and this understanding frightened Her. She said, 'This Cupid, who has conquered the whole world and entered My heart, is My greatest enemy, for He does not allow Me to forget Him.'

TEXT 58

ঔৎসুক্যের প্রাবীণ্যে,   জিতি' অন্য ভাব-সৈন্যে,
উদয় হৈল নিজ-রাজ্য-মনে ।
মনে হইল লালস,   না হয় আপন-বশ,
দুঃখে মনে করেন ভর্ৎসনে ॥ ৫৮ ॥

autsukyera prāvīṇye,   jiti' anya bhāva-sainye,
udaya haila nija-rājya-mane
mane ha-ila lālasa,   nā haya āpana-vaśa,
duḥkhe mane karena bhartsane

SYNONYMS

autsukyera—of eagerness; *prāvīṇye*—because of high development; *jiti'*—conquering; *anya*—other; *bhāva-sainye*—soldiers of ecstasy; *udaya*—arising; *haila*—there was; *nija-rājya-mane*—within the kingdom of Her own mind; *mane*—within the mind; *ha-ila*—there was; *lālasa*—greed; *nā*—not; *haya*—becomes; *āpana-vaśa*—within Her own control; *duḥkhe*—in unhappiness; *mane*—to the mind; *karena*—does; *bhartsane*—chastisement.

TRANSLATION

"Then great eagerness conquered all the other soldiers of ecstasy, and an uncontrollable desire arose in the kingdom of Śrīmatī Rādhārāṇī's mind. Greatly unhappy, She then chastised Her own mind.

TEXT 59

"মন মোর বাম-দীন,   জল বিনা যেন মীন,
কৃষ্ণ বিনা ক্ষণে মরি' যায় ।
মধুর-হাস্য-বদনে,   মন-নেত্র-রসায়নে,
কৃষ্ণতৃষ্ণা দ্বিগুণ বাড়ায় ॥ ৫৯ ॥

"mana mora vāma-dīna,   jala vinā yena mīna,
kṛṣṇa vinā kṣaṇe mari' yāya

madhura-hāsya-vadane, mana-netra-rasāyane,
kṛṣṇa-tṛṣṇā dviguṇa bāḍāya

SYNONYMS

mana mora—My mind; *vāma-dīna*—unagreeably poor; *jala*—water; *vinā*—without; *yena*—as if; *mīna*—a fish; *kṛṣṇa*—Lord Kṛṣṇa; *vinā*—without; *kṣaṇe*—in a moment; *mari' yāya*—dies; *madhura*—sweet; *hāsya*—smiling; *vadane*—face; *mana*—the mind; *netra*—the eyes; *rasa-āyane*—very pleasing to; *kṛṣṇa-tṛṣṇā*—the thirst for Kṛṣṇa; *dvi-guṇa*—twice as much; *bāḍāya*—increases.

TRANSLATION

" 'If I do not think of Kṛṣṇa, My impoverished mind will die within a moment like a fish out of water. But when I see Kṛṣṇa's sweetly smiling face, My mind and eyes are so pleased that My desire for Him redoubles.

TEXT 60

হা হা কৃষ্ণ প্রাণধন, হা হা পদ্মলোচন,
হাহা দিব্য সদ্‌গুণ-সাগর !
হা হা শ্যামসুন্দর, হা হা পীতাম্বরধর,
হা হা রাসবিলাস নাগর ॥ ৬০ ॥

hā hā kṛṣṇa prāṇa-dhana, hā hā padma-locana,
hā hā divya sad-guṇa-sāgara!
hā hā śyāma-sundara, hā hā pītāmbara-dhara,
hā hā rāsa-vilāsa nāgara

SYNONYMS

hā hā—alas; *kṛṣṇa*—O Kṛṣṇa; *prāṇa-dhana*—the treasure of My life; *hā hā*—alas; *padma-locana*—the lotus-eyed one; *hā hā*—alas; *divya*—divine; *sat-guṇa-sāgara*—ocean of transcendental attributes; *hā hā*—alas; *śyāma-sundara*—the beautiful, blackish youth; *hā hā*—alas; *pīta-ambara-dhara*—one who wears yellow garments; *hā hā*—alas; *rāsa-vilāsa*—of the *rāsa* dance; *nāgara*—the hero.

TRANSLATION

" 'Alas! Where is Kṛṣṇa, the treasure of My life? Where is the lotus-eyed one? Alas! Where is the divine ocean of all transcendental qualities? Alas! Where is the beautiful, blackish youth dressed in yellow garments? Alas! Where is the hero of the rāsa dance?

TEXT 61

কাহাঁ গেলে তোমা পাই, তুমি কহ,—তাহাঁ যাই”,
এত কহি’ চলিলা ধাঞা।
স্বরূপ উঠি’ কোলে করি’, প্রভুরে আনিল ধরি’,
নিজস্থানে বসাইলা লৈঞা ॥ ৬১ ॥

kāhāṅ gele tomā pāi, tumi kaha,——tāhāṅ yāi",
eta kahi' calilā dhāñā
svarūpa uṭhi' kole kari', prabhure ānila dhari',
nija-sthāne vasāilā laiñā

SYNONYMS

kāhāṅ—where; *gele*—going; *tomā*—You; *pāi*—I can get; *tumi*—You; *kaha*—please tell; *tāhāṅ*—there; *yāi*—I shall go; *eta kahi'*—saying this; *calilā dhāñā*—began to run; *svarūpa*—Svarūpa Dāmodara Gosvāmī; *uṭhi'*—getting up; *kole kari'*—taking on His lap; *prabhure*—Śrī Caitanya Mahāprabhu; *ānila*—brought back; *dhari'*—catching; *nija-sthāne*—in His own place; *vasāilā*—sat down; *laiñā*—taking.

TRANSLATION

" 'Where shall I go? Where can I find You? Please tell Me. I shall go there.' " Speaking in this way, Śrī Caitanya Mahāprabhu began running. Svarūpa Dāmodara Gosvāmī, however, stood up, caught Him and took Him on his lap. Then Svarūpa Dāmodara brought Him back to His place and made Him sit down.

TEXT 62

ক্ষণেকে প্রভুর বাহ্য হৈল, স্বরূপেরে আজ্ঞা দিল,
“স্বরূপ, কিছু কর মধুর গান।”
স্বরূপ গায় বিদ্যাপতি, গীতগোবিন্দ-গীতি,
শুনি’ প্রভুর জুড়াইল কাণ ॥ ৬২ ॥

kṣaṇeke prabhura bāhya haila, svarūpere ājñā dila,
"svarūpa, kichu kara madhura gāna"
svarūpa gāya vidyāpati, gīta-govinda-gīti,
śuni' prabhura juḍāila kāṇa

SYNONYMS

kṣaṇeke—within a moment; *prabhura*—of Śrī Caitanya Mahāprabhu; *bāhya*—external consciousness; *haila*—there was; *svarūpere ājñā dila*—He ordered Svarūpa Dāmodara Gosvāmī; *svarūpa*—My dear Svarūpa; *kichu*—some; *kara*—make; *madhura*—sweet; *gāna*—songs; *svarūpa*—Svarūpa Dāmodara; *gāya*—sings; *vidyāpati*—songs by Vidyāpati; *gīta-govinda-gīti*—songs from *Gīta-govinda; śuni'*—hearing; *prabhura*—of Śrī Caitanya Mahāprabhu; *juḍāila*—became satisfied; *kāṇa*—ears.

TRANSLATION

Suddenly Śrī Caitanya Mahāprabhu returned to external consciousness and said to Svarūpa Dāmodara Gosvāmī, "My dear Svarūpa, please sing some sweet songs." The Lord's ears were satisfied when He heard Svarūpa Dāmodara sing songs from Gīta-govinda and those by the poet Vidyāpati.

TEXT 63

এইমত মহাপ্রভু প্রতি-রাত্রি-দিনে ।
উন্মাদ চেষ্টিত হয় প্রলাপ-বচনে ॥ ৬৩ ॥

ei-mata mahāprabhu prati-rātri-dine
unmāda ceṣṭita haya pralāpa-vacane

SYNONYMS

ei-mata—in this way; *mahāprabhu*—Śrī Caitanya Mahāprabhu; *prati-rātri-dine*—every night and day; *unmāda*—mad; *ceṣṭita*—activities; *haya*—are; *pralāpa-vacane*—talking like a madman.

TRANSLATION

Each day and night, Śrī Caitanya Mahāprabhu would become deranged in this way and talk like a madman.

TEXT 64

একদিনে যত হয় ভাবের বিকার ।
সহস্রমুখে বর্ণে যদি, নাহি পায় পার ॥ ৬৪ ॥

eka-dine yata haya bhāvera vikāra
sahasra-mukhe varṇe yadi, nāhi pāya pāra

SYNONYMS

eka-dine—in one day; *yata haya*—as many as there are; *bhāvera*—of ecstasy; *vikāra*—transformations; *sahasra-mukhe*—possessing thousands of mouths; *varṇe yadi*—if describes; *nāhi pāya*—cannot reach; *pāra*—the limit.

TRANSLATION

Even Anantadeva, who possesses thousands of mouths, cannot fully describe the ecstatic transformations that Śrī Caitanya Mahāprabhu experienced in a single day.

TEXT 65

জীব দীন কি করিবে তাহার বর্ণন ?
শাখা-চন্দ্র-ন্যায় করি' দিগ্‌দরশন ॥ ৬৫ ॥

jīva dīna ki karibe tāhāra varṇana?
śākhā-candra-nyāya kari' dig-daraśana

SYNONYMS

jīva—a living entity; *dīna*—very poor; *ki*—what; *karibe*—will do; *tāhāra*—of that; *varṇana*—description; *śākhā-candra-nyāya*—the logic of showing the moon through the branches of a tree; *kari'*—I make; *dik-daraśana*—seeing the direction.

TRANSLATION

What can a poor creature like me describe of those transformations? I can give only a hint of them, as if showing the moon through the branches of a tree.

TEXT 66

ইহা যেই শুনে, তার জুড়ায় মন-কাণ ।
অলৌকিক গূঢ়প্রেম-চেষ্টা হয় জ্ঞান ॥ ৬৬ ॥

ihā yei śune, tāra juḍāya mana-kāṇa
alaukika gūḍha-prema-ceṣṭā haya jñāna

SYNONYMS

ihā—this; *yei śune*—anyone who hears; *tāra*—his; *juḍāya*—become satisfied; *mana-kāṇa*—mind and ears; *alaukika*—uncommon; *gūḍha-prema*—of deep ecstatic love for Kṛṣṇa; *ceṣṭā*—activities; *haya jñāna*—he can understand.

TRANSLATION

This description, however, will satisfy the mind and ears of anyone who hears it, and he will be able to understand these uncommon activities of deep ecstatic love for Kṛṣṇa.

TEXT 67

অদ্ভুত নিগূঢ় প্রেমের মাধুর্য-মহিমা ।
আপনি আস্বাদি' প্রভু দেখাইলা সীমা ॥ ৬৭ ॥

adbhuta nigūḍha premera mādhurya-mahimā
āpani āsvādi' prabhu dekhāilā sīmā

SYNONYMS

adbhuta—wonderful; *nigūḍha*—deep; *premera*—of ecstatic love for Kṛṣṇa; *mādhurya-mahimā*—the glories of the sweetness; *āpani*—personally; *āsvādi'*—tasting; *prabhu*—Śrī Caitanya Mahāprabhu; *dekhāilā*—showed; *sīmā*—the extreme limit.

TRANSLATION

Ecstatic love for Kṛṣṇa is wonderfully deep. By personally tasting the glorious sweetness of that love, Śrī Caitanya Mahāprabhu showed us its extreme limit.

TEXT 68

অদ্ভুত-দয়ালু চৈতন্য—অদ্ভুত-বদান্য !
ঐছে দয়ালু দাতা লোকে নাহি শুনি অন্য ॥ ৬৮ ॥

adbhuta-dayālu caitanya——adbhuta-vadānya!
aiche dayālu dātā loke nāhi śuni anya

SYNONYMS

adbhuta—wonderfully; *dayālu*—merciful; *caitanya*—Śrī Caitanya Mahāprabhu; *adbhuta-vadānya*—wonderfully magnanimous; *aiche*—such; *dayālu*—merciful; *dātā*—charitable person; *loke*—within this world; *nāhi*—not; *śuni*—we have heard of; *anya*—other.

TRANSLATION

Śrī Caitanya Mahāprabhu is wonderfully merciful and wonderfully magnanimous. We have heard of no one else within this world so merciful and charitable.

TEXT 69

সর্বভাবে ভজ, লোক, চৈতন্য-চরণ ।
যাহা হৈতে পাইবা কৃষ্ণপ্রেমামৃত-ধন ॥ ৬৯ ॥

sarva-bhāve bhaja, loka, caitanya-caraṇa
yāhā haite pāibā kṛṣṇa-premāmṛta-dhana

SYNONYMS

sarva-bhāve—in all respects; *bhaja*—worship; *loka*—O entire world; *caitanya-caraṇa*—the lotus feet of Śrī Caitanya Mahāprabhu; *yāhā haite*—by which; *pāibā*—you will get; *kṛṣṇa-prema*—of love of Kṛṣṇa; *amṛta*—of the nectar; *dhana*—the treasure.

TRANSLATION

Worship the lotus feet of Śrī Caitanya Mahāprabhu in all respects. Only in this way will you achieve the nectarean treasure of ecstatic love for Kṛṣṇa.

TEXT 70

এই ত' কহিলুঁ 'কূর্মাকৃতি'-অনুভাব ।
উন্মাদ-চেষ্টিত তাতে উন্মাদ-প্রলাপ ॥ ৭০ ॥

ei ta' kahiluṅ 'kūrmākṛti'-anubhāva
unmāda-ceṣṭita tāte unmāda-pralāpa

SYNONYMS

ei ta' kahiluṅ—thus I have described; *kūrma-ākṛti*—of becoming like a tortoise; *anubhāva*—the ecstatic symptom; *unmāda-ceṣṭita*—enacted in madness; *tāte*—in that; *unmāda-pralāpa*—talking like a madman.

TRANSLATION

Thus I have described Śrī Caitanya Mahāprabhu's ecstatic transformation of becoming like a tortoise. In that ecstasy, He talked and acted like a madman.

TEXT 71

এই লীলা স্বগ্রন্থে রঘুনাথ-দাস ।
গৌরাঙ্গস্তবকল্পবৃক্ষে কৈরাছেন প্রকাশ ॥ ৭১ ॥

ei līlā sva-granthe raghunātha-dāsa
gaurāṅga-stava-kalpavṛkṣe kairāchena prakāśa

SYNONYMS

ei līlā—this pastime; *sva-granthe*—in his book; *raghunātha-dāsa*—Raghunātha dāsa Gosvāmī; *gaurāṅga-stava-kalpa-vṛkṣe*—named *Gaurāṅga-stava-kalpavṛkṣa; kairāchena prakāśa*—has fully described.

TRANSLATION

Śrīla Raghunātha dāsa Gosvāmī has fully described this pastime in his book Gaurāṅga-stava-kalpavṛkṣa.

TEXT 72

অনুদ্ঘাট্য দ্বারত্রয়মুরু চ ভিত্তিত্রয়মহো
বিলঙ্ঘ্যোচ্চৈঃ কালিঙ্গিক-সুরভিমধ্যে নিপতিতঃ ।
তনূদ্যৎসঙ্কোচাৎ কমঠ ইব কৃষ্ণোরুবিরহাদ্
বিরাজন্ গৌরাঙ্গো হৃদয় উদয়ন্মাং মদয়তি ॥ ৭২ ॥

anudghāṭya dvāra-trayam uru ca bhitti-trayam aho
vilaṅghyoccaiḥ kāliṅgika-surabhi-madhye nipatitaḥ
tanūdyat-saṅkocāt kamaṭha iva kṛṣṇoru-virahād
virājan gaurāṅgo hṛdaya udayan māṁ madayati

SYNONYMS

anudghāṭya—without opening; *dvāra-trayam*—the three doors; *uru*—strong; *ca*—and; *bhitti-trayam*—three walls; *aho*—how wonderful; *vilaṅghya*—crossing over; *uccaiḥ*—very high; *kāliṅgika*—of Kāliṅga-deśa, which is in the district of Tailaṅga; *surabhi-madhye*—among the cows; *nipatitaḥ*—fallen down; *tanu-udyat-saṅkocāt*—by contracting within the body; *kamaṭhaḥ*—a tortoise; *iva*—like; *kṛṣṇa-uru-virahāt*—because of strong feelings of separation from Kṛṣṇa; *virājan*—appearing; *gaurāṅgaḥ*—Lord Śrī Caitanya Mahāprabhu; *hṛdaye*—in my heart; *udayan*—rising; *mām*—me; *madayati*—maddens.

TRANSLATION

"How wonderful it is! Śrī Caitanya Mahāprabhu left His residence without opening the three strongly bolted doors. Then He crossed over three high walls, and later, because of strong feelings of separation from Kṛṣṇa, He fell down amidst the cows of the Tailaṅga district and retracted all the limbs of His body like a tortoise. Śrī Caitanya Mahāprabhu, who appeared in that way, rises in my heart and maddens me."

TEXT 73

শ্রীরূপ-রঘুনাথ-পদে যার আশ।
চৈতন্যচরিতামৃত কহে কৃষ্ণদাস ॥ ৭৩ ॥

śrī-rūpa-raghunātha-pade yāra āśa
caitanya-caritāmṛta kahe kṛṣṇadāsa

SYNONYMS

śrī-rūpa—Śrīla Rūpa Gosvāmī; *raghunātha*—Śrīla Raghunātha dāsa Gosvāmī; *pade*—at the lotus feet; *yāra*—whose; *āśa*—expectation; *caitanya-caritāmṛta*—the book named *Caitanya-caritāmṛta; kahe*—describes; *kṛṣṇadāsa*—Śrīla Kṛṣṇadāsa Kavirāja Gosvāmī.

TRANSLATION

Praying at the lotus feet of Śrī Rūpa and Śrī Raghunātha, always desiring their mercy, I, Kṛṣṇadāsa, narrate Śrī Caitanya-caritāmṛta, following in their footsteps.

Thus end the Bhaktivedanta purports to the Śrī Caitanya-caritāmṛta, Antya-līlā, *Seventeenth Chapter, describing Śrī Caitanya Mahāprabhu's pastime of retracting His limbs like a tortoise.*

CHAPTER 18

Rescuing the Lord from the Sea

A summary of the Eighteenth Chapter is given by Śrīla Bhaktivinoda Ṭhākura in his *Amṛta-pravāha-bhāṣya*. On an autumn evening when the moon was full, Śrī Caitanya Mahāprabhu walked along the seashore near the Āiṭoṭā temple. Mistaking the sea for the Yamunā River, He jumped into it, hoping to see the water pastimes of Kṛṣṇa and Śrīmatī Rādhārāṇī and the other *gopīs*. As He floated in the sea, however, He was washed away to the Koṇārka temple, where a fisherman, thinking that the Lord's body was a big fish, caught Him in his net and brought Him ashore. Śrī Caitanya Mahāprabhu was unconscious, and His body had become unusually transformed. As soon as the fisherman touched the Lord's body, he became mad in ecstatic love of Kṛṣṇa. His own madness frightened him, however, because he thought that he was being haunted by a ghost. As he was about to seek a ghost charmer, he met Svarūpa Dāmodara Gosvāmī and the other devotees on the beach, who had been looking everywhere for the Lord. After some inquiries, Svarūpa Dāmodara could understand that the fisherman had caught Lord Śrī Caitanya Mahāprabhu in his net. Since the fisherman was afraid of being haunted by a ghost, Svarūpa Dāmodara gave him a slap and chanted Hare Kṛṣṇa, which immediately pacified him. Thereafter, when the devotees chanted the Hare Kṛṣṇa *mahā-mantra* loudly, Śrī Caitanya Mahāprabhu came to His external consciousness. Then they brought Him back to His own residence.

TEXT 1

শরজ্জ্যোৎস্না-সিন্ধোরবকলনয়া জাতযমুনা-
ভ্রমাদ্ধাবন্ যোঽস্মিন্ হরিবিরহতাপার্ণব ইব ।
নিমগ্নো মূর্চ্ছালঃ পয়সি নিবসন্ রাত্রিমখিলাং
প্রভাতে প্রাপ্তঃ স্বৈরবতু স শচীসূনুরিহ নঃ ॥ ১ ॥

śaraj-jyotsnā-sindhor avakalanayā jāta-yamunā-
bhramād dhāvan yo 'smin hari-viraha-tāpārṇava iva
nimagno mūrcchālaḥ payasi nivasan rātrim akhilāṁ
prabhāte prāptaḥ svair avatu sa śacī-sūnur iha naḥ

SYNONYMS

śarat-jyotsnā—in the moonlight of autumn; *sindhoḥ*—of the sea; *avakalanayā*—by sight; *jāta*—appeared; *yamunā*—the River Yamunā; *bhramāt*—by mistake; *dhāvan*—running; *yaḥ*—He who; *asmin*—in this; *hari-viraha*—due to separation from Hari; *tāpa*—of suffering; *arṇave*—in the ocean; *iva*—as if; *nimagnaḥ*—dove; *mūrcchālaḥ*—unconscious; *payasi*—in the water; *nivasan*—staying; *rātrim*—the night; *akhilām*—whole; *prabhāte*—in the morning; *prāptaḥ*—was gotten; *svaiḥ*—by His personal associates; *avatu*—may protect; *saḥ*—He; *śacī-sūnuḥ*—the son of mother Śacī; *iha*—here; *naḥ*—us.

TRANSLATION

In the brilliant autumn moonlight, Śrī Caitanya Mahāprabhu mistook the sea for the River Yamunā. Greatly afflicted by separation from Kṛṣṇa, He ran and dove into the sea and remained unconscious in the water the entire night. In the morning, He was found by His personal devotees. May that Śrī Caitanya Mahāprabhu, the son of mother Śacī, protect us by His transcendental pastimes.

TEXT 2

জয় জয় শ্রীচৈতন্য জয় নিত্যানন্দ ।
জয়াদ্বৈতচন্দ্র জয় গৌরভক্তবৃন্দ ॥ ২ ॥

jaya jaya śrī-caitanya jaya nityānanda
jayādvaita-candra jaya gaura-bhakta-vṛnda

SYNONYMS

jaya jaya—all glories; *śrī-caitanya*—to Lord Śrī Caitanya Mahāprabhu; *jaya*—all glories; *nityānanda*—to Nityānanda Prabhu; *jaya*—all glories; *advaita-candra*—to Advaita Ācārya; *jaya*—all glories; *gaura-bhakta-vṛnda*—to the devotees of Śrī Caitanya Mahāprabhu.

TRANSLATION

All glories to Śrī Caitanya Mahāprabhu! All glories to Nityānanda Prabhu! All glories to Advaita Ācārya! And all glories to all the devotees of Śrī Caitanya Mahāprabhu!

TEXT 3

এইমতে মহাপ্রভু নীলাচলে বৈসে ।
রাত্রি-দিনে কৃষ্ণবিচ্ছেদার্ণবে ভাসে ॥ ৩ ॥

ei-mate mahāprabhu nīlācale vaise
rātri-dine kṛṣṇa-vicchedārṇave bhāse

SYNONYMS

ei-mate—in this way; *mahāprabhu*—Śrī Caitanya Mahāprabhu; *nīlācale*—at Jagannātha Purī; *vaise*—resides; *rātri-dine*—night and day; *kṛṣṇa-viccheda*—of separation from Kṛṣṇa; *arṇave*—in the ocean; *bhāse*—floats.

TRANSLATION

While thus living at Jagannātha Purī, Śrī Caitanya Mahāprabhu floated all day and night in an ocean of separation from Kṛṣṇa.

TEXT 4

শরৎকালের রাত্রি, সব চন্দ্রিকা-উজ্জ্বল ।
প্রভু নিজগণ লঞা বেড়ান রাত্রি-সকল ॥ ৪ ॥

śarat-kālera rātri, saba candrikā-ujjvala
prabhu nija-gaṇa lañā beḍāna rātri-sakala

SYNONYMS

śarat-kālera—of autumn; *rātri*—night; *saba*—all; *candrikā-ujjvala*—brightened by the moonlight; *prabhu*—Śrī Caitanya Mahāprabhu; *nija-gaṇa*—His own associates; *lañā*—taking; *beḍāna*—walks; *rātri-sakala*—the whole night.

TRANSLATION

During a night of the autumn season when a full moon brightened everything, Śrī Caitanya Mahāprabhu wandered all night long with His devotees.

TEXT 5

উদ্যানে উদ্যানে ভ্রমেন কৌতুক দেখিতে ।
রাসলীলার গীত-শ্লোক পড়িতে শুনিতে ॥ ৫ ॥

udyāne udyāne bhramena kautuka dekhite
rāsa-līlāra gīta-śloka paḍite śunite

SYNONYMS

udyāne udyāne—from garden to garden; *bhramena*—He walks; *kautuka dekhite*—seeing the fun; *rāsa-līlāra*—of the *rāsa* dance; *gīta-śloka*—songs and verses; *paḍite śunite*—reciting and hearing.

TRANSLATION

He walked from garden to garden, seeing the pastimes of Lord Kṛṣṇa and hearing and reciting songs and verses concerning the rāsa-līlā.

TEXT 6

প্রভু প্রেমাবেশে করেন গান, নর্তন।
কভু ভাবাবেশে রাসলীলানুকরণ ॥ ৬ ॥

prabhu premāveśe karena gāna, nartana
kabhu bhāvāveśe rāsa-līlānukaraṇa

SYNONYMS

prabhu—Śrī Caitanya Mahāprabhu; *prema-āveśe*—in ecstatic love; *karena*—does; *gāna*—singing; *nartana*—dancing; *kabhu*—sometimes; *bhāva-āveśe*—in ecstatic emotion; *rāsa-līlā*—the *rāsa-līlā* dance; *anukaraṇa*—imitating.

TRANSLATION

He sang and danced in ecstatic love and sometimes imitated the rāsa dance in emotional ecstasy.

TEXT 7

কভু ভাবোন্মাদে প্রভু ইতি-উতি ধায়।
ভূমে পড়ি' কভু মূর্চ্ছা, কভু গড়ি' যায় ॥ ৭ ॥

kabhu bhāvonmāde prabhu iti-uti dhāya
bhūme paḍi' kabhu mūrcchā, kabhu gaḍi' yāya

SYNONYMS

kabhu—sometimes; *bhāva-unmāde*—in the madness of ecstatic love; *prabhu*—Śrī Caitanya Mahāprabhu; *iti-uti*—here and there; *dhāya*—runs; *bhūme paḍi'*—falling on the ground; *kabhu mūrcchā*—sometimes unconscious; *kabhu*—sometimes; *gaḍi' yāya*—rolls on the ground.

TRANSLATION

He sometimes ran here and there in the madness of ecstasy and sometimes fell and rolled on the ground. Sometimes He became completely unconscious.

TEXT 8

রাসলীলার এক শ্লোক যবে পড়ে, শুনে।
পূর্ববৎ তবে অর্থ করেন আপনে ॥ ৮ ॥

rāṣa-līlāra eka śloka yabe paḍe, śune
pūrvavat tabe artha karena āpane

SYNONYMS

rāsa-līlāra—of the *rāsa-līlā; eka*—one; *śloka*—verse; *yabe*—when; *paḍe*—recites; *śune*—hears; *pūrva-vat*—as previously; *tabe*—then; *artha karena*—explains; *āpane*—personally.

TRANSLATION

When He heard Svarūpa Dāmodara recite a verse concerning the rāsa-līlā or He Himself recited one, He would personally explain it, as He had previously done.

TEXT 9

এইমত রাসলীলায় হয় যত শ্লোক ।
সবার অর্থ করে, পায় কভু হর্ষ-শোক ॥ ৯ ॥

ei-mata rāsa-līlāya haya yata śloka
sabāra artha kare, pāya kabhu harṣa-śoka

SYNONYMS

ei-mata—in this way; *rāsa-līlāya*—in the pastimes of the *rāsa-līlā; haya*—there are; *yata śloka*—as many verses; *sabāra*—of all of them; *artha kare*—He explains the meaning; *pāya*—gets; *kabhu*—sometimes; *harṣa-śoka*—happiness and lamentation.

TRANSLATION

In this way, He explained the meaning of all the verses concerning the rāsa-līlā. Sometimes He would be very sad and sometimes very happy.

TEXT 10

সে সব শ্লোকের অর্থ, সে সব 'বিকার' ।
সে সব বর্ণিতে গ্রন্থ হয় অতি-বিস্তার ॥ ১০ ॥

se saba ślokera artha, se saba 'vikāra'
se saba varṇite grantha haya ati-vistāra

SYNONYMS

se saba—all those; *ślokera*—of verses; *artha*—meanings; *se*—those; *saba*—all; *vikāra*—transformations; *se saba*—all of them; *varṇite*—to describe; *grantha haya*—the book becomes; *ati-vistāra*—very, very large.

TRANSLATION

To explain fully all those verses and all the transformations that took place in the Lord's body would require a very large volume.

TEXT 11

দ্বাদশ বৎসরে যে যে লীলা ক্ষণে-ক্ষণে ।
অতিবাহুল্য-ভয়ে গ্রন্থ না কৈলুঁ লিখনে ॥ ১১ ॥

dvādaśa vatsare ye ye līlā kṣaṇe-kṣaṇe
ati-bāhulya-bhaye grantha nā kailuṅ likhane

SYNONYMS

dvādaśa vatsare—in twelve years; *ye ye*—whatever; *līlā*—pastimes; *kṣaṇe-kṣaṇe*—moment after moment; *ati-bāhulya*—too abundant; *bhaye*—being afraid of; *grantha*—book; *nā*—not; *kailuṅ likhane*—I have written.

TRANSLATION

So as not to increase the size of this book, I have not written about all the Lord's pastimes, for He performed them every moment of every day for twelve years.

TEXT 12

পূর্বে যেই দেখাঞাছি দিগ্‌দরশন ।
তৈছে জানিহ 'বিকার' 'প্রলাপ' বর্ণন ॥ ১২ ॥

pūrve yei dekhāñāchi dig-daraśana
taiche jāniha 'vikāra' 'pralāpa' varṇana

SYNONYMS

pūrve—previously; *yei*—as; *dekhāñāchi*—I have shown; *dik-daraśana*—only an indication; *taiche*—similarly; *jāniha*—you may know; *vikāra*—transformations; *pralāpa*—crazy talks; *varṇana*—description.

TRANSLATION

As I have previously indicated, I am describing the mad speeches and bodily transformations of the Lord only in brief.

TEXT 13

সহস্র-বদনে যবে কহয়ে 'অনন্ত' ।
একদিনের লীলার তবু নাহি পায় অন্ত ॥ ১৩ ॥

sahasra-vadane yabe kahaye 'ananta'
eka-dinera līlāra tabu nāhi pāya anta

SYNONYMS

sahasra-vadane—in thousands of mouths; *yabe*—when; *kahaye*—says; *ananta*—Lord Ananta; *eka-dinera*—of one day; *līlāra*—of pastimes; *tabu*—still; *nāhi*—does not; *pāya*—reach; *anta*—the limit.

TRANSLATION

If Ananta, with His one thousand hoods, tried to describe even one day's pastimes of Śrī Caitanya Mahāprabhu, He would find them impossible to describe fully.

TEXT 14

কোটিযুগ পর্যন্ত যদি লিখয়ে গণেশ ।
একদিনের লীলার তবু নাহি পায় শেষ ॥ ১৪ ॥

koṭi-yuga paryanta yadi likhaye gaṇeśa
eka-dinera līlāra tabu nāhi pāya śeṣa

SYNONYMS

koṭi-yuga—millions of millenniums; *paryanta*—to the extent of; *yadi*—if; *likhaye*—writes; *gaṇeśa*—the demigod Gaṇeśa (son of Lord Śiva); *eka-dinera*—of one day; *līlāra*—of pastimes; *tabu*—still; *nāhi pāya*—cannot reach; *śeṣa*—the limit.

TRANSLATION

If Gaṇeśa, Lord Śiva's son and the expert scribe of the demigods, tried for millions of millenniums to fully describe one day of the Lord's pastimes, he would be unable to find their limit.

TEXT 15

ভক্তের প্রেম-বিকার দেখি' কৃষ্ণের চমৎকার ।
কৃষ্ণ যার না পায় অন্ত, কেবা ছার আর ? ১৫ ॥

bhaktera prema-vikāra dekhi' kṛṣṇera camatkāra!
kṛṣṇa yāra nā pāya anta, kebā chāra āra?

SYNONYMS

bhaktera—of a devotee; *prema-vikāra*—transformations of ecstatic emotion; *dekhi'*—seeing; *kṛṣṇera*—of Lord Kṛṣṇa; *camatkāra*—wonder; *kṛṣṇa*—Lord Kṛṣṇa; *yāra*—of which; *nā pāya*—cannot get; *anta*—the limit; *kebā*—who; *chāra*—insignificant; *āra*—others.

TRANSLATION

Even Lord Kṛṣṇa is struck with wonder at seeing the transformations of ecstasy in His devotees. If Kṛṣṇa Himself cannot estimate the limits of such emotions, how could others?

TEXTS 16-17

ভক্ত-প্রেমার যত দশা, যে গতি প্রকার।
যত দুঃখ, যত সুখ, যতেক বিকার ॥ ১৬ ॥
কৃষ্ণ তাহা সম্যক্ না পারে জানিতে।
ভক্তভাব অঙ্গীকরে তাহা আস্বাদিতে ॥ ১৭ ॥

bhakta-premāra yata daśā, ye gati prakāra
yata duḥkha, yata sukha, yateka vikāra

kṛṣṇa tāhā samyak nā pāre jānite
bhakta-bhāva aṅgīkare tāhā āsvādite

SYNONYMS

bhakta-premāra—of the ecstatic emotion of the devotee; *yata*—all; *daśā*—conditions; *ye*—which; *gati prakāra*—mode of progress; *yata*—all; *duḥkha*—unhappiness; *yata*—all; *sukha*—happiness; *yateka*—all; *vikāra*—transformation; *kṛṣṇa*—Lord Kṛṣṇa; *tāhā*—that; *samyak*—fully; *nā pāre jānite*—cannot understand; *bhakta-bhāva*—the mood of a devotee; *aṅgīkare*—He accepts; *tāhā*—that; *āsvādite*—to taste.

TRANSLATION

Kṛṣṇa Himself cannot fully understand the conditions, the mode of progress, the happiness and unhappiness, and the moods of ecstatic love of His devotees. He therefore accepts the role of a devotee to taste these emotions fully.

TEXT 18

কৃষ্ণেরে নাচায় প্রেমা, ভক্তেরে নাচায় ।
আপনে নাচয়ে,—তিনে নাচে একঠাঞি ॥ ১৮ ॥

kṛṣṇere nācāya premā, bhaktere nācāya
āpane nācaye,——tine nāce eka-ṭhāñi

SYNONYMS

kṛṣṇere—Kṛṣṇa; *nācāya*—causes to dance; *premā*—love of Kṛṣṇa; *bhaktere*—the devotee; *nācāya*—causes to dance; *āpane*—personally; *nācaye*—dances; *tine*—all three; *nāce*—dance; *eka-ṭhāñi*—in one place.

TRANSLATION

Ecstatic love of Kṛṣṇa makes Kṛṣṇa and His devotees dance, and it also dances personally. In this way, all three dance together in one place.

TEXT 19

প্রেমার বিকার বর্ণিতে চাহে যেই জন ।
চান্দ ধরিতে চাহে, যেন হঞা 'বামন' ॥ ১৯ ॥

premāra vikāra varṇite cāhe yei jana
cānda dharite cāhe, yena hañā 'vāmana'

SYNONYMS

premāra—of ecstatic love of Kṛṣṇa; *vikāra*—transformations; *varṇite*—to describe; *cāhe*—wants; *yei jana*—which person; *cānda dharite*—to catch the moon; *cāhe*—he wants; *yena*—as if; *hañā*—being; *vāmana*—a dwarf.

TRANSLATION

One who wants to describe the transformations of ecstatic love of Kṛṣṇa is like a dwarf trying to catch the moon in the sky.

TEXT 20

বায়ু যৈছে সিন্ধু-জলের হরে এক 'কণ' ।
কৃষ্ণপ্রেম-কণ তৈছে জীবের স্পর্শন ॥ ২০ ॥

vāyu yaiche sindhu-jalera hare eka 'kaṇa'
kṛṣṇa-prema-kaṇa taiche jīvera sparśana

SYNONYMS

vāyu—the wind; *yaiche*—as; *sindhu-jalera*—of the water of the ocean; *hare*—takes away; *eka kaṇa*—one particle; *kṛṣṇa-prema-kaṇa*—one particle of love of Kṛṣṇa; *taiche*—similarly; *jīvera sparśana*—a living entity can touch.

TRANSLATION

As the wind can carry away but a drop of the water in the ocean, a living entity can touch only a particle of the ocean of love of Kṛṣṇa.

TEXT 21

ক্ষণে ক্ষণে উঠে প্রেমার তরঙ্গ অনন্ত ।
জীব ছার কাহাঁ তার পাইবেক অন্ত ? ২১ ॥

kṣaṇe kṣaṇe uṭhe premāra taraṅga ananta
jīva chāra kāhāṅ tāra pāibeka anta?

SYNONYMS

kṣaṇe kṣaṇe—moment after moment; *uṭhe*—rise; *premāra*—of love of Kṛṣṇa; *taraṅga*—waves; *ananta*—unlimited; *jīva*—a living entity; *chāra*—insignificant; *kāhāṅ*—where; *tāra*—of that; *pāibeka*—will get; *anta*—the limit.

TRANSLATION

Endless waves arise moment after moment in that ocean of love. How could an insignificant living entity estimate their limits?

TEXT 22

শ্রীকৃষ্ণচৈতন্য যাহা করেন আস্বাদন ।
সবে এক জানে তাহা স্বরূপাদি 'গণ' ॥ ২২ ॥

śrī-kṛṣṇa-caitanya yāhā karena āsvādana
sabe eka jāne tāhā svarūpādi 'gaṇa'

SYNONYMS

śrī-kṛṣṇa-caitanya—Lord Śrī Caitanya Mahāprabhu; *yāhā*—whatever; *karena*—does; *āsvādana*—tasting; *sabe*—fully; *eka*—one; *jāne*—knows; *tāhā*—that; *svarūpa-ādi gaṇa*—devotees like Svarūpa Dāmodara Gosvāmī.

TRANSLATION

Only a person on the level of Svarūpa Dāmodara Gosvāmī can fully know what Lord Śrī Caitanya Mahāprabhu tastes in His love for Kṛṣṇa.

TEXT 23

জীব হঞা করে যেই তাহার বর্ণন ।
আপনা শোধিতে তার ছোঁয়ে এক 'কণ' ॥ ২৩ ॥

jīva hañā kare yei tāhāra varṇana
āpanā śodhite tāra choṅye eka 'kaṇa'

SYNONYMS

jīva hañā—being an ordinary living entity; *kare*—makes; *yei*—whoever; *tāhāra*—of that; *varṇana*—description; *āpanā*—himself; *śodhite*—to purify; *tāra*—of that; *choṅye*—touches; *eka kaṇa*—one particle.

TRANSLATION

When an ordinary living entity describes the pastimes of Śrī Caitanya Mahāprabhu, he purifies himself by touching one drop of that great ocean.

TEXT 24

এইমত রাসের শ্লোক-সকলই পড়িলা ।
শেষে জলকেলির শ্লোক পড়িতে লাগিলা ॥ ২৪ ॥

ei-mata rāsera śloka-sakala-i paḍilā
śeṣe jala-kelira śloka paḍite lāgilā

SYNONYMS

ei-mata—in this way; *rāsera*—of the *rāsa* dance; *śloka*—verses; *sakala-i*—all; *paḍilā*—recited; *śeṣe*—at the end; *jala-kelira*—of pastimes in the water; *śloka*—verse; *paḍite lāgilā*—began to recite.

TRANSLATION

Thus all the verses about the rāsa-līlā dance were recited. Then finally the verse concerning the pastimes in the water was recited.

TEXT 25

তাভির্যুতঃ শ্রমমপোহিতুমঙ্গসঙ্গ-
ঘৃষ্টস্রজঃ স কুচকুঙ্কুমরঞ্জিতায়াঃ ।
গন্ধর্বপালিভিরনুদ্রুত আবিশদ্বাঃ
শ্রান্তো গজীভিরিভরাড়িব ভিন্নসেতুঃ ॥ ২৫ ॥

tābhir yutaḥ śramam apohitum aṅga-saṅga-
ghṛṣṭa-srajaḥ sa kuca-kuṅkuma-rañjitāyāḥ
gandharva-pālibhir anudruta āviśad vāḥ
śrānto gajībhir ibha-rāḍ iva bhinna-setuḥ

SYNONYMS

tābhiḥ—by them (the *gopīs*); *yutaḥ*—accompanied; *śramam*—fatigue; *apohitum*—to remove; *aṅga-saṅga*—by touching of the bodies; *ghṛṣṭa*—crushed; *srajaḥ*—from the flower garland; *saḥ*—He; *kuca-kuṅkuma*—by *kuṅkuma* on the breasts; *rañjitāyāḥ*—colored; *gandharva-pa*—like celestial beings of Gandharvaloka; *alibhiḥ*—by bees; *anudrutaḥ*—followed; *āviśat*—entered; *vāḥ*—the water; *śrāntaḥ*—being fatigued; *gajībhiḥ*—by she-elephants; *ibha*—of elephants; *rāṭ*—the king; *iva*—like; *bhinna-setuḥ*—beyond the Vedic principles of morality.

TRANSLATION

"As an independent leader among elephants enters the water with its female elephants, Kṛṣṇa, who is transcendental to the Vedic principles of morality, entered the water of the Yamunā with the gopīs. His chest had brushed against their breasts, crushing His flower garland and coloring it with red kuṅkuma powder. Attracted by the fragrance of that garland, humming bumblebees followed Kṛṣṇa like celestial beings of Gandharvaloka. In this way, Lord Kṛṣṇa mitigated the fatigue of the rāsa dance."

PURPORT

This verse is from *Śrīmad-Bhāgavatam* (10.33.23).

TEXT 26

এইমত মহাপ্রভু ভ্রমিতে ভ্রমিতে ।
আইটোটা হৈতে সমুদ্র দেখেন আচম্বিতে ॥ ২৬ ॥

ei-mata mahāprabhu bhramite bhramite
āiṭoṭā haite samudra dekhena ācambite

SYNONYMS

ei-mata—in this way; *mahāprabhu*—Śrī Caitanya Mahāprabhu; *bhramite bhramite*—while wandering; *āiṭoṭā haite*—from the temple of Āiṭoṭā; *samudra*—the sea; *dekhena*—sees; *ācambite*—suddenly.

TRANSLATION

While thus wandering near the temple of Āiṭoṭā, Śrī Caitanya Mahāprabhu suddenly saw the sea.

TEXT 27

চন্দ্রকান্ত্যে উছলিত তরঙ্গ উজ্জ্বল ।
ঝলমল করে,—যেন 'যমুনার জল' ॥ ২৭ ॥

candra-kāntye uchalita taraṅga ujjvala
jhalamala kare,——yena 'yamunāra jala'

SYNONYMS

candra-kāntye—by the shining of the moon; *uchalita*—swollen high; *taraṅga*—waves; *ujjvala*—very bright; *jhalamala kare*—glitter; *yena*—as if; *yamunāra jala*—the water of the River Yamunā.

TRANSLATION

Brightened by the shining light of the moon, the high waves of the sea glittered like the waters of the River Yamunā.

TEXT 28

যমুনার ভ্রমে প্রভু ধাঞা চলিলা ।
অলক্ষিতে যাই' সিন্ধু-জলে ঝাঁপ দিলা ॥ ২৮ ॥

yamunāra bhrame prabhu dhāñā calilā
alakṣite yāi' sindhu-jale jhāṅpa dilā

SYNONYMS

yamunāra bhrame—by mistaking for the Yamunā; *prabhu*—Śrī Caitanya Mahāprabhu; *dhāñā calilā*—began to run very swiftly; *alakṣite*—without being seen; *yāi'*—going; *sindhu-jale*—into the water of the sea; *jhāṅpa dilā*—He jumped.

TRANSLATION

Mistaking the sea for the Yamunā, the Lord ran swiftly and jumped into the water, unseen by the others.

TEXT 29

পড়িতেই হৈল মূর্চ্ছা, কিছুই না জানে ।
কভু ডুবায়, কভু ভাসায় তরঙ্গের গণে ॥ ২৯ ॥

paḍitei haila mūrcchā, kichui nā jāne
kabhu ḍubāya, kabhu bhāsāya taraṅgera gaṇe

SYNONYMS

paḍitei—falling down; *haila mūrcchā*—He became unconscious; *kichui*—anything; *nā jāne*—did not understand; *kabhu*—sometimes; *ḍubāya*—cause to sink; *kabhu*—sometimes; *bhāsāya*—float; *taraṅgera gaṇe*—the waves.

TRANSLATION

Falling into the sea, He lost consciousness and could not understand where He was. Sometimes He sank beneath the waves, and sometimes He floated above them.

TEXT 30

তরঙ্গে বহিয়া ফিরে,—যেন শুষ্ক কাষ্ঠ।
কে বুঝিতে পারে এই চৈতন্যের নাট ? ৩০ ॥

taraṅge vahiyā phire,——yena śuṣka kāṣṭha
ke bujhite pāre ei caitanyera nāṭa?

SYNONYMS

taraṅge—the waves; *vahiyā phire*—carry here and there; *yena*—like; *śuṣka kāṣṭha*—a piece of dry wood; *ke*—who; *bujhite pāre*—can understand; *ei*—this; *caitanyera nāṭa*—dramatic performance of Lord Śrī Caitanya Mahāprabhu.

TRANSLATION

The waves carried Him here and there like a piece of dry wood. Who can understand this dramatic performance by Śrī Caitanya Mahāprabhu?

TEXT 31

কোণার্কের দিকে প্রভুরে তরঙ্গে লঞা যায়।
কভু ডুবাঞা রাখে, কভু ভাসাঞা লঞা যায়॥ ৩১ ॥

koṇārkera dike prabhure taraṅge lañā yāya
kabhu ḍubāñā rākhe, kabhu bhāsāñā lañā yāya

SYNONYMS

koṇārkera dike—toward the Koṇārka temple; *prabhure*—Śrī Caitanya Mahāprabhu; *taraṅge*—the waves; *lañā yāya*—take away; *kabhu*—sometimes; *ḍubāñā*—causing to sink; *rākhe*—keep; *kabhu*—sometimes; *bhāsāñā*—floating; *lañā yāya*—take away.

TRANSLATION

Keeping the Lord sometimes submerged and sometimes afloat, the waves carried Him toward the Koṇārka temple.

PURPORT

Koṇārka, generally known as Arka-tīrtha, is a temple of Lord Sūrya, the sun-god. It is situated on the seashore, nineteen miles north of Jagannātha Purī. It was constructed of black stone in the beginning of the thirteenth century of the Śaka Era, and it shows expert craftsmanship and architecture.

TEXT 32

যমুনাতে জলকেলি গোপীগণ-সঙ্গে ।
কৃষ্ণ করেন—মহাপ্রভু মগ্ন সেই রঙ্গে ॥ ৩২ ॥

yamunāte jala-keli gopī-gaṇa-saṅge
kṛṣṇa karena——mahāprabhu magna sei raṅge

SYNONYMS

yamunāte—in the River Yamunā; *jala-keli*—pastimes in the water; *gopī-gaṇa-saṅge*—with the *gopīs; kṛṣṇa karena*—Kṛṣṇa performs; *mahāprabhu*—Śrī Caitanya Mahāprabhu; *magna*—fully merged; *sei raṅge*—in those pastimes.

TRANSLATION

Lord Kṛṣṇa performed pastimes with the gopīs in the waters of the Yamunā, and Śrī Caitanya Mahāprabhu fully merged in those pastimes.

TEXT 33

ইহাঁ স্বরূপাদিগণ প্রভু না দেখিয়া ।
'কাহাঁ গেলা প্রভু ?' কহে চমকিত হঞা ॥ ৩৩ ॥

ihāṅ svarūpādi-gaṇa prabhu nā dekhiyā
'kāhāṅ gelā prabhu?' kahe camakita hañā

SYNONYMS

ihāṅ—here; *svarūpa-ādi-gaṇa*—the devotees headed by Svarūpa Dāmodara; *prabhu*—Śrī Caitanya Mahāprabhu; *nā dekhiyā*—not seeing; *kāhāṅ*—where; *gelā*—has gone; *prabhu*—Śrī Caitanya Mahāprabhu; *kahe*—say; *camakita hañā*—being astonished.

TRANSLATION

Meanwhile, all the devotees, headed by Svarūpa Dāmodara, lost sight of Śrī Caitanya Mahāprabhu. Astonished, they began searching for Him, asking, "Where has the Lord gone?"

TEXT 34

মনোবেগে গেলা প্রভু, দেখিতে নারিলা ।
প্রভুরে না দেখিয়া সংশয় করিতে লাগিলা ॥ ৩৪ ॥

mano-vege gelā prabhu, dekhite nārilā
prabhure nā dekhiyā saṁśaya karite lāgilā

SYNONYMS

manaḥ-vege—at the speed of mind; *gelā*—went; *prabhu*—Śrī Caitanya Mahāprabhu; *dekhite nārilā*—no one could see; *prabhure*—the Lord; *nā dekhiyā*—not seeing; *saṁśaya*—doubts; *karite lāgilā*—began to feel.

TRANSLATION

Śrī Caitanya Mahāprabhu had run off at the speed of mind. No one could see Him. Thus everyone was puzzled as to His whereabouts.

TEXT 35

'জগন্নাথ দেখিতে কিবা দেবালয়ে গেলা ?
অন্য উদ্যানে কিবা উন্মাদে পড়িলা ? ৩৫ ॥

'jagannātha dekhite kibā devālaye gelā?
anya udyāne kibā unmāde paḍilā?

SYNONYMS

jagannātha—Lord Jagannātha; *dekhite*—to see; *kibā*—whether; *devālaye*—to the temple; *gelā*—went; *anya*—other; *udyāne*—in a garden; *kibā*—or; *unmāde*—in madness; *paḍilā*—fell down.

TRANSLATION

"Has the Lord gone to the temple of Jagannātha, or has He fallen down in madness in some garden?

TEXT 36

গুণ্ডিচা-মন্দিরে গেলা, কিবা নরেন্দ্রেরে ?
চটক-পর্বতে গেলা, কিবা কোণার্কেরে ?' ৩৬ ॥

guṇḍicā-mandire gelā, kibā narendrere?
caṭaka-parvate gelā, kibā koṇārkere?'

SYNONYMS

guṇḍicā-mandire—to the Guṇḍicā temple; *gelā*—has gone; *kibā*—or; *narendrere*—to the Narendra Lake; *caṭaka-parvate*—to Caṭaka-parvata; *gelā*—has gone; *kibā*—or; *koṇārkere*—to the Koṇārka temple.

TRANSLATION

"Perhaps He went to the Guṇḍicā temple, or to Lake Narendra, or to the Caṭaka-parvata. Maybe He went to the temple at Koṇārka."

TEXT 37

এত বলি' সবে ফিরে প্রভুরে চাহিয়া ।
সমুদ্রের তীরে আইলা কত জন লঞা ॥ ৩৭ ॥

eta bali' sabe phire prabhure cāhiyā
samudrera tīre āilā kata jana lañā

SYNONYMS

eta bali'—saying this; *sabe*—all of them; *phire*—wander; *prabhure cāhiyā*—looking for Śrī Caitanya Mahāprabhu; *samudrera tīre*—on the seashore; *āilā*—arrived; *kata*—many; *jana*—people; *lañā*—accompanied by.

TRANSLATION

Talking like this, the devotees wandered here and there looking for the Lord. Finally they came to the shore, accompanied by many others.

TEXT 38

চাহিয়ে বেড়াইতে ঐছে রাত্রি-শেষ হৈল ।
'অন্তর্ধান হইলা প্রভু',—নিশ্চয় করিল ॥ ৩৮ ॥

cāhiye beḍāite aiche rātri-śeṣa haila
'antardhāna ha-ilā prabhu',——niścaya karila

SYNONYMS

cāhiye—looking; *beḍāite*—wandering; *aiche*—in this way; *rātri-śeṣa haila*—the night ended; *antardhāna ha-ilā*—has disappeared; *prabhu*—the Lord; *niścaya karila*—they decided.

TRANSLATION

While they were searching for the Lord, the night ended, and thus they all decided, "Lord Śrī Caitanya Mahāprabhu has now disappeared."

TEXT 39

প্রভুর বিচ্ছেদে কার দেহে নাহি প্রাণ ।
অনিষ্টাশঙ্কা বিনা কার মনে নাহি আন ॥ ৩৯ ॥

prabhura vicchede kāra dehe nāhi prāṇa
aniṣṭā-śaṅkā vinā kāra mane nāhi āna

SYNONYMS

prabhura—from the Lord; *vicchede*—due to separation; *kāra*—of all of them; *dehe*—in the body; *nāhi prāṇa*—there was practically no life; *aniṣṭā-śaṅkā*—doubts of some mishap; *vinā*—besides; *kāra*—of all of them; *mane*—in the mind; *nāhi āna*—there is nothing else.

TRANSLATION

In separation from the Lord, everyone felt as though he had lost his very life. They concluded that there must have been some mishap. They could not think of anything else.

TEXT 40

"অনিষ্টাশঙ্কীনি বন্ধুহৃদয়ানি ভবন্তি হি ।" ৪০ ॥

"aniṣṭā-śaṅkīni bandhu-hṛdayāni bhavanti hi"

SYNONYMS

aniṣṭā—of some mishap; *śaṅkīni*—possessing doubts; *bandhu*—of friends or relatives; *hṛdayāni*—hearts; *bhavanti*—become; *hi*—certainly.

TRANSLATION

"A relative or intimate friend is always fearful of some injury to his beloved."

PURPORT

This is a quotation from the *Abhijñāna-śakuntala-nāṭaka*.

TEXT 41

সমুদ্রের তীরে আসি' যুকতি করিলা ।
চিরায়ু-পর্বত-দিকে কতজন গেলা ॥ ৪১ ॥

samudrera tīre āsi' yukati karilā
cirāyu-parvata-dike kata-jana gelā

SYNONYMS

samudrera tīre—on the seashore; *āsi'*—coming; *yukati karilā*—they consulted among themselves; *cirāyu-parvata*—of Caṭaka-parvata; *dike*—in the direction; *kata-jana*—some of them; *gelā*—went.

TRANSLATION

When they arrived at the seashore, they conferred among themselves. Then some of them sought out Śrī Caitanya Mahāprabhu at Caṭaka-parvata.

TEXT 42

পূর্ব-দিশায় চলে স্বরূপ লঞা কত জন ।
সিন্ধু-তীরে-নীরে করেন প্রভুর অন্বেষণ ॥ ৪২ ॥

pūrva-diśāya cale svarūpa lañā kata jana
sindhu-tīre-nīre karena prabhura anveṣaṇa

SYNONYMS

pūrva-diśāya—in the eastern direction; *cale*—goes; *svarūpa*—Svarūpa Dāmodara Gosvāmī; *lañā*—taking; *kata jana*—some persons; *sindhu-tīre*—on the seashore; *nīre*—in the water; *karena*—does; *prabhura*—of Śrī Caitanya Mahāprabhu; *anveṣaṇa*—searching.

TRANSLATION

Svarūpa Dāmodara proceeded east with others, looking for the Lord on the beach or in the water.

TEXT 43

বিষাদে বিহ্বল সবে, নাহিক 'চেতন' ।
তবু প্রেমে বুলে করি' প্রভুর অন্বেষণ ॥ ৪৩ ॥

viṣāde vihvala sabe, nāhika 'cetana'
tabu preme bule kari' prabhura anveṣaṇa

SYNONYMS

viṣāde—in great moroseness; *vihvala*—overwhelmed; *sabe*—in everyone; *nāhika*—there was not; *cetana*—consciousness; *tabu*—still; *preme*—in love; *bule*—wander; *kari'*—doing; *prabhura*—Śrī Caitanya Mahāprabhu; *anveṣaṇa*—searching for.

TRANSLATION

Everyone was overwhelmed with moroseness and almost unconscious, but out of ecstatic love they continued to wander here and there, searching for the Lord.

TEXT 44

দেখেন—এক জালিয়া আইসে কান্ধে জাল করি'।
হাসে, কান্দে, নাচে, গায়, বলে 'হরি' 'হরি' ॥ ৪৪ ॥

dekhena——eka jāliyā āise kāndhe jāla kari'
hāse, kānde, nāce, gāya, bale 'hari' 'hari'

SYNONYMS

dekhena—they see; *eka jāliyā*—one fisherman; *āise*—comes; *kāndhe*—on the shoulder; *jāla kari'*—carrying a net; *hāse*—laughs; *kānde*—cries; *nāce*—dances; *gāya*—sings; *bale*—says; *hari hari*—Hari, Hari.

TRANSLATION

Passing along the beach, they saw a fisherman approaching with his net over his shoulder. Laughing, crying, dancing and singing, he kept repeating the holy name "Hari, Hari."

TEXT 45

জালিয়ার চেষ্টা দেখি' সবার চমৎকার।
স্বরূপ-গোসাঞি তারে পুছেন সমাচার ॥ ৪৫ ॥

jāliyāra ceṣṭā dekhi' sabāra camatkāra
svarūpa-gosāñi tāre puchena samācāra

SYNONYMS

jāliyāra—of the fisherman; *ceṣṭā*—activity; *dekhi'*—seeing; *sabāra*—of everyone; *camatkāra*—astonishment; *svarūpa-gosāñi*—Svarūpa Dāmodara Gosāñi; *tāre*—unto him; *puchena*—inquires; *samācāra*—news.

TRANSLATION

Seeing the activities of the fisherman, everyone was astonished. Svarūpa Dāmodara Gosvāmī, therefore, asked him for information.

TEXT 46

“কহ, জালিয়া, এই দিকে দেখিলা একজন ?
তোমার এই দশা কেনে,—কহত' কারণ ?” ৪৬ ॥

"kaha, jāliyā, ei dike dekhilā eka-jana?
tomāra ei daśā kene,——kahata' kāraṇa?"

SYNONYMS

kaha—please say; *jāliyā*—O fisherman; *ei dike*—in this direction; *dekhilā*—did you see; *eka-jana*—someone; *tomāra*—your; *ei*—this; *daśā*—condition; *kene*—why; *kahata'*—kindly speak; *kāraṇa*—the cause.

TRANSLATION

"My dear fisherman," he said, "why are you behaving like this? Have you seen someone hereabouts? What is the cause of your behavior? Please tell us."

TEXT 47

জালিয়া কহে,—“ইহাঁ এক মনুষ্য না দেখিল ।
জাল বাহিতে এক মৃতক মোর জালে আইল ॥ ৪৭ ॥

jāliyā kahe,——"ihāṅ eka manuṣya nā dekhila
jāla vāhite eka mṛtaka mora jāle āila

SYNONYMS

jāliyā kahe—the fisherman said; *ihāṅ*—here; *eka*—one; *manuṣya*—man; *nā dekhila*—I did not see; *jāla vāhite*—while I was working with the net; *eka*—one; *mṛtaka*—dead body; *mora jāle*—in my net; *āila*—came.

TRANSLATION

The fisherman replied, "I have not seen a single person here, but while casting my net in the water, I captured a dead body.

TEXT 48

বড় মৎস্য বলি' আমি উঠাইলুঁ যতনে ।
মৃতক দেখিতে মোর ভয় হৈল মনে ॥ ৪৮ ॥

baḍa matsya bali' āmi uṭhāiluṅ yatane
mṛtaka dekhite mora bhaya haila mane

SYNONYMS

baḍa—great; *matsya*—fish; *bali'*—thinking to be; *āmi*—I; *uṭhāiluṅ*—lifted; *yatane*—with care; *mṛtaka*—the dead body; *dekhite*—seeing; *mora*—my; *bhaya*—fear; *haila*—there was; *mane*—in the mind.

TRANSLATION

"I lifted it with great care, thinking it a big fish, but as soon as I saw that it was a corpse, great fear arose in my mind.

TEXT 49

জাল খসাইতে তার অঙ্গ-স্পর্শ হইল ।
স্পর্শমাত্রে সেই ভূত হৃদয়ে পশিল ॥ ৪৯ ॥

jāla khasāite tāra aṅga-sparśa ha-ila
sparśa-mātre sei bhūta hṛdaye paśila

SYNONYMS

jāla—the net; *khasāite*—releasing; *tāra*—his; *aṅga-sparśa*—touch of the body; *ha-ila*—there was; *sparśa-mātre*—as soon as I touched it; *sei*—that; *bhūta*—ghost; *hṛdaye*—in my heart; *paśila*—entered.

TRANSLATION

"As I tried to release the net, I touched the body, and as soon as I touched it, a ghost entered my heart.

TEXT 50

ভয়ে কম্প হৈল, মোর নেত্রে বহে জল ।
গদগদ বাণী, রোম উঠিল সকল ॥ ৫০ ॥

bhaye kampa haila, mora netre vahe jala
gadgada vāṇī, roma uṭhila sakala

SYNONYMS

bhaye—out of fear; *kampa*—shivering; *haila*—there was; *mora*—my; *netre*—in the eyes; *vahe*—flow; *jala*—tears; *gadgada*—faltering; *vāṇī*—voice; *roma*—body hair; *uṭhila*—stood up; *sakala*—all.

TRANSLATION

"I shivered in fear and shed tears. My voice faltered, and all the hairs on my body stood up.

TEXT 51

কিবা ব্রহ্মদৈত্য, কিবা ভূত, কহনে না যায়।
দর্শনমাত্রে মনুষ্যের পৈশে সেই কায়॥ ৫১॥

kibā brahma-daitya, kibā bhūta, kahane nā yāya
darśana-mātre manuṣyera paiśe sei kāya

SYNONYMS

kibā—whether; *brahma-daitya*—a *brāhmaṇa* ghost; *kibā*—or; *bhūta*—an ordinary ghost; *kahane nā yāya*—I cannot say; *darśana-mātre*—as soon as one sees; *manuṣyera*—of a man; *paiśe*—enters; *sei kāya*—that body.

TRANSLATION

"I do not know whether it was the ghost of a dead brāhmaṇa or an ordinary man, but as soon as one looks upon it, it enters his body.

TEXT 52

শরীর দীঘল তার — হাত পাঁচ-সাত।
একেক-হস্ত-পদ তার, তিন তিন হাত॥ ৫২॥

śarīra dīghala tāra——hāta pāṅca-sāta
ekeka-hasta-pada tāra, tina tina hāta

SYNONYMS

śarīra—body; *dīghala*—long; *tāra*—his; *hāta*—cubits (one cubit approximately equals a foot and a half); *pāṅca-sāta*—five to seven; *ekeka*—each and every; *hasta-pada*—arm and leg; *tāra*—of that; *tina*—three; *tina*—three; *hāta*—cubits.

TRANSLATION

"The body of this ghost is very long, five to seven cubits. Each of its arms and legs is as much as three cubits long.

TEXT 53

অস্থি-সন্ধি ছুটিলে চর্ম করে নড়-বড়ে ।
তাহা দেখি' প্রাণ কা'র নাহি রহে ধড়ে ॥ ৫৩ ॥

asthi-sandhi chuṭile carma kare naḍa-baḍe
tāhā dekhi' prāṇa kā'ra nāhi rahe dhaḍe

SYNONYMS

asthi-sandhi—the joints of the bones; *chuṭile*—being separated; *carma*—the skin; *kare*—does; *naḍa-baḍe*—hanging; *tāhā*—that; *dekhi'*—seeing; *prāṇa*—life; *kā'ra*—whose; *nāhi*—does not; *rahe*—remain; *dhaḍe*—in the body.

TRANSLATION

"Its joints are all separated beneath the skin, which is completely slack. No one could see it and remain alive in his body.

TEXT 54

মড়া-রূপ ধরি' রহে উত্তান-নয়ন ।
কভু গোঁ-গোঁ করে, কভু রহে অচেতন ॥ ৫৪ ॥

maḍā-rūpa dhari' rahe uttāna-nayana
kabhu goṅ-goṅ kare, kabhu rahe acetana

SYNONYMS

maḍā—of a dead body; *rūpa*—the form; *dhari'*—accepting; *rahe*—remains; *uttāna-nayana*—with open eyes; *kabhu*—sometimes; *goṅ-goṅ*—the sound *goṅ-goṅ; kare*—makes; *kabhu*—sometimes; *rahe*—remains; *acetana*—unconscious.

TRANSLATION

"That ghost has taken the form of a corpse, but he keeps his eyes open. Sometimes he utters the sounds 'goṅ-goṅ,' and sometimes he remains unconscious.

TEXT 55

সাক্ষাৎ দেখেছোঁ,—মোরে পাইল সেই ভূত ।
মুই মৈলে মোর কৈছে জীবে স্ত্রী-পুত্ ॥ ৫৫ ॥

sākṣāt dekhechoṅ,—more pāila sei bhūta
mui maile mora kaiche jīve strī-put

SYNONYMS

sākṣāt—directly; *dekhechoṅ*—I have seen; *more*—me; *pāila*—has entered; *sei*—that; *bhūta*—ghost; *mui maile*—if I die; *mora*—my; *kaiche*—how; *jīve*—will live; *strī-put*—wife and children.

TRANSLATION

"I have seen that ghost directly, and he is haunting me. But if I die, who will take care of my wife and children?

TEXT 56

সেই ত' ভূতের কথা কহন না যায়।
ওঝা-ঠাঞি যাইছোঁ,—যদি সে ভূত ছাড়ায় ॥ ৫৬ ॥

sei ta' bhūtera kathā kahana nā yāya
ojhā-ṭhāñi yāichoṅ,——yadi se bhūta chāḍāya

SYNONYMS

sei—that; *ta'*—certainly; *bhūtera*—of the ghost; *kathā*—topics; *kahana*—to speak; *nā yāya*—is not possible; *ojhā-ṭhāñi*—to the exorcist; *yāichoṅ*—I am going; *yadi*—if; *se*—that; *bhūta*—the ghost; *chāḍāya*—he can cause to leave.

TRANSLATION

"The ghost is certainly very difficult to talk about, but I am going to find an exorcist and ask him if he can release me from it.

TEXT 57

একা রাত্র্যে বুলি' মৎস্য মারিয়ে নির্জনে।
ভূত-প্রেত আমার না লাগে 'নৃসিংহ'-স্মরণে ॥ ৫৭ ॥

ekā rātrye buli' matsya māriye nirjane
bhūta-preta āmāra nā lāge 'nṛsiṁha'-smaraṇe

SYNONYMS

ekā—alone; *rātrye*—at night; *buli'*—wandering; *matsya*—fish; *māriye*—I kill; *nirjane*—in solitary places; *bhūta-preta*—ghosts; *āmāra*—me; *nā lāge*—cannot touch; *nṛsiṁha-smaraṇe*—by remembering Nṛsiṁha.

TRANSLATION

"I wander alone at night killing fish in solitary places, but because I remember the hymn to Lord Nṛsiṁha, ghosts do not touch me.

TEXT 58

এই ভূত নৃসিংহ-নামে চাপয়ে দ্বিগুণে।
তাহার আকার দেখিতে ভয় লাগে মনে ॥ ৫৮ ॥

ei bhūta nṛsiṁha-nāme cāpaye dviguṇe
tāhāra ākāra dekhite bhaya lāge mane

SYNONYMS

ei bhūta—this ghost; *nṛsiṁha-nāme*—by the holy name of Lord Nṛsiṁha; *cāpaye*—comes over me; *dvi-guṇe*—with doubled strength; *tāhāra*—his; *ākāra*—form; *dekhite*—seeing; *bhaya*—fear; *lāge mane*—arises in the mind.

TRANSLATION

"This ghost, however, overcomes me with redoubled strength when I chant the Nṛsiṁha mantra. When I even see the form of this ghost, great fear arises in my mind.

TEXT 59

ওথা না যাইহ, আমি নিষেধি তোমারে।
তাহাঁ গেলে সেই ভূত লাগিবে সবারে॥" ৫৯ ॥

othā nā yāiha, āmi niṣedhi tomāre
tāhāṅ gele sei bhūta lāgibe sabāre"

SYNONYMS

othā—there; *nā yāiha*—do not go; *āmi*—I; *niṣedhi*—forbid; *tomāre*—you; *tāhāṅ*—there; *gele*—if you go; *sei bhūta*—that ghost; *lāgibe*—will catch; *sabāre*—all of you.

TRANSLATION

"Do not go near there. I forbid you. If you go, that ghost will catch you all."

TEXT 60

এত শুনি' স্বরূপ-গোসাঞি সব তত্ত্ব জানি'।
জালিয়ারে কিছু কয় সুমধুর বাণী ॥ ৬০ ॥

eta śuni' svarūpa-gosāñi saba tattva jāni'
jāliyāre kichu kaya sumadhura vāṇī

SYNONYMS

eta śuni'—hearing this; *svarūpa-gosāñi*—Svarūpa Dāmodara Gosvāmī; *saba*—all; *tattva*—truth; *jāni'*—understanding; *jāliyāre*—unto the fisherman; *kichu*—some; *kaya*—said; *su-madhura*—sweet; *vāṇī*—words.

TRANSLATION

Hearing this, Svarūpa Dāmodara could understand the full truth of the matter. He spoke sweetly to the fisherman.

TEXT 61

'আমি—বড় ওঝা জানি ভূত ছাড়াইতে'।
মন্ত্র পড়ি' শ্রীহস্ত দিলা তাহার মাথাতে ॥ ৬১ ॥

'āmi——baḍa ojhā jāni bhūta chāḍāite'
mantra paḍi' śrī-hasta dilā tāhāra māthāte

SYNONYMS

āmi—I; *baḍa*—big; *ojhā*—exorcist; *jāni*—I know; *bhūta*—ghost; *chāḍāite*—how to exorcise; *mantra paḍi'*—chanting hymns; *śrī-hasta*—his hand; *dilā*—placed; *tāhāra māthāte*—on his head.

TRANSLATION

"I am a famous exorcist," he said, "and I know how to rid you of this ghost." He then chanted some mantras and placed his hand on the top of the fisherman's head.

TEXT 62

তিন চাপড় মারি' কহে,—'ভূত পলাইল।
ভয় না পাইহ'—বলি' সুস্থির করিল ॥ ৬২ ॥

tina cāpaḍa māri' kahe,——'bhūta palāila
bhaya nā pāiha'——bali' susthira karila

SYNONYMS

tina cāpaḍa māri'—slapping three times; *kahe*—says; *bhūta*—the ghost; *palāila*—has gone away; *bhaya nā pāiha*—do not be afraid; *bali'*—saying; *su-sthira karila*—pacified him.

TRANSLATION

He slapped the fisherman three times and said, "Now the ghost has gone away. Do not be afraid." By saying this, he pacified the fisherman.

TEXT 63

একে প্রেম, আরে ভয়,—দ্বিগুণ অস্থির ।
ভয়-অংশ গেল,—সে হৈল কিছু ধীর ॥ ৬৩ ॥

eke prema, āre bhaya,——dviguṇa asthira
bhaya-aṁśa gela,——se haila kichu dhīra

SYNONYMS

eke—on one hand; *prema*—ecstatic love; *āre*—on the other hand; *bhaya*—fear; *dvi-guṇa*—doubly; *asthira*—agitated; *bhaya-aṁśa*—the fear part; *gela*—disappeared; *se*—he; *haila*—became; *kichu*—somewhat; *dhīra*—sober.

TRANSLATION

The fisherman was affected by ecstatic love, but he was also fearful. He had thus become doubly agitated. Now that his fear had subsided, however, he had become somewhat normal.

TEXT 64

স্বরূপ কহে,—"যাঁরে তুমি কর 'ভূত'-জ্ঞান ।
ভূত নহে—তেঁহো কৃষ্ণচৈতন্য ভগবান্ ॥ ৬৪ ॥

svarūpa kahe,——"yāṅre tumi kara 'bhūta'-jñāna
bhūta nahe——teṅho kṛṣṇa-caitanya bhagavān

SYNONYMS

svarūpa kahe—Svarūpa Dāmodara Gosvāmī said; *yāṅre*—the person whom; *tumi*—you; *kara bhūta-jñāna*—consider a ghost; *bhūta nahe*—is not a ghost; *teṅho*—He; *kṛṣṇa-caitanya*—Lord Śrī Caitanya Mahāprabhu; *bhagavān*—the Supreme Personality of Godhead.

TRANSLATION

Svarūpa Dāmodara said to the fisherman, "My dear sir, the person whom you are thinking a ghost is not actually a ghost but the Supreme Personality of Godhead, Śrī Kṛṣṇa Caitanya Mahāprabhu.

TEXT 65

প্রেমাবেশে পড়িলা তেঁহো সমুদ্রের জলে ।
তাঁরে তুমি উঠাইলা আপনার জালে ॥ ৬৫ ॥

premāveśe paḍilā teṅho samudrera jale
tāṅre tumi uṭhāilā āpanāra jāle

SYNONYMS

prema-āveśe—out of ecstatic emotion; *paḍilā*—fell down; *teṅho*—He; *samudrera jale*—in the water of the sea; *tāṅre*—Him; *tumi*—you; *uṭhāilā*—brought out; *āpanāra jāle*—in your net.

TRANSLATION

"Because of ecstatic love, the Lord fell into the sea, and you have caught Him in your net and rescued Him.

TEXT 66

তাঁর স্পর্শে হইল তোমার কৃষ্ণপ্রেমোদয় ।
ভূত-প্রেত-জ্ঞানে তোমার হৈল মহাভয় ॥ ৬৬ ॥

tāṅra sparśe ha-ila tomāra kṛṣṇa-premodaya
bhūta-preta-jñāne tomāra haila mahā-bhaya

SYNONYMS

tāṅra sparśe—by His touch; *ha-ila*—there was; *tomāra*—your; *kṛṣṇa-prema-udaya*—awakening of ecstatic love for Kṛṣṇa; *bhūta-preta-jñāne*—by thinking to be a ghost; *tomāra*—your; *haila*—there was; *mahā-bhaya*—great fear.

TRANSLATION

"Simply touching Him has awakened your dormant love of Kṛṣṇa, but because you thought Him a ghost, you were very much afraid of Him.

TEXT 67

এবে ভয় গেল, তোমার মন হৈল স্থিরে ।
কাহাঁ তাঁরে উঠাঞাছ, দেখাহ আমারে ॥” ৬৭ ॥

ebe bhaya gela, tomāra mana haila sthire
kāhāṅ tāṅre uṭhāñācha, dekhāha āmāre"

SYNONYMS

ebe—now; *bhaya*—fear; *gela*—has gone; *tomāra*—your; *mana*—mind; *haila*—has become; *sthire*—pacified; *kāhāṅ*—where; *tāṅre*—Him; *uṭhāñācha*—have you lifted; *dekhāha*—please show; *āmāre*—me.

TRANSLATION

"Now that your fear has gone and your mind is peaceful, please show me where He is."

TEXT 68

জালিয়া কহে,—"প্রভুরে দেখ্যাছোঁ বারবার ।
তেঁহো নহেন, এই অতিবিকৃত আকার ॥" ৬৮ ॥

jāliyā kahe,——"prabhure dekhyāchoṅ bāra-bāra
teṅho nahena, ei ati-vikṛta ākāra"

SYNONYMS

jāliyā kahe—the fisherman said; *prabhure*—Lord Śrī Caitanya Mahāprabhu; *dekhyāchoṅ*—I have seen; *bāra-bāra*—many times; *teṅho*—He; *nahena*—it is not; *ei*—this; *ati-vikṛta*—very deformed; *ākāra*—body.

TRANSLATION

The fisherman replied, "I have seen the Lord many times, but this is not He. This body is very deformed."

TEXT 69

স্বরূপ কহে,—"তাঁর হয় প্রেমের বিকার ।
অস্থি-সন্ধি ছাড়ে, হয় অতি দীর্ঘাকার ॥" ৬৯ ॥

svarūpa kahe,——"tāṅra haya premera vikāra
asthi-sandhi chāḍe, haya ati dīrghākāra"

SYNONYMS

svarūpa kahe—Svarūpa Dāmodara said; *tāṅra*—of Him; *haya*—there are; *premera*—of love of Godhead; *vikāra*—transformations of the body; *asthi-sandhi*—the joints of the bones; *chāḍe*—become separated; *haya*—there is; *ati*—very; *dīrgha-ākāra*—elongated body.

TRANSLATION

Svarūpa Dāmodara said, "The Lord's body becomes transformed in His love for God. Sometimes the joints of His bones separate, and His body becomes very elongated."

TEXT 70

শুনি' সেই জালিয়া আনন্দিত হইল।
সবা লঞা গেল, মহাপ্রভুরে দেখাইল ॥ ৭০ ॥

śuni' sei jāliyā ānandita ha-ila
sabā lañā gela, mahāprabhure dekhāila

SYNONYMS

śuni'—hearing; *sei*—that; *jāliyā*—fisherman; *ānandita ha-ila*—became very happy; *sabā lañā*—taking everyone; *gela*—went; *mahāprabhure*—Śrī Caitanya Mahāprabhu; *dekhāila*—showed.

TRANSLATION

Hearing this, the fisherman was very happy. He brought all the devotees with him and showed them the body of Śrī Caitanya Mahāprabhu.

TEXT 71

ভূমিতে পড়ি' আছে প্রভু দীর্ঘ সব কায়।
জলে শ্বেত-তনু, বালু লাগিয়াছে গায় ॥ ৭১ ॥

bhūmite paḍi' āche prabhu dīrgha saba kāya
jale śveta-tanu, vālu lāgiyāche gāya

SYNONYMS

bhūmite—on the ground; *paḍi'*—lying; *āche*—was; *prabhu*—Śrī Caitanya Mahāprabhu; *dīrgha*—elongated; *saba kāya*—the whole body; *jale*—by the water; *śveta-tanu*—white body; *vālu*—sand; *lāgiyāche gāya*—was smeared over the body.

TRANSLATION

The Lord was lying on the ground, His body elongated and bleached white by the water. He was covered from head to foot with sand.

TEXT 72

অতিদীর্ঘ শিথিল তনু-চর্ম নট্‌কায়।
দূর পথ উঠাঞা ঘরে আনান না যায় ॥ ৭২ ॥

ati-dīrgha śithila tanu-carma naṭkāya
dūra patha uṭhāñā ghare ānāna nā yāya

SYNONYMS

ati-dīrgha—very elongated; *śithila*—slackened; *tanu*—body; *carma*—skin; *naṭkāya*—hanging; *dūra patha*—long distance; *uṭhāñā*—lifting; *ghare*—home; *ānāna*—bringing; *nā yāya*—was not possible.

TRANSLATION

The Lord's body was stretched, and His skin was slack and hanging loose. To lift Him and take Him the long distance home would have been impossible.

TEXT 73

আর্দ্র কৌপীন দূর করি' শুষ্ক পরাঞা।
বহির্বাসে শোয়াইলা বালুকা ছাড়াঞা ॥ ৭৩ ॥

ārdra kaupīna dūra kari' śuṣka parāñā
bahirvāse śoyāilā vālukā chāḍāñā

SYNONYMS

ārdra—wet; *kaupīna*—underwear; *dūra kari'*—removing; *śuṣka*—dry; *parāñā*—putting on; *bahirvāse*—on a covering cloth; *śoyāilā*—put down; *vālukā*—sand; *chāḍāñā*—removing.

TRANSLATION

The devotees removed His wet undergarment and replaced it with a dry one. Then, laying the Lord on an outer cloth, they cleaned the sand from His body.

TEXT 74

সবে মেলি' উচ্চ করি' করেন সঙ্কীর্তনে।
উচ্চ করি' কৃষ্ণনাম কহেন প্রভুর কাণে ॥ ৭৪ ॥

sabe meli' ucca kari' karena saṅkīrtane
ucca kari' kṛṣṇa-nāma kahena prabhura kāṇe

SYNONYMS

sabe meli'—all together; *ucca kari'*—very loudly; *karena*—performed; *saṅkīrtane*—chanting of the holy name; *ucca kari'*—loudly; *kṛṣṇa-nāma*—the holy name of Kṛṣṇa; *kahena*—said; *prabhura kāṇe*—in the ear of Śrī Caitanya Mahāprabhu.

TRANSLATION

They all performed saṅkīrtana, loudly chanting the holy name of Kṛṣṇa into the Lord's ear.

TEXT 75

কতক্ষণে প্রভুর কাণে শব্দ পরশিল ।
হুঙ্কার করিয়া প্রভু তবহি উঠিল ॥ ৭৫ ॥

kata-kṣaṇe prabhura kāṇe śabda paraśila
huṅkāra kariyā prabhu tabahi uṭhila

SYNONYMS

kata-kṣaṇe—after some time; *prabhura*—of Śrī Caitanya Mahāprabhu; *kāṇe*—within the ear; *śabda*—the sound; *paraśila*—entered; *huṅkāra kariyā*—making a loud sound; *prabhu*—Śrī Caitanya Mahāprabhu; *tabahi*—immediately; *uṭhila*—got up.

TRANSLATION

After some time, the sound of the holy name entered the ear of the Lord, who immediately got up, making a great noise.

TEXT 76

উঠিতেই অস্থি সব লাগিল নিজ-স্থানে ।
'অর্ধবাহ্যে' ইতি-উতি করেন দরশনে ॥ ৭৬ ॥

uṭhitei asthi saba lāgila nija-sthāne
'ardha-bāhye' iti-uti karena daraśane

SYNONYMS

uṭhitei—as soon as He got up; *asthi*—bones; *saba*—all; *lāgila*—contracted; *nija-sthāne*—in their own places; *ardha-bāhye*—in half-external consciousness; *iti-uti*—here and there; *karena daraśane*—looks.

TRANSLATION

As soon as He got up, His bones assumed their proper places. With half-external consciousness, the Lord looked here and there.

TEXT 77

'তিন-দশায় মহাপ্রভু রহেন সর্বকাল ।
'অন্তর্দশা', 'বাহ্যদশা', 'অর্ধবাহ্য' আর ॥ ৭৭ ॥

tina-daśāya mahāprabhu rahena sarva-kāla
'antar-daśā', 'bāhya-daśā', 'ardha-bāhya' āra

SYNONYMS

tina-daśāya—in three conditions; *mahāprabhu*—Śrī Caitanya Mahāprabhu; *rahena*—remains; *sarva-kāla*—at all times; *antaḥ-daśā*—internal condition; *bāhya-daśā*—external condition; *ardha-bāhya*—half-external consciousness; *āra*—and.

TRANSLATION

The Lord remains in one of three different states of consciousness at all times: internal, external, and half-external.

TEXT 78

অন্তর্দশার কিছু ঘোর, কিছু বাহ্য-জ্ঞান ।
সেই দশা কহে ভক্ত 'অর্ধবাহ্য-নাম ॥ ৭৮ ॥

antar-daśāra kichu ghora, kichu bāhya-jñāna
sei daśā kahe bhakta 'ardha-bāhya'-nāma

SYNONYMS

antaḥ-daśāra—of the internal condition; *kichu*—some; *ghora*—deep state; *kichu*—some; *bāhya-jñāna*—external consciousness; *sei daśā*—that condition; *kahe*—say; *bhakta*—devotees; *ardha-bāhya*—half-external consciousness; *nāma*—name.

TRANSLATION

When the Lord is deeply absorbed in internal consciousness but He nevertheless exhibits some external consciousness, devotees call His condition ardha-bāhya, or half-external consciousness.

TEXT 79

'অর্ধবাহ্যে' কহেন প্রভু প্রলাপ-বচনে।
আকাশে কহেন প্রভু, শুনেন ভক্তগণে ॥ ৭৯ ॥

'ardha-bāhye' kahena prabhu pralāpa-vacane
ākāśe kahena prabhu, śunena bhakta-gaṇe

SYNONYMS

ardha-bāhye—in half-external consciousness; *kahena*—says; *prabhu*—Śrī Caitanya Mahāprabhu; *pralāpa-vacane*—crazy words; *ākāśe*—to the sky; *kahena*—speaks; *prabhu*—Śrī Caitanya Mahāprabhu; *śunena*—hear; *bhakta-gaṇe*—the devotees.

TRANSLATION

In this half-external consciousness, Śrī Caitanya Mahāprabhu talked like a madman. The devotees could distinctly hear Him speaking to the sky.

TEXT 80

"কালিন্দী দেখিয়া আমি গেলাঙ বৃন্দাবন।
দেখি,—জলক্রীড়া করেন ব্রজেন্দ্রনন্দন ॥ ৮০ ॥

"kālindī dekhiyā āmi gelāṅa vṛndāvana
dekhi,——jala-krīḍā karena vrajendra-nandana

SYNONYMS

kālindī—River Yamunā; *dekhiyā*—seeing; *āmi*—I; *gelāṅa*—went; *vṛndāvana*—to Vṛndāvana; *dekhi*—I see; *jala-krīḍā*—pastimes in the water; *karena*—performs; *vrajendra-nandana*—Kṛṣṇa, the son of Nanda Mahārāja.

TRANSLATION

"Seeing the River Yamunā," He said, "I went to Vṛndāvana. There I saw the son of Nanda Mahārāja performing His sporting pastimes in the water.

TEXT 81

রাধিকাদি গোপীগণ-সঙ্গে একত্র মেলি'।
যমুনার জলে মহারঙ্গে করেন কেলি ॥ ৮১ ॥

rādhikādi gopī-gaṇa-saṅge ekatra meli'
yamunāra jale mahā-raṅge karena keli

SYNONYMS

rādhikā-ādi—headed by Śrīmatī Rādhārāṇī; *gopī-gaṇa-saṅge*—with the *gopīs; ekatra meli'*—meeting together; *yamunāra*—of the River Yamunā; *jale*—in the water; *mahā-raṅge*—in a great sporting attitude; *karena keli*—performs pastimes.

TRANSLATION

"Lord Kṛṣṇa was in the water of the Yamunā in the company of the gopīs, headed by Śrīmatī Rādhārāṇī. They were performing pastimes in a great sporting manner.

TEXT 82

তীরে রহি' দেখি আমি সখীগণ-সঙ্গে ।
একসখী সখীগণে দেখায় সেই রঙ্গে ॥ ৮২ ॥

tīre rahi' dekhi āmi sakhī-gaṇa-saṅge
eka-sakhī sakhī-gaṇe dekhāya sei raṅge

SYNONYMS

tīre—on the bank; *rahi'*—standing; *dekhi*—see; *āmi*—I; *sakhī-gaṇa-saṅge*—with the *gopīs; eka-sakhī*—one *gopī; sakhī-gaṇe*—to other *gopīs; dekhāya*—shows; *sei raṅge*—that pastime.

TRANSLATION

"I saw this pastime as I stood on the bank of the Yamunā in the company of the gopīs. One gopī was showing some other gopīs the pastimes of Rādhā and Kṛṣṇa in the water.

TEXT 83

পট্টবস্ত্র, অলঙ্কারে, সমর্পিয়া সখী-করে,
সূক্ষ্ম-শুক্লবস্ত্র-পরিধান ।
কৃষ্ণ লঞা কান্তাগণ, কৈলা জলাবগাহন,
জলকেলি রচিলা সুঠাম ॥ ৮৩ ॥

paṭṭa-vastra, alaṅkāre, samarpiyā sakhī-kare,
sūkṣma-śukla-vastra-paridhāna
kṛṣṇa lañā kāntā-gaṇa, kailā jalāvagāhana,
jala-keli racilā suṭhāma

SYNONYMS

paṭṭa-vastra—silk garments; *alaṅkāre*—ornaments; *samarpiyā*—entrusting; *sakhī-kare*—in the hands of their *gopī* friends; *sūkṣma*—very fine; *śukla-vastra*—white cloth; *paridhāna*—putting on; *kṛṣṇa*—Lord Kṛṣṇa; *lañā*—taking; *kāntā-gaṇa*—the beloved *gopīs; kailā*—performed; *jala-avagāhana*—bathing in the water; *jala-keli*—pastimes in the water; *racilā*—planned; *su-ṭhāma*—very nice.

TRANSLATION

"All the gopīs entrusted their silken garments and ornaments to the care of their friends and then put on fine white cloth. Taking His beloved gopīs with Him, Lord Kṛṣṇa bathed and performed very nice pastimes in the water of the Yamunā.

TEXT 84

সখি হে, দেখ কৃষ্ণের জলকেলি-রঙ্গে ।
কৃষ্ণ মত্ত করিবর, চঞ্চল কর-পুষ্কর,
গোপীগণ করিণীর সঙ্গে ॥ ৮৪ ॥ ধ্রু ॥

sakhi he, dekha kṛṣṇera jala-keli-raṅge
kṛṣṇa matta kari-vara, cañcala kara-puṣkara,
gopī-gaṇa kariṇīra saṅge

SYNONYMS

sakhi he—O my dear friends; *dekha*—just see; *kṛṣṇera*—of Lord Kṛṣṇa; *jala-keli*—of the pastimes in the water; *raṅge*—the sporting mood; *kṛṣṇa*—Lord Kṛṣṇa; *matta*—maddened; *kari-vara*—chief elephant; *cañcala*—restless; *kara-puṣkara*—lotus palms; *gopī-gaṇa*—the *gopīs; kariṇīra*—of the she-elephants; *saṅge*—in the company.

TRANSLATION

"My dear friends, just see Lord Kṛṣṇa's sporting pastimes in the water. Kṛṣṇa's restless palms resemble lotus flowers. He is just like a chief of mad elephants, and the gopīs who accompany Him are like she-elephants.

TEXT 85

আরম্ভিলা জলকেলি, অন্যোঽন্যে জল ফেলাফেলি,
হুড়াহুড়ি, বর্ষে জলধার ।

সবে জয়-পরাজয়, নাহি কিছু নিশ্চয়,
জলযুদ্ধ বাড়িল অপার ॥ ৮৫ ॥

ārambhilā jala-keli, anyo'nye jala phelāpheli,
huḍāhuḍi, varṣe jala-dhāra
sabe jaya-parājaya, nāhi kichu niścaya,
jala-yuddha bāḍila apāra

SYNONYMS

ārambhilā—began; *jala-keli*—pastimes in the water; *anyo'nye*—at one another; *jala*—water; *phelāpheli*—throwing back and forth; *huḍāhuḍi*—tumultuous activities; *varṣe*—in rains; *jala-dhāra*—showers of water; *sabe*—all of them; *jaya-parājaya*—victory and defeat; *nāhi*—not; *kichu*—any; *niścaya*—certainty; *jala-yuddha*—the fight in the water; *bāḍila*—increased; *apāra*—unlimitedly.

TRANSLATION

"The sporting pastimes in the water began, and everyone started splashing water back and forth. In the tumultuous showers of water, no one could be certain which party was winning and which was losing. This sporting water fight increased unlimitedly.

TEXT 86

বর্ষে স্থির তড়িদ্গণ, সিঞ্চে শ্যাম নবঘন,
ঘন বর্ষে তড়িৎ-উপরে।
সখীগণের নয়ন, তৃষিত চাতকগণ,
সেই অমৃত সুখে পান করে ॥ ৮৬ ॥

varṣe sthira taḍid-gaṇa, siñce śyāma nava-ghana,
ghana varṣe taḍit-upare
sakhī-gaṇera nayana, tṛṣita cātaka-gaṇa,
sei amṛta sukhe pāna kare

SYNONYMS

varṣe—in that shower; *sthira*—fixed; *taḍit-gaṇa*—streaks of lightning; *siñce*—sprinkle; *śyāma*—blackish; *nava-ghana*—new cloud; *ghana*—the cloud; *varṣe*—rains; *taḍit-upare*—upon the streaks of lightning; *sakhī-gaṇera*—of the *gopīs;* *nayana*—the eyes; *tṛṣita*—thirsty; *cātaka-gaṇa*—*cātaka* birds; *sei amṛta*—that nectar; *sukhe*—in happiness; *pāna kare*—drink.

TRANSLATION

"The gopīs were like steady streaks of lightning, and Kṛṣṇa resembled a blackish cloud. The lightning began sprinkling water upon the cloud, and the cloud upon the lightning. Like thirsty cātaka birds, the eyes of the gopīs joyously drank the nectarean water from the cloud.

TEXT 87

প্রথমে যুদ্ধ 'জলাজলি', তবে যুদ্ধ 'করাকরি',
তার পাছে যুদ্ধ 'মুখামুখি'।
তবে যুদ্ধ 'হৃদাহৃদি', তবে হৈল 'রদারদি',
তবে হৈল যুদ্ধ 'নখানখি' ॥ ৮৭ ॥

prathame yuddha 'jalājali', tabe yuddha 'karākari',
tāra pāche yuddha 'mukhāmukhi'
tabe yuddha 'hṛdāhṛdi', tabe haila 'radāradi',
tabe haila yuddha 'nakhānakhi'

SYNONYMS

prathame—in the beginning; *yuddha*—the fight; *jalājali*—throwing water upon one another; *tabe*—thereafter; *yuddha*—the fight; *karākari*—hand to hand; *tāra pāche*—after that; *yuddha*—the fight; *mukhāmukhi*—face to face; *tabe*—thereafter; *yuddha*—the fight; *hṛdāhṛdi*—chest to chest; *tabe*—thereafter; *haila*—was; *radāradi*—teeth to teeth; *tabe*—thereafter; *haila*—there was; *yuddha*—the fight; *nakhānakhi*—nail to nail.

TRANSLATION

"As the fight began, they splashed water on one another. Then they fought hand to hand, then face to face, then chest to chest, teeth to teeth and finally nail to nail.

TEXT 88

সহস্র-করে জল সেকে, সহস্র নেত্রে গোপী দেখে,
সহস্র-পদে নিকট গমনে।
সহস্রমুখ-চুম্বনে, সহস্রবপু-সঙ্গমে,
গোপীনর্ম শুনে সহস্র-কাণে ॥ ৮৮ ॥

sahasra-kare jala seke, sahasra netre gopī dekhe,
sahasra-pade nikaṭa gamane

sahasra-mukha-cumbane, sahasra-vapu-saṅgame,
gopī-narma śune sahasra-kāṇe

SYNONYMS

sahasra—thousands; *kare*—with hands; *jala*—water; *seke*—throw; *sahasra*—thousands; *netre*—with eyes; *gopī*—the *gopīs; dekhe*—see; *sahasra*—thousands; *pade*—with legs; *nikaṭa*—near; *gamane*—in going; *sahasra*—thousands; *mukha*—faces; *cumbane*—kissing; *sahasra*—thousands; *vapu*—bodies; *saṅgame*—in embracing; *gopī*—the *gopīs; narma*—joking; *śune*—hear; *sahasra*—thousands; *kāṇe*—in ears.

TRANSLATION

"Thousands of hands splashed water, and the gopīs saw Kṛṣṇa with thousands of eyes. With thousands of legs they came near Him and kissed Him with thousands of faces. Thousands of bodies embraced Him. The gopīs heard His joking words with thousands of ears.

TEXT 89

কৃষ্ণ রাধা লঞা বলে, গেলা কণ্ঠদঘ্ন জলে,
ছাড়িলা তাহাঁ, যাহাঁ অগাধ পানী ।
তেঁহো কৃষ্ণকণ্ঠ ধরি', ভাসে জলের উপরি,
গজোৎখাতে যৈছে কমলিনী ॥ ৮৯ ॥

kṛṣṇa rādhā lañā bale, gelā kaṇṭha-daghna jale,
chāḍilā tāhāṅ, yāhāṅ agādha pānī
teṅho kṛṣṇa-kaṇṭha dhari', bhāse jalera upari,
gajotkhāte yaiche kamalinī

SYNONYMS

kṛṣṇa—Lord Kṛṣṇa; *rādhā*—Śrīmatī Rādhārāṇī; *lañā*—taking; *bale*—forcibly; *gelā*—went; *kaṇṭha-daghna*—up to the neck; *jale*—in water; *chāḍilā*—let go; *tāhāṅ*—there; *yāhāṅ*—where; *agādha*—very deep; *pānī*—water; *teṅho*—She; *kṛṣṇa-kaṇṭha*—the neck of Kṛṣṇa; *dhari'*—capturing; *bhāse*—floats; *jalera upari*—on the water; *gaja-utkhāte*—plucked by an elephant; *yaiche*—as; *kamalinī*—a lotus flower.

TRANSLATION

"Kṛṣṇa forcibly swept Rādhārāṇī away and took Her into water up to Her neck. Then He released Her where the water was very deep. She grasped

Kṛṣṇa's neck, however, and floated on the water like a lotus flower plucked by the trunk of an elephant.

TEXT 90

যত গোপ-সুন্দরী, কৃষ্ণ তত রূপ ধরি',
সবার বস্ত্র করিলা হরণে ।
যমুনা-জল নির্মল, অঙ্গ করে ঝলমল,
সুখে কৃষ্ণ করে দরশনে ॥ ৯০ ॥

yata gopa-sundarī, kṛṣṇa tata rūpa dhari',
sabāra vastra karilā haraṇe
yamunā-jala nirmala, aṅga kare jhalamala,
sukhe kṛṣṇa kare daraśane

SYNONYMS

yata—as many; *gopa-sundarī*—beautiful *gopīs;* *kṛṣṇa*—Lord Kṛṣṇa; *tata*—that many; *rūpa*—forms; *dhari'*—accepting; *sabāra*—of all; *vastra*—covering cloths; *karilā haraṇe*—took away; *yamunā-jala*—the water of the Yamunā; *nirmala*—very clear; *aṅga*—bodies; *kare jhalamala*—glitter; *sukhe*—happily; *kṛṣṇa*—Lord Kṛṣṇa; *kare daraśane*—sees.

TRANSLATION

"Kṛṣṇa expanded Himself into as many forms as there were gopīs and then took away all the garments that covered them. The water of the River Yamunā was crystal clear, and Kṛṣṇa saw the glittering bodies of the gopīs in great happiness.

TEXT 91

পদ্মিনীলতা—সখীচয়, কৈল কারো সহায়,
তরঙ্গ-হস্তে পত্র সমর্পিল ।
কেহ মুক্ত-কেশপাশ, আগে কৈল অধোবাস,
হস্তে কেহ কঞ্চুলি ধরিল ॥ ৯১ ॥

padminī-latā——sakhī-caya, kaila kāro sahāya,
taraṅga-haste patra samarpila
keha mukta-keśa-pāśa, āge kaila adhovāsa,
haste keha kañculi dharila

SYNONYMS

padminī-latā—the stems of lotus flowers; *sakhī-caya*—friends of the *gopīs; kaila*—gave; *kāro*—to some of the *gopīs; sahāya*—help; *taraṅga-haste*—by the waves of the Yamunā, which are compared to hands; *patra*—the lotus leaves; *samarpila*—supplied; *keha*—someone; *mukta*—released; *keśa-pāśa*—the bunches of hair; *āge*—in front; *kaila*—made; *adhovāsa*—a lower dress; *haste*—the hands; *keha*—some; *kañculi*—as a top dress; *dharila*—held.

TRANSLATION

"The lotus stems were friends of the gopīs and therefore helped them by offering them lotus leaves. The lotuses pushed their large, round leaves over the surface of the water with their hands, the waves of the Yamunā, to cover the gopīs' bodies. Some gopīs undid their hair and kept it in front of them as dresses to cover the lower portions of their bodies and used their hands as bodices to cover their breasts.

TEXT 92

কৃষ্ণের কলহ রাধা-সনে, গোপীগণ সেইক্ষণে,
হেমাব্জ-বনে গেলা লুকাইতে ।
আকণ্ঠ-বপু জলে পৈশে, মুখমাত্র জলে ভাসে,
পদ্মে-মুখে না পারি চিনিতে ॥ ৯২ ॥

kṛṣṇera kalaha rādhā-sane, gopī-gaṇa sei-kṣaṇe,
hemābja-vane gelā lukāite
ākaṇṭha-vapu jale paiśe, mukha-mātra jale bhāse,
padme-mukhe nā pāri cinite

SYNONYMS

kṛṣṇera—of Kṛṣṇa; *kalaha*—quarrel; *rādhā-sane*—with Rādhā; *gopī-gaṇa*—the *gopīs; sei-kṣaṇe*—at that moment; *hema-abja*—of white lotus flowers; *vane*—in the forest; *gelā*—went; *lukāite*—to hide; *ākaṇṭha*—up to the neck; *vapu*—body; *jale*—into the water; *paiśe*—enter; *mukha-mātra*—only the lotus flowers and the faces; *jale*—in the water; *bhāse*—float; *padme-mukhe*—between the lotus flowers and the faces; *nā pāri*—not able; *cinite*—to discern.

TRANSLATION

"Then Kṛṣṇa quarreled with Rādhārāṇī, and all the gopīs hid themselves in a cluster of white lotus flowers. They submerged their bodies up to their necks in the water. Only their faces floated above the surface, and the faces were indistinguishable from the lotuses.

TEXT 93

এথা কৃষ্ণ রাধা-সনে, কৈলা যে আছিল মনে,
গোপীগণ অন্বেষিতে গেলা ।
তবে রাধা সূক্ষ্মমতি, জানিয়া সখীর স্থিতি,
সখী-মধ্যে আসিয়া মিলিলা ॥ ৯৩ ॥

ethā kṛṣṇa rādhā-sane, kailā ye āchila mane,
gopī-gaṇa anveṣite gelā
tabe rādhā sūkṣma-mati, jāniyā sakhīra sthiti,
sakhī-madhye āsiyā mililā

SYNONYMS

ethā—here; *kṛṣṇa*—Lord Kṛṣṇa; *rādhā-sane*—with Śrīmatī Rādhārāṇī; *kailā*—performed; *ye*—what; *āchila*—was; *mane*—in the mind; *gopī-gaṇa*—all the *gopīs; anveṣite*—to search out; *gelā*—went; *tabe*—at that time; *rādhā*—Śrīmatī Rādhārāṇī; *sūkṣma-mati*—very finely intelligent; *jāniyā*—knowing; *sakhīra*—of the *gopīs; sthiti*—situation; *sakhī-madhye*—among the friends; *āsiyā*—coming; *mililā*—mixed.

TRANSLATION

"In the absence of the other gopīs, Lord Kṛṣṇa behaved with Śrīmatī Rādhārāṇī as freely as He desired. When the gopīs began searching for Kṛṣṇa, Śrīmatī Rādhārāṇī, being of very fine intelligence and thus knowing the situation of Her friends, immediately mingled in their midst.

TEXT 94

যত হেমাব্জ জলে ভাসে, তত নীলাব্জ তার পাশে,
আসি' আসি' করয়ে মিলন ।
নীলাব্জে হেমাব্জে ঠেকে, যুদ্ধ হয় প্রত্যেকে,
কৌতুকে দেখে তীরে সখীগণ ॥ ৯৪ ॥

yata hemābja jale bhāse, tata nīlābja tāra pāśe,
āsi' āsi' karaye milana
nīlābje hemābje ṭheke, yuddha haya pratyeke,
kautuke dekhe tīre sakhī-gaṇa

SYNONYMS

yata—as many as there were; *hema-abja*—white lotus flowers; *jale*—on the water; *bhāse*—float; *tata*—that many; *nīla-abja*—bluish lotus flowers; *tāra pāśe*—by their side; *āsi' āsi'*—coming closer; *karaye milana*—they meet; *nīla-abje*—the bluish lotus flowers; *hema-abje*—with the white lotus flowers; *ṭheke*—collide; *yuddha*—a fight; *haya*—there is; *prati-eke*—with one another; *kautuke*—in great fun; *dekhe*—see; *tīre*—on the bank; *sakhī-gaṇa*—the *gopīs.*

TRANSLATION

"Many white lotus flowers were floating in the water, and as many bluish lotus flowers came nearby. As they came close together, the white and blue lotuses collided and began fighting with one another. The gopīs on the bank of the Yamunā watched with great amusement.

TEXT 95

চক্রবাক-মণ্ডল, পৃথক্ পৃথক্ যুগল,
জল হৈতে করিল উদ্গম ।
উঠিল পদ্মমণ্ডল, পৃথক্ পৃথক্ যুগল,
চক্রবাকে কৈল আচ্ছাদন ॥ ৯৫ ॥

cakravāka-maṇḍala, pṛthak pṛthak yugala,
jala haite karila udgama
uṭhila padma-maṇḍala, pṛthak pṛthak yugala,
cakravāke kaila ācchādana

SYNONYMS

cakravāka-maṇḍala—the globes of *cakravāka* birds; *pṛthak pṛthak*—separate; *yugala*—couples; *jala haite*—from the water; *karila*—made; *udgama*—appearance; *uṭhila*—arose; *padma-maṇḍala*—the circle of lotus flowers; *pṛthak pṛthak*—separate; *yugala*—couples; *cakravāke*—the *cakravāka* birds; *kaila*—did; *ācchādana*—covering.

TRANSLATION

"When the raised breasts of the gopīs, which resembled the globelike bodies of cakravāka birds, emerged from the water in separate couples, the bluish lotuses of Kṛṣṇa's hands rose to cover them.

TEXT 96

উঠিল বহু রক্তোৎপল, পৃথক্ পৃথক্ যুগল,
পদ্মগণের কৈল নিবারণ ।

'পদ্ম' চাহে লুটি' নিতে, 'উৎপল' চাহে রাখিতে',
'চক্রবাক' লাগি' দুঁহার রণ ॥ ৯৬ ॥

uṭhila bahu raktotpala, pṛthak pṛthak yugala,
padma-gaṇera kaila nivāraṇa
'padma' cāhe luṭi' nite, 'utpala' cāhe rākhite',
'cakravāka' lāgi' duṅhāra raṇa

SYNONYMS

uṭhila—arose; *bahu*—many; *rakta-utpala*—red lotus flowers; *pṛthak pṛthak*—separate; *yugala*—couples; *padma-gaṇera*—of the bluish lotus flowers; *kaila*—did; *nivāraṇa*—obstruction; *padma*—the blue lotus flowers; *cāhe*—want; *luṭi'*—stealing; *nite*—to take; *utpala*—the red lotus flowers; *cāhe rākhite'*—wanted to protect; *cakravāka lāgi'*—for the *cakravāka* birds; *duṅhāra*—between the two, (the red and blue lotus flowers); *raṇa*—fight.

TRANSLATION

"The hands of the gopīs, which resembled red lotus flowers, arose from the water in pairs to obstruct the bluish flowers. The blue lotuses tried to plunder the white cakravāka birds, and the red lotuses tried to protect them. Thus there was a fight between the two.

TEXT 97

পদ্মোৎপল —অচেতন, চক্রবাক —সচেতন,
চক্রবাকে পদ্ম আস্বাদয় ।
ইহাঁ দুঁহার উল্টা স্থিতি, ধর্ম হৈল বিপরীতি,
কৃষ্ণের রাজ্যে ঐছে ন্যায় হয় ॥ ৯৭ ॥

padmotpala——acetana, cakravāka——sacetana,
cakravāke padma āsvādaya
ihāṅ duṅhāra ulṭā sthiti, dharma haila viparīti,
kṛṣṇera rājye aiche nyāya haya

SYNONYMS

padma-utpala—the blue and red lotus flowers; *acetana*—unconscious; *cakravāka*—the *cakravāka* birds; *sa-cetana*—conscious; *cakravāke*—the *cakravāka* birds; *padma*—the blue lotus flowers; *āsvādaya*—taste; *ihāṅ*—here; *duṅhāra*—of both of them; *ulṭā sthiti*—the reverse situation; *dharma*—

characteristic nature; *haila*—became; *viparīti*—reversed; *kṛṣṇera*—of Lord Kṛṣṇa; *rājye*—in the kingdom; *aiche*—such; *nyāya*—principle; *haya*—there is.

TRANSLATION

"Blue and red lotus flowers are unconscious objects, whereas cakravākas are conscious and alive. Nevertheless, in ecstatic love, the blue lotuses began to taste the cakravākas. This is a reversal of their natural behavior, but in Lord Kṛṣṇa's kingdom such reversals are a principle of His pastimes.

PURPORT

Generally the *cakravāka* bird tastes the lotus flower, but in Kṛṣṇa's pastimes the lotus, which is usually lifeless, tastes the *cakravāka* bird.

TEXT 98

মিত্রের মিত্র সহবাসী, চক্রবাকে লুটে আসি',
কৃষ্ণের রাজ্যে ঐছে ব্যবহার ।
অপরিচিত শত্রুর মিত্র, রাখে উৎপল,– এ বড় চিত্র,
এই বড় 'বিরোধ-অলঙ্কার' ॥ ৯৮ ॥

mitrera mitra saha-vāsī, cakravāke luṭe āsi',
kṛṣṇera rājye aiche vyavahāra
aparicita śatrura mitra, rākhe utpala,——e baḍa citra,
ei baḍa 'virodha-alaṅkāra'

SYNONYMS

mitrera—of the sun-god; *mitra*—the friend; *saha-vāsī*—living together with the *cakravāka* birds; *cakravāke*—the *cakravāka* birds; *luṭe*—plunder; *āsi'*—coming; *kṛṣṇera rājye*—in the kingdom of Kṛṣṇa; *aiche*—such; *vyavahāra*—behavior; *aparicita*—unacquainted; *śatrura mitra*—the friend of the enemy; *rākhe*—protects; *utpala*—the red lotus flower; *e*—this; *baḍa citra*—very wonderful; *ei*—this; *baḍa*—great; *virodha-alaṅkāra*—metaphor of contradiction.

TRANSLATION

"The blue lotuses are friends of the sun-god, and though they all live together, the blue lotuses plunder the cakravākas. The red lotuses, however, blossom at night and are therefore strangers or enemies to the cakravākas. Yet

in Kṛṣṇa's pastimes the red lotuses, which are the hands of the gopīs, protect their cakravāka breasts. This is a metaphor of contradiction."

PURPORT

Because the blue lotus flower blossoms with the rising of the sun, the sun is the friend of the blue lotus. The *cakravāka* birds also appear when the sun rises, and therefore the *cakravākas* and blue lotuses meet. Although the blue lotus is a friend of the sun, in Kṛṣṇa's pastimes it nevertheless plunders their mutual friend the *cakravāka.* Normally, *cakravākas* move about whereas lotuses stand still, but herein Kṛṣṇa's hands, which are compared to blue lotuses, attack the breasts of the *gopīs,* which are compared to *cakravākas.* This is called a reverse analogy. At night the red lotus blossoms, whereas in sunlight it closes. Therefore the red lotus is an enemy to the sun and is unknown to the sun's friend the *cakravāka.* The *gopīs'* breasts, however, are compared to *cakravākas* and their hands to red lotuses protecting them. This is a wonderful instance of reverse analogy.

TEXT 99

অতিশয়োক্তি, বিরোধাভাস, দুই অলঙ্কার প্রকাশ,
করি' কৃষ্ণ প্রকট দেখাইল ।
যাহা করি' আস্বাদন, আনন্দিত মোর মন,
নেত্র-কর্ণ-যুগ্ম জুড়াইল ॥ ৯৯ ॥

atiśayokti, virodhābhāsa, dui alaṅkāra prakāśa,
kari' kṛṣṇa prakaṭa dekhāila
yāhā kari' āsvādana, ānandita mora mana,
netra-karṇa-yugma juḍāila

SYNONYMS

atiśaya-ukti—exaggerated language; *virodha-ābhāsa*—incongruent analogy; *dui alaṅkāra*—two metaphors; *prakāśa*—manifestations; *kari'*—making; *kṛṣṇa*—Lord Kṛṣṇa; *prakaṭa*—exhibited; *dekhāila*—showed; *yāhā*—which; *kari' āsvādana*—tasting; *ānandita*—pleased; *mora mana*—My mind; *netra-karṇa*—of eyes and ears; *yugma*—the couples; *juḍāila*—became satisfied.

TRANSLATION

Śrī Caitanya Mahāprabhu continued, "In His pastimes, Kṛṣṇa displayed the two ornaments of hyperbole and reverse analogy. Tasting them brought gladness to My mind and fully satisfied My ears and eyes.

TEXT 100

ঐছে বিচিত্র ক্রীড়া করি', তীরে আইলা শ্রীহরি,
সঙ্গে লঞা সব কান্তাগণ ।
গন্ধ-তৈল-মর্দন, আমলকী-উদ্বর্তন,
সেবা করে তীরে সখীগণ ॥ ১০০ ॥

aiche vicitra krīḍā kari', tīre āilā śrī-hari,
saṅge lañā saba kāntā-gaṇa
gandha-taila-mardana, āmalakī-udvartana,
sevā kare tīre sakhī-gaṇa

SYNONYMS

aiche—such; *vicitra*—wonderful; *krīḍā*—pastimes; *kari'*—performing; *tīre*—on the bank; *āilā*—arrived; *śrī-hari*—Lord Śrī Kṛṣṇa; *saṅge*—with Him; *lañā*—taking; *saba kāntā-gaṇa*—all the beloved *gopīs; gandha*—scented; *taila*—oil; *mardana*—massaging; *āmalakī*—of the *āmalakī* fruit; *udvartana*—annointing with paste; *sevā kare*—render service; *tīre*—on the bank of the Yamunā; *sakhī-gaṇa*—all the *gopīs.*

TRANSLATION

"After performing such wonderful pastimes, Lord Śrī Kṛṣṇa got up on the shore of the Yamunā River, taking with Him all His beloved gopīs. Then the gopīs on the riverbank rendered service by massaging Kṛṣṇa and the other gopīs with scented oil and smearing paste of āmalakī fruit on their bodies.

TEXT 101

পুনরপি কৈল স্নান, শুষ্কবস্ত্র পরিধান,
রত্ন-মন্দিরে কৈলা আগমন ।
বৃন্দা-কৃত সম্ভার, গন্ধপুষ্প-অলঙ্কার,
বন্যবেশ করিল রচন ॥ ১০১ ॥

punarapi kaila snāna, śuṣka-vastra paridhāna,
ratna-mandire kailā āgamana
vṛndā-kṛta sambhāra, gandha-puṣpa-alaṅkāra,
vanya-veśa karila racana

SYNONYMS

punarapi—again; *kaila*—took; *snāna*—bath; *śuṣka-vastra*—dry cloth; *paridhāna*—putting on; *ratna-mandire*—in a small house of jewels; *kailā*—did;

āgamana—arrival; *vṛndā-kṛta*—arranged by the *gopī* Vṛndā; *sambhāra*—all kinds of articles; *gandha-puṣpa-alaṅkāra*—scented flowers and ornaments; *vanya-veśa*—forest dress; *karila*—did; *racana*—arrangement.

TRANSLATION

"Then they all bathed again, and after putting on dry clothing, they went to a small jeweled house, where the gopī Vṛndā arranged to dress them in forest clothing by decorating them with fragrant flowers, green leaves and all kinds of other ornaments.

TEXT 102

বৃন্দাবনে তরুলতা, অদ্ভুত তাহার কথা,
বারমাস ধরে ফুল-ফল ।
বৃন্দাবনে দেবীগণ, কুঞ্জদাসী যত জন,
ফল পাড়ি' আনিয়া সকল ॥ ১০২ ॥

vṛndāvane taru-latā, adbhuta tāhāra kathā,
bāra-māsa dhare phula-phala
vṛndāvane devī-gaṇa, kuñja-dāsī yata jana,
phala pāḍi' āniyā sakala

SYNONYMS

vṛndāvane—at Vṛndāvana; *taru-latā*—trees and creepers; *adbhuta*—wonderful; *tāhāra kathā*—their story; *bāra-māsa*—twelve months; *dhare*—produce; *phula-phala*—fruits and flowers; *vṛndāvane*—at Vṛndāvana; *devī-gaṇa*—all the *gopīs; kuñja-dāsī*—maidservants in the bowers; *yata jana*—as many persons as there are; *phala pāḍi'*—picking fruits; *āniyā*—bringing; *sakala*—all varieties.

TRANSLATION

"In Vṛndāvana, the trees and creepers are wonderful because throughout the entire year they produce all kinds of fruits and flowers. The gopīs and maidservants in the bowers of Vṛndāvana pick these fruits and flowers and bring them before Rādhā and Kṛṣṇa.

TEXT 103

উত্তম সংস্কার করি', বড় বড় থালী ভরি',
রত্ন-মন্দিরে পিণ্ডার উপরে ।
ভক্ষণের ক্রম করি', ধরিয়াছে সারি সারি,
আগে আসন বসিবার তরে ॥ ১০৩ ॥

uttama saṁskāra kari', baḍa baḍa thālī bhari',
ratna-mandire piṇḍāra upare
bhakṣaṇera krama kari', dhariyāche sāri sāri,
āge āsana vasibāra tare

SYNONYMS

uttama—topmost; *saṁskāra*—cleaning; *kari'*—doing; *baḍa baḍa*—big; *thālī*—plates; *bhari'*—filling up; *ratna-mandire*—in the house of jewels; *piṇḍāra upare*—on the platform; *bhakṣaṇera krama kari'*—making arrangements for eating; *dhariyāche*—have kept; *sāri sāri*—one after another; *āge*—in front; *āsana*—sitting place; *vasibāra tare*—to sit down.

TRANSLATION

"The gopīs peeled all the fruits and placed them together on large plates on a platform in the jeweled cottage. They arranged the fruit in orderly rows for eating, and in front of it they made a place to sit.

TEXT 104

এক নারিকেল নানা-জাতি, এক আম্র নানা ভাতি,
কলা, কোলি—বিবিধপ্রকার।
পনস, খর্জুর, কমলা, নারঙ্গ, জাম, সন্তরা,
দ্রাক্ষা, বাদাম, মেওয়া যত আর ॥ ১০৪ ॥

eka nārikela nānā-jāti, eka āmra nānā bhāti,
kalā, koli——vividha-prakāra
panasa, kharjura, kamalā, nāraṅga, jāma, santarā,
drākṣā, bādāma, meoyā yata āra

SYNONYMS

eka—one item; *nārikela*—coconut; *nānā-jāti*—of many varieties; *eka*—one; *āmra*—mango; *nānā bhāti*—of many different qualities; *kalā*—banana; *koli*—berries; *vividha-prakāra*—of different varieties; *panasa*—jackfruit; *kharjura*—dates; *kamalā*—tangerines; *nāraṅga*—oranges; *jāma*—blackberries; *santarā*—another type of tangerine; *drākṣā*—grapes; *bādāma*—almonds; *meoyā*—dried fruits; *yata*—as many as there are; *āra*—and.

TRANSLATION

"Among the fruits were many varieties of coconut and mango, bananas, berries, jackfruits, dates, tangerines, oranges, blackberries, santarās, grapes, almonds and all kinds of dried fruit.

TEXT 105

খরমুজা, ক্ষীরিকা, তাল, কেশুর, পানীফল, মৃণাল,
বিল্ব, পীলু, দাড়িম্বাদি যত।
কোন দেশে কার খ্যাতি, বৃন্দাবনে সব-প্রাপ্তি,
সহস্রজাতি, লেখা যায় কত ? ১০৫ ॥

kharamujā, kṣīrikā, tāla, keśura, pānī-phala, mṛṇāla,
bilva, pīlu, dāḍimbādi yata
kona deśe kāra khyāti, vṛndāvane saba-prāpti,
sahasra-jāti, lekhā yāya kata?

SYNONYMS

kharamujā—cantaloupe; *kṣīrikā*—*kṣīrikā* fruit; *tāla*—palm or palmyra fruit *keśura*—*keśura* fruit; *pānī-phala*—a fruit produced in the water of rivers; *mṛṇāla*—a fruit from lotus flowers; *bilva*—bel fruit; *pīlu*—a special fruit in Vṛndāvana; *dāḍimba-ādi*—the pomegranate and other similar fruits; *yata*—as many as there are; *kona deśe*—in some country; *kāra*—of which; *khyāti*—of fame; *vṛndāvane*—in Vṛndāvana; *saba-prāpti*—obtainment of all; *sahasra-jāti*—thousands of varieties; *lekhā yāya*—one is able to write; *kata*—how much.

TRANSLATION

"There were cantaloupes, kṣirikās, palmfruits, keśuras, waterfruits, lotus fruits, bel, pīlu, pomegranate and many others. Some of them are variously known in different places, but in Vṛndāvana they are always available in so many thousands of varieties that no one can fully describe them.

TEXT 106

গঙ্গাজল, অমৃতকেলি, পীযূষগ্রন্থি, কর্পূরকেলি,
সরপূরী, অমৃতি, পদ্মচিনি।
খণ্ডক্ষীরিসার-বৃক্ষ, ঘরে করি' নানা ভক্ষ্য,
রাধা যাহা কৃষ্ণ লাগি' আনি ॥ ১০৬ ॥

gaṅgājala, amṛtakeli, pīyūṣagranthi, karpūrakeli,
sarapūrī, amṛti, padmacini
khaṇḍa-kṣīrisāra-vṛkṣa, ghare kari' nānā bhakṣya,
rādhā yāhā kṛṣṇa lāgi' āni

SYNONYMS

gaṅgā-jala—the sweetmeat *gaṅgājala; amṛta-keli*—a sweetmeat made of milk; *pīyūṣa-granthi*—*pīyūṣagranthi; karpūra-keli*—*karpūrakeli; sara-pūrī*—a sweet made from milk; *amṛti*—a sweet prepared from rice flour; *padma-cini*—a sweet preparation made from lotus flowers; *khaṇḍa-kṣīri-sāra-vṛkṣa*—sugar sweets made in the shape of trees; *ghare*—at home; *kari'*—making; *nānā bhakṣya*—varieties of eatables; *rādhā*—Śrīmatī Rādhārāṇī; *yāhā*—which; *kṛṣṇa lāgi'*—for Kṛṣṇa; *āni*—brought.

TRANSLATION

"At home Śrīmatī Rādhārāṇī had made various types of sweetmeats from milk and sugar, such as gaṅgājala, amṛtakeli, pīyūṣagranthi, karpūrakeli, sarapūrī, amṛti, padmacini and khaṇḍa-kṣīrisāra-vṛkṣa. She had then brought them all for Kṛṣṇa.

TEXT 107

ভক্ষ্যের পরিপাটী দেখি', কৃষ্ণ হৈলা মহাসুখী,
বসি' কৈল বন্য ভোজন।
সঙ্গে লঞা সখীগণ, রাধা কৈলা ভোজন,
দুঁহে কৈলা মন্দিরে শয়ন ॥ ১০৭ ॥

bhakṣyera paripāṭī dekhi', kṛṣṇa hailā mahā-sukhī,
vasi' kaila vanya bhojana
saṅge lañā sakhī-gaṇa, rādhā kailā bhojana,
duṅhe kailā mandire śayana

SYNONYMS

bhakṣyera—of eatables; *paripāṭī*—the arrangements; *dekhi'*—seeing; *kṛṣṇa*—Lord Kṛṣṇa; *hailā*—became; *mahā-sukhī*—very happy; *vasi'*—sitting down; *kaila*—performed; *vanya bhojana*—a picnic in the forest; *saṅge*—in association; *lañā*—taking; *sakhī-gaṇa*—all the *gopīs; rādhā*—Śrīmatī Rādhārāṇī; *kailā bhojana*—took the remnants; *duṅhe*—both of them; *kailā*—did; *mandire*—in the jeweled house; *śayana*—lying down.

TRANSLATION

"When Kṛṣṇa saw the very nice arrangement of food, He happily sat down and had a forest picnic. Then, after Śrīmatī Rādhārāṇī and Her gopī friends partook of the remnants, Rādhā and Kṛṣṇa lay down together in the jeweled house.

TEXT 108

কেহ করে বীজন, কেহ পাদসম্বাহন,
কেহ করায় তাম্বূল ভক্ষণ ।
রাধাকৃষ্ণ নিদ্রা গেলা, সখীগণ শয়ন কৈলা,
দেখি' আমার সুখী হৈল মন ॥ ১০৮ ॥

keha kare vījana, keha pāda-saṁvāhana,
keha karāya tāmbūla bhakṣaṇa
rādhā-kṛṣṇa nidrā gelā, sakhī-gaṇa śayana kailā,
dekhi' āmāra sukhī haila mana

SYNONYMS

keha—someone; *kare*—does; *vījana*—fanning; *keha*—someone; *pāda-saṁvāhana*—massaging of the feet; *keha*—someone; *karāya*—made them do; *tāmbūla bhakṣaṇa*—eating a preparation of betel leaves; *rādhā-kṛṣṇa*—Rādhā and Kṛṣṇa; *nidrā gelā*—went to sleep; *sakhī-gaṇa*—all the *gopīs; śayana kailā*—lay down; *dekhi'*—seeing; *āmāra*—My; *sukhī*—happy; *haila*—became; *mana*—mind.

TRANSLATION

"Some of the gopīs fanned Rādhā and Kṛṣṇa, others massaged Their feet, and some fed Them betel leaves to chew. When Rādhā and Kṛṣṇa fell asleep, all the other gopīs also lay down. When I saw this, My mind was very happy.

TEXT 109

হেনকালে মোরে ধরি', মহাকোলাহল করি',
তুমি-সব ইহঁা লঞা আইলা ।
কাঁহা যমুনা, বৃন্দাবন, কাঁহা কৃষ্ণ, গোপীগণ,
সেই সুখ ভঙ্গ করাইলা !" ১০৯ ॥

hena-kāle more dhari', mahā-kolāhala kari',
tumi-saba ihāṅ lañā āilā
kāṅhā yamunā, vṛndāvana, kāṅhā kṛṣṇa, gopī-gaṇa,
sei sukha bhaṅga karāilā!"

SYNONYMS

hena-kāle—at that time; *more dhari'*—picking Me up; *mahā-kolāhala kari'*—and making a great tumult; *tumi-saba*—all of you; *ihāṅ*—here; *lañā āilā*—

brought; *kāṅhā*—where; *yamunā*—the Yamunā River; *vṛndāvana*—Vṛndāvana; *kāṅhā*—where; *kṛṣṇa*—Kṛṣṇa; *gopī-gaṇa*—the *gopīs; sei sukha*—that happiness; *bhaṅga karāilā*—you have broken.

TRANSLATION

"Suddenly, all of you created a great tumult and picked Me up and brought Me back here. Where now is the River Yamunā? Where is Vṛndāvana? Where are Kṛṣṇa and the gopīs? You have broken My happy dream!"

TEXT 110

এতেক কহিতে প্রভুর কেবল 'বাহ্য' হৈল ।
স্বরূপ-গোসাঞিরে দেখি' তাঁহারে পুছিল ॥ ১১০ ॥

eteka kahite prabhura kevala 'bāhya' haila
svarūpa-gosāñire dekhi' tāṅhāre puchila

SYNONYMS

eteka—this; *kahite*—while speaking; *prabhura*—of Śrī Caitanya Mahāprabhu; *kevala*—only; *bāhya*—external consciousness; *haila*—there was; *svarūpa-gosāñire*—Svarūpa Gosāñi; *dekhi'*—seeing; *tāṅhāre puchila*—He asked him.

TRANSLATION

Speaking in this way, Śrī Caitanya Mahāprabhu fully returned to external consciousness. Seeing Svarūpa Dāmodara Gosvāmī, the Lord questioned him.

TEXT 111

'ইহাঁ কেনে তোমরা আমারে লঞা আইলা ?'
স্বরূপ-গোসাঞি তবে কহিতে লাগিলা ॥ ১১১ ॥

'ihāṅ kene tomarā āmāre lañā āilā?'
svarūpa-gosāñi tabe kahite lāgilā

SYNONYMS

ihāṅ—here; *kene*—why; *tomarā*—you; *āmāre*—Me; *lañā āilā*—have brought; *svarūpa-gosāñi*—Svarūpa Dāmodara Gosāñi; *tabe*—at that time; *kahite lāgilā*—began to speak.

TRANSLATION

"Why have you brought Me here?" He asked. Then Svarūpa Dāmodara answered Him.

TEXT 112

"যমুনার ভ্রমে তুমি সমুদ্রে পড়িলা ।
সমুদ্রের তরঙ্গে আসি, এত দূর আইলা ! ১১২ ॥

"yamunāra bhrame tumi samudre paḍilā
samudrera taraṅge āsi, eta dūra āilā!

SYNONYMS

yamunāra bhrame—in mistaking for the Yamunā; *tumi*—You; *samudre*—in the sea; *paḍilā*—fell; *samudrera taraṅge*—by the waves of the sea; *āsi*—coming; *eta*—this; *dūra*—far; *āilā*—You have come.

TRANSLATION

"You mistook the sea for the Yamunā River," he said, "and You jumped into it. You have been carried this far by the waves of the sea.

TEXT 113

এই জালিয়া জালে করি' তোমা উঠাইল ।
তোমার পরশে এই প্রেমে মত্ত হইল ॥ ১১৩ ॥

ei jāliyā jāle kari' tomā uṭhāila
tomāra paraśe ei preme matta ha-ila

SYNONYMS

ei jāliyā—this fisherman; *jāle*—in the net; *kari'*—catching; *tomā*—You; *uṭhāila*—rescued from the water; *tomāra paraśe*—by Your touch; *ei*—this man; *preme*—in ecstatic love; *matta ha-ila*—became maddened.

TRANSLATION

"This fisherman caught You in his net and rescued You from the water. Because of Your touch, he is now mad with ecstatic love for Kṛṣṇa.

TEXT 114

সব রাত্রি সবে বেড়াই তোমারে অন্বেষিয়া ।
জালিয়ার মুখে শুনি' পাইনু আসিয়া ॥ ১১৪ ॥

saba rātri sabe beḍāi tomāre anveṣiyā
jāliyāra mukhe śuni' pāinu āsiyā

SYNONYMS

saba rātri—the whole night; *sabe*—all of us; *beḍāi*—walked; *tomāre*—You; *anveṣiyā*—searching for; *jāliyāra mukhe*—from the mouth of this fisherman; *śuni'*—hearing; *pāinu*—we found; *āsiyā*—coming.

TRANSLATION

"Throughout the night, we all walked about in search of You. After hearing from this fisherman, we came here and found You.

TEXT 115

তুমি মূর্চ্ছা-ছলে বৃন্দাবনে দেখ ক্রীড়া।
তোমার মূর্চ্ছা দেখি' সবে মনে পাই পীড়া ॥ ১১৫ ॥

tumi mūrcchā-chale vṛndāvane dekha krīḍā
tomāra mūrcchā dekhi' sabe mane pāi pīḍā

SYNONYMS

tumi—You; *mūrcchā-chale*—pretending to be unconscious; *vṛndāvane*—at Vṛndāvana; *dekha*—see; *krīḍā*—the pastimes; *tomāra mūrcchā dekhi'*—seeing Your unconsciousness; *sabe*—all of us; *mane*—in the mind; *pāi*—get; *pīḍā*—agony.

TRANSLATION

"While apparently unconscious, You witnessed the pastimes in Vṛndāvana, but when we saw You unconscious, we suffered great agony in our minds.

TEXT 116

কৃষ্ণনাম লইতে তোমার 'অর্ধবাহ্য' হইল।
তাতে যে প্রলাপ কৈলা, তাহা যে শুনিল ॥" ১১৬ ॥

kṛṣṇa-nāma la-ite tomāra 'ardha-bāhya' ha-ila
tāte ye pralāpa kailā, tāhā ye śunila"

SYNONYMS

kṛṣṇa-nāma la-ite—chanting the holy name of Kṛṣṇa; *tomāra*—Your; *ardha-bāhya*—half-consciousness; *ha-ila*—there was; *tāte*—thereafter; *ye*—whatever; *pralāpa*—crazy talks; *kailā*—You did; *tāhā*—that; *ye*—which; *śunila*—have heard.

TRANSLATION

"When we chanted the holy name of Kṛṣṇa, however, You came to semi-consciousness, and we have all been hearing You speak like a madman."

TEXT 117

প্রভু কহে,—"স্বপ্নে দেখি' গেলাঙ বৃন্দাবনে ।
দেখি,—কৃষ্ণ রাস করেন গোপীগণ-সনে ॥ ১১৭ ॥

prabhu kahe,——"svapne dekhi' gelāṅa vṛndāvane
dekhi,——kṛṣṇa rāsa karena gopīgaṇa-sane

SYNONYMS

prabhu kahe—Śrī Caitanya Mahāprabhu said; *svapne dekhi'*—dreaming; *gelāṅa vṛndāvane*—I went to Vṛndāvana; *dekhi*—I see; *kṛṣṇa*—Lord Kṛṣṇa; *rāsa karena*—performs the *rāsa* dance; *gopī-gaṇa-sane*—with the *gopīs*.

TRANSLATION

Śrī Caitanya Mahāprabhu said, "In My dream I went to Vṛndāvana, where I saw Lord Kṛṣṇa perform the rāsa dance with all the gopīs.

TEXT 118

জলক্রীড়া করি' কৈলা বন্য-ভোজনে ।
দেখি' আমি প্রলাপ কৈলুঁ—হেন লয় মনে ॥"১১৮॥

jala-krīḍā kari' kailā vanya-bhojane
dekhi' āmi pralāpa kailuṅ——hena laya mane"

SYNONYMS

jala-krīḍā—sports in the water; *kari'*—performing; *kailā*—had; *vanya-bhojane*—a picnic; *dekhi'*—seeing; *āmi*—I; *pralāpa kailuṅ*—talked crazily; *hena*—such; *laya*—takes; *mane*—in My mind.

TRANSLATION

"After sporting in the water, Kṛṣṇa enjoyed a picnic. I can understand that after seeing this, I must certainly have talked like a madman."

TEXT 119

তবে স্বরূপ-গোসাঞি তাঁরে স্নান করাঞা ।
প্রভুরে লঞা ঘর আইলা আনন্দিত হঞা ॥ ১১৯ ॥

tabe svarūpa-gosāñi tāṅre snāna karāñā
prabhure lañā ghara āilā ānandita hañā

SYNONYMS

tabe—thereafter; *svarūpa-gosāñi*—Svarūpa Dāmodara Gosāñi; *tāṅre*—Him; *snāna karāñā*—causing to bathe; *prabhure*—Śrī Caitanya Mahāprabhu; *lañā*—taking; *ghara āilā*—came back to His house; *ānandita hañā*—being very happy.

TRANSLATION

Thereafter, Svarūpa Dāmodara Gosvāmī had Lord Śrī Caitanya Mahāprabhu bathe in the sea, and then he very happily brought Him back home.

TEXT 120

এই ত' কহিলুঁ প্রভুর সমুদ্র-পতন ।
ইহা যেই শুনে, পায় চৈতন্য-চরণ ॥ ১২০ ॥

ei ta' kahiluṅ prabhura samudra-patana
ihā yei śune, pāya caitanya-caraṇa

SYNONYMS

ei ta'—thus; *kahiluṅ*—I have described; *prabhura*—of Śrī Caitanya Mahāprabhu; *samudra-patana*—the falling into the sea; *ihā*—this story; *yei śune*—anyone who hears; *pāya*—obtains; *caitanya-caraṇa*—shelter at the lotus feet of Śrī Caitanya Mahāprabhu.

TRANSLATION

Thus I have described the incident of Lord Śrī Caitanya Mahāprabhu's falling into the ocean. Anyone who listens to this pastime will certainly attain shelter at the lotus feet of Śrī Caitanya Mahāprabhu.

TEXT 121

শ্রীরূপ রঘুনাথ-পদে যার আশ ।
চৈতন্যচরিতামৃত কহে কৃষ্ণদাস ॥ ১২১ ॥

śrī-rūpa-raghunātha pade yāra āśa
caitanya-caritāmṛta kahe kṛṣṇadasa

SYNONYMS

śrī-rūpa—Śrīla Rūpa Gosvāmī; *raghunātha*—Śrīla Raghunātha dāsa Gosvāmī; *pade*—at the lotus feet; *yāra*—whose; *āśa*—expectation; *caitanya-caritāmṛta*—the book named *Caitanya-caritāmṛta; kahe*—describes; *kṛṣṇadāsa*—Śrīla Kṛṣṇadāsa Kavirāja Gosvāmī.

TRANSLATION

Praying at the lotus feet of Śrī Rūpa and Śrī Raghunātha, always desiring their mercy, I, Kṛṣṇadāsa, narrate Śrī Caitanya-caritāmṛta, following in their footsteps.

Thus end the Bhaktivedanta purports to the Śrī Caitanya-caritāmṛta, Antya-līlā, *Eighteenth Chapter, describing Lord Śrī Caitanya Mahāprabhu's falling into the water of the sea.*

CHAPTER 19

The Inconceivable Behavior of Lord Śrī Caitanya Mahāprabhu

The following summary of Chapter Nineteen is given by Śrīla Bhaktivinoda Ṭhākura in his *Amṛta-pravāha-bhāṣya.*

Every year, Śrī Caitanya Mahāprabhu asked Jagadānanda Paṇḍita to visit His mother in Navadvīpa with gifts of cloth and *prasāda.* After one such visit, Jagadānanda Paṇḍita returned to Purī with a sonnet that Advaita Ācārya had written. When Śrī Caitanya Mahāprabhu read it, His ecstasy was so great that all the devotees feared that the Lord would very soon pass away. The Lord's condition was so serious that at night He would bruise and bloody His face by rubbing it against the walls. To stop this, Svarūpa Dāmodara asked Śaṅkara Paṇḍita to stay at night in the same room with the Lord.

This chapter further describes how Lord Śrī Caitanya Mahāprabhu entered the Jagannātha-vallabha garden during the full-moon night of Vaiśākha (April-May) and experienced various transcendental ecstasies. Overwhelmed with ecstatic love at sucdenly seeing Lord Śrī Kṛṣṇa beneath an *aśoka* tree, He exhibited various symptoms of spiritual madness.

TEXT 1

বন্দে তং কৃষ্ণচৈতন্যং মাতৃভক্তশিরোমণিম্ ।
প্রলপ্য মুখসংঘর্ষী মধূদ্যানে ললাস যঃ ॥ ১ ॥

vande taṁ kṛṣṇa-caitanyaṁ
mātṛ-bhakta-śiromaṇim
pralapya mukha-saṅgharṣī
madhūdyāne lalāsa yaḥ

SYNONYMS

vande—I offer my respectful obeisances; *tam*—unto Him; *kṛṣṇa-caitanyam*—Lord Śrī Caitanya Mahāprabhu; *mātṛ-bhakta*—of great devotees of mothers; *śiromaṇim*—the crown jewel; *pralapya*—talking like a madman; *mukha-*

saṅgharṣī—who used to rub His face; *madhu-udyāne*—in the garden known as Jagannātha-vallabha; *lalāsa*—enjoyed; *yaḥ*—who.

TRANSLATION

Lord Śrī Caitanya Mahāprabhu, the most exalted of all devotees of mothers, spoke like a madman and rubbed His face against the walls. Overwhelmed by emotions of ecstatic love, He would sometimes enter the Jagannātha-vallabha garden to perform His pastimes. I offer my respectful obeisances unto Him.

TEXT 2

জয় জয় শ্রীচৈতন্য জয় নিত্যানন্দ ।
জয়াদ্বৈতচন্দ্র জয় গৌরভক্তবৃন্দ ॥ ২ ॥

jaya jaya śrī-caitanya jaya nityānanda
jayādvaita-candra jaya gaura-bhakta-vṛnda

SYNONYMS

jaya jaya—all glories; *śrī-caitanya*—to Lord Śrī Caitanya Mahāprabhu; *jaya*—all glories; *nityānanda*—to Nityānanda Prabhu; *jaya*—all glories; *advaita-candra*—to Advaita Ācārya; *jaya*—all glories; *gaura-bhakta-vṛnda*—to the devotees of Lord Gaurāṅga.

TRANSLATION

All glories to Śrī Caitanya Mahāprabhu! All glories to Lord Nityānanda! All glories to Advaita Ācārya! And all glories to all the devotees of Lord Caitanya Mahāprabhu!

TEXT 3

এইমতে মহাপ্রভু কৃষ্ণপ্রেমাবেশে ।
উন্মাদ-প্রলাপ করে রাত্রি-দিবসে ॥ ৩ ॥

ei-mate mahāprabhu kṛṣṇa-premāveśe
unmāda-pralāpa kare rātri-divase

SYNONYMS

ei-mate—in this way; *mahāprabhu*—Śrī Caitanya Mahāprabhu; *kṛṣṇa-prema-āveśe*—in ecstatic emotional love of Kṛṣṇa; *unmāda*—madness; *pralāpa*—and crazy talk; *kare*—performs; *rātri-divase*—throughout the entire day and night.

TRANSLATION

In the ecstasy of love of Kṛṣṇa, Śrī Caitanya Mahāprabhu thus behaved like a madman, talking insanely all day and night.

TEXT 4

প্রভুর অত্যন্ত প্রিয় পণ্ডিত-জগদানন্দ ।
যাহার চরিত্রে প্রভু পায়েন আনন্দ ॥ ৪ ॥

prabhura atyanta priya paṇḍita-jagadānanda
yāhāra caritre prabhu pāyena ānanda

SYNONYMS

prabhura—of Śrī Caitanya Mahāprabhu; *atyanta*—very; *priya*—affectionate; *paṇḍita-jagadānanda*—Jagadānanda Paṇḍita; *yāhāra caritre*—in whose activities; *prabhu*—Śrī Caitanya Mahāprabhu; *pāyena*—gets; *ānanda*—great pleasure.

TRANSLATION

Jagadānanda Paṇḍita was a very dear devotee of Śrī Caitanya Mahāprabhu. The Lord derived great pleasure from his activities.

TEXT 5

প্রতিবৎসর প্রভু তাঁরে পাঠান নদীয়াতে ।
বিচ্ছেদ-দুঃখিতা জানি' জননী আশ্বাসিতে ॥ ৫ ॥

prati-vatsara prabhu tāṅre pāṭhāna nadīyāte
viccheda-duḥkhitā jāni' jananī āśvāsite

SYNONYMS

prati-vatsara—every year; *prabhu*—Śrī Caitanya Mahāprabhu; *tāṅre*—him; *pāṭhāna*—sends; *nadīyāte*—to Navadvīpa; *viccheda-duḥkhitā jāni'*—knowing her affliction due to separation; *jananī*—His mother; *āśvāsite*—to console.

TRANSLATION

Knowing His mother to be greatly afflicted by separation, the Lord would send Jagadānanda Paṇḍita to Navadvīpa every year to console her.

TEXT 6

"নদীয়া চলহ, মাতারে কহিহ নমস্কার ।
আমার নামে পাদপদ্ম ধরিহ তাঁহার ॥ ৬ ॥

"nadīyā calaha, mātāre kahiha namaskāra
āmāra nāme pāda-padma dhariha tāṅhāra

SYNONYMS

nadīyā calaha—start for Nadia; *mātāre*—unto My mother; *kahiha*—tell; *namaskāra*—My obeisances; *āmāra nāme*—in My name; *pāda-padma*—the lotus feet; *dhariha*—catch; *tāṅhāra*—her.

TRANSLATION

Śrī Caitanya Mahāprabhu told Jagadānanda Paṇḍita, "Go to Nadia and offer My obeisances to My mother. Touch her lotus feet in My name.

TEXT 7

কহিহ তাঁহারে—'তুমি করহ স্মরণ ।
নিত্য আসি' আমি তোমার বন্দিয়ে চরণ ॥ ৭ ॥

kahiha tāṅhāre—'tumi karaha smaraṇa
nitya āsi' āmi tomāra vandiye caraṇa

SYNONYMS

kahiha tāṅhāre—inform her; *tumi karaha smaraṇa*—please remember; *nitya āsi'*—coming daily; *āmi*—I; *tomāra*—your; *vandiye caraṇa*—offer respect to the lotus feet.

TRANSLATION

"Tell her for Me, 'Please remember that I come here every day and offer My respects to your lotus feet.

TEXT 8

যে-দিনে তোমার ইচ্ছা করাইতে ভোজন ।
সে-দিনে আসি' অবশ্য করিয়ে ভক্ষণ ॥ ৮ ॥

ye-dine tomāra icchā karāite bhojana
se-dine āsi' avaśya kariye bhakṣaṇa

SYNONYMS

ye-dine—any day; *tomāra*—your; *icchā*—desire; *karāite bhojana*—to feed Me; *se-dine*—on that day; *āsi'*—coming; *avaśya*—certainly; *kariye bhakṣaṇa*—I eat.

TRANSLATION

" 'Any day you desire to feed Me, I certainly come and accept what you offer.

TEXT 9

তোমার সেবা ছাড়ি' আমি করিলুঁ সন্ন্যাস।
'বাউল' হঞা আমি কৈলুঁ ধর্মনাশ ॥ ৯ ॥

tomāra sevā chāḍi' āmi kariluṅ sannyāsa
'bāula' hañā āmi kailuṅ dharma-nāśa

SYNONYMS

tomāra sevā chāḍi'—giving up your service; *āmi*—I; *kariluṅ*—accepted; *sannyāsa*—the renounced order of life; *bāula hañā*—becoming mad; *āmi*—I; *kailuṅ*—did; *dharma-nāśa*—destruction of religion.

TRANSLATION

" 'I have given up service to you and have accepted the vow of sannyāsa. I have thus become mad and have destroyed the principles of religion.

TEXT 10

এই অপরাধ তুমি না লইহ আমার।
তোমার অধীন আমি—পুত্র সে তোমার ॥ ১০ ॥

ei aparādha tumi nā la-iha āmāra
tomāra adhīna āmi——putra se tomāra

SYNONYMS

ei aparādha—this offense; *tumi*—you; *nā*—do not; *la-iha*—take; *āmāra*—of Me; *tomāra*—your; *adhīna*—dependent; *āmi*—I; *putra*—son; *se*—that; *tomāra*—of you.

TRANSLATION

" 'Mother, please do not take this as an offense, for I, your son, am completely dependent upon you.

TEXT 11

নীলাচলে আছি আমি তোমার আজ্ঞাতে।
যাবৎ জীব, তাবৎ আমি নারিব ছাড়িতে॥' ১১ ॥

nīlācale āchi āmi tomāra ājñāte
yāvat jība, tāvat āmi nāriba chāḍite'

SYNONYMS

nīlācale—Jagannātha Purī, Nīlācala; *āchi āmi*—I am; *tomāra ājñāte*—on the basis of your order; *yāvat jība*—as long as I live; *tāvat*—so long; *āmi*—I; *nāriba*—shall not be able; *chāḍite*—to leave.

TRANSLATION

" 'I am staying here at Nīlācala, Jagannātha Purī, according to your order. As long as I live, I shall not leave this place.' "

TEXT 12

গোপ-লীলায় পাইলা যেই প্রসাদ-বসনে।
মাতারে পাঠান তাহা পুরীর বচনে॥ ১২ ॥

gopa-līlāya pāilā yei prasāda-vasane
mātāre pāṭhāna tāhā purīra vacane

SYNONYMS

gopa-līlāya—in His pastimes as a cowherd boy; *pāilā*—got; *yei*—whatever; *prasāda*—remnant; *vasane*—clothing; *mātāre*—unto His mother; *pāṭhāna*—sent; *tāhā*—that; *purīra vacane*—on the order of Paramānanda Purī.

TRANSLATION

Following the order of Paramānanda Purī, Śrī Caitanya Mahāprabhu sent His mother the prasāda clothing left by Lord Jagannātha after His pastimes as a cowherd boy.

TEXT 13

জগন্নাথের উত্তম প্রসাদ আনিয়া যতনে।
মাতারে পৃথক্ পাঠান, আর ভক্তগণে॥ ১৩ ॥

jagannāthera uttama prasāda āniyā yatane
mātāre pṛthak pāṭhāna, āra bhakta-gaṇe

SYNONYMS

jagannāthera—of Lord Jagannātha; *uttama*—first class; *prasāda*—remnants of food; *āniyā yatane*—bringing very carefully; *mātāre*—unto His mother; *pṛthak*—separately; *pāṭhāna*—sends; *āra bhakta-gaṇe*—and to the other devotees.

TRANSLATION

Śrī Caitanya Mahāprabhu very carefully brought first-class prasāda from Lord Jagannātha and sent it in separate packages to His mother and the devotees at Nadia.

TEXT 14

মাতৃভক্তগণের প্রভু হন শিরোমণি ।
সন্ন্যাস করিয়া সদা সেবেন জননী ॥ ১৪ ॥

mātṛ-bhakta-gaṇera prabhu hana śiromaṇi
sannyāsa kariyā sadā sevena jananī

SYNONYMS

mātṛ-bhakta-gaṇera—of the devotees of mothers; *prabhu*—Śrī Caitanya Mahāprabhu; *hana*—is; *śiromaṇi*—the topmost jewel; *sannyāsa kariyā*—even after taking the *sannyāsa* order; *sadā*—always; *sevena*—renders service; *jananī*—to His mother.

TRANSLATION

Śrī Caitanya Mahāprabhu is the topmost gem of all devotees of mothers. He rendered service to His mother even after He had accepted the vow of sannyāsa.

TEXT 15

জগদানন্দ নদীয়া গিয়া মাতারে মিলিলা ।
প্রভুর যত নিবেদন, সকল কহিলা ॥ ১৫ ॥

jagadānanda nadīyā giyā mātāre mililā
prabhura yata nivedana, sakala kahilā

SYNONYMS

jagadānanda—Jagadānanda; *nadīyā*—to Navadvīpa; *giyā*—going; *mātāre*—mother Śacī; *mililā*—met; *prabhura*—of Śrī Caitanya Mahāprabhu; *yata nivedana*—all kinds of salutations; *sakala*—everything; *kahilā*—he told.

TRANSLATION

Jagadānanda Paṇḍita thus returned to Nadia, and when he met Śacīmātā, he conveyed to her all the Lord's salutations.

TEXT 16

আচার্যাদি ভক্তগণে মিলিলা প্রসাদ দিয়া।
মাতা-ঠাঞি আজ্ঞা লইলা মাসেক রহিয়া॥ ১৬॥

ācāryādi bhakta-gaṇe mililā prasāda diyā
mātā-ṭhāñi ājñā la-ilā māseka rahiyā

SYNONYMS

ācārya-ādi—beginning with Advaita Ācārya; *bhakta-gaṇe*—all the devotees; *mililā*—he met; *prasāda diyā*—delivering the *prasāda* of Lord Jagannātha; *mātā-ṭhāñi*—from mother Śacī; *ājñā la-ilā*—took permission to leave; *māseka rahiyā*—remaining for one month.

TRANSLATION

He then met all the other devotees, headed by Advaita Ācārya, and gave them the prasāda of Jagannātha. After staying for one month, he took permission from mother Śacī to leave.

TEXT 17

আচার্যের ঠাঞি গিয়া আজ্ঞা মাগিলা।
আচার্য-গোসাঞি প্রভুরে সন্দেশ কহিলা॥ ১৭॥

ācāryera ṭhāñi giyā ājñā māgilā
ācārya-gosāñi prabhure sandeśa kahilā

SYNONYMS

ācāryera ṭhāñi—to Advaita Ācārya; *giyā*—going; *ājñā māgilā*—begged for permission to leave; *ācārya-gosāñi*—Advaita Ācārya; *prabhure*—unto Śrī Caitanya Mahāprabhu; *sandeśa kahilā*—sent a message.

TRANSLATION

When he went to Advaita Ācārya and also asked His permission to return, Advaita Prabhu gave him a message to deliver to Śrī Caitanya Mahāprabhu.

TEXT 18

তরজা-প্রহেলী আচার্য কহেন ঠারে-ঠোরে ।
প্রভু মাত্র বুঝেন, কেহ বুঝিতে না পারে ॥ ১৮ ॥

tarajā-prahelī ācārya kahena ṭhāre-ṭhore
prabhu mātra bujhena, keha bujhite nā pāre

SYNONYMS

tarajā-prahelī—a sonnet in equivocal language; *ācārya*—Advaita Ācārya; *kahena*—spoke; *ṭhāre-ṭhore*—making some indications; *prabhu*—Śrī Caitanya Mahāprabhu; *mātra*—only; *bujhena*—could understand; *keha bujhite nā pāre*—others could not understand.

TRANSLATION

Advaita Ācārya had written a sonnet in equivocal language with an import that Śrī Caitanya Mahāprabhu could understand but others could not.

TEXT 19

"প্রভুরে কহিহ আমার কোটি নমস্কার ।
এই নিবেদন তাঁর চরণে আমার ॥ ১৯ ॥

"prabhure kahiha āmāra koṭi namaskāra
ei nivedana tāṅra caraṇe āmāra

SYNONYMS

prabhure kahiha—just inform Lord Caitanya; *āmāra*—My; *koṭi namaskāra*—hundreds and thousands of obeisances; *ei nivedana*—this is the submission; *tāṅra*—His; *caraṇe*—unto the lotus feet; *āmāra*—My.

TRANSLATION

In His sonnet, Advaita Prabhu first offered His obeisances hundreds and thousands of times unto the lotus feet of Lord Śrī Caitanya Mahāprabhu. He then submitted the following statement at His lotus feet.

TEXT 20

বাউলকে কহিহ,—লোক হইল বাউল ।
বাউলকে কহিহ,—হাটে না বিকায় চাউল ॥ ২০ ॥

bāulake kahiha,——loka ha-ila bāula
bāulake kahiha,——hāṭe nā vikāya cāula

SYNONYMS

bāulake kahiha—please inform Śrī Caitanya Mahāprabhu, who is playing the part of a madman in ecstatic love; *loka*—the people in general; *ha-ila*—have become; *bāula*—also mad in ecstatic love; *bāulake kahiha*—again inform Lord Śrī Caitanya Mahāprabhu, the *bāula; hāṭe*—in the market; *nā*—not; *vikāya*—sells; *cāula*—rice.

TRANSLATION

"Please inform Śrī Caitanya Mahāprabhu, who is acting like a madman, that everyone here has become mad like Him. Inform Him also that in the marketplace, rice is no longer in demand.

TEXT 21

বাউলকে কহিহ,– কাযে নাহিক আউল।
বাউলকে কহিহ,—ইহা কহিয়াছে বাউল ॥" ২১ ॥

bāulake kahiha,——kāye nāhika āula
bāulake kahiha,——ihā kahiyāche bāula"

SYNONYMS

bāulake kahiha—again inform the *bāula,* Śrī Caitanya Mahāprabhu; *kāye*—in business; *nāhika*—there is not; *āula*—persons who have become mad in ecstatic love; *bāulake kahiha*—again inform the *bāula,* Śrī Caitanya Mahāprabhu; *ihā*—this; *kahiyāche*—has spoken; *bāula*—another madman, Śrī Advaita Prabhu Himself.

TRANSLATION

"Those now mad in ecstatic love are no longer interested in the material world. Tell Śrī Caitanya Mahāprabhu that Advaita Prabhu, who has also become a madman in ecstatic love, has spoken these words."

TEXT 22

এত শুনি' জগদানন্দ হাসিতে লাগিলা।
নীলাচলে আসি' তবে প্রভুরে কহিলা ॥ ২২ ॥

eta śuni' jagadānanda hāsite lāgilā
nīlācale āsi' tabe prabhure kahilā

SYNONYMS

eta śuni'—hearing this; *jagadānanda*—Jagadānanda Paṇḍita; *hāsite lāgilā*—began to laugh; *nīlācale*—to Jagannātha Purī; *āsi'*—returning; *tabe*—then; *prabhure kahilā*—he told all this to Śrī Caitanya Mahāprabhu.

TRANSLATION

When he heard Advaita Ācārya's statement, Jagadānanda Paṇḍita began to laugh, and when he returned to Jagannātha Purī, Nīlācala, he informed Caitanya Mahāprabhu of everything.

TEXT 23

তরজা শুনি' মহাপ্রভু ঈষৎ হাসিলা।
'তাঁর যেই আজ্ঞা'– বলি' মৌন ধরিলা ॥ ২৩ ॥

tarajā śuni' mahāprabhu īṣat hāsilā
'tāṅra yei ājñā'——bali' mauna dharilā

SYNONYMS

tarajā śuni'—hearing the sonnet; *mahāprabhu*—Śrī Caitanya Mahāprabhu; *īṣat hāsilā*—quietly smiled; *tāṅra yei ājñā*—that is His order; *bali'*—saying; *mauna dharilā*—became silent.

TRANSLATION

After hearing the equivocal sonnet by Advaita Ācārya, Śrī Caitanya Mahāprabhu quietly smiled. "That is His order," He said. Then He fell silent.

TEXT 24

জানিয়াও স্বরূপ গোসাঞি প্রভুরে পুছিল।
'এই তরজার অর্থ বুঝিতে নারিল' ॥ ২৪ ॥

jāniyāo svarūpa gosāñi prabhure puchila
'ei tarajāra artha bujhite nārila'

SYNONYMS

jāniyāo—although knowing; *svarūpa gosāñi*—Svarūpa Dāmodara Gosvāmī; *prabhure puchila*—inquired from Śrī Caitanya Mahāprabhu; *ei tarajāra artha*—the meaning of this sonnet; *bujhite*—to understand; *nārila*—I was not able.

TRANSLATION

Although he knew the secret, Svarūpa Dāmodara Gosvāmī inquired from the Lord, "What is the meaning of this sonnet? I could not understand it."

TEXT 25

প্রভু কহেন,—'আচার্য হয় পূজক প্রবল ।
আগম-শাস্ত্রের বিধি-বিধানে কুশল ॥ ২৫ ॥

prabhu kahena,—'ācārya haya pūjaka prabala
āgama-śāstrera vidhi-vidhāne kuśala

SYNONYMS

prabhu kahena—Śrī Caitanya Mahāprabhu said; *ācārya haya pūjaka prabala*—Advaita Ācārya is a great worshiper; *āgama-śāstrera*—of the Vedic literature; *vidhi-vidhāne kuśala*—very expert in the regulative principles.

TRANSLATION

Śrī Caitanya Mahāprabhu replied, "Advaita Ācārya is a great worshiper of the Lord and is very expert in the regulative principles enjoined in the Vedic literatures.

TEXT 26

উপাসনা লাগি' দেবের করেন আবাহন ।
পূজা লাগি' কত কাল করেন নিরোধন ॥ ২৬ ॥

upāsanā lāgi' devera karena āvāhana
pūjā lāgi' kata kāla karena nirodhana

SYNONYMS

upāsanā lāgi'—for worshiping the Deity; *devera*—of the Lord; *karena āvāhana*—invites to come; *pūjā lāgi'*—to perform the worship; *kata kāla*—for some time; *karena nirodhana*—He keeps the Deity.

TRANSLATION

"Advaita Ācārya invites the Lord to come and be worshiped, and to perform the worship He keeps the Deity for some time.

TEXT 27

পূজা-নির্বাহণ হৈলে পাছে করেন বিসর্জন ।
তরজার না জানি অর্থ, কিবা তাঁর মন ॥ ২৭ ॥

pūjā-nirvāhaṇa haile pāche karena visarjana
tarajāra nā jāni artha, kibā tāṅra mana

SYNONYMS

pūjā-nirvāhaṇa—finishing of the worship; *haile*—when there is; *pāche*—at last; *karena visarjana*—sends back the Deity; *tarajāra*—of the sonnet; *nā jāni*—I do not know; *artha*—the meaning; *kibā tāṅra mana*—what is in His mind.

TRANSLATION

"After the worship is completed, He sends the Deity somewhere else. I do not know the meaning of this sonnet, nor do I know what is in Advaita Prabhu's mind.

TEXT 28

মহাযোগেশ্বর আচার্য— তরজাতে সমর্থ ।
আমিহ বুঝিতে নারি তরজার অর্থ ॥' ২৮ ॥

mahā-yogeśvara ācārya——tarajāte samartha
āmiha bujhite nāri tarajāra artha'

SYNONYMS

mahā-yogeśvara—the greatest mystic; *ācārya*—Advaita Ācārya; *tarajāte samartha*—very expert in writing sonnets; *āmiha*—and yet I; *bujhite*—to understand; *nāri*—am not able; *tarajāra*—of the sonnet; *artha*—the meaning.

TRANSLATION

"Advaita Ācārya is a great mystic. No one can understand Him. He is expert in writing sonnets that even I Myself cannot understand."

TEXT 29

শুনিয়া বিস্মিত হইলা সব ভক্তগণ ।
স্বরূপ-গোসাঞি কিছু হইলা বিমন ॥ ২৯ ॥

śuniyā vismita ha-ilā saba bhakta-gaṇa
svarūpa-gosāñi kichu ha-ilā vimana

SYNONYMS

śuniyā—hearing; *vismita*—astonished; *ha-ilā*—became; *saba*—all; *bhakta-gaṇa*—the devotees; *svarūpa-gosāñi*—Svarūpa Dāmodara Gosvāmī; *kichu*—somewhat; *ha-ilā*—became; *vimana*—morose.

TRANSLATION

Hearing this, all the devotees were astonished, especially Svarūpa Dāmodara, who became somewhat morose.

TEXT 30

সেই দিন হৈতে প্রভুর আর দশা হইল।
কৃষ্ণের বিচ্ছেদ-দশা দ্বিগুণ বাড়িল ॥ ৩০ ॥

sei dina haite prabhura āra daśā ha-ila
kṛṣṇera viccheda-daśā dviguṇa bāḍila

SYNONYMS

sei dine haite—from that day on; *prabhura*—of Śrī Caitanya Mahāprabhu; *āra*—another; *daśā*—condition; *ha-ila*—there was; *kṛṣṇera*—from Lord Kṛṣṇa; *viccheda-daśā*—the condition of separation; *dvi-guṇa*—twice; *bāḍila*—increased.

TRANSLATION

From that day on, Śrī Caitanya Mahāprabhu's emotional state changed markedly; His feelings of separation from Kṛṣṇa doubled in intensity.

TEXT 31

উন্মাদ-প্রলাপ-চেষ্টা করে রাত্রি-দিনে।
রাধা-ভাবাবেশে বিরহ বাড়ে অনুক্ষণে ॥ ৩১ ॥

unmāda-pralāpa-ceṣṭā kare rātri-dine
rādhā-bhāvāveśe viraha bāḍe anukṣaṇe

SYNONYMS

unmāda—madness; *pralāpa*—craziness; *ceṣṭā*—activities; *kare rātri-dine*—He performed day and night; *rādhā-bhāva-āveśe*—in the ecstatic emotion of Śrīmatī Rādhārāṇī; *viraha*—separation; *bāḍe*—increases; *anukṣaṇe*—every moment.

TRANSLATION

As His feelings of separation in the ecstasy of Śrīmatī Rādhārāṇī increased at every moment, the Lord's activities, both day and night, were now wild, insane performances.

TEXT 32

আচম্বিতে স্ফুরে কৃষ্ণের মথুরা-গমন ।
উদ্‌ঘূর্ণা-দশা হৈল উন্মাদ-লক্ষণ ॥ ৩২ ॥

ācambite sphure kṛṣṇera mathurā-gamana
udghūrṇā-daśā haila unmāda-lakṣaṇa

SYNONYMS

ācambite—suddenly; *sphure*—there awoke; *kṛṣṇera*—of Lord Kṛṣṇa; *mathurā-gamana*—the departure for Mathurā; *udghūrṇā-daśā*—the ecstatic condition known as *udghūrṇā; haila*—there was; *unmāda-lakṣaṇa*—the symptom of madness.

TRANSLATION

Suddenly there awoke within Śrī Caitanya Mahāprabhu the scene of Lord Kṛṣṇa's departure to Mathurā, and He began exhibiting the symptom of ecstatic madness known as udghūrṇā.

TEXT 33

রামানন্দের গলা ধরি' করেন প্রলাপন ।
স্বরূপে পুছেন মানি' নিজ-সখীগণ ॥ ৩৩ ॥

rāmānandera galā dhari' karena pralāpana
svarūpe puchena māni' nija-sakhī-gaṇa

SYNONYMS

rāmānandera—of Rāmānanda Rāya; *galā dhari'*—holding the neck; *karena pralāpana*—begins talking like a crazy man; *svarūpe puchena*—inquired from Svarūpa Dāmodara; *māni'*—accepting; *nija-sakhī-gaṇa*—as a *gopī* friend.

TRANSLATION

Śrī Caitanya Mahāprabhu spoke like a madman, holding Rāmānanda Rāya by the neck, and He questioned Svarūpa Dāmodara, thinking him to be His gopī friend.

TEXT 34

পূর্বে যেন বিশাখারে রাধিকা পুছিলা ।
সেই শ্লোক পড়ি' প্রলাপ করিতে লাগিলা ॥ ৩৪ ॥

pūrve yena viśākhāre rādhikā puchilā
sei śloka paḍi' pralāpa karite lāgilā

SYNONYMS

pūrve—formerly; *yena*—as; *viśākhāre*—unto Viśākhā; *rādhikā*—Śrīmatī Rādhārāṇī; *puchilā*—inquired; *sei śloka*—that verse; *paḍi'*—reading; *pralāpa*—talking like a crazy man; *karite lāgilā*—began to do.

TRANSLATION

Just as Śrīmatī Rādhārāṇī inquired from Her personal friend Viśākhā, Śrī Caitanya Mahāprabhu, reading that very verse, began speaking like a madman.

TEXT 35

ক্ব নন্দকুলচন্দ্রমাঃ ক্ব শিখিচন্দ্রকালঙ্কৃতিঃ
ক্ব মন্দ্রমুরলীরবঃ ক্ব নু সুরেন্দ্রনীলদ্যুতিঃ ।
ক্ব রাসরসতাণ্ডবী ক্ব সখি জীবরক্ষৌষধি-
নিধির্মম সুহৃত্তমঃ ক্ব বত হন্ত হা ধিগ্বিধিম্ ॥ ৩৫ ॥

kva nanda-kula-candramāḥ kva śikhi-candrakālaṅkṛtiḥ
kva mandra-muralī-ravaḥ kva nu surendra-nīla-dyutiḥ
kva rāsa-rasa-tāṇḍavī kva sakhi jīva-rakṣauṣadhir
nidhir mama suhṛttamaḥ kva bata hanta hā dhig-vidhim

SYNONYMS

kva—where; *nanda-kula-candramāḥ*—Kṛṣṇa, who has arisen like the moon in the ocean of the dynasty of Nanda Mahārāja; *kva*—where; *śikhi-candraka-alaṅkṛtiḥ*—Kṛṣṇa, whose head is decorated with a peacock feather; *kva*—where; *mandra-muralī-ravaḥ*—Kṛṣṇa, whose flute produces a deep sound; *kva*—where; *nu*—certainly; *surendra-nīla-dyutiḥ*—Kṛṣṇa, whose bodily luster is like the jewel called *indranīla; kva*—where; *rāsa-rasa-tāṇḍavī*—Kṛṣṇa, who is expert in dancing in the *rāsa* dance; *kva*—where; *sakhi*—O My dear friend; *jīva-rakṣa-auṣadhiḥ*—Kṛṣṇa, who is the medicine that can save one's life; *nidhiḥ*—treasure; *mama*—My; *suhṛt-tamaḥ*—best of friends; *kva*—where; *bata*—I am so sorry; *hanta*—alas; *hā*—oh; *dhik-vidhim*—condemnation to Vidhi, the maker of my destiny.

TRANSLATION

" 'My dear friend, where is Kṛṣṇa, who is like the moon rising from the ocean of Mahārāja Nanda's dynasty? Where is Kṛṣṇa, His head decorated with a peacock feather? Where is He? Where is Kṛṣṇa, whose flute produces such a deep sound? Oh, where is Kṛṣṇa, whose bodily luster is like the luster of the blue indranīla jewel? Where is Kṛṣṇa, who is so expert in rāsa dancing? Oh, where is He who can save My life? Kindly tell Me where to find Kṛṣṇa, the treasure of My life and best of My friends. Feeling separation from Him, I hereby condemn Providence, the shaper of My destiny.'

PURPORT

This verse is found in the *Lalita-mādhava* (3.25) of Śrīla Rūpa Gosvāmī.

TEXT 36

"ব্রজেন্দ্রকুল—দুগ্ধসিন্ধু, কৃষ্ণ তাহে পূর্ণ ইন্দু,
জন্মি' কৈলা জগৎ উজোর।
কান্ত্যমৃত যেবা পিয়ে, নিরন্তর পিয়া জিয়ে,
ব্রজ-জনের নয়ন-চকোর ॥ ৩৬ ॥

"vrajendra-kula——dugdha-sindhu, kṛṣṇa tāhe pūrṇa indu,
janmi' kailā jagat ujora
kānty-amṛta yebā piye, nirantara piyā jiye,
vraja-janera nayana-cakora

SYNONYMS

vrajendra-kula—the dynasty of Mahārāja Nanda in Vrajabhūmi; *dugdha-sindhu*—like the ocean of milk; *kṛṣṇa*—Lord Kṛṣṇa; *tāhe*—in that; *pūrṇa*—full; *indu*—moon; *janmi'*—arising; *kailā*—has made; *jagat*—the whole world; *ujora*—illuminated; *kānti-amṛta*—the nectar of His bodily luster; *yebā piye*—anyone who drinks; *nirantara*—always; *piyā*—drinking; *jiye*—sustains life; *vraja-janera*—of the inhabitants of Vṛndāvana; *nayana-cakora*—eyes that are like *cakora* birds.

TRANSLATION

"The family of Mahārāja Nanda is just like an ocean of milk, wherein Lord Kṛṣṇa has arisen like the full moon to illuminate the entire universe. The eyes of the residents of Vraja are like cakora birds that continuously drink the nectar of His bodily luster and thus live peacefully.

TEXT 37

সখি হে, কোথা কৃষ্ণ, করাহ দরশন ।
ক্ষণেকে যাহার মুখ, না দেখিলে ফাটে বুক,
শীঘ্র দেখাহ, না রহে জীবন ॥ ৩৭ ॥ ধ্রু ॥

sakhi he, kothā kṛṣṇa, karāha daraśana
kṣaṇeke yāhāra mukha, nā dekhile phāṭe buka,
śīghra dekhāha, nā rahe jīvana

SYNONYMS

sakhi he—O My dear friend; *kothā kṛṣṇa*—where is Lord Kṛṣṇa; *karāha daraśana*—please let Me see Him; *kṣaṇeke*—within a moment; *yāhāra*—whose; *mukha*—face; *nā dekhile*—if not seeing; *phāṭe buka*—My heart is breaking; *śīghra*—quickly; *dekhāha*—show; *nā rahe jīvana*—My life is expiring.

TRANSLATION

"My dear friend, where is Kṛṣṇa? Kindly let Me see Him. My heart breaks at not seeing His face even for a moment. Kindly show Him to Me immediately; otherwise I cannot live.

TEXT 38

এই ব্রজের রমণী, কামার্কতপ্ত-কুমুদিনী,
নিজ-করামৃত দিয়া দান ।
প্রফুল্লিত করে যেই, কাহাঁ মোর চন্দ্র সেই,
দেখাহ, সখি, রাখ মোর প্রাণ ॥ ৩৮ ॥

ei vrajera ramaṇī, kāmārka-tapta-kumudinī,
nija-karāmṛta diyā dāna
praphullita kare yei, kāhāṅ mora candra sei,
dekhāha, sakhi, rākha mora prāṇa

SYNONYMS

ei—these; *vrajera ramaṇī*—women of Vṛndāvana; *kāma-arka-tapta-kumudinī*—exactly like lilies becoming very hot in the sun of lusty desire; *nija*—own; *kara-amṛta*—nectar of hands; *diyā*—giving; *dāna*—charity; *praphullita*—jubilant; *kare*—makes; *yei*—one who; *kāhāṅ*—where; *mora*—My; *candra*—moon; *sei*—that; *dekhāha*—please show; *sakhi*—O My dear friend; *rākha*—please save; *mora prāṇa*—My life.

TRANSLATION

"The women of Vṛndāvana are just like lilies growing hot in the sun of lusty desires. But moonlike Kṛṣṇa makes them all jubilant by bestowing upon them the nectar of His hands. O My dear friend, where is My moon now? Save My life by showing Him to Me!

TEXT 39

কাহাঁ সে চূড়ার ঠাম, শিখিপিঞ্ছের উড়ান,
নব-মেঘে যেন ইন্দ্রধনু।
পীতাম্বর—তড়িদ্দ্যুতি, মুক্তামালা—বকপাঁতি,
নবাম্বুদ জিনি' শ্যামতনু ॥ ৩৯ ॥

kāhāṅ se cūḍāra ṭhāma, śikhi-piñchera uḍāna,
nava-meghe yena indra-dhanu
pītāmbara——taḍid-dyuti, muktā-mālā——baka-pāṅti,
navāmbuda jini' śyāma-tanu

SYNONYMS

kāhāṅ—where; *se*—that; *cūḍāra ṭhāma*—beauty of the helmet; *śikhi-piñchera uḍāna*—upon which there is a peacock feather; *nava-meghe*—in a new cloud; *yena*—just like; *indra-dhanu*—the rainbow; *pīta-ambara*—yellow garments; *taḍit-dyuti*—like the illumination of lightning; *muktā-mālā*—pearl necklace; *baka-pāṅti*—like rows of ducks; *nava-ambuda*—a new rain cloud; *jini'*—conquering; *śyāma-tanu*—the blackish body.

TRANSLATION

"My dear friend, where is that beautiful helmet with a peacock feather upon it like a rainbow upon a new cloud? Where are those yellow garments, shining like lightning? And where is that necklace of pearls that resemble flocks of ducks flying in the sky? The blackish body of Kṛṣṇa triumphs over the new blackish rain cloud.

TEXT 40

একবার যার নয়নে লাগে, সদা তার হৃদয়ে জাগে,
কৃষ্ণতনু—যেন আম্র-আঠা।
নারী-মনে পৈশে হায়, যত্নে নাহি বাহিরায়,
তনু নহে,—সেয়াকুলের কাঁটা ॥ ৪০ ॥

eka-bāra yāra nayane lāge, sadā tāra hṛdaye jāge,
kṛṣṇa-tanu——yena āmra-āṭhā
nārī-mane paiśe hāya, yatne nāhi bāhirāya,
tanu nahe,——seyā-kulera kāṅṭā

SYNONYMS

eka-bāra—once; *yāra*—whose; *nayane*—eyes; *lāge*—capture; *sadā*—always; *tāra*—his; *hṛdaye*—in the heart; *jāge*—remains prominent; *kṛṣṇa-tanu*—the body of Kṛṣṇa; *yena*—like; *āmra-āṭhā*—the sap of the mango tree; *nārī-mane*—in the minds of women; *paiśe*—enters; *hāya*—alas; *yatne*—even with great endeavor; *nāhi*—does not; *bāhirāya*—come out; *tanu nahe*—is not an ordinary body; *seyā-kulera kāṅṭā*—it is like the thorn of the *seyā* berry tree.

TRANSLATION

"If a person's eyes even once capture that beautiful body of Kṛṣṇa's, it remains always prominent within his heart. Kṛṣṇa's body resembles the sap of the mango tree, for when it enters the minds of women, it will not come out, despite great endeavor. Thus Kṛṣṇa's extraordinary body is like a thorn of the seyā berry tree.

TEXT 41

জিনিয়া তমালদ্যুতি, ইন্দ্রনীল-সম কান্তি,
সে কান্তিতে জগৎ মাতায়।
শৃঙ্গার-রস-সার ছানি', তাতে চন্দ্র-জ্যোৎস্না সানি',
জানি বিধি নিরমিলা তায় ॥ ৪১ ॥

jiniyā tamāla-dyuti, indranīla-sama kānti,
se kāntite jagat mātāya
śṛṅgāra-rasa-sāra chāni', tāte candra-jyotsnā sāni',
jāni vidhi niramilā tāya

SYNONYMS

jiniyā—being victorious over; *tamāla-dyuti*—the luster of the *tamāla* tree; *in-dra-nīla*—the gem known as *indranīla; sama kānti*—the luster like; *se kāntite*—by that luster; *jagat mātāya*—the whole world becomes maddened; *śṛṅgāra-rasa*—of the mellow of conjugal love; *sāra*—essence; *chāni'*—filtering; *tāte*—in that; *candra-jyotsnā*—the illumination of the full moon; *sāni'*—mixing; *jāni*—I know; *vidhi*—Providence; *niramilā*—made very clear; *tāya*—that.

TRANSLATION

"Kṛṣṇa's bodily luster shines like the indranīla gem and surpasses the luster of the tamāla tree. The luster of His body drives the entire world mad because Providence has made it transparent by refining the essence of the mellow of conjugal love and mixing it with moonshine.

TEXT 42

কাহাঁ সে মুরলীধ্বনি, নবাভ্র-গর্জিত জিনি',
জগৎ আকর্ষে শ্রবণে যাহার।
উঠি' ধায় ব্রজ-জন, তৃষিত চাতকগণ,
আসি' পিয়ে কান্ত্যমৃত-ধার ॥ ৪২ ॥

kāhāṅ se muralī-dhvani, navābhra-garjita jini',
jagat ākarṣe śravaṇe yāhāra
uṭhi' dhāya vraja-jana, tṛṣita cātaka-gaṇa,
āsi' piye kānty-amṛta-dhāra

SYNONYMS

kāhāṅ—where; *se*—that; *muralī-dhvani*—the vibration of the flute; *nava-abhra-garjita jini'*—conquering the vibrations of new clouds; *jagat*—the whole world; *ākarṣe*—attracts; *śravaṇe*—the hearing; *yāhāra*—whose; *uṭhi'*—standing up; *dhāya*—run; *vraja-jana*—the inhabitants of Vrajabhūmi; *tṛṣita cātaka-gaṇa*—like lusty *cātaka* birds; *āsi'*—coming; *piye*—drink; *kānti-amṛta-dhāra*—the showers of the nectar of Kṛṣṇa's bodily luster.

TRANSLATION

"The deep vibration of Kṛṣṇa's flute surpasses the thundering of new clouds and attracts the aural reception of the entire world. Thus the inhabitants of Vṛndāvana rise and pursue that sound, drinking the showering nectar of Kṛṣṇa's bodily luster like thirsty cātaka birds.

TEXT 43

মোর সেই কলানিধি, প্রাণরক্ষা-মহৌষধি,
সখি, মোর তেঁহো সুহৃত্তম।
দেহ জীয়ে তাঁহা বিনে, ধিক্ এই জীবনে,
বিধি করে এত বিড়ম্বন !" ৪৩ ॥

mora sei kalā-nidhi, prāṇa-rakṣā-mahauṣadhi,
sakhi, mora teṅho suhṛttama
deha jīye tāṅhā vine, dhik ei jīvane,
vidhi kare eta viḍambana!"

SYNONYMS

mora—of Me; *sei*—that; *kalā-nidhi*—reservoir of art and culture; *prāṇa-rakṣā-mahā-auṣaudhi*—the panacea for saving My life; *sakhi*—O My dear friend; *mora*—My; *teṅho*—He; *suhṛt-tama*—the best of friends; *deha jīye*—My body lives; *tāṅhā vine*—without Him; *dhik*—condemnation; *ei jīvane*—to this life; *vidhi*—Providence; *kare*—does; *eta viḍambana*—so much cheating.

TRANSLATION

"Kṛṣṇa is the reservoir of art and culture, and He is the panacea that saves My life. O My dear friend, since I live without Him, who is the best among My friends, I condemn the duration of My life. I think that Providence has cheated Me in many ways.

TEXT 44

'যে-জন জীতে নাহি চায়, তারে কেনে জীয়ায়',
বিধিপ্রতি উঠে ক্রোধ-শোক ।
বিধিরে করে ভর্ৎসন, কৃষ্ণে দেন ওলাহন,
পড়ি' ভাগবতের এক শ্লোক ॥ ৪৪ ॥

'ye-jana jīte nāhi cāya, tāre kene jīyāya',
vidhi-prati uṭhe krodha-śoka
vidhire kare bhartsana, kṛṣṇe dena olāhana,
paḍi' bhāgavatera eka śloka

SYNONYMS

ye-jana—that person who; *jīte*—to live; *nāhi cāya*—does not want; *tāre*—him; *kene*—why; *jīyāya*—he makes life continue; *vidhi-prati*—towards Providence; *uṭhe*—awakens; *krodha-śoka*—anger and lamentation; *vidhire*—unto Providence; *kare*—does; *bhartsana*—chastisement; *kṛṣṇe*—unto Lord Kṛṣṇa; *dena*—gives; *olāhana*—accusation; *paḍi'*—reading; *bhāgavatera*—of *Śrīmad-Bhāgavatam; eka śloka*—one verse.

TRANSLATION

"Why does Providence continue the life of one who does not wish to live?" This thought aroused anger and lamentation. Śrī Caitanya Mahāprabhu then

read a verse from Śrīmad-Bhāgavatam that chastises Providence and makes an accusation against Kṛṣṇa.

TEXT 45

অহো বিধাতস্তব ন কচিদ্দয়া
সংযোজ্য মৈত্র্যা প্রণয়েন দেহিনঃ ।
তাংশ্চাকৃতার্থান্ বিযুনঙ্ক্ষ্যপার্থকং
বিচেষ্টিতং তেঽর্ভকচেষ্টিতং যথা ॥ ৪৫ ॥

aho vidhātas tava na kvacid dayā
saṁyojya maitryā praṇayena dehinaḥ
tāṁś cākṛtārthān viyunaṅkṣy apārthakaṁ
viceṣṭitaṁ te 'rbhaka-ceṣṭitaṁ yathā

SYNONYMS

aho—alas; *vidhātaḥ*—O Providence; *tava*—your; *na*—not; *kvacit*—at any time; *dayā*—mercy; *saṁyojya*—making connections; *maitryā*—by friendship; *praṇayena*—and by affection; *dehinaḥ*—of the embodied souls; *tān*—them; *ca*—and; *akṛta-arthān*—without achievement; *viyunaṅkṣi*—you cause to happen; *apārthakam*—separation; *viceṣṭitam*—activities; *te*—your; *arbhaka*—of a boy; *ceṣṭitam*—the childish play; *yathā*—like.

TRANSLATION

" 'O Providence, you have no mercy! You bring embodied souls together through friendship and affection, but before their desires are fulfilled, you separate them. Your activities are like the foolish pranks of children.'

PURPORT

This verse, quoted from *Śrīmad-Bhāgavatam* (10.39.19), was chanted by the damsels of Vraja when Kṛṣṇa left Vṛndāvana for Mathurā with Akrūra and Balarāma. The *gopīs* lamented that providence had made it possible for them to meet Kṛṣṇa and Balarāma in affection and love and had then separated them.

TEXT 46

"না জানিস্ প্রেম-মর্ম, ব্যর্থ করিস্ পরিশ্রম,
তোর চেষ্টা—বালক-সমান ।
'তোর যদি লাগ্ পাইয়ে, তবে তোরে শিক্ষা দিয়ে,
এমন যেন না করিস্ বিধান ॥ ৪৬ ॥

"nā jānis prema-marma, vyartha karis pariśrama,
tora ceṣṭā——bālaka-samāna
'tora yadi lāg pāiye, tabe tore śikṣā diye,
emana yena nā karis vidhāna

SYNONYMS

nā jānis—you do not know; *prema-marma*—the purport of loving affairs; *vyartha karis*—you baffle; *pariśrama*—all labor; *tora ceṣṭā*—your activities; *bālaka-samāna*—like the childish activities of a boy; *tora yadi lāg pāiye*—if I get the opportunity to meet you; *tabe*—then; *tore*—unto you; *śikṣā diye*—I shall give some lessons; *emana*—like this; *yena*—so that; *nā karis vidhāna*—will not make arrangements.

TRANSLATION

"Providence, you do not know the purport of loving affairs, and therefore you baffle all our endeavors. This is very childish of you. If we could catch you, we would give you such a lesson that you would never again make such arrangements.

TEXT 47

অরে বিধি, তুই বড়ই নিঠুর ।
অন্যোঽন্য দুর্লভ জন, প্রেমে করাঞা সম্মিলন,
'অকৃতার্থান্' কেনে করিস্ দূর ? ৪৭ ॥ ধ্রু ॥

are vidhi, tui baḍa-i niṭhura
anyo 'nya durlabha jana, preme karāñā sammilana,
'akṛtārthān' kene karis dūra?

SYNONYMS

are—oh; *vidhi*—Providence; *tui*—you; *baḍa-i*—very; *niṭhura*—cruel; *anyo 'nya*—for one another; *durlabha jana*—persons rarely obtained; *preme*—in love; *karāñā sammilana*—causing to meet together; *akṛta-arthān*—unsuccessful; *kene*—why; *karis*—you do; *dūra*—far apart.

TRANSLATION

"Oh, cruel Providence! You are very unkind, for you bring together in love people who are rarely in touch with each other. Then, after you have made them meet but before they are fulfilled, you again spread them far apart.

TEXT 48

অরে বিধি অকরুণ, দেখাঞা কৃষ্ণানন,
নেত্র-মন লোভাইলা মোর ।
ক্ষণেকে করিতে পান, কাড়ি' নিলা অন্য স্থান,
পাপ কৈলি 'দত্ত-অপহার' ॥ ৪৮ ॥

are vidhi akaruṇa, dekhāñā kṛṣṇānana,
netra-mana lobhāilā mora
kṣaṇeke karite pāna, kāḍi' nilā anya sthāna
pāpa kaili 'datta-apahāra'

SYNONYMS

are—oh; *vidhi*—Providence; *akaruṇa*—most unkind; *dekhāñā*—showing; *kṛṣṇa-ānana*—the beautiful face of Kṛṣṇa; *netra-mana*—mind and eyes; *lobhāilā*—have made greedy; *mora*—My; *kṣaṇeke karite pāna*—drinking only for a moment; *kāḍi' nilā*—took it away; *anya sthāna*—to another place; *pāpa kaili*—have performed a most sinful act; *datta-apahāra*—taking back things given in charity.

TRANSLATION

"O Providence, you are so unkind! You reveal the beautiful face of Kṛṣṇa and make the mind and eyes greedy, but after they have drunk that nectar for only a moment, you whisk Kṛṣṇa away to another place. This is a great sin because you thus take away what you have given as charity.

TEXT 49

'অক্রূর করে তোমার দোষ,আমায় কেনে কর রোষ',
ইহা যদি কহ 'দুরাচার' ।
তুই অক্রূর-মূর্তি ধরি', কৃষ্ণ নিলি চুরি করি',
অন্যের নহে ঐছে ব্যবহার ॥ ৪৯ ॥

'akrūra kare tomāra doṣa, āmāya kene kara roṣa',
ihā yadi kaha 'durācāra'
tui akrūra-mūrti dhari', kṛṣṇa nili curi kari',
anyera nahe aiche vyavahāra

SYNONYMS

akrūra—Akrūra; *kare*—does; *tomāra doṣa*—fault to you; *āmāya*—unto me; *kene*—why; *kara*—you do; *roṣa*—anger; *ihā*—this; *yadi*—if; *kaha*—you say; *durācāra*—O misbehaved (Providence); *tui*—you; *akrūra-mūrti dhari'*—taking the form of Akrūra; *kṛṣṇa*—Lord Kṛṣṇa; *nili*—you have taken; *curi kari'*—stealing; *anyera*—of others; *nahe*—there is not; *aiche*—this type of; *vyavahāra*—behavior.

TRANSLATION

"O misbehaved Providence! If you reply to us, 'Akrūra is actually at fault; why are you angry with me?' then I say to you, 'Providence, you have taken the form of Akrūra and have stolen Kṛṣṇa away. No one else would behave like this.'

TEXT 50

আপনার কর্ম-দোষ, তোরে কিবা করি রোষ,
তোয়-মোয় সম্বন্ধ বিদূর ।
যে আমার প্রাণনাথ, একত্র রহি যাঁর সাথ,
সেই কৃষ্ণ হইলা নিঠুর ! ৫০ ॥

āpanāra karma-doṣa, tore kibā kari roṣa,
toya-moya sambandha vidūra
ye āmāra prāṇa-nātha, ekatra rahi yāṅra sātha,
sei kṛṣṇa ha-ilā niṭhura!

SYNONYMS

āpanāra karma-doṣa—it is the result of My own fate; *tore*—unto you; *kibā*—what; *kari roṣa*—I give accusations; *toya-moya*—between you and Me; *sambandha*—the relationship; *vidūra*—very far; *ye*—the one who is; *āmāra*—My; *prāṇa-nātha*—life and soul; *ekatra*—together; *rahi*—We remain; *yāṅra sātha*—with whom; *sei kṛṣṇa*—that Kṛṣṇa; *ha-ilā niṭhura*—has become so cruel.

TRANSLATION

"But this is the fault of My own destiny. Why should I needlessly accuse you? There is no intimate relationship between you and Me. Kṛṣṇa, however, is My life and soul. It is We who live together, and it is He who has become so cruel.

TEXT 51

সব ত্যজি' ভজি যাঁরে, সেই আপন-হাতে মারে,
নারীবধে কৃষ্ণের নাহি ভয়।
তাঁর লাগি' আমি মরি, উলটি' না চাহে হরি,
ক্ষণমাত্রে ভাঙ্গিল প্রণয় ॥ ৫১ ॥

saba tyaji' bhaji yāṅre, sei āpana-hāte māre,
nārī-vadhe kṛṣṇera nāhi bhaya
tāṅra lāgi' āmi mari, ulaṭi' nā cāhe hari,
kṣaṇa-mātre bhāṅgila praṇaya

SYNONYMS

saba tyaji'—leaving everything aside; *bhaji yāṅre*—the person whom I worship; *sei*—that person; *āpana-hāte*—by His own hand; *māre*—kills; *nārī-vadhe*—in killing one woman; *kṛṣṇera*—of Kṛṣṇa; *nāhi bhaya*—there is no fear; *tāṅra lāgi'*—for Him; *āmi mari*—I die; *ulaṭi'*—turning back; *nā cāhe hari*—Kṛṣṇa does not look; *kṣaṇa-mātre*—within a moment; *bhāṅgila*—has broken; *praṇaya*—all loving affairs.

TRANSLATION

"He for whom I have left everything is personally killing Me with His own hands. Kṛṣṇa has no fear of killing women. Indeed, I am dying for Him, but He doesn't even turn back to look at Me. Within a moment, He has broken off our loving affairs.

TEXT 52

কৃষ্ণে কেনে করি রোষ, আপন দুর্দৈব-দোষ,
পাকিল মোর এই পাপফল।
যে কৃষ্ণ—মোর প্রেমাধীন, তারে কৈল উদাসীন,
এই মোর অভাগ্য প্রবল ॥" ৫২ ॥

kṛṣṇe kene kari roṣa, āpana durdaiva-doṣa,
pākila mora ei pāpa-phala
ye kṛṣṇa——mora premādhīna, tāre kaila udāsīna,
ei mora abhāgya prabala"

SYNONYMS

kṛṣṇe—unto Kṛṣṇa; *kene*—why; *kari roṣa*—I am angry; *āpana*—of My own; *durdaiva*—of misfortune; *doṣa*—fault; *pākila*—has ripened; *mora*—My; *ei*—this;

pāpa-phala—sinful reaction; *ye*—that; *kṛṣṇa*—Kṛṣṇa; *mora*—My; *prema-adhīna*—dependent on love; *tāre*—Him; *kaila*—has made; *udāsīna*—indifferent; *ei mora*—this is My; *abhāgya*—misfortune; *prabala*—very strong.

TRANSLATION

"Yet why should I be angry with Kṛṣṇa? It is the fault of My own misfortune. The fruit of my sinful activities has ripened, and therefore Kṛṣṇa, who has always been dependent on My love, is now indifferent. This means that My misfortune is very strong."

TEXT 53

এইমত গৌর-রায়, বিষাদে করে হায় হায়,
'হা হা কৃষ্ণ, তুমি গেলা কতি ?'
গোপীভাব হৃদয়ে, তার বাক্যে বিলাপয়ে,
'গোবিন্দ দামোদর মাধবেতি' ॥ ৫৩ ॥

ei-mata gaura-rāya, viṣāde kare hāya hāya,
'hā hā kṛṣṇa, tumi gelā kati?'
gopī-bhāva hṛdaye, tāra vākye vilāpaye,
'govinda dāmodara mādhaveti'

SYNONYMS

ei-mata—in this way; *gaura-rāya*—Lord Śrī Caitanya Mahāprabhu; *viṣāde*—in lamentation due to separation; *kare hāya hāya*—always says "alas, alas"; *hā hā kṛṣṇa*—oh, oh Kṛṣṇa; *tumi gelā kati*—where have You gone; *gopī-bhāva hṛdaye*—with the ecstatic love of the *gopīs* in His heart; *tāra vākye*—in their words; *vilāpaye*—He laments; *govinda dāmodara mādhava*—O Govinda, O Dāmodara, O Mādhava; *iti*—thus.

TRANSLATION

In this way, Śrī Caitanya Mahāprabhu lamented in the mood of separation, "Alas, alas! O Kṛṣṇa, where have You gone?" Feeling in His heart the ecstatic emotions of the gopīs, Śrī Caitanya Mahāprabhu agonized in their words, saying, "O Govinda! O Dāmodara! O Mādhava!"

TEXT 54

তবে স্বরূপ-রামরায়, করি' নানা উপায়,
মহাপ্রভুর করে আশ্বাসন ।

গায়েন সঙ্গম-গীত, প্রভুর ফিরাইলা চিত,
প্রভুর কিছু স্থির হৈল মন ॥ ৫৪ ॥

tabe svarūpa-rāma-rāya, kari' nānā upāya,
mahāprabhura kare āśvāsana
gāyena saṅgama-gīta, prabhura phirāilā cita,
prabhura kichu sthira haila mana

SYNONYMS

tabe—thereafter; *svarūpa-rāma-rāya*—Svarūpa Dāmodara Gosvāmī and Rāmānanda Rāya; *kari' nānā upāya*—devising many means; *mahāprabhura*—Śrī Caitanya Mahāprabhu; *kare āśvāsana*—pacify; *gāyena*—they sang; *saṅgama-gīta*—meeting songs; *prabhura*—of Śrī Caitanya Mahāprabhu; *phirāilā cita*—transformed the heart; *prabhura*—of Śrī Caitanya Mahāprabhu; *kichu*—somewhat; *sthira*—peaceful; *haila*—became; *mana*—the mind.

TRANSLATION

Svarūpa Dāmodara and Rāmānanda Rāya then devised various means to pacify the Lord. They sang songs of meeting that transformed His heart and made His mind peaceful.

TEXT 55

এইমত বিলপিতে অর্ধরাত্রি গেল ।
গম্ভীরাতে স্বরূপ-গোসাঞি প্রভুরে শোয়াইল ॥৫৫ ॥

ei-mata vilapite ardha-rātri gela
gambhīrāte svarūpa-gosāñi prabhure śoyāila

SYNONYMS

ei-mata—in this way; *vilapite*—speaking in lamentation; *ardha-rātri gela*—half the night passed; *gambhīrāte*—in the room known as the Gambhīrā; *svarūpa-gosāñi*—Svarūpa Dāmodara Gosvāmī; *prabhure śoyāila*—made the Lord lie down.

TRANSLATION

As Śrī Caitanya Mahāprabhu lamented in this way, half the night passed. Then Svarūpa Dāmodara made the Lord lie down in the room known as the Gambhīrā.

TEXT 56

প্রভুরে শোয়াঞা রামানন্দ গেলা ঘরে ।
স্বরূপ, গোবিন্দ শুইলা গম্ভীরার দ্বারে ॥ ৫৬ ॥

prabhure śoyāñā rāmānanda gelā ghare
svarūpa, govinda śuilā gambhīrāra dvāre

SYNONYMS

prabhure—Lord Śrī Caitanya Mahāprabhu; *śoyāñā*—making lie down; *rāmānanda*—Rāmānanda Rāya; *gelā ghare*—returned to his home; *svarūpa*—Svarūpa Dāmodara Gosvāmī; *govinda*—Govinda; *śuilā*—lay down; *gambhīrāra dvāre*—at the door of the Gambhīrā.

TRANSLATION

After the Lord was made to lie down, Rāmānanda Rāya returned home, and Svarūpa Dāmodara and Govinda lay down at the door of the Gambhīrā.

TEXT 57

প্রেমাবেশে মহাপ্রভুর গর-গর মন ।
নামসঙ্কীর্তন করি' করেন জাগরণ ॥ ৫৭ ॥

premāveśe mahāprabhura gara-gara mana
nāma-saṅkīrtana kari' karena jāgaraṇa

SYNONYMS

prema-āveśe—in greatly ecstatic emotion; *mahāprabhura*—of Śrī Caitanya Mahāprabhu; *gara-gara mana*—the mind was fully overwhelmed; *nāma-saṅkīrtana kari'*—chanting the Hare Kṛṣṇa *mantra; karena*—does; *jāgaraṇa*—wakefulness.

TRANSLATION

Śrī Caitanya Mahāprabhu stayed awake all night, chanting the Hare Kṛṣṇa *mahā-mantra*, His mind overwhelmed by spiritual ecstasy.

TEXT 58

বিরহে ব্যাকুল প্রভু উদ্বেগে উঠিলা ।
গম্ভীরার ভিত্ত্যে মুখ ঘষিতে লাগিলা ॥ ৫৮ ॥

virahe vyākula prabhu udvege uṭhilā
gambhīrāra bhittye mukha ghaṣite lāgilā

SYNONYMS

virahe—in the lamentation of separation; *vyākula*—very agitated; *prabhu*—Śrī Caitanya Mahāprabhu; *udvege*—in great anxiety; *uṭhilā*—stood up; *gambhīrāra*—of the Gambhīrā; *bhittye*—on the walls; *mukha*—face; *ghaṣite*—to rub; *lāgilā*—began.

TRANSLATION

Feeling separation from Kṛṣṇa, Śrī Caitanya Mahāprabhu was so distraught that in great anxiety He stood up and began rubbing His face against the walls of the Gambhīrā.

TEXT 59

মুখে, গণ্ডে, নাকে ক্ষত হইল অপার ।
ভাবাবেশে না জানেন প্রভু, পড়ে রক্তধার ॥ ৫৯ ॥

mukhe, gaṇḍe, nāke kṣata ha-ila apāra
bhāvāveśe nā jānena prabhu, paḍe rakta-dhāra

SYNONYMS

mukhe—on the mouth; *gaṇḍe*—on the cheeks; *nāke*—on the nose; *kṣata*—injuries; *ha-ila*—there were; *apāra*—many; *bhāva-āveśe*—in ecstatic emotion; *nā jānena*—could not understand; *prabhu*—Śrī Caitanya Mahāprabhu; *paḍe*—oozes out; *rakta-dhāra*—a flow of blood.

TRANSLATION

Blood oozed from the many injuries on His mouth, nose and cheeks, but due to His ecstatic emotions, the Lord did not know it.

TEXT 60

সর্বরাত্রি করেন ভাবে মুখ সংঘর্ষণ ।
গোঁ-গোঁ-শব্দ করেন,—স্বরূপ শুনিলা তখন ॥ ৬০ ॥

sarva-rātri karena bhāve mukha saṅgharṣaṇa
goṅ-goṅ-śabda karena,——svarūpa śunilā takhana

SYNONYMS

sarva-rātri—the whole night; *karena*—does; *bhāve*—in emotion; *mukha saṅgharṣaṇa*—rubbing of the face; *goṅ-goṅ-śabda karena*—makes a peculiar sound, *goṅ-goṅ; svarūpa*—Svarūpa Dāmodara Gosvāmī; *śunilā*—heard; *takhana*—then.

TRANSLATION

In ecstasy, Śrī Caitanya Mahāprabhu rubbed His face against the walls all night long, making a peculiar sound, "goṅ-goṅ," which Svarūpa Dāmodara could hear through the door.

TEXT 61

দীপ জ্বালি' ঘরে গেলা, দেখি' প্রভুর মুখ।
স্বরূপ, গোবিন্দ দুঁহার হৈল বড় দুঃখ ॥ ৬১ ॥

dīpa jvāli' ghare gelā, dekhi' prabhura mukha
svarūpa, govinda duṅhāra haila baḍa duḥkha

SYNONYMS

dīpa jvāli'—lighting the lamp; *ghare*—in the room; *gelā*—went; *dekhi'*—seeing; *prabhura mukha*—the face of the Lord; *svarūpa*—Svarūpa Dāmodara Gosvāmī; *govinda*—and Govinda; *duṅhāra*—of both of them; *haila baḍa duḥkha*—there was great unhappiness.

TRANSLATION

Lighting a lamp, Svarūpa Dāmodara and Govinda entered the room. When they saw the Lord's face, both of them were full of sorrow.

TEXT 62

প্রভুরে শয্যাতে আনি' সুস্থির করাইলা।
'কাঁহে কৈলা এই তুমি?'—স্বরূপ পুছিলা ॥ ৬২ ॥

prabhure śayyāte āni' susthira karāilā
'kāṅhe kailā ei tumi?'——svarūpa puchilā

SYNONYMS

prabhure—Śrī Caitanya Mahāprabhu; *śayyāte*—to the bed; *āni'*—bringing; *susthira karāilā*—made Him pacified; *kāṅhe*—why; *kailā*—have done; *ei*—this; *tumi*—You; *svarūpa puchilā*—Svarūpa Dāmodara Gosvāmī inquired.

TRANSLATION

They brought the Lord to His bed, calmed Him and then asked, "Why have You done this to Yourself?"

TEXT 63

প্রভু কহেন,—"উদ্বেগে ঘরে না পারি রহিতে ।
দ্বার চাহি' বুলি' শীঘ্র বাহির হইতে ॥ ৬৩ ॥

prabhu kahena,——"udvege ghare nā pāri rahite
dvāra cāhi' buli' śīghra bāhira ha-ite

SYNONYMS

prabhu kahena—Śrī Caitanya Mahāprabhu replied; *udvege*—out of great agitation; *ghare*—within the room; *nā pāri*—I was not able; *rahite*—to stay; *dvāra cāhi'*—looking for the door; *buli'*—wandering; *śīghra*—quickly; *bāhira ha-ite*—to get out.

TRANSLATION

Śrī Caitanya Mahāprabhu replied, "I was in such anxiety that I could not stay in the room. I wanted to go out, and therefore I wandered about the room, looking for the door.

TEXT 64

দ্বার নাহি' পাঞা মুখ লাগে চারিভিতে ।
ক্ষত হয়, রক্ত পড়ে, না পাই যাইতে ॥" ৬৪ ॥

dvāra nāhi' pāñā mukha lāge cāri-bhite
kṣata haya, rakta paḍe, nā pāi yāite"

SYNONYMS

dvāra nāhi' pāñā—not finding the door; *mukha lāge*—My face strikes; *cāri-bhite*—on the four walls; *kṣata haya*—there was injury; *rakta paḍe*—blood came out; *nā pāi yāite*—still I could not get out.

TRANSLATION

"Unable to find the door, I kept hitting the four walls with My face. My face was injured, and it bled, but I still could not get out."

TEXT 65

উন্মাদ-দশায় প্রভুর স্থির নহে মন ।
যেই করে, যেই বোলে সব,—উন্মাদ-লক্ষণ ॥ ৬৫ ॥

unmāda-daśāya prabhura sthira nahe mana
yei kare, yei bole saba,——unmāda-lakṣaṇa

SYNONYMS

unmāda-daśāya—in such a state of madness; *prabhura*—of Śrī Caitanya Mahāprabhu; *sthira nahe mana*—the mind is not steady; *yei kare*—whatever He does; *yei bole*—whatever He says; *saba*—all; *unmāda-lakṣaṇa*—simply symptoms of madness.

TRANSLATION

In this state of madness, Śrī Caitanya Mahāprabhu's mind was unsteady. Whatever He said or did was all symptomatic of madness.

TEXT 66

স্বরূপ-গোসাঞি তবে চিন্তা পাইলা মনে ।
ভক্তগণ লঞা বিচার কৈলা আর দিনে ॥ ৬৬ ॥

svarūpa-gosāñi tabe cintā pāilā mane
bhakta-gaṇa lañā vicāra kailā āra dine

SYNONYMS

svarūpa-gosāñi—Svarūpa Dāmodara Gosvāmī; *tabe*—thereafter; *cintā*—an anxiety or thought; *pāilā mane*—got in his mind; *bhakta-gaṇa lañā*—among all the devotees; *vicāra kailā*—considered; *āra dine*—the next day.

TRANSLATION

Svarūpa Dāmodara was very anxious, but then he had an idea. The following day, he and the other devotees considered it together.

TEXT 67

সব ভক্ত মেলি' তবে প্রভুরে সাধিল ।
শঙ্কর-পণ্ডিতে প্রভুর সঙ্গে শোয়াইল ॥ ৬৭ ॥

saba bhakta meli' tabe prabhure sādhila
śaṅkara-paṇḍite prabhura saṅge śoyāila

SYNONYMS

saba bhakta meli'—all the devotees, meeting together; *tabe*—thereupon; *prabhure sādhila*—entreated Śrī Caitanya Mahāprabhu; *śaṅkara-paṇḍite*—

Śaṅkara Paṇḍita; *prabhura*—Śrī Caitanya Mahāprabhu; *saṅge*—with; *śoyāila*—made to lie down.

TRANSLATION

After consulting with one another, they entreated Śrī Caitanya Mahāprabhu to allow Śaṅkara Paṇḍita to lie down in the same room with Him.

TEXT 68

প্রভু-পাদতলে শঙ্কর করেন শয়ন ।
প্রভু তাঁর উপর করেন পাদ-প্রসারণ ॥ ৬৮ ॥

prabhu-pāda-tale śaṅkara karena śayana
prabhu tāṅra upara karena pāda-prasāraṇa

SYNONYMS

prabhu-pāda-tale—at the lotus feet of Śrī Caitanya Mahāprabhu; *śaṅkara*—Śaṅkara; *karena śayana*—lies down; *prabhu*—Śrī Caitanya Mahāprabhu; *tāṅra*—of him; *upara*—on the body; *karena*—does; *pāda-prasāraṇa*—extending His legs.

TRANSLATION

Thus Śaṅkara Paṇḍita lay at the feet of Śrī Caitanya Mahāprabhu, and the Lord placed His legs upon Śaṅkara's body.

TEXT 69

'প্রভু-পাদোপাধান' বলি' তাঁর নাম হইল ।
পূর্বে বিদুরে যেন শ্রীশুক বর্ণিল ॥ ৬৯ ॥

'prabhu-pādopādhāna' bali' tāṅra nāma ha-ila
pūrve vidure yena śrī-śuka varṇila

SYNONYMS

prabhu-pāda-upādhāna—the pillow of Śrī Caitanya Mahāprabhu's legs; *bali'*—calling as such; *tāṅra nāma*—his name; *ha-ila*—became; *pūrve*—formerly; *vidure*—Vidura; *yena*—as; *śrī-śuka varṇila*—Śrī Śukadeva Gosvāmī described.

TRANSLATION

Śaṅkara became celebrated by the name "the pillow of Śrī Caitanya Mahāprabhu." He was like Vidura, as Śukadeva Gosvāmī previously described him.

TEXT 70

ইতি ব্রুবাণং বিদুরং বিনীতং সহস্রশীর্ষ্ণশ্চরণোপধানম্ ।
প্রহৃষ্টরোমা ভগবৎকথায়াং প্রণীয়মানো মুনিরভ্যচষ্ট ॥ ৭০ ॥

iti bruvāṇaṁ viduraṁ vinītaṁ
sahasra-śīrṣṇaś caraṇopadhānam
prahṛṣṭa-romā bhagavat-kathāyāṁ
praṇīyamāno munir abhyacaṣṭa

SYNONYMS

iti—thus; *bruvāṇam*—speaking; *viduram*—to Vidura; *vinītam*—submissive; *sahasra-śīrṣṇaḥ*—of Lord Kṛṣṇa; *caraṇa-upadhānam*—the resting pillow for the legs; *prahṛṣṭa-romā*—whose hairs on the body were standing; *bhagavat-kathāyām*—in topics of the Supreme Personality of Godhead; *praṇīyamānaḥ*—being induced; *muniḥ*—the great sage Maitreya; *abhyacaṣṭa*—began to speak.

TRANSLATION

"When submissive Vidura, the resting place of the legs of Lord Kṛṣṇa, had thus spoken to Maitreya, Maitreya began speaking, his hair standing on end due to the transcendental pleasure of discussing topics concerning Lord Kṛṣṇa."

PURPORT

This is a quotation from *Śrīmad-Bhāgavatam* (3.13.5).

TEXT 71

শঙ্কর করেন প্রভুর পাদ-সম্বাহন ।
ঘুমাঞা পড়েন, তৈছে করেন শয়ন ॥ ৭১ ॥

śaṅkara karena prabhura pāda-samvāhana
ghumāñā paḍena, taiche karena śayana

SYNONYMS

śaṅkara—Śaṅkara; *karena*—does; *prabhura*—of Śrī Caitanya Mahāprabhu; *pāda-samvāhana*—massaging the legs; *ghumāñā paḍena*—he falls asleep; *taiche*—in that way; *karena śayana*—he lies down.

TRANSLATION

Śaṅkara massaged the legs of Śrī Caitanya Mahāprabhu, but while massaging he would fall asleep and thus lie down.

TEXT 72

উঘাড়-অঙ্গে পড়িয়া শঙ্কর নিদ্রা যায়।
প্রভু উঠি' আপন-কাঁথা তাহারে জড়ায় ॥ ৭২ ॥

ughāḍa-aṅge paḍiyā śaṅkara nidrā yāya
prabhu uṭhi' āpana-kāṅthā tāhāre jaḍāya

SYNONYMS

ughāḍa-aṅge—without a covering over the body; *paḍiyā*—lying down; *śaṅkara*—Śaṅkara; *nidrā yāya*—goes to sleep; *prabhu*—Śrī Caitanya Mahāprabhu; *uṭhi'*—getting up; *āpana-kāṅthā*—His own quilt; *tāhāre jaḍāya*—wraps him with.

TRANSLATION

He would lie asleep without a covering on his body, and Śrī Caitanya Mahāprabhu would get up and wrap him with His own quilt.

TEXT 73

নিরন্তর ঘুমায় শঙ্কর শীঘ্র-চেতন।
বসি' পাদ চাপি' করে রাত্রি-জাগরণ ॥ ৭৩ ॥

nirantara ghumāya śaṅkara śīghra-cetana
vasi' pāda cāpi' kare rātri-jāgaraṇa

SYNONYMS

nirantara—incessantly; *ghumāya*—sleeps; *śaṅkara*—Śaṅkara; *śīghra*—very quickly; *cetana*—waking up; *vasi'*—sitting; *pāda cāpi'*—massaging the legs; *kare*—does; *rātri-jāgaraṇa*—keeps awake at night.

TRANSLATION

Śaṅkara Paṇḍita would always fall asleep, but he would quickly awaken, sit up and again begin massaging the legs of Śrī Caitanya Mahāprabhu. In this way he would stay awake the entire night.

TEXT 74

তাঁর ভয়ে নারেন প্রভু বাহিরে যাইতে।
তাঁর ভয়ে নারেন ভিত্ত্যে মুখাব্জ ঘষিতে ॥ ৭৪ ॥

tāṅra bhaye nārena prabhu bāhire yāite
tāṅra bhaye nārena bhittye mukhābja ghaṣite

SYNONYMS

tāṅra bhaye—because of fear of him; *nārena*—was not able; *prabhu*—Śrī Caitanya Mahāprabhu; *bāhire yāite*—to go out; *tāṅra bhaye*—because of fear of him; *nārena*—was not able; *bhittye*—on the walls; *mukha-abja ghaṣite*—to rub His lotuslike face.

TRANSLATION

Out of fear of Śaṅkara, Śrī Caitanya Mahāprabhu could neither leave His room nor rub His lotuslike face against the walls.

TEXT 75

এই লীলা মহাপ্রভুর রঘুনাথ-দাস ।
গৌরাঙ্গ-স্তবকল্পবৃক্ষে করিয়াছে প্রকাশ ॥ ৭৫ ॥

ei līlā mahāprabhura raghunātha-dāsa
gaurāṅga-stava-kalpavṛkṣe kariyāche prakāśa

SYNONYMS

ei līlā—this pastime; *mahāprabhura*—of Śrī Caitanya Mahāprabhu; *raghunātha-dāsa*—Raghunātha dāsa Gosvāmī; *gaurāṅga-stava-kalpa-vṛkṣe*—in his book known as *Gaurāṅga-stava-kalpavṛkṣa; kariyāche prakāśa*—has described very nicely.

TRANSLATION

This pastime of Śrī Caitanya Mahāprabhu's has been described very nicely by Raghunātha dāsa Gosvāmī in his book known as Gaurāṅga-stava-kalpavṛkṣa.

TEXT 76

স্বকীয়স্য প্রাণার্বুদসদৃশ-গোষ্ঠস্য বিরহাৎ
প্রলাপানুন্মাদাৎ সততমতি কুর্বন্ বিকলধীঃ ।
দধদ্ভিত্তৌ শশ্বদ্বদনবিধুঘর্ষেণ রুধিরং
ক্ষতোত্থং গৌরাঙ্গো হৃদয় উদয়ন্মাং মদয়তি ॥ ৭৬ ॥

svakīyasya prāṇārbuda-sadṛśa-goṣṭhasya virahāt
pralāpān unmādāt satatam ati kurvan vikala-dhīḥ
dadhad bhittau śaśvad vadana-vidhu-gharṣeṇa rudhiraṁ
kṣatotthaṁ gaurāṅgo hṛdaya udayan māṁ madayati

SYNONYMS

svakīyasya—His own; *prāṇa-arbuda*—uncountable breaths of life; *sadṛśa*—like; *goṣṭhasya*—of Vṛndāvana; *virahāt*—because of separation; *pralāpān*—crazy talks; *unmādāt*—because of madness; *satatam*—always; *ati*—very much; *kurvan*—doing; *vikala-dhīḥ*—whose intelligence was disturbed; *dadhat*—oozing forth; *bhittau*—on the walls; *śaśvat*—always; *vadana-vidhu*—of His moonlike face; *gharṣeṇa*—by rubbing; *rudhiram*—blood; *kṣāta-uttham*—coming forth from injuries; *gaurāṅgaḥ*—Lord Śrī Caitanya Mahāprabhu; *hṛdaye*—in my heart; *udayan*—rising; *mām*—me; *madayati*—maddens.

TRANSLATION

"Because of separation from His many friends in Vṛndāvana, who were like His own life, Śrī Caitanya Mahāprabhu spoke like a madman. His intelligence was transformed. Day and night He rubbed His moonlike face against the walls, and blood flowed from the injuries. May that Śrī Caitanya Mahāprabhu rise in my heart and make me mad with love."

TEXT 77

এইমত মহাপ্রভু রাত্রি-দিবসে ।
প্রেমসিন্ধু-মগ্ন রহে, কভু ডুবে, ভাসে ॥ ৭৭ ॥

ei-mata mahāprabhu rātri-divase
prema-sindhu-magna rahe, kabhu ḍube, bhāse

SYNONYMS

ei-mata—in this way; *mahāprabhu*—Śrī Caitanya Mahāprabhu; *rātri-divase*—day and night; *prema-sindhu-magna rahe*—remains merged in the ocean of love of Kṛṣṇa; *kabhu ḍube*—sometimes drowns; *bhāse*—floats.

TRANSLATION

Śrī Caitanya Mahāprabhu in this way stayed immersed day and night in an ocean of ecstatic love for Kṛṣṇa. Sometimes He was submerged, and sometimes He floated.

TEXT 78

এককালে বৈশাখের পৌর্ণমাসী-দিনে ।
রাত্রিকালে মহাপ্রভু চলিলা উদ্যানে ॥ ৭৮ ॥

eka-kāle vaiśākhera paurṇamāsī-dine
rātri-kāle mahāprabhu calilā udyāne

SYNONYMS

eka-kāle—at one time; *vaiśākhera*—of the month of Vaiśākha, (April-May); *paurṇamāsī-dine*—on the full-moon night; *rātri-kāle*—at night; *mahāprabhu*—Śrī Caitanya Mahāprabhu; *calilā*—went; *udyāne*— to a garden.

TRANSLATION

One full-moon night in the month of Vaiśākha [April and May], Śrī Caitanya Mahāprabhu went to a garden.

TEXT 79

'জগন্নাথবল্লভ' নাম উদ্যানপ্রধানে ।
প্রবেশ করিলা প্রভু লঞা ভক্তগণে ॥ ৭৯ ॥

'jagannātha-vallabha' nāma udyāna-pradhāne
praveśa karilā prabhu lañā bhakta-gaṇe

SYNONYMS

jagannātha-vallabha—Jagannātha-vallabha; *nāma*—named; *udyāna-pradhāne*—one of the best gardens; *praveśa karilā*—entered; *prabhu*—Śrī Caitanya Mahāprabhu; *lañā*—taking; *bhakta-gaṇe*—the devotees.

TRANSLATION

The Lord, along with His devotees, entered one of the nicest gardens, called Jagannātha-vallabha.

TEXT 80

প্রফুল্লিত বৃক্ষ-বল্লী,—যেন বৃন্দাবন ।
শুক, শারী, পিক, ভৃঙ্গ করে আলাপন ॥ ৮০ ॥

praphullita vṛkṣa-vallī,——yena vṛndāvana
śuka, śārī, pika, bhṛṅga kare ālāpana

SYNONYMS

praphullita—fully blossomed; *vṛkṣa-vallī*—trees and creepers; *yena vṛndāvana*—exactly resembling Vṛndāvana; *śuka*—the *śuka* birds; *śārī*—the *śārī* birds; *pika*—the *pika* birds; *bhṛṅga*—the bumblebees; *kare*—do; *ālāpana*—talking with one another.

TRANSLATION

In the garden were fully blossomed trees and creepers exactly like those in Vṛndāvana. Bumblebees and birds like the śuka, śārī and pika talked with one another.

TEXT 81

পুষ্পগন্ধ লঞা বহে মলয়-পবন ।
'গুরু' হঞা তরুলতায় শিখায় নাচন ॥ ৮১ ॥

puṣpa-gandha lañā vahe malaya-pavana
'guru' hañā taru-latāya śikhāya nācana

SYNONYMS

puṣpa-gandha—the fragrance of the flowers; *lañā*—taking; *vahe*—blows; *malaya-pavana*—the mild breeze; *guru hañā*—becoming the spiritual master; *taru-latāya*—to the trees and creepers; *śikhāya*—instructs; *nācana*—dancing.

TRANSLATION

A mild breeze was blowing, carrying the fragrance of aromatic flowers. The breeze had become a guru and was teaching all the trees and creepers how to dance.

TEXT 82

পূর্ণচন্দ্র-চন্দ্রিকায় পরম উজ্জ্বল ।
তরুলতাদি জ্যোৎস্নায় করে ঝলমল ॥ ৮২ ॥

pūrṇa-candra-candrikāya parama ujjvala
taru-latādi jyotsnāya kare jhalamala

SYNONYMS

pūrṇa-candra—of the full moon; *candrikāya*—by the shine; *parama*—very; *ujjvala*—bright; *taru-latā-ādi*—the creepers, trees and so on; *jyotsnāya*—in the illumination of the moonshine; *kare*—do; *jhalamala*—glittering.

TRANSLATION

Brightly illuminated by the full moon, the trees and creepers glittered in the light.

TEXT 83

ছয় ঋতুগণ যাহাঁ বসন্ত প্রধান ।
দেখি' আনন্দিত হৈলা গৌর ভগবান্ ॥ ৮৩ ॥

chaya ṛtu-gaṇa yāhāṅ vasanta pradhāna
dekhi' ānandita hailā gaura bhagavān

SYNONYMS

chaya—six; *ṛtu-gaṇa*—seasons; *yāhāṅ*—where; *vasanta pradhāna*—the spring season was chief; *dekhi'*—seeing; *ānandita*—very pleased; *hailā*—became; *gaura*—Śrī Caitanya Mahāprabhu; *bhagavān*—the Supreme Personality of Godhead.

TRANSLATION

The six seasons, especially spring, seemed present there. Seeing the garden, Śrī Caitanya Mahāprabhu, the Supreme Personality of Godhead, was very happy.

TEXT 84

"ললিত-লবঙ্গলতা" পদ গাওয়াঞা ।
নৃত্য করি' বুলেন প্রভু নিজগণ লঞা ॥ ৮৪ ॥

"lalita-lavaṅga-latā" pada gāoyāñā
nṛtya kari' bulena prabhu nija-gaṇa lañā

SYNONYMS

lalita-lavaṅga-latā—beginning with the words *lalita-lavaṅga-latā; pada*—the verse; *gāoyāñā*—making sing; *nṛtya kari'*—dancing; *bulena*—wanders; *prabhu*—Śrī Caitanya Mahāprabhu; *nija-gaṇa lañā*—accompanied by His personal associates.

TRANSLATION

In this atmosphere, the Lord had His associates sing a verse from the Gīta-govinda, beginning with the words "lalita-lavaṅga-latā," as He danced and wandered about with them.

TEXT 85

প্রতিবৃক্ষবল্লী ঐছে ভ্রমিতে ভ্রমিতে ।
অশোকের তলে কৃষ্ণে দেখেন আচম্বিতে ॥ ৮৫ ॥

prati-vṛkṣa-vallī aiche bhramite bhramite
aśokera tale kṛṣṇe dekhena ācambite

SYNONYMS

prati-vṛkṣa-vallī—around each and every tree and creeper; *aiche*—in that way; *bhramite bhramite*—wandering; *aśokera tale*—underneath an *aśoka* tree; *kṛṣṇe*—Lord Kṛṣṇa; *dekhena*—He sees; *ācambite*—suddenly.

TRANSLATION

As He thus wandered around every tree and creeper, He came beneath an *aśoka* tree and suddenly saw Lord Kṛṣṇa.

TEXT 86

কৃষ্ণ দেখি' মহাপ্রভু ধাঞা চলিলা।
আগে দেখি' হাসি' কৃষ্ণ অন্তর্ধান হইলা ॥ ৮৬ ॥

kṛṣṇa dekhi' mahāprabhu dhāñā calilā
āge dekhi' hāsi' kṛṣṇa antardhāna ha-ilā

SYNONYMS

kṛṣṇa dekhi'—seeing Kṛṣṇa; *mahāprabhu*—Śrī Caitanya Mahāprabhu; *dhāñā calilā*—began to run very swiftly; *āge*—ahead; *dekhi'*—seeing; *hāsi'*—smiling; *kṛṣṇa*—Lord Kṛṣṇa; *antardhāna ha-ilā*—disappeared.

TRANSLATION

When He saw Kṛṣṇa, Śrī Caitanya Mahāprabhu began running very swiftly, but Kṛṣṇa smiled and disappeared.

TEXT 87

আগে পাইলা কৃষ্ণে, তাঁরে পুনঃ হারাঞা।
ভূমেতে পড়িলা প্রভু মূর্চ্ছিত হঞা ॥ ৮৭ ॥

āge pāilā kṛṣṇe, tāṅre punaḥ hārāñā
bhūmete paḍilā prabhu mūrcchita hañā

SYNONYMS

āge—in the beginning; *pāilā*—got; *kṛṣṇe*—Lord Kṛṣṇa; *tāṅre*—Him; *punaḥ*—again; *hārāñā*—losing; *bhūmete*—on the ground; *paḍilā*—fell down; *prabhu*—Lord Śrī Caitanya Mahāprabhu; *mūrcchita*—unconscious; *hañā*—becoming.

TRANSLATION

Having first gotten Kṛṣṇa and then having lost Him again, Śrī Caitanya Mahāprabhu fell to the ground unconscious.

TEXT 88

কৃষ্ণের শ্রীঅঙ্গগন্ধে ভরিছে উদ্যানে ।
সেই গন্ধ পাঞা প্রভু হৈলা অচেতনে ॥ ৮৮ ॥

kṛṣṇera śrī-aṅga-gandhe bhariche udyāne
sei gandha pāñā prabhu hailā acetane

SYNONYMS

kṛṣṇera—of Lord Kṛṣṇa; *śrī-aṅga-gandhe*—the aroma of the transcendental body; *bhariche*—filled; *udyāne*—in the garden; *sei gandha pāñā*—getting that aroma; *prabhu*—Śrī Caitanya Mahāprabhu; *hailā*—became; *acetane*—unconscious.

TRANSLATION

The entire garden was filled with the scent of Lord Śrī Kṛṣṇa's transcendental body. When Śrī Caitanya Mahāprabhu smelled it, He fell unconscious at once.

TEXT 89

নিরন্তর নাসায় পশে কৃষ্ণ-পরিমল ।
গন্ধ আস্বাদিতে প্রভু হইলা পাগল ॥ ৮৯ ॥

nirantara nāsāya paśe kṛṣṇa-parimala
gandha āsvādite prabhu ha-ilā pāgala

SYNONYMS

nirantara—incessantly; *nāsāya*—in the nostrils; *paśe*—enters; *kṛṣṇa-parimala*—the scent of Kṛṣṇa's body; *gandha āsvādite*—to relish the fragrance; *prabhu*—Śrī Caitanya Mahāprabhu; *ha-ilā pāgala*—became mad.

TRANSLATION

The scent of Kṛṣṇa's body, however, incessantly entered His nostrils, and the Lord became mad to relish it.

TEXT 90

কৃষ্ণগন্ধ-লুব্ধা রাধা সখীরে যে কহিলা ।
সেই শ্লোক পড়ি' প্রভু অর্থ করিলা ॥ ৯০ ॥

kṛṣṇa-gandha-lubdhā rādhā sakhīre ye kahilā
sei śloka paḍi' prabhu artha karilā

SYNONYMS

kṛṣṇa-gandha—the scent of the body of Kṛṣṇa; *lubdhā*—hankering after; *rādhā*—Śrīmatī Rādhārāṇī; *sakhīre*—to the *gopī* friends; *ye kahilā*—whatever She said; *sei*—that; *śloka*—verse; *paḍi'*—reciting; *prabhu*—Śrī Caitanya Mahāprabhu; *artha karilā*—explained its meaning.

TRANSLATION

Śrīmatī Rādhārāṇī expressed to Her gopī friends how She hankers for the transcendental scent of Kṛṣṇa's body. Śrī Caitanya Mahāprabhu recited that same verse and made its meaning clear.

TEXT 91

কুরঙ্গমদজিদ্বপুঃপরিমলোর্মিকৃষ্টাঙ্গনঃ
স্বকাঙ্গ-নলিনাষ্টকে শশিযুতাব্জগন্ধপ্রথঃ ।
মদেন্দুবরচন্দনাগুরুসুগন্ধিচর্চার্চিতঃ
স মে মদনমোহনঃ সখি তনোতি নাসাস্পৃহাম্ ॥ ৯১ ॥

kuraṅga-mada-jid-vapuḥ-parimalormi-kṛṣṭāṅganaḥ
svakāṅga-nalināṣṭake śaśi-yutābja-gandha-prathaḥ
madenduvara-candanāguru-sugandhi-carcārcitaḥ
sa me madana-mohanaḥ sakhi tanoti nāsā-spṛhām

SYNONYMS

kuraṅga-mada-jit—conquering the aromatic smell of musk; *vapuḥ*—of His transcendental body; *parimala-ūrmi*—with waves of scent; *kṛṣṭa-aṅganaḥ*—attracting the *gopīs* of Vṛndāvana; *svaka-aṅga-nalina-aṣṭake*—on all eight different lotuslike parts of the body (face, navel, eyes, palms and feet); *śaśi-yuta-abja-gandha-prathaḥ*—who distributes the scent of lotus mixed with camphor; *mada-induvara-candana-aguru-sugandhi-carca-arcitaḥ*—smeared with the unguents of musk, camphor, white sandalwood and *aguru; saḥ*—He; *me*—My; *madana-mohanaḥ*—Lord Kṛṣṇa, who enchants even Cupid; *sakhi*—O My dear friends; *tanoti*—increases; *nāsā-spṛhām*—the desire of My nostrils.

TRANSLATION

" 'The scent of Kṛṣṇa's transcendental body surpasses the aroma of musk and attracts the minds of all women. The eight lotuslike parts of His body distribute the fragrance of lotuses mixed with that of camphor. His body is anointed with aromatic substances like musk, camphor, sandalwood and aguru. O My dear friend, that Personality of Godhead, also known as the enchanter of Cupid, always increases the desire of My nostrils.'

PURPORT

This is a verse found in *Govinda-līlāmṛta* (8.6).

TEXT 92

কস্তূরিকা-নীলোৎপল, তার যেই পরিমল,
তাহা জিনি' কৃষ্ণ-অঙ্গ-গন্ধ ।
ব্যাপে চৌদ্দ-ভুবনে, করে সর্ব আকর্ষণে,
নারীগণের আঁখি করে অন্ধ ॥ ৯২ ॥

kastūrikā-nīlotpala, tāra yei parimala,
tāhā jini' kṛṣṇa-aṅga-gandha
vyāpe caudda-bhuvane, kare sarva ākarṣaṇe,
nārī-gaṇera āṅkhi kare andha

SYNONYMS

kastūrikā—musk; *nīlotpala*—combined with the bluish lotus flower; *tāra*—its; *yei*—whatever; *parimala*—scent; *tāhā*—that; *jini'*—conquering; *kṛṣṇa-aṅga*—of the transcendental body of Kṛṣṇa; *gandha*—the scent; *vyāpe*—spreads; *caudda-bhuvane*—throughout the fourteen worlds; *kare*—does; *sarva ākarṣaṇe*—attracting everyone; *nārī-gaṇera*—of the women; *āṅkhi*—the eyes; *kare*—makes; *andha*—blind.

TRANSLATION

"The scent of Kṛṣṇa's body surpasses the fragrances of musk and the bluish lotus flower. Spreading throughout the fourteen worlds, it attracts everyone and makes the eyes of all women blind.

TEXT 93

সখি হে, কৃষ্ণগন্ধ জগৎ মাতায় ।
নারীর নাসাতে পশে, সর্বকাল তাহাঁ বৈসে,
কৃষ্ণপাশ ধরি' লঞা যায় ॥ ৯৩ ॥ ধ্রু ॥

sakhi he, kṛṣṇa-gandha jagat mātāya
nārīra nāsāte paśe, sarva-kāla tāhāṅ vaise,
kṛṣṇa-pāśa dhari' lañā yāya

SYNONYMS

sakhi he—O My dear friend; *kṛṣṇa-gandha*—the fragrance of the body of Kṛṣṇa; *jagat mātāya*—enchants the whole world; *nārīra*—of women; *nāsāte*—in the nostrils; *paśe*—enters; *sarva-kāla*—always; *tāhāṅ*—there; *vaise*—remains; *kṛṣṇa-pāśa*—to the side of Lord Kṛṣṇa; *dhari'*—catching; *lañā yāya*—takes one.

TRANSLATION

"My dear friend, the scent of Kṛṣṇa's body enchants the entire world. It especially enters the nostrils of women and remains seated there. Thus it captures them and forcibly brings them to Kṛṣṇa.

TEXT 94

নেত্র-নাভি, বদন, কর-যুগ চরণ,
এই অষ্টপদ্ম কৃষ্ণ-অঙ্গে ।
কর্পূর-লিপ্ত কমল, তার যৈছে পরিমল,
সেই গন্ধ অষ্টপদ্ম-সঙ্গে ॥ ৯৪ ॥

netra-nābhi, vadana, kara-yuga caraṇa,
ei aṣṭa-padma kṛṣṇa-aṅge
karpūra-lipta kamala, tāra yaiche parimala,
sei gandha aṣṭa-padma-saṅge

SYNONYMS

netra—the eyes; *nābhi*—the navel; *vadana*—the face; *kara-yuga*—the palms; *caraṇa*—the feet; *ei*—these; *aṣṭa*—eight; *padma*—lotus flowers; *kṛṣṇa-aṅge*—in the body of Kṛṣṇa; *karpūra*—with camphor; *lipta*—smeared; *kamala*—the lotus flower; *tāra*—of that; *yaiche*—like; *parimala*—the fragrance; *sei gandha*—that fragrance; *aṣṭa-padma-saṅge*—is associated with the eight lotus flowers.

TRANSLATION

"Kṛṣṇa's eyes, navel and face, hands and feet are like eight lotus flowers on His body. From those eight lotuses emanates a fragrance like a mixture of camphor and lotus. That is the scent associated with His body.

TEXT 95

হেম-কীলিত চন্দন, তাহা করি' ঘর্ষণ,
তাহে অগুরু, কুঙ্কুম, কস্তূরী।
কর্পূর-সনে চর্চা অঙ্গে, পূর্ব অঙ্গের গন্ধ সঙ্গে,
মিলি' তারে যেন কৈল চুরি ॥ ৯৫ ॥

hema-kīlita candana, tāhā kari' gharṣaṇa,
tāhe aguru, kuṅkuma, kastūrī
karpūra-sane carcā aṅge, pūrva aṅgera gandha saṅge,
mili' tāre yena kaila curi

SYNONYMS

hema—with gold; *kīlita*—bedecked; *candana*—white sandalwood; *tāhā*—that; *kari'*—doing; *gharṣaṇa*—rubbing; *tāhe*—in that; *aguru*—the *aguru* flavor; *kuṅkuma*—*kuṅkuma;* *kastūrī*—and musk; *karpūra*—camphor; *sane*—with; *carcā*—smearing; *aṅge*—on the body; *pūrva*—previous; *aṅgera*—of the body; *gandha*—scent; *saṅge*—with; *mili'*—combining; *tāre*—that; *yena*—as if; *kaila*—did; *curi*—stealing or covering.

TRANSLATION

"When sandalwood pulp with aguru, kuṅkuma and musk is mixed with camphor and spread on Kṛṣṇa's body, it combines with Kṛṣṇa's own original bodily perfume and seems to cover it.

PURPORT

In another version, the last line of this verse reads, *kāmadevera mana kaila curi.* This means "the scent of all these substances mixes with the previous scent of Kṛṣṇa's body and steals away the mind of Cupid."

TEXT 96

হরে নারীর তনুমন, নাসা করে ঘূর্ণন,
খসায় নীবি, ছুটায় কেশবন্ধ।
করিয়া আগে বাউরী, নাচায় জগৎ-নারী,
হেন ডাকাতিয়া কৃষ্ণাঙ্গগন্ধ ॥ ৯৬ ॥

hare nārīra tanu-mana, nāsā kare ghūrṇana,
khasāya nīvi, chuṭāya keśa-bandha

kariyā āge bāurī, nācāya jagat-nārī,
hena ḍākātiyā kṛṣṇāṅga-gandha

SYNONYMS

hare—enchants; *nārīra*—of women; *tanu-mana*—the minds and bodies; *nāsā*—the nostrils; *kare ghūrṇana*—bewilders; *khasāya*—slackens; *nīvi*—the belt; *chuṭāya*—loosens; *keśa-bandha*—the bunch of hair; *kariyā*—acting; *āge*—in front; *bāurī*—like madwomen; *nācāya*—causes to dance; *jagat-nārī*—all the women of the world; *hena*—such; *ḍākātiyā*—a plunderer; *kṛṣṇa-aṅga-gandha*—the scent of Kṛṣṇa's body.

TRANSLATION

"The scent of Kṛṣṇa's transcendental body is so attractive that it enchants the bodies and minds of all women. It bewilders their nostrils, loosens their belts and hair, and makes them madwomen. All the women of world come under its influence, and therefore the scent of Kṛṣṇa's body is like a plunderer.

TEXT 97

সেই গন্ধবশ নাসা, সদা করে গন্ধের আশা,
কভু পায়, কভু নাহি পায় ।
পাইলে পিয়া পেট ভরে, পিঙ পিঙ তবু করে,
না পাইলে তৃষ্ণায় মরি' যায় ॥ ৯৭ ॥

sei gandha-vaśa nāsā, sadā kare gandhera āśā,
kabhu pāya, kabhu nāhi pāya
pāile piyā peṭa bhare, piṅa piṅa tabu kare,
nā pāile tṛṣṇāya mari' yāya

SYNONYMS

sei—that; *gandha-vaśa*—under the control of the fragrance; *nāsā*—the nostrils; *sadā*—always; *kare*—make; *gandhera*—for the fragrance; *āśā*—hope; *kabhu pāya*—sometimes they obtain; *kabhu nāhi pāya*—sometimes do not obtain; *pāile*—if obtaining; *piyā*—drinking; *peṭa*—the belly; *bhare*—fills; *piṅa*—let me drink; *piṅa*—let me drink; *tabu*—still: *kare*—they hanker; *nā pāile*—if they do not get; *tṛṣṇāya*—out of thirst; *mari' yāya*—they die.

TRANSLATION

"Falling completely under its influence, the nostrils yearn for it continuously, although sometimes they obtain it and sometimes not. When they do they drink their fill, though they still want more and more, but if they don't, out of thirst they die.

TEXT 98

মদনমোহন-নাট, পসারি গন্ধের হাট,
জগন্নারী-গ্রাহকে লোভায়।
বিনা-মূল্যে দেয় গন্ধ, গন্ধ দিয়া করে অন্ধ,
ঘর যাইতে পথ নাহি পায়॥" ৯৮ ॥

madana-mohana-nāṭa, pasāri gandhera hāṭa,
jagan-nārī-grāhake lobhāya
vinā-mūlye deya gandha, gandha diyā kare andha,
ghara yāite patha nāhi pāya"

SYNONYMS

madana-mohana-nāṭa—the dramatic player Madana-mohana; *pasāri*—a dealer; *gandhera hāṭa*—in a market of scents; *jagat-nārī*—of the women of the whole world; *grāhake*—to the customers; *lobhāya*—attracts; *vinā-mūlye*—without a price; *deya*—distributes; *gandha*—the scent; *gandha diyā*—delivering the scent; *kare andha*—makes the customers blind; *ghara yāite*—to return home; *patha*—the path; *nāhi pāya*—do not find.

TRANSLATION

"The dramatic actor Madana-mohana has opened a shop of scents that attract the women of the world to be His customers. He delivers the scents freely, but they make the women all so blind they cannot find the path returning home."

TEXT 99

এইমত গৌরহরি, গন্ধে কৈল মন চুরি,
ভৃঙ্গপ্রায় ইতি-উতি ধায়।
যায় বৃক্ষলতা-পাশে, কৃষ্ণ স্ফুরে—সেই আশে,
কৃষ্ণ না পায়, গন্ধমাত্র পায়॥ ৯৯ ॥

ei-mata gaurahari, gandhe kaila mana curi,
bhṛṅga-prāya iti-uti dhāya
yāya vṛkṣa-latā-pāśe, kṛṣṇa sphure——sei āśe,
kṛṣṇa nā pāya, gandha-mātra pāya

SYNONYMS

ei-mata—in this way; *gaurahari*—Śrī Caitanya Mahāprabhu; *gandhe*—by the scent; *kaila*—did; *mana curi*—stealing of the mind; *bhṛṅga-prāya*—just like a bumblebee; *iti-uti dhāya*—wanders here and there; *yāya*—goes; *vṛkṣa-latā-pāśe*—by the side of the trees and creepers; *kṛṣṇa sphure*—Lord Kṛṣṇa will appear; *sei āśe*—by that hope; *kṛṣṇa nā pāya*—does not obtain Kṛṣṇa; *gandha-mātra pāya*—gets only the scent.

TRANSLATION

Śrī Caitanya Mahāprabhu, His mind thus stolen by that scent, ran here and there like a bumblebee. He ran to the trees and plants, hoping that Lord Kṛṣṇa would appear, but instead He found only the scent of Kṛṣṇa's body.

TEXT 100

স্বরূপ-রামানন্দ গায়, প্রভু নাচে, সুখ পায়,
এইমতে প্রাতঃকাল হৈল ।
স্বরূপ-রামানন্দরায়, করি নানা উপায়,
মহাপ্রভুর বাহ্যস্ফূর্তি কৈল ॥ ১০০ ॥

svarūpa-rāmānanda gāya, prabhu nāce, sukha pāya,
ei-mate prātaḥ-kāla haila
svarūpa-rāmānanda-rāya, kari nānā upāya,
mahāprabhura bāhya-sphūrti kaila

SYNONYMS

svarūpa-rāmānanda gāya—Svarūpa Dāmodara Gosvāmī and Rāmānanda Rāya sing; *prabhu nāce*—Lord Śrī Caitanya Mahāprabhu dances; *sukha pāya*—enjoys happiness; *ei-mate*—in this way; *prātaḥ-kāla haila*—morning arrived; *svarūpa-rāmānanda-rāya*—both Svarūpa Dāmodara Gosvāmī and Rāmānanda Rāya; *kari*—devising; *nānā*—various; *upāya*—means; *mahāprabhura*—of Śrī Caitanya Mahāprabhu; *bāhya-sphūrti kaila*—awakened the external consciousness.

TRANSLATION

Both Svarūpa Dāmodara and Rāmānanda Rāya sang to the Lord, who danced and enjoyed happiness until the morning arrived. Then they devised a plan to revive the Lord to external consciousness.

TEXT 101

মাতৃভক্তি, প্রলাপন, ভিত্ত্যে মুখ-ঘর্ষণ,
কৃষ্ণগন্ধ-স্ফূর্ত্যে দিব্যনৃত্য ।
এই চারিলীলা-ভেদে, গাইল এই পরিচ্ছেদে,
কৃষ্ণদাস রূপগোসাঞি-ভৃত্য ॥ ১০১ ॥

mātṛ-bhakti, pralāpana, bhittye mukha-gharṣaṇa,
kṛṣṇa-gandha-sphūrtye divya-nṛtya
ei cāri-līlā-bhede, gāila ei paricchede,
kṛṣṇadāsa rūpa-gosāñi-bhṛtya

SYNONYMS

mātṛ-bhakti—devotion to His mother; *pralāpana*—words of madness; *bhittye*—on the walls; *mukha-gharṣaṇa*—rubbing His face; *kṛṣṇa-gandha*—of Lord Kṛṣṇa's fragrance; *sphūrtye*—on the appearance; *divya-nṛtya*—transcendental dancing; *ei*—these; *cāri*—four; *līlā*—pastimes; *bhede*—different; *gāila*—has sung; *ei paricchede*—in this chapter; *kṛṣṇadāsa*—Kṛṣṇadāsa Kavirāja; *rūpa-gosāñi-bhṛtya*—servant of Śrīla Rūpa Gosvāmī.

TRANSLATION

Thus, I, Kṛṣṇadāsa, the servant of Śrīla Rūpa Gosvāmī, have sung of four divisions of the Lord's pastimes in this chapter: the Lord's devotion to His mother, His words of madness, His rubbing His face against the walls at night, and His dancing at the appearance of Lord Kṛṣṇa's fragrance.

PURPORT

Kṛṣṇadāsa Kavirāja Gosvāmī says that he has been able to describe these four pastimes of Śrī Caitanya Mahāprabhu by the blessings of Śrīla Rūpa Gosvāmī. Kṛṣṇadāsa Kavirāja Gosvāmī was not actually a direct disciple of Śrīla Rūpa Gosvāmī , but he followed the instructions given by Śrīla Rūpa Gosvāmī in *Bhakti-rasāmṛta-sindhu.* He therefore acted according to the directions of Rūpa Gosvāmī and prayed in every chapter for his mercy.

TEXT 102

এইমত মহাপ্রভু পাঞা চেতন ।
স্নান করি' কৈল জগন্নাথ-দরশন ॥ ১০২ ॥

ei-mata mahāprabhu pāñā cetana
snāna kari' kaila jagannātha-daraśana

SYNONYMS

ei-mata—in this way; *mahāprabhu*—Śrī Caitanya Mahāprabhu; *pāñā cetana*—becoming conscious; *snāna kari'*—after bathing; *kaila jagannātha-daraśana*—saw Lord Jagannātha.

TRANSLATION

Śrī Caitanya Mahāprabhu thus returned to consciousness. He then bathed and went to see Lord Jagannātha.

TEXT 103

অলৌকিক কৃষ্ণলীলা, দিব্যশক্তি তার ।
তর্কের গোচর নহে চরিত্র যাহার ॥ ১০৩ ॥

alaukika kṛṣṇa-līlā, divya-śakti tāra
tarkera gocara nahe caritra yāhāra

SYNONYMS

alaukika—uncommon; *kṛṣṇa-līlā*—pastimes of Lord Kṛṣṇa; *divya-śakti*—transcendental potency; *tāra*—of that; *tarkera*—of argument; *gocara*—within the purview; *nahe*—is not; *caritra*—the characteristics; *yāhāra*—of which.

TRANSLATION

The pastimes of Lord Kṛṣṇa are uncommonly full of transcendental potency. It is a characteristic of such pastimes that they do not fall within the jurisdiction of experimental logic and arguments.

TEXT 104

এই প্রেম সদা জাগে যাহার অন্তরে ।
পণ্ডিতেহ তার চেষ্টা বুঝিতে না পারে ॥ ১০৪ ॥

ei prema sadā jāge yāhāra antare
paṇḍiteha tāra ceṣṭā bujhite nā pāre

SYNONYMS

ei—this; *prema*—love of Godhead; *sadā*—always; *jāge*—awakens; *yāhāra*—of whom; *antare*—within the heart; *paṇḍiteha*—even a learned scholar; *tāra*—his; *ceṣṭā*—activities; *bujhite*—to understand; *nā pāre*—cannot.

TRANSLATION

When transcendental love of Kṛṣṇa awakens in one's heart, even a learned scholar cannot comprehend one's activities.

TEXT 105

ধন্যস্যায়ং নবঃ প্রেমা যস্যোন্মীলতি চেতসি ।
অন্তর্বাণীভিরপ্যস্য মুদ্রা সুষ্ঠু সুদুর্গমা ॥ ১০৫ ॥

dhanyasyāyaṁ navaḥ premā
yasyonmīlati cetasi
antarvāṇībhir apy asya
mudrā suṣṭhu sudurgamā

SYNONYMS

dhanyasya—of a most fortunate person; *ayam*—this; *navaḥ*—new; *premā*—love of Godhead; *yasya*—of whom; *unmīlati*—manifests; *cetasi*—in the heart; *antarvāṇībhiḥ*—by persons well versed in *śāstras; api*—even; *asya*—of him; *mudrā*—the symptoms; *suṣṭhu*—exceedingly; *sudurgamā*—difficult to understand.

TRANSLATION

"The activities and symptoms of that exalted personality in whose heart love of Godhead has awakened cannot be understood even by the most learned scholar."

PURPORT

This verse is quoted from *Bhakti-rasāmṛta-sindhu* (1.4.17).

TEXT 106

অলৌকিক প্রভুর 'চেষ্টা', 'প্রলাপ' শুনিয়া ।
তর্ক না করিহ, শুন বিশ্বাস করিয়া ॥ ১০৬ ॥

alaukika prabhura 'ceṣṭā', 'pralāpa' śuniyā
tarka nā kariha, śuna viśvāsa kariyā

SYNONYMS

alaukika—uncommon; *prabhura*—of Śrī Caitanya Mahāprabhu; *ceṣṭā*—the activities; *pralāpa*—talking in madness; *śuniyā*—hearing; *tarka*—unnecessary arguments; *nā kariha*—do not make; *śuna*—simply hear; *viśvāsa kariyā*—having full faith.

TRANSLATION

The activities of Śrī Caitanya Mahāprabhu are undoubtedly uncommon, especially His talking like a madman. Therefore, one who hears of these pastimes should not put forward mundane arguments. He should simply hear the pastimes with full faith.

TEXT 107

ইহার সত্যত্বে প্রমাণ শ্রীভাগবতে ।
শ্রীরাধার প্রেম-প্রলাপ 'ভ্রমর-গীতা'তে ॥ ১০৭ ॥

ihāra satyatve pramāṇa śrī-bhāgavate
śrī-rādhāra prema-pralāpa 'bhramara-gītā'te

SYNONYMS

ihāra—of these talks; *satyatve*—in the truthfulness; *pramāṇa*—the evidence; *śrī-bhāgavate*—in *Śrīmad-Bhāgavatam; śrī-rādhāra*—of Śrīmatī Rādhārāṇī; *prema-pralāpa*—talking crazily in ecstatic love; *bhramara-gītāte*—in the section known as *Bhramara-gītā.*

TRANSLATION

The evidence of the truth of these talks is found in Śrīmad-Bhāgavatam. There, in the section of the Tenth Canto known as the Bhramara-gītā, "the Song to the Bumblebee," Śrīmatī Rādhārāṇī speaks insanely in ecstatic love for Kṛṣṇa.

PURPORT

When Uddhava arrived from Mathurā carrying a message for the *gopīs,* the *gopīs* began talking about Kṛṣṇa and crying. Then one important *gopī* saw a bumblebee and began speaking to it like someone mad, thinking that the bee was a messenger of Uddhava's or was someone very dear to him and Kṛṣṇa. The verses are as follows (*Bhāg.* 10.47.12-21):

madhupa kitava-bandho mā spṛśāṅghriṁ sapatnyāḥ
kuca-vilulita-mālā-kuṅkuma-śmaśrubhir naḥ
vahatu madhu-patis tan-māninīnāṁ prasādaṁ
yadu-sadasi viḍambyaṁ yasya dūtas tvam īdṛk

"My dear bumblebee, you are a very cunning friend of Uddhava and Kṛṣṇa. You are very expert in touching people's feet, but I am not going to be misled by this. You appear to have sat on the breasts of one of Kṛṣṇa's friends, for I see that you have *kuṅkuma* dust on your mustache. Kṛṣṇa is now engaged in flattering all His young girl friends in Mathurā. Therefore, now that He can be called a friend of the residents of Mathurā, He does not need the help of the residents of Vṛndāvana. He has no reason to satisfy us *gopīs.* Since you are the messenger of such a person as He, what is the use of your presence here? Certainly Kṛṣṇa would be ashamed of your presence in this assembly."

How has Kṛṣṇa offended the *gopīs* so that they want to reject Him from their minds? The answer is given as follows:

sakṛd adhara-sudhāṁ svāṁ mohinīṁ pāyayitvā
sumanasa iva sadyas tatyaje 'smān bhavādṛk
paricarati kathaṁ tat-pāda-padmaṁ tu padmā
hy api bata hṛta-cetā uttama-śloka-jalpaiḥ

"Kṛṣṇa no longer gives us the enchanting nectar of His lips; instead, He now gives that nectar to the women of Mathurā. Kṛṣṇa directly attracts our minds, yet He resembles a bumblebee like you because He gives up the association of a beautiful flower and goes to a flower that is inferior. That is the way Kṛṣṇa has treated us. I do not know why the goddess of fortune continues to serve His lotus feet instead of leaving them aside. Apparently she believes in Kṛṣṇa's false words. We *gopīs,* however, are not unintelligent like Lakṣmī."

After hearing the bumblebee's sweet songs and recognizing that the bee was singing about Kṛṣṇa for Her satisfaction, the *gopī* replied,

kim iha bahu ṣaḍaṅghre gāyasi tvaṁ yadūnām
adhipatim agṛhāṇām agrato naḥ purāṇam
vijaya-sakha-sakhīnāṁ gīyatāṁ tat-prasaṅgaḥ
kṣapita-kucarujas te kalpayantīṣṭam iṣṭāḥ

"Dear bumblebee, Lord Kṛṣṇa has no residence here, but we know Him as Yadupati [the King of the Yadu dynasty]. We know Him very well, and therefore we are not interested in hearing any more songs about Him. It would be better for you to go sing to those who are now very dear to Kṛṣṇa. Those women of Mathurā have now achieved the opportunity to be embraced by Him. They are His beloveds now, and therefore He has relieved the burning in their breasts. If you go there and sing your songs to those fortunate women, they will be very pleased, and they will honor you."

divi bhuvi ca rasāyāṁ kāḥ striyas tad durāpāḥ
kapaṭa-rucira-hāsa-bhrūvi-jṛmbhasya yāḥ syuḥ
caraṇa-raja upāste yasya bhūtir vayaṁ kā
api ca kṛpaṇa-pakṣe hy uttamaśloka-śabdaḥ

"O collector of honey, Kṛṣṇa must be very sorry not to see us *gopīs*. Surely He is afflicted by memories of our pastimes. Therefore He has sent you as a messenger to satisfy us. Do not speak to us! All the women in the three worlds where death is inevitable—the heavenly, middle and lower planets—are very easily available to Kṛṣṇa because His curved eyebrows are so attractive. Moreover, He is always served very faithfully by the goddess of fortune. In comparison with her, we are most insignificant. Indeed, we are nothing. Yet although He is very cunning, Kṛṣṇa is also very charitable. You may inform Him that He is praised for His kindness to unfortunate persons and that He is therefore known as Uttamaśloka, one who is praised by chosen words and verses."

visṛja śirasi pādaṁ vedmy ahaṁ cāṭukārair
anunaya-viduṣas te 'bhyetya dautyair mukundāt
svakṛta iha visṛṣṭāpatya-paty-anya-lokā
vyasṛjad akṛta-cetāḥ kiṁ nu sandheyam asmin

"You are buzzing at My feet just to be forgiven for your past offenses. Kindly go away from My feet! I know that Mukunda has taught you to speak very sweet, flattering words like this and to act as His messenger. These are certainly clever tricks, My dear bumblebee, but I can understand them. This is Kṛṣṇa's offense. Do not tell Kṛṣṇa what I have said, although I know that you are very envious. We *gopīs* have given up our husbands, our sons, and all the religious principles that promise better births, and now we have no other business then serving Kṛṣṇa. Yet Kṛṣṇa, by controlling His mind, has easily forgotten us. Therefore, don't speak of Him any more. Let us forget our relationship."

mṛgayur iva kapīndraṁ vivyadhe lubdha-dharmā
striyam akṛta-virūpāṁ strī-jitaḥ kāmayānām
balim api balim attvāveṣṭayad dhvāṅkṣavad yas
tad alam asita-sakhyair dustyajas tat-kathārthaḥ

"When we remember the past births of Kṛṣṇa, My dear bumblebee, we are very afraid of Him. In His incarnation as Lord Rāmacandra, He acted just like a hunter and unjustly killed His friend Vāli. Lusty Śūrpaṇakhā came to satisfy Rāmacandra's desires, but He was so attached to Sītādevī that He cut off Śūrpaṇakhā's nose. In His incarnation as Vāmanadeva, He plundered Bali Mahārāja and took all his possessions, cheating him on the pretext of accepting worship from him. Vāmanadeva caught Bali Mahārāja exactly as one catches a crow. My dear bumblebee, it is not very good to make friends with such a person. I know that once one begins to talk about Kṛṣṇa, it is very difficult to stop, and I admit that I have insufficient strength to give up talking about Him."

yad-anucarita-līlā-karṇa-pīyuṣa-vipruṭ
sakṛd adana-vidhūta-dvandva-dharmā vinaṣṭāḥ
sapadi gṛha-kuṭumbaṁ dīnam utsṛjya dīnā
bahava iha vihaṅgā bhikṣu-caryāṁ caranti

"Topics about Kṛṣṇa are so powerful that they destroy the four religious principles—religion, economic development, sense gratification and liberation. Anyone who drinks even a small drop of *kṛṣṇa-kathā* through aural reception is freed from all material attachment and envy. Like a bird with no means of subsistence, such a person becomes a mendicant and lives by begging. Ordinary household affairs become miserable for him, and without attachment he suddenly gives up everything. Although such renunciation is quite suitable, because I am a woman I am unable to adopt it."

vayam ṛtam iva jihma-vyāhṛtaṁ śraddadhānāḥ
kulikarutam ivājñāḥ kṛṣṇa-vadhvo hiraṇyaḥ
dadṛśur asakṛd etat tan-nakha-sparśatīvra-
smararuja upamantrin bhaṇyatām anya-vārtā

"O My dear messenger, I am just like a foolish bird that hears the sweet songs of a hunter, believes in them due to simplicity, and is then pierced in the heart and made to suffer all kinds of miseries. Because we believed in Kṛṣṇa's words, we have suffered great pain. Indeed, the touch of Kṛṣṇa's nails has injured our faces. He has caused us so much pain! Therefore, you should give up topics concerning Him and talk about something else."

After hearing all these statements from Śrīmatī Rādhikā, the bumblebee left and then returned. After some thought, the *gopī* said:

priya-sakha punar āgāḥ preyasā preṣitaḥ kiṁ
varaya kim anurundhe mānanīyo 'si me 'ṅga
nayasi katham ihāsmān dustyaja-dvandva-pārśvaṁ
satatam urasi saumya śrīr vadhūḥ sākamāste

"You are Kṛṣṇa's very dear friend, and by His order you have come here again. Therefore you are worshipable for Me. O best of messengers, tell Me now, what is your request? What do you want? Kṛṣṇa cannot give up conjugal love, and therefore I understand that you have come here to take us to Him. But how will you do that? We know many goddesses of fortune now reside at Kṛṣṇa's chest, and they constantly serve Kṛṣṇa better than we can."

Praising the bumblebee for its sobriety, She began to speak in great jubilation.

api bata madhu-puryām ārya-putro 'dhunā 'ste
smarati sa pitṛ-gehān saumya bandhūṁś ca gopān

kvacid api sa kathā naḥ kiṅkarīṇāṁ gṛṇīte
bhujam aguru-sugandhaṁ mūrdhny adhāsyat kadā nu

"Kṛṣṇa is now living like a gentleman at the Gurukula in Mathurā, forgetting all the *gopīs* of Vṛndāvana. But does He not remember the sweet house of His father, Nanda Mahārāja? We are all naturally His maidservants. Does He not remember us? Does He ever speak about us, or has He forgotten us completely? Will He ever forgive us and once again touch us with those hands fragrant with the scent of *aguru?*"

TEXT 108

মহিষীর গীত যেন 'দশমে'র শেষে।
পণ্ডিতে না বুঝে তার অর্থবিশেষে ॥ ১০৮ ॥

mahiṣīra gīta yena 'daśame'ra śeṣe
paṇḍite nā bujhe tāra artha-viśeṣe

SYNONYMS

mahiṣīra—of the queens; *gīta*—the songs; *yena*—just as; *daśamera*—of the Tenth Canto; *śeṣe*—at the end; *paṇḍite*—very learned scholars; *nā*—not; *bujhe*—understand; *tāra*—its; *artha-viśeṣe*—particular meaning.

TRANSLATION

The songs of the queens at Dvārakā, which are mentioned at the end of the Tenth Canto of Śrīmad-Bhāgavatam, have a very special meaning. They are not understood even by the most learned scholars.

PURPORT

These songs of *Śrīmad-Bhāgavatam* are verses 15-24 of the Ninetieth Chapter of the Tenth Canto.

kurari vilapasi tvaṁ vīta-nidrā na śeṣe
svapiti jagati rātryām īśvaro gupta-bodhaḥ
vayam iva sakhi kaccid gāḍha-nirbhinna-cetā
nalina-nayana-hāsodāra-līlekṣitena

All the queens incessantly thought of Kṛṣṇa. After their pastimes in the water, the queens said, "Our dear friend the osprey, Kṛṣṇa is now asleep, but we stay awake at night because of Him. You laugh at us when you see us awake at night, but why are you not sleeping? You seem absorbed in thoughts of Kṛṣṇa. Have you also been pierced by Kṛṣṇa's smile? His smile is very sweet. One who is pierced by such an arrow is very fortunate."

netre nimīlayasi naktam adṛṣṭa-bandhus
tvam roravīṣi karuṇaṁ bata cakravāki
dāsyaṁ gatā vayam ivācyuta-pāda-juṣṭāṁ
kiṁ vā srajaṁ spṛhayase kabareṇa voḍhum

"O *cakravāki,* you keep your eyes wide open at night because you cannot see your friend. Indeed, you are suffering very much. Is it because of compassion that you are crying, or are you trying to capture Kṛṣṇa by remembering Him? Having been touched by the lotus feet of Kṛṣṇa, all the queens are very happy. Are you crying to wear Kṛṣṇa's garland on your head? Please answer these questions clearly, O *cakravāki,* so that we can understand."

bho bhoḥ sadā niṣṭanase udanvann
alabdha-nidro 'dhigata-prajāgaraḥ
kiṁ vā mukundāpahṛtātma-lāñchanaḥ
prāptāṁ daśāṁ tvaṁ ca gato duratyayām

"O ocean, you have no opportunity to sleep quietly at night. Instead, you are always awake and crying. You have received this benediction, and your heart is broken just like ours. Mukunda's business with us is simply to smear our marks of *kuṅkuma.* O ocean, you suffer as much as we."

tvaṁ yakṣmaṇā balavatāsi gṛhīta indo
kṣīṇas tamo na nija-dīdhitibhiḥ kṣiṇoṣi
kaccin mukunda-gaditāni yathā vayaṁ tvaṁ
vismṛtya bhoḥ sthagita-gīr upalakṣyase naḥ

"O moon, you appear to be suffering from a severe fever, perhaps tuberculosis. Indeed, your effulgence does not have the strength to destroy the darkness. Have you become mad after hearing the songs of Kṛṣṇa? Is that why you are silent? Seeing your suffering, we feel that you are one of us."

kiṁ tvācaritam asmābhir
malayānila te 'priyam
govindāpāṅga-nirbhinne
hṛdīrayasi naḥ smaran

"O Malayan breeze, kindly tell us what wrong we have done to you. Why do you fan the flames of desire in our hearts? We have been pierced by the arrow of Govinda's glance, for He is perfect in the art of awakening the influence of Cupid."

megha śrīmaṁs tvam asi dayito yādavendrasya nūnaṁ
śrīvatsāṅkaṁ vayam iva bhavān dhyāyati prema-baddhaḥ
atyutkaṇṭhaḥ śabala-hṛdayo 'smad-vidho bāṣpa-dhārāḥ
smṛtvā smṛtvā visṛjasi muhur duḥkha-das tat-prasaṅgaḥ

"Dear cloud, O friend of Kṛṣṇa's, are you thinking of the Śrīvatsa symbol on Kṛṣṇa's chest like us queens engaged in loving affairs with Him? You are absorbed in meditation, remembering the association of Kṛṣṇa, and thus you shed tears of misery."

priya-rāva-padāni bhāṣase
mṛta-saṁjīvikayānayā girā
karavāṇi kim adya te priyaṁ
vada me valgita-kaṇṭha kokila

"Dear cuckoo, you possess a very sweet voice, and you are very expert in imitating others. You could excite even a dead body with your voice. Therefore, tell the queens that good behavior is their proper duty."

na calasi na vadasy udāra-buddhe
kṣiti-dhara cintyase mahāntam artham
api bata vasudeva-nandanāṅghriṁ
vayam iva kāmayase stanair vidhartum

"O magnanimous mountain, you are very grave and sober, absorbed in thoughts of doing something very great. Like us, you have vowed to keep within your heart the lotus feet of Kṛṣṇa, the son of Vasudeva."

śuṣyad-ghradāḥ karśitā bata sindhu-patnyaḥ
sampraty-apāsta-kamala-śriya-iṣṭa-bhartuḥ
yadvad vayaṁ madhu-pateḥ praṇayāvalokam
aprāpya muṣṭa-hṛdayāḥ puru-karṣitāḥ sma

"O rivers, wives of the ocean, we see that the ocean does not give you happiness. Thus you have almost dried up, and you no longer bear beautiful lotuses. The lotuses have become skinny, and even in the sunshine they are devoid of all pleasure. Similarly, the hearts of us poor queens are all dried up, and our bodies are skinny because we are now devoid of loving affairs with Madhupati. Are you, like us, dry and without beauty because you are devoid of Kṛṣṇa's loving glance?"

haṁsa svāgatam āsyatāṁ piba payo brūhy aṅga śaureḥ kathāṁ
dūtaṁ tvāṁ nu vidāma kaccid ajitaḥ svasty āsta uktaṁ purā

kiṁ vā naś cala-sauhṛdaḥ smarati taṁ kasmād bhajāmo vayaṁ
kṣaudrālāpaya-kāmadaṁ śriyamṛte saivaika-niṣṭhā striyām

"O swan, you have come here so happily! Let us welcome you. We understand that you are always Kṛṣṇa's messenger. Now while you drink this milk, tell us what His message is. Has Kṛṣṇa said something about us to you? May we inquire from you whether Kṛṣṇa is happy? We want to know. Does He remember us? We know that the goddess of fortune is serving Him alone. We are simply maidservants. How can we worship He who speaks sweet words but never fulfills our desires?"

TEXT 109

মহাপ্রভু-নিত্যানন্দ, দোঁহার দাসের দাস।
যারে কৃপা করেন, তার হয় ইথে বিশ্বাস ॥ ১০৯ ॥

mahāprabhu-nityānanda, doṅhāra dāsera dāsa
yāre kṛpā karena, tāra haya ithe viśvāsa

SYNONYMS

mahāprabhu—Śrī Caitanya Mahāprabhu; *nityānanda*—Lord Nityānanda; *doṅhāra dāsera dāsa*—I am a servant of the servant of the servants of these two personalities; *yāre kṛpā karena*—if anyone is favored by Them; *tāra haya*—he certainly maintains; *ithe viśvāsa*—faith in all these affairs.

TRANSLATION

If one becomes a servant of the servants of Śrī Caitanya Mahāprabhu and Lord Nityānanda Prabhu and is favored by Them, he can believe in all these discourses.

TEXT 110

শ্রদ্ধা করি, শুন ইহা, শুনিতে মহাসুখ।
খণ্ডিবে আধ্যাত্মিকাদি কুতর্কাদি-দুঃখ ॥ ১১০ ॥

śraddhā kari, śuna ihā, śunite mahā-sukha
khaṇḍibe ādhyātmikādi kutarkādi-duḥkha

SYNONYMS

śraddhā kari—with great faith; *śuna*—hear; *ihā*—all these topics; *śunite*—even to hear; *mahā-sukha*—great pleasure; *khaṇḍibe*—it will destroy; *ādhyātmika-*

ādi—all distresses due to the body, mind and so on; *kutarka-ādi-duḥkha*—and the miserable conditions arising from the use of false arguments.

TRANSLATION

Just try to hear these topics with faith, for there is great pleasure even in hearing them. That hearing will destroy all miseries pertaining to the body, mind and other living entities, and the unhappiness of false arguments as well.

TEXT 111

চৈতন্যচরিতামৃত—নিত্য-নূতন ।
শুনিতে শুনিতে জুড়ায় হৃদয়-শ্রবণ ॥ ১১১ ॥

caitanya-caritāmṛta——nitya-nūtana
śunite śunite juḍāya hṛdaya-śravaṇa

SYNONYMS

caitanya-carita-amṛta—the book named *Caitanya-caritāmṛta; nitya-nūtana*—always fresh; *śunite śunite*—by hearing and hearing; *juḍāya*—becomes pacified; *hṛdaya-śravaṇa*—the ear and heart.

TRANSLATION

Caitanya-caritāmṛta is ever-increasingly fresh. Continuously hearing it pacifies one's heart and ear.

TEXT 112

শ্রীরূপ-রঘুনাথ-পদে যার আশ ।
চৈতন্যচরিতামৃত কহে কৃষ্ণদাস ॥ ১১২ ॥

śrī-rūpa-raghunātha-pade yāra āśa
caitanya-caritāmṛta kahe kṛṣṇadāsa

SYNONYMS

śrī-rūpa—Śrīla Rūpa Gosvāmī; *raghunātha*—Śrīla Raghunātha dāsa Gosvāmī; *pade*—at the lotus feet; *yāra*—whose; *āśa*—expectation; *caitanya-caritāmṛta*—the book named *Caitanya-caritāmṛta; kahe*—describes; *kṛṣṇadāsa*—Śrīla Kṛṣṇadāsa Kavirāja Gosvāmī.

TRANSLATION

Praying at the lotus feet of Śrī Rūpa and Śrī Raghunātha, always desiring their mercy, I, Kṛṣṇadāsa, narrate Śrī Caitanya-caritāmṛta, following in their footsteps.

Thus end the Bhaktivedanta purports to the Śrī Caitanya-caritāmṛta, Antya-līlā, *Nineteenth Chapter, describing the Lord's devotion to His mother, His mad speeches in separation from Kṛṣṇa, His rubbing His face against the walls, and His dancing in the Jagannātha-vallabha garden.*

CHAPTER 20

The Śikṣāṣṭaka Prayers

The following summary study of the Twentieth Chapter is given by Śrīla Bhaktivinoda Ṭhākura in his *Amṛta-pravāha-bhāṣya.* Śrī Caitanya Mahāprabhu passed His nights tasting the meaning of *Śikṣāṣṭaka* in the company of Svarūpa Dāmodara Gosvāmī and Rāmānanda Rāya. Sometimes He recited verses from Jayadeva Gosvāmī's *Gīta-govinda,* from *Śrīmad-Bhāgavatam,* from Śrī Rāmānanda Rāya's *Jagannātha-vallabha-nāṭaka* or from Śrī Bilvamaṅgala Ṭhākura's *Kṛṣṇa-karṇāmṛta.* In this way, He became absorbed in ecstatic emotions. For the twelve years Śrī Caitanya Mahāprabhu lived at Jagannātha Purī, He relished the taste of reciting such transcendental verses. The Lord was present in this mortal world for forty-eight years altogether. After hinting about the Lord's disappearance, the author of *Caitanya-caritāmṛta* gives a short description of the entire *Antya-līlā* and then ends his book.

TEXT 1

প্রেমোদ্ভাবিতহর্ষের্ষ্যোদ্বেগদৈন্যার্তিমিশ্রিতম্ ।
লপিতং গৌরচন্দ্রস্য ভাগ্যবদ্ভির্নিষেব্যতে ॥ ১ ॥

premodbhāvita-harṣerṣyod-
vega-dainyārti-miśritam
lapitaṁ gauracandrasya
bhāgyavadbhir niṣevyate

SYNONYMS

prema-udbhāvita—produced from ecstatic love and emotion; *harṣa*—jubilation; *īrṣyā*—envy; *udvega*—agitation; *dainya*—submissiveness; *ārti*—grief; *miśritam*—mixed with; *lapitam*—talks like those of a crazy man; *gaura-candrasya*—of Śrī Caitanya Mahāprabhu; *bhāgyavadbhiḥ*—by the most fortunate; *niṣevyate*—is enjoyable.

TRANSLATION

Only the most fortunate will relish the mad words of Śrī Caitanya Mahāprabhu, which mixed with jubilation, envy, agitation, submissiveness and grief, all produced by ecstatic loving emotions.

TEXT 2

জয় জয় গৌরচন্দ্র জয় নিত্যানন্দ ।
জয়াদ্বৈতচন্দ্র জয় গৌরভক্তবৃন্দ ॥ ২ ॥

jaya jaya gauracandra jaya nityānanda
jayādvaita-candra jaya gaura-bhakta-vṛnda

SYNONYMS

jaya jaya—all glories; *gauracandra*—to Lord Śrī Caitanya Mahāprabhu; *jaya*—all glories; *nityānanda*—to Lord Nityānanda Prabhu; *jaya*—all glories; *advaita-candra*—to Advaita Prabhu; *jaya*—all glories; *gaura-bhakta-vṛnda*—to the devotees of Śrī Caitanya Mahāprabhu.

TRANSLATION

All glories to Lord Śrī Caitanya Mahāprabhu! All glories to Lord Nityānanda! All glories to Advaitacandra! And all glories to all the devotees of Śrī Caitanya Mahāprabhu!

TEXT 3

এইমত মহাপ্রভু বৈসে নীলাচলে ।
রজনী-দিবসে কৃষ্ণবিরহে বিহ্বলে ॥ ৩ ॥

ei-mata mahāprabhu vaise nīlācale
rajanī-divase kṛṣṇa-virahe vihvale

SYNONYMS

ei-mata—in this way; *mahāprabhu*—Śrī Caitanya Mahāprabhu; *vaise nīlācale*—resided at Nīlācala; *rajanī-divase*—day and night; *kṛṣṇa-virahe*—because of separation from Kṛṣṇa; *vihvale*—overwhelmed.

TRANSLATION

While Śrī Caitanya Mahāprabhu thus resided at Jagannātha Purī [Nīlācala], He was continuously overwhelmed, night and day, by separation from Kṛṣṇa.

TEXT 4

স্বরূপ, রামানন্দ,—এই দুইজন-সনে ।
রাত্রি-দিনে রস-গীত-শ্লোক আস্বাদনে ॥ ৪ ॥

svarūpa, rāmānanda,——ei duijana-sane
rātri-dine rasa-gīta-śloka āsvādane

SYNONYMS

svarūpa—Svarūpa Dāmodara Gosvāmī; *rāmānanda*—Rāmānanda Rāya; *ei*—these; *dui-jana-sane*—with two persons; *rātri-dine*—night and day; *rasa-gīta-śloka*—verses and songs containing the mellows of transcendental bliss; *āsvādane*—in tasting.

TRANSLATION

Day and night He tasted transcendental blissful songs and verses with two associates, namely Svarūpa Dāmodara Gosvāmī and Rāmānanda Rāya.

TEXT 5

নানা-ভাব উঠে প্রভুর হর্ষ, শোক, রোষ ।
দৈন্যোদ্বেগ-আর্তি উৎকণ্ঠা, সন্তোষ ॥ ৫ ॥

nānā-bhāva uṭhe prabhura harṣa, śoka, roṣa
dainyodvega-ārti utkaṇṭhā, santoṣa

SYNONYMS

nānā-bhāva—all kinds of emotion; *uṭhe*—awaken; *prabhura*—of Śrī Caitanya Mahāprabhu; *harṣa*—jubilation; *śoka*—lamentation; *roṣa*—anger; *dainya*—humility; *udvega*—anxiety; *ārti*—grief; *utkaṇṭhā*—more eagerness; *santoṣa*—satisfaction.

TRANSLATION

He relished the symptoms of various transcendental emotions such as jubilation, lamentation, anger, humility, anxiety, grief, eagerness and satisfaction.

TEXT 6

সেই সেই ভাবে নিজ-শ্লোক পড়িয়া ।
শ্লোকের অর্থ আস্বাদয়ে দুইবন্ধু লঞা ॥ ৬ ॥

sei sei bhāve nija-śloka paḍiyā
ślokera artha āsvādaye dui-bandhu lañā

SYNONYMS

sei sei bhāve—in that particular emotion; *nija-śloka paḍiyā*—reciting His own verses; *ślokera*—of the verses; *artha*—meaning; *āsvādaye*—tastes; *dui-bandhu lañā*—with two friends.

TRANSLATION

He would recite His own verses, expressing their meanings and emotions, and thus enjoy tasting them with these two friends.

TEXT 7

কোন দিনে কোন ভাবে শ্লোক-পঠন ।
সেই শ্লোক আস্বাদিতে রাত্রি-জাগরণ ॥ ৭ ॥

kona dine kona bhāve śloka-paṭhana
sei śloka āsvādite rātri-jāgaraṇa

SYNONYMS

kona dine—sometimes; *kona bhāve*—in some emotion; *śloka-paṭhana*—reciting the verses; *sei śloka*—those verses; *āsvādite*—to taste; *rātri-jāgaraṇa*—keeping awake at night.

TRANSLATION

Sometimes the Lord would be absorbed in a particular emotion and would stay awake all night reciting related verses and relishing their taste.

TEXT 8

হর্ষে প্রভু কহেন,—"শুন স্বরূপ-রামরায় ।
নামসঙ্কীর্তন—কলৌ পরম উপায় ॥ ৮ ॥

harṣe prabhu kahena,—"śuna svarūpa-rāma-rāya
nāma-saṅkīrtana—kalau parama upāya

SYNONYMS

harṣe—in jubilation; *prabhu*—Śrī Caitanya Mahāprabhu; *kahena*—says; *śuna*—please hear; *svarūpa-rāma-rāya*—My dear Svarūpa Dāmodara Gosvāmī and Rāmānanda Rāya; *nāma-saṅkīrtana*—chanting of the holy name of the Lord; *kalau*—in the age of Kali; *parama upāya*—the most feasible means for deliverance.

TRANSLATION

In great jubilation, Śrī Caitanya Mahāprabhu said, "My dear Svarūpa Dāmodara and Rāmānanda Rāya, know from me that chanting of the holy names is the most feasible means of salvation in this age of Kali.

TEXT 9

সঙ্কীর্তনযজ্ঞে কলৌ কৃষ্ণ-আরাধন ।
সেই ত' সুমেধা পায় কৃষ্ণের চরণ ॥ ৯ ॥

saṅkīrtana-yajñe kalau kṛṣṇa-ārādhana
sei ta' sumedhā pāya kṛṣṇera caraṇa

SYNONYMS

saṅkīrtana-yajñe—performing the *yajña* of chanting the Hare Kṛṣṇa *mantra; kalau*—in this age of Kali; *kṛṣṇa-ārādhana*—the process of worshiping Kṛṣṇa; *sei ta'*—such persons; *su-medhā*—greatly intelligent; *pāya*—get; *kṛṣṇera caraṇa*—shelter at the lotus feet of Kṛṣṇa.

TRANSLATION

"In this age of Kali, the process of worshiping Kṛṣṇa is to perform sacrifice by chanting the holy name of the Lord. One who does so is certainly very intelligent, and he attains shelter at the lotus feet of Kṛṣṇa.

PURPORT

For further information, one may refer to the *Ādi-līlā,* Chapter Three, texts 77-78.

TEXT 10

কৃষ্ণবর্ণং ত্বিষাহকৃষ্ণং সাঙ্গোপাঙ্গাস্ত্রপার্ষদম্ ।
যজ্ঞৈঃ সঙ্কীর্তনপ্রায়ৈর্যজন্তি হি সুমেধসঃ ॥ ১০ ॥

kṛṣṇa-varṇaṁ tviṣākṛṣṇaṁ
sāṅgopāṅgāstra-pārṣadam
yajñaiḥ saṅkīrtana-prāyair
yajanti hi sumedhasaḥ

SYNONYMS

kṛṣṇa-varṇam—repeating the syllables *kṛṣ-ṇa; tviṣā*—with a luster; *akṛṣṇam*—not black (golden); *sa-aṅga*—with associates; *upāṅga*—servitors; *astra*—weapons; *pārṣadam*—confidential companions; *yajñaiḥ*—by sacrifice; *saṅkīrtana-prāyaiḥ*—consisting chiefly of congregational chanting; *yajanti*—they worship; *hi*—certainly; *su-medhasaḥ*—intelligent persons.

TRANSLATION

" 'In the age of Kali, intelligent persons perform congregational chanting to worship the incarnation of Godhead who constantly sings the name of Kṛṣṇa. Although His complexion is not blackish, He is Kṛṣṇa Himself. He is accompanied by His associates, servants, weapons and confidential companions.'

PURPORT

This verse is spoken by Saint Karabhājana in *Śrīmad-Bhāgavatam* (11.5.32). For further information, see *Ādi-līlā,* Chapter Three, text 52.

TEXT 11

নামসঙ্কীর্তন হৈতে সর্বানর্থ-নাশ ।
সর্ব-শুভোদয়, কৃষ্ণ-প্রেমের উল্লাস ॥ ১১ ॥

nāma-saṅkīrtana haite sarvānartha-nāśa
sarva-śubhodaya, kṛṣṇa-premera ullāsa

SYNONYMS

nāma-saṅkīrtana—chanting of the holy names of the Lord; *haite*—from; *sarva-anartha-nāśa*—destruction of all undesirable things; *sarva-śubha-udaya*—awakening of all good fortune; *kṛṣṇa-premera ullāsa*—the beginning of the flow of love of Kṛṣṇa.

TRANSLATION

"Simply by chanting the holy name of Lord Kṛṣṇa, one can be freed from all undesirable habits. This is the means of awakening all good fortune and initiating the flow of waves of love for Kṛṣṇa.

TEXT 12

চেতোদর্পণমার্জনং ভবমহাদাবাগ্নিনির্বাপণং
শ্রেয়ঃকৈরবচন্দ্রিকাবিতরণং বিদ্যাবধূজীবনম্ ।
আনন্দাম্বুধিবর্ধনং প্রতিপদং পূর্ণামৃতাস্বাদনং
সর্বাত্মস্নপনং পরং বিজয়তে শ্রীকৃষ্ণসঙ্কীর্তনম্ ॥ ১২ ॥

ceto-darpaṇa-mārjanaṁ bhava-mahādāvāgni-nirvāpaṇaṁ
śreyaḥ-kairava-candrikā-vitaraṇaṁ vidyā-vadhū-jīvanam
ānandāmbudhi-vardhanaṁ prati-padaṁ pūrṇāmṛtāsvādanaṁ
sarvātma-snapanaṁ paraṁ vijayate śrī-kṛṣṇa-saṅkīrtanam

SYNONYMS

cetaḥ—of the heart; *darpaṇa*—the mirror; *mārjanam*—cleansing; *bhava*—of material existence; *mahā-dāvāgni*—the blazing forest fire; *nirvāpaṇam*—extinguishing; *śreyaḥ*—of good fortune; *kairava*—the white lotus; *candrikā*—the moonshine; *vitaraṇam*—spreading; *vidyā*—of all education; *vadhū*—wife; *jīvanam*—the life; *ānanda*—of bliss; *ambudhi*—the ocean; *vardhanam*—increasing; *prati-padam*—at every step; *pūrṇa-amṛta*—of the full nectar; *āsvādanam*—giving a taste; *sarva*—for everyone; *ātma-snapanam*—bathing of the self; *param*—transcendental; *vijayate*—let there be victory; *śrī-kṛṣṇa-saṅkīrtanam*—for the congregational chanting of the holy name of Kṛṣṇa.

TRANSLATION

"Let there be all victory for the chanting of the holy name of Lord Kṛṣṇa, which can cleanse the mirror of the heart and stop the miseries of the blazing fire of material existence. That chanting is the waxing moon that spreads the white lotus of good fortune for all living entities. It is the life and soul of all education. The chanting of the holy name of Kṛṣṇa expands the blissful ocean of transcendental life. It gives a cooling effect to everyone and enables one to taste full nectar at every step.

PURPORT

This is the first verse of Śrī Caitanya Mahāprabhu's *Śikṣāṣṭaka*. The other seven verses are found in texts 16, 21, 29, 32, 36, 39 and 47.

TEXT 13

সঙ্কীর্তন হৈতে পাপ-সংসার-নাশন ।
চিত্তশুদ্ধি, সর্বভক্তিসাধন-উদ্গম ॥ ১৩ ॥

saṅkīrtana haite pāpa-saṁsāra-nāśana
citta-śuddhi, sarva-bhakti-sādhana-udgama

SYNONYMS

saṅkīrtana haite—from the process of chanting the holy name; *pāpa-saṁsāra-nāśana*—annihilation of materialistic life resulting from sins; *citta-śuddhi*—

cleansing of the heart; *sarva-bhakti*—all kinds of devotional service; *sādhana*—of the performances; *udgama*—awakening.

TRANSLATION

"By performing congregational chanting of the Hare Kṛṣṇa mantra, one can destroy the sinful condition of material existence, purify the unclean heart and awaken all varieties of devotional service.

TEXT 14

কৃষ্ণপ্রেমোদ্গম, প্রেমামৃত-আস্বাদন ।
কৃষ্ণপ্রাপ্তি, সেবামৃত-সমুদ্রে মজ্জন ॥ ১৪ ॥

kṛṣṇa-premodgama, premāmṛta-āsvādana
kṛṣṇa-prāpti, sevāmṛta-samudre majjana

SYNONYMS

kṛṣṇa-prema-udgama—awakening of love for Kṛṣṇa; *prema-amṛta-āsvādana*—tasting of the transcendental bliss of love for Kṛṣṇa; *kṛṣṇa-prāpti*—attainment of the lotus feet of Kṛṣṇa; *sevā-amṛta*—of the nectar of service; *samudre*—in the ocean; *majjana*—immersing.

TRANSLATION

"The result of chanting is that one awakens his love for Kṛṣṇa and tastes transcendental bliss. Ultimately, one attains the association of Kṛṣṇa and engages in His devotional service, as if immersing himself in a great ocean of love."

TEXT 15

উঠিল বিষাদ, দৈন্য,—পড়ে আপন-শ্লোক ।
যাহার অর্থ শুনি' সব যায় দুঃখ-শোক ॥ ১৫ ॥

uṭhila viṣāda, dainya,——paḍe āpana-śloka
yāhāra artha śuni' saba yāya duḥkha-śoka

SYNONYMS

uṭhila viṣāda—there was awakening of lamentation; *dainya*—humility; *paḍe*—reads; *āpana-śloka*—His own verse; *yāhāra*—of which; *artha śuni'*—hearing the meaning; *saba*—all; *yāya*—go away; *duḥkha-śoka*—unhappiness and lamentation.

TRANSLATION

Lamentation and humility awoke within Śrī Caitanya Mahāprabhu, and He began reciting another of His own verses. By hearing the meaning of that verse, one can forget all unhappiness and lamentation.

TEXT 16

নাম্নামকারি বহুধা নিজসর্বশক্তি-
স্তত্রার্পিতা নিয়মিতঃ স্মরণে ন কালঃ ।
এতাদৃশী তব কৃপা ভগবন্মমাপি
দুর্দৈবমীদৃশমিহাজনি নানুরাগঃ ॥ ১৬ ॥

nāmnām akāri bahudhā nija-sarva-śaktis
tatrārpitā niyamitaḥ smaraṇe na kālaḥ
etādṛśī tava kṛpā bhagavan mamāpi
durdaivam īdṛśam ihājani nānurāgaḥ

SYNONYMS

nāmnām—of the holy names of the Lord; *akāri*—manifested; *bahudhā*—various kinds; *nija-sarva-śaktiḥ*—all kinds of personal potency; *tatra*—in that; *arpitā*—bestowed; *niyamitaḥ*—restricted; *smaraṇe*—in remembering; *na*—not; *kālaḥ*—consideration of time; *etādṛśī*—so much; *tava*—Your; *kṛpā*—mercy; *bhagavan*—O Lord; *mama*—My; *api*—although; *durdaivam*—misfortune; *īdṛśam*—such; *iha*—in this (the holy name); *ajani*—was born; *na*—not; *anurāgaḥ*—attachment.

TRANSLATION

"My Lord, O Supreme Personality of Godhead, in Your holy name there is all good fortune for the living entity, and therefore You have many names, such as Kṛṣṇa and Govinda, by which You expand Yourself. You have invested all Your potencies in those names, and there are no hard and fast rules for remembering them. My dear Lord, although You bestow such mercy upon the fallen, conditioned souls by liberally teaching Your holy names, I am so unfortunate that I commit offenses while chanting the holy name, and therefore I do not achieve attachment for chanting.

TEXT 17

অনেক-লোকের বাঞ্ছা—অনেক-প্রকার ।
কৃপাতে করিল অনেক-নামের প্রচার ॥ ১৭ ॥

aneka-lokera vāñchā——aneka-prakāra
kṛpāte karila aneka-nāmera pracāra

SYNONYMS

aneka-lokera—of many persons; *vāñchā*—the desires; *aneka-prakāra*—of many varieties; *kṛpāte*—by Your mercy; *karila*—You have done; *aneka*—various; *nāmera*—of the holy names; *pracāra*—broadcasting.

TRANSLATION

"Because people vary in their desires, You have distributed various holy names by Your mercy.

TEXT 18

খাইতে শুইতে যথা তথা নাম লয়।
কাল-দেশ-নিয়ম নাহি, সর্ব সিদ্ধি হয় ॥ ১৮ ॥

khāite śuite yathā tathā nāma laya
kāla-deśa-niyama nāhi, sarva siddhi haya

SYNONYMS

khāite—eating; *śuite*—lying down; *yathā*—as; *tathā*—so; *nāma laya*—one takes the holy name; *kāla*—in time; *deśa*—in place; *niyama*—regulation; *nāhi*—there is not; *sarva siddhi haya*—there is all perfection.

TRANSLATION

"Regardless of time or place, one who chants the holy name, even while eating or sleeping, attains all perfection.

TEXT 19

"সর্বশক্তি নামে দিলা করিয়া বিভাগ।
আমার দুর্দৈব,—নামে নাহি অনুরাগ !!" ১৯ ॥

"sarva-śakti nāme dilā kariyā vibhāga
āmāra durdaiva,——nāme nāhi anurāga!!"

SYNONYMS

sarva-śakti—all potencies; *nāme*—in the holy name; *dilā*—You have bestowed; *kariyā vibhāga*—making separation; *āmāra durdaiva*—My misfortune; *nāme*—for chanting the holy names; *nāhi*—there is not; *anurāga*—attachment.

TRANSLATION

"You have invested Your full potencies in each individual holy name, but I am so unfortunate that I have no attachment for chanting Your holy names."

TEXT 20

যেরূপে লইলে নাম প্রেম উপজয়।
তাহার লক্ষণ শুন, স্বরূপ-রামরায় ॥ ২০ ॥

ye-rūpe la-ile nāma prema upajaya
tāhāra lakṣaṇa śuna, svarūpa-rāma-rāya

SYNONYMS

ye-rūpe—by which process; *la-ile*—if chanting; *nāma*—the holy name; *prema upajaya*—dormant love of Kṛṣṇa awakens; *tāhāra lakṣaṇa śuna*—just hear the symptom of that; *svarūpa-rāma-rāya*—O Svarūpa Dāmodara and Rāmānanda Rāya.

TRANSLATION

Śrī Caitanya Mahāprabhu continued, "O Svarūpa Dāmodara Gosvāmī and Rāmānanda Rāya, hear from Me the symptoms of how one should chant the Hare Kṛṣṇa mahā-mantra to awaken very easily one's dormant love for Kṛṣṇa.

TEXT 21

তৃণাদপি সুনীচেন তরোরিব সহিষ্ণুনা।
অমানিনা মানদেন কীর্তনীয়ঃ সদা হরিঃ ॥ ২১ ॥

tṛṇād api sunīcena
taror iva sahiṣṇunā
amāninā mānadena
kīrtanīyaḥ sadā hariḥ

SYNONYMS

tṛṇāt api—than downtrodden grass; *sunīcena*—being lower; *taroḥ*—than a tree; *iva*—like; *sahiṣṇunā*—with tolerance; *amāninā*—without being puffed up by false pride; *mānadena*—giving respect to all; *kīrtanīyaḥ*—to be chanted; *sadā*—always; *hariḥ*—the holy name of the Lord.

TRANSLATION

"One who thinks himself lower than the grass, who is more tolerant than a tree, and who does not expect personal honor but is always prepared to give all respect to others, can very easily always chant the holy name of the Lord.

TEXT 22

উত্তম হঞা আপনাকে মানে তৃণাধম ।
দুইপ্রকারে সহিষ্ণুতা করে বৃক্ষসম ॥ ২২ ॥

uttama hañā āpanāke māne tṛṇādhama
dui-prakāre sahiṣṇutā kare vṛkṣa-sama

SYNONYMS

uttama hañā—although being very exalted; *āpanāke*—himself; *māne*—thinks; *tṛṇa-adhama*—lower than a blade of the grass on the ground; *dui-prakāre*—in two ways; *sahiṣṇutā*—tolerance; *kare*—performs; *vṛkṣa-sama*—like the tree.

TRANSLATION

"These are the symptoms of one who chants the Hare Kṛṣṇa mahā-mantra. Although he is very exalted, he thinks himself lower than the grass on the ground, and like a tree, he tolerates everything in two ways.

TEXT 23

বৃক্ষ যেন কাটিলেহ কিছু না বোলয় ।
শুকাঞা মৈলেহ কারে পানী না মাগয় ॥ ২৩ ॥

vṛkṣa yena kāṭileha kichu nā bolaya
śukāñā maileha kāre pānī nā māgaya

SYNONYMS

vṛkṣa—a tree; *yena*—as; *kāṭileha*—when it is cut; *kichu nā bolaya*—does not say anything; *śukāñā*—drying up; *maileha*—if dying; *kāre*—anyone; *pānī*—water; *nā māgaya*—does not ask for.

TRANSLATION

"When a tree is cut down, it does not protest, and even when drying up, it does not ask anyone for water.

TEXT 24

যেই যে মাগয়ে, তারে দেয় আপন-ধন ।
ঘর্ম-বৃষ্টি সহে, আনের করয়ে রক্ষণ ॥ ২৪ ॥

yei ye māgaye, tāre deya āpana-dhana
gharma-vṛṣṭi sahe, ānera karaye rakṣaṇa

SYNONYMS

yei ye māgaye—if anyone asks anything from the tree; *tāre*—unto him; *deya*—gives; *āpana-dhana*—its own wealth; *gharma-vṛṣṭi*—the scorching heat of the sun and torrents of rain; *sahe*—tolerates; *ānera*—to others; *karaye rakṣaṇa*—gives protection.

TRANSLATION

"The tree delivers its fruits, flowers and whatever it possesses to anyone and everyone. It tolerates scorching heat and torrents of rain, yet it still gives shelter to others.

TEXT 25

উত্তম হঞা বৈষ্ণব হবে নিরভিমান ।
জীবে সম্মান দিবে জানি' 'কৃষ্ণ'-অধিষ্ঠান ॥ ২৫ ॥

uttama hañā vaiṣṇava habe nirabhimāna
jīve sammāna dibe jāni' 'kṛṣṇa'-adhiṣṭhāna

SYNONYMS

uttama hañā—although being very exalted; *vaiṣṇava*—a devotee; *habe*—should become; *nirabhimāna*—without pride; *jīve*—to all living entities; *sammāna dibe*—should give respect; *jāni'*—knowing; *kṛṣṇa-adhiṣṭhāna*—the residing place of Kṛṣṇa.

TRANSLATION

"Although a Vaiṣṇava is the most exalted person, he is prideless and gives all respect to everyone, knowing everyone to be the resting place of Kṛṣṇa.

TEXT 26

এইমত হঞা যেই কৃষ্ণনাম লয় ।
শ্রীকৃষ্ণচরণে তাঁর প্রেম উপজয় ॥ ২৬ ॥

ei-mata hañā yei kṛṣṇa-nāma laya
śrī-kṛṣṇa-caraṇe tāṅra prema upajaya

SYNONYMS

ei-mata—in this way; *hañā*—becoming; *yei*—anyone who; *kṛṣṇa-nāma laya*—chants the holy name of Kṛṣṇa; *śrī-kṛṣṇa-caraṇe*—at the lotus feet of Lord Kṛṣṇa; *tāṅra*—his; *prema upajaya*—love of Kṛṣṇa awakens.

TRANSLATION

"If one chants the holy name of Lord Kṛṣṇa in this manner, he will certainly awaken his dormant love for Kṛṣṇa's lotus feet."

TEXT 27

কহিতে কহিতে প্রভুর দৈন্য বাড়িলা ।
'শুদ্ধভক্তি' কৃষ্ণ-ঠাঞি মাগিতে লাগিলা ॥ ২৭ ॥

kahite kahite prabhura dainya bāḍilā
'śuddha-bhakti' kṛṣṇa-ṭhāñi māgite lāgilā

SYNONYMS

kahite kahite—speaking like this; *prabhura*—of Śrī Caitanya Mahāprabhu; *dainya*—humility; *bāḍilā*—increased; *śuddha-bhakti*—pure devotional service; *kṛṣṇa-ṭhāñi*—from Kṛṣṇa; *māgite lāgilā*—began to pray for.

TRANSLATION

As Lord Caitanya spoke in this way, His humility increased, and He began praying to Kṛṣṇa that He could discharge pure devotional service.

TEXT 28

প্রেমের স্বভাব—যাহাঁ প্রেমের সম্বন্ধ ।
সেই মানে,—'কৃষ্ণে মোর নাহি প্রেম-গন্ধ' ॥ ২৮ ॥

premera svabhāva——yāhāṅ premera sambandha
sei māne,——'kṛṣṇe mora nāhi prema-gandha'

SYNONYMS

premera sva-bhāva—the nature of love of Godhead; *yāhāṅ*—where; *premera sambandha*—a relationship of love of Godhead; *sei māne*—he recognizes;

kṛṣṇe—unto Lord Kṛṣṇa; *mora*—my; *nāhi*—there is not; *prema-gandha*—even a scent of love of Godhead.

TRANSLATION

Wherever there is a relationship of love of Godhead, its natural symptom is that the devotee does not think himself a devotee. Instead, he always thinks that he has not even a drop of love for Kṛṣṇa.

PURPORT

Śrīla Bhaktisiddhānta Sarasvatī Ṭhākura comments that persons who are actually very poor because they possess not even a drop of love of Godhead or pure devotional service falsely advertise themselves as great devotees, although they cannot at any time relish the transcendental bliss of devotional service. A class of so-called devotees known as *prākṛta-sahajiyās* sometimes display devotional symptoms to exhibit their good fortune. They are pretending, however, because these devotional features are only external. The *prākṛta-sahajiyās* exhibit these symptoms to advertise their so-called advancement in love of Kṛṣṇa, but instead of praising the *prākṛta-sahajiyās* for their symptoms of transcendental ecstasy, pure devotees do not like to associate with them. It is not advisable to equate the *prākṛta-sahajiyās* with pure devotees. When one is actually advanced in ecstatic love of Kṛṣṇa, he does not try to advertise himself. Instead, he endeavors more and more to render service to the Lord.

The *prākṛta-sahajiyās* sometimes criticize pure devotees by calling them philosophers, learned scholars, knowers of the truth, or minute observers, but not devotees. On the other hand, they depict themselves as the most advanced, transcendentally blissful devotees, deeply absorbed in devotional service and mad to taste transcendental mellows. They also describe themselves as the most advanced devotees in spontaneous love, as knowers of transcendental mellows, as the topmost devotees in conjugal love of Kṛṣṇa, and so on. Not actually knowing the transcendental nature of love of God, they accept their material emotions to be indicative of advancement. In this way they pollute the process of devotional service. To try to become writers of Vaiṣṇava literature, they introduce their material conceptions of life into pure devotional service. Because of their material conceptions, they advertise themselves as knowers of transcendental mellows, but they do not understand the transcendental nature of devotional service.

TEXT 29

ন ধনং ন জনং ন সুন্দরীং কবিতাং বা জগদীশ কাময়ে।
মম জন্মনি জন্মনীশ্বরে ভবতাদ্ভক্তিরহৈতুকী ত্বয়ি ॥ ২৯ ॥

na dhanaṁ na janaṁ na sundarīṁ
kavitāṁ vā jagadīśa kāmaye
mama janmani jamanīśvare
bhavatād bhaktir ahaitukī tvayi

SYNONYMS

na—not; *dhanam*—riches; *na*—not; *janam*—followers; *na*—not; *sundarīm*—a very beautiful woman; *kavitām*—fruitive activities described in flowery language; *vā*—or; *jagat-īśa*—O Lord of the universe; *kāmaye*—I desire; *mama*—My; *janmani*—in birth; *janmani*—after birth; *īśvare*—unto the Supreme Personality of Godhead; *bhavatāt*—let there be; *bhaktiḥ*—devotional service; *ahaitukī*—with no motives; *tvayi*—unto You.

TRANSLATION

"O Lord of the universe, I do not desire material wealth, materialistic followers, a beautiful wife or fruitive activities described in flowery language. All I want, life after life, is unmotivated devotional service to You.

TEXT 30

"ধন, জন নাহি মাগোঁ, কবিতা সুন্দরী ।
'শুদ্ধভক্তি' দেহ' মোরে, কৃষ্ণ কৃপা করি' ॥ ৩০ ॥

dhana, jana nāhi māgoṅ, kavitā sundarī
'śuddha-bhakti' deha' more, kṛṣṇa kṛpā kari'

SYNONYMS

dhana—wealth; *jana*—followers; *nāhi*—do not; *māgoṅ*—I want; *kavitā sundarī*—a beautiful wife or fruitive activities; *śuddha-bhakti*—pure devotional service; *deha'*—please award; *more*—unto Me; *kṛṣṇa*—O Lord Kṛṣṇa; *kṛpā kari'*—becoming merciful.

TRANSLATION

"My dear Lord Kṛṣṇa, I do not want material wealth from You, nor do I want followers, a beautiful wife or the results of fruitive activities. I only pray that by Your causeless mercy You give Me pure devotional service to You, life after life.

TEXT 31

অতিদৈন্যে পুনঃ মাগে দাস্যভক্তি-দান ।
আপনারে করে সংসারী জীব-অভিমান ॥ ৩১ ॥

ati-dainye punaḥ māge dāsya-bhakti-dāna
āpanāre kare saṁsārī jīva-abhimāna

SYNONYMS

ati-dainye—in great humility; *punaḥ*—again; *māge*—begs; *dāsya-bhakti-dāna*—the awarding of devotion in servitude; *āpanāre*—to Himself; *kare*—does; *saṁsārī*—materialistic; *jīva-abhimāna*—conception as a conditioned soul.

TRANSLATION

In great humility, considering Himself a conditioned soul of the material world, Śrī Caitanya Mahāprabhu again expressed His desire to be endowed with service to the Lord.

TEXT 32

অয়ি নন্দতনুজ কিঙ্করং পতিতং মাং বিষমে ভবাম্বুধৌ ।
কৃপয়া তব পাদপঙ্কজস্থিতধূলীসদৃশং বিচিন্তয় ॥ ৩২ ॥

ayi nanda-tanuja kiṅkaraṁ
patitaṁ māṁ viṣame bhavāmbudhau
kṛpayā tava pāda-paṅkaja-
sthita-dhūlī-sadṛśaṁ vicintaya

SYNONYMS

ayi—oh, My Lord; *nanda-tanuja*—the son of Nanda Mahārāja, Kṛṣṇa; *kiṅkaram*—the servant; *patitam*—fallen; *mām*—Me; *viṣame*—horrible; *bhava-ambudhau*—in the ocean of nescience; *kṛpayā*—by causeless mercy; *tava*—Your; *pāda-paṅkaja*—lotus feet; *sthita*—situated at; *dhūlī-sadṛśam*—like a particle of dust; *vicintaya*—kindly consider.

TRANSLATION

"Oh, My Lord, O Kṛṣṇa, son of Mahārāja Nanda, I am Your eternal servant, but because of My own fruitive acts, I have fallen in this horrible ocean of nescience. Now please be causelessly merciful to Me. Consider Me a particle of dust at Your lotus feet.

TEXT 33

"তোমার নিত্যদাস মুই, তোমা পাসরিয়া ।
পড়িয়াছোঁ ভবার্ণবে মায়াবদ্ধ হঞা ॥ ৩৩ ॥

"tomāra nitya-dāsa mui, tomā pāsariyā
paḍiyāchoṅ bhavārṇave māyā-baddha hañā

SYNONYMS

tomāra—Your; *nitya-dāsa*—eternal servant; *mui*—I; *tomā pāsariyā*—forgetting Your Lordship; *paḍiyāchoṅ*—I have fallen; *bhava-arṇave*—in the ocean of nescience; *māyā-baddha hañā*—becoming conditioned by the external energy.

TRANSLATION

"I am Your eternal servant, but I forgot Your Lordship. Now I have fallen in the ocean of nescience and have been conditioned by the external energy.

TEXT 34

কৃপা করি' কর মোরে পদধূলি-সম ।
তোমার সেবক করোঁ তোমার সেবন ॥" ৩৪ ॥

kṛpā kari' kara more pada-dhūli-sama
tomāra sevaka karoṅ tomāra sevana"

SYNONYMS

kṛpā kari'—being merciful; *kara*—make; *more*—Me; *pada-dhūli-sama*—like a particle of dust at Your lotus feet; *tomāra sevaka*—as I am Your eternal servant; *karoṅ*—let Me be engaged; *tomāra sevana*—in Your service.

TRANSLATION

"Be causelessly merciful to Me by giving Me a place with the particles of dust at Your lotus feet so that I may engage in the service of Your Lordship as Your eternal servant."

TEXT 35

পুনঃ অতি-উৎকণ্ঠা, দৈন্য হইল উদ্গম ।
কৃষ্ণ-ঠাঞি মাগে প্রেম-নামসঙ্কীর্তন ॥ ৩৫ ॥

punaḥ ati-utkaṇṭhā, dainya ha-ila udgama
kṛṣṇa-ṭhāñi māge prema-nāma-saṅkīrtana

SYNONYMS

punaḥ—again; *ati-utkaṇṭhā*—great eagerness; *dainya*—humility; *ha-ila udgama*—was awakened; *kṛṣṇa-ṭhāñi*—from Lord Kṛṣṇa; *māge*—prays for; *prema*—in ecstatic love; *nāma-saṅkīrtana*—chanting the *mahā-mantra.*

TRANSLATION

Natural humility and eagerness then awoke in Lord Śrī Caitanya Mahāprabhu. He prayed to Kṛṣṇa to be able to chant the mahā-mantra in ecstatic love.

TEXT 36

নয়নং গলদশ্রুধারয়া, বদনং গদ্গদ-রুদ্ধয়া গিরা।
পুলকৈর্নিচিতং বপুঃ কদা, তব নাম-গ্রহণে ভবিষ্যতি ॥৩৬॥

nayanaṁ galad-aśru-dhārayā
vadanaṁ gadgada-ruddhayā girā
pulakair nicitaṁ vapuḥ kadā,
tava nāma-grahaṇe bhaviṣyati

SYNONYMS

nayanam—the eyes; *galat-aśru-dhārayā*—by streams of tears running down; *vadanam*—mouth; *gadgada*—faltering; *ruddhayā*—choked up; *girā*—with words; *pulakaiḥ*—with erection of the hairs due to transcendental happiness; *nicitam*—covered; *vapuḥ*—the body; *kadā*—when; *tava*—Your; *nāma-grahaṇe*—in chanting the name; *bhaviṣyati*—will be.

TRANSLATION

"My dear Lord, when will My eyes be beautified by filling with tears that constantly glide down as I chant Your holy name? When will My voice falter and all the hairs on My body stand erect in transcendental happiness as I chant Your holy name?

TEXT 37

"প্রেমধন বিনা ব্যর্থ দরিদ্র জীবন।
'দাস' করি' বেতন মোরে দেহ প্রেমধন ॥" ৩৭ ॥

"prema-dhana vinā vyartha daridra jīvana
'dāsa' kari' vetana more deha prema-dhana"

SYNONYMS

prema-dhana—the wealth of ecstatic love; *vinā*—without; *vyartha*—useless; *daridra jīvana*—poor life; *dāsa kari'*—accepting as Your eternal servant; *vetana*—salary; *more*—unto Me; *deha*—give; *prema-dhana*—the treasure of love of Godhead.

TRANSLATION

"Without love of Godhead, My life is useless. Therefore I pray that You accept Me as Your servant and give Me the salary of ecstatic love of God."

TEXT 38

রসান্তরাবেশে হইল বিয়োগ-স্ফুরণ ।
উদ্বেগ, বিষাদ, দৈন্যে করে প্রলপন ॥ ৩৮ ॥

rasāntarāveśe ha-ila viyoga-sphuraṇa
udvega, viṣāda, dainye kare pralapana

SYNONYMS

rasa-antara-āveśe—in the ecstatic love of different mellows; *ha-ila*—there was; *viyoga-sphuraṇa*—awakening of separation; *udvega*—distress; *viṣāda*—moroseness; *dainye*—humility; *kare pralapana*—speaks like a crazy person.

TRANSLATION

Separation from Kṛṣṇa awoke various mellows of distress, lamentation and humility. Thus Śrī Caitanya Mahāprabhu spoke like a crazy man.

TEXT 39

যুগায়িতং নিমেষেণ চক্ষুষা প্রাবৃষায়িতম্ ।
শূন্যায়িতং জগৎ সর্বং গোবিন্দ-বিরহেণ মে ॥ ৩৯ ॥

yugāyitaṁ nimeṣeṇa
cakṣuṣā prāvṛṣāyitam
śūnyāyitaṁ jagat sarvaṁ
govinda-viraheṇa me

SYNONYMS

yugāyitam—appearing like a great millennium; *nimeṣeṇa*—by a moment; *cakṣuṣā*—from the eyes; *prāvṛṣāyitam*—tears falling like torrents of rain; *śūnyāyitam*—appearing void; *jagat*—the world; *sarvam*—all; *govinda*—from Lord Govinda, Kṛṣṇa; *viraheṇa me*—by My separation.

TRANSLATION

"My Lord Govinda, because of separation from You, I consider even a moment a great millennium. Tears flow from My eyes like torrents of rain, and I see the entire world as void.

TEXT 40

উদ্বেগে দিবস না যায়, 'ক্ষণ' হৈল 'যুগ'-সম ।
বর্ষার মেঘপ্রায় অশ্রু বরিষে নয়ন ॥ ৪০ ॥

udvege divasa nā yāya 'kṣaṇa' haila 'yuga'-sama
varṣāra megha-prāya aśru variṣe nayana

SYNONYMS

udvege—by great agitation; *divasa*—day; *nā*—not; *yāya*—passes; *kṣaṇa*—a moment; *haila*—became; *yuga-sama*—like a great millennium; *varṣāra*—of the rainy season; *megha-prāya*—like clouds; *aśru*—tears; *variṣe*—fall down; *nayana*—from the eyes.

TRANSLATION

"In My agitation, a day never ends, for every moment seems like a millennium. Pouring incessant tears, My eyes are like clouds in the rainy season.

TEXT 41

গোবিন্দ-বিরহে শূন্য হইল ত্রিভুবন ।
তুষানলে পোড়ে,—যেন না যায় জীবন ॥ ৪১ ॥

govinda-virahe śūnya ha-ila tribhuvana
tuṣānale poḍe,——yena nā yāya jīvana

SYNONYMS

govinda-virahe—by separation from Govinda; *śūnya*—void; *ha-ila*—became; *tri-bhuvana*—the three worlds; *tuṣa-anale*—in the slow fire; *poḍe*—burns; *yena*—just like; *nā yāya*—does not go; *jīvana*—life.

TRANSLATION

"The three worlds have become void because of separation from Govinda. I feel as if I were burning alive in a slow fire.

TEXT 42

কৃষ্ণ উদাসীন হইলা করিতে পরীক্ষণ ।
সখী সব কহে,—'কৃষ্ণে কর উপেক্ষণ' ॥ ৪২ ॥

kṛṣṇa udāsīna ha-ilā karite parīkṣaṇa
sakhī saba kahe,——'kṛṣṇe kara upekṣaṇa'

SYNONYMS

kṛṣṇa—Lord Kṛṣṇa; *udāsīna*—indifferent; *ha-ilā*—became; *karite*—to make; *parīkṣaṇa*—testing; *sakhī saba kahe*—all the friends say; *kṛṣṇe*—unto Kṛṣṇa; *kara*—just do; *upekṣaṇa*—neglecting.

TRANSLATION

"Lord Kṛṣṇa has become indifferent to Me just to test My love, and My friends say, 'Better to disregard Him.' "

TEXT 43

এতেক চিন্তিতে রাধার নির্মল হৃদয়।
স্বাভাবিক প্রেমার স্বভাব করিল উদয়॥ ৪৩॥

eteka cintite rādhāra nirmala hṛdaya
svābhāvika premāra svabhāva karila udaya

SYNONYMS

eteka—thus; *cintite*—thinking; *rādhāra*—of Śrīmatī Rādhārāṇī; *nirmala hṛdaya*—possessing a pure heart; *svābhāvika*—natural; *premāra*—of love of Kṛṣṇa; *sva-bhāva*—the character; *karila udaya*—awakes.

TRANSLATION

While Śrīmatī Rādhārāṇī was thinking in this way, the characteristics of natural love became manifest because of Her pure heart.

TEXT 44

ঈর্ষ্যা, উৎকণ্ঠা, দৈন্য, প্রৌঢ়ি, বিনয়।
এত ভাব এক-ঠাঞি করিল উদয়॥ ৪৪॥

īrṣyā, utkaṇṭhā, dainya, prauḍhi, vinaya
eta bhāva eka-ṭhāñi karila udaya

SYNONYMS

īrṣyā—envy; *utkaṇṭhā*—eagerness; *dainya*—humility; *prauḍhi*—zeal; *vinaya*—solicitation; *eta bhāva*—all these transcendental ecstasies; *eka-ṭhāñi*—in one place; *karila udaya*—awoke.

TRANSLATION

The ecstatic symptoms of envy, great eagerness, humility, zeal and supplication all became manifest at once.

TEXT 45

এত ভাবে রাধার মন অস্থির হইলা।
সখীগণ-আগে প্রৌঢ়ি-শ্লোক যে পড়িলা ॥ ৪৫ ॥

eta bhāve rādhāra mana asthira ha-ilā
sakhī-gaṇa-āge prauḍhi-śloka ye paḍilā

SYNONYMS

eta bhāve—in that mood; *rādhāra*—of Śrīmatī Rādhārāṇī; *mana*—the mind; *asthira ha-ilā*—became agitated; *sakhī-gaṇa-āge*—before the friends, the *gopīs;* *prauḍhi-śloka*—advanced devotional verse; *ye*—which; *paḍilā*—She recited.

TRANSLATION

In that mood, the mind of Śrīmatī Rādhārāṇī was agitated, and therefore She spoke a verse of advanced devotion to Her gopī friends.

TEXT 46

সেই ভাবে প্রভু সেই শ্লোক উচ্চারিলা।
শ্লোক উচ্চারিতে তদ্রূপ আপনে হইলা ॥ ৪৬ ॥

sei bhāve prabhu sei śloka uccārilā
śloka uccārite tad-rūpa āpane ha-ilā

SYNONYMS

sei bhāve—in that ecstatic mood; *prabhu*—Śrī Caitanya Mahāprabhu; *sei*—that; *śloka*—verse; *uccārilā*—recited; *śloka*—the verse; *uccārite*—by reciting; *tat-rūpa*—like Śrīmatī Rādhārāṇī; *āpane*—Himself; *ha-ilā*—became.

TRANSLATION

In the same spirit of ecstasy, Śrī Caitanya Mahāprabhu recited that verse, and as soon as He did so, He felt like Śrīmatī Rādhārāṇī.

TEXT 47

আশ্লিষ্য বা পাদরতাং পিনষ্টু মা-
মদর্শনান্মর্মহতাং করোতু বা।
যথা তথা বা বিদধাতু লম্পটো
মৎপ্রাণনাথস্তু স এব নাপরঃ ॥ ৪৭ ॥

āśliṣya vā pāda-ratāṁ pinaṣṭu mām
adarśanān marma-hatāṁ karotu vā
yathā tathā vā vidadhātu lampaṭo
mat-prāṇa-nāthas tu sa eva nāparaḥ

SYNONYMS

āśliṣya—embracing with great pleasure; *vā*—or; *pāda-ratām*—who is fallen at the lotus feet; *pinaṣṭu*—let Him trample; *mām*—Me; *adarśanāt*—by not being visible; *marma-hatām*—brokenhearted; *karotu*—let Him make; *vā*—or; *yathā*—as (He likes); *tathā*—so; *vā*—or; *vidadhātu*—let Him do; *lampaṭaḥ*—a debauchee, who mixes with other women; *mat-prāṇa-nāthaḥ*—the Lord of My life; *tu*—but; *saḥ*—He; *eva*—only; *na aparaḥ*—not anyone else.

TRANSLATION

"Let Kṛṣṇa tightly embrace this maidservant, who has fallen at His lotus feet. Let Him trample Me or break My heart by never being visible to Me. He is a debauchee, after all, and can do whatever He likes, but He is still no one other than the worshipable Lord of My heart.

TEXT 48

"আমি—কৃষ্ণপদ-দাসী, তেঁহো—রসসুখরাশি,
আলিঙ্গিয়া করে আত্মসাথ।
কিবা না দেয় দরশন, জারেন মোর তনুমন,
তবু তেঁহো—মোর প্রাণনাথ ॥ ৪৮ ॥

"āmi——kṛṣṇa-pada-dāsī, teṅho——rasa-sukha-rāśi,
āliṅgiyā kare ātma-sātha
kibā nā deya daraśana, jārena mora tanu-mana,
tabu teṅho——mora prāṇa-nātha

SYNONYMS

āmi—I; *kṛṣṇa-pada-dāsī*—a maidservant at the lotus feet of Kṛṣṇa; *teṅho*—He; *rasa-sukha-rāśi*—the reservoir of transcendental mellows; *āliṅgiyā*—by embracing; *kare*—makes; *ātma-sātha*—merged; *kibā*—or; *nā deya*—does not give; *daraśana*—audience; *jārena*—corrodes; *mora*—My; *tanu-mana*—body and mind; *tabu*—still; *teṅho*—He; *mora prāṇa-nātha*—the Lord of My life.

TRANSLATION

"I am a maidservant at the lotus feet of Kṛṣṇa. He is the embodiment of transcendental happiness and mellows. If He likes He can tightly embrace Me

and make Me feel oneness with Him, or by not giving Me His audience, He may corrode My mind and body. Nevertheless, it is He who is the Lord of My life.

TEXT 49

সখি হে, শুন মোর মনের নিশ্চয় ।
কিবা অনুরাগ করে,   কিবা দুঃখ দিয়া মারে,
মোর প্রাণেশ্বর কৃষ্ণ—অন্য নয় ॥ ৪৯ ॥

sakhi he, śuna mora manera niścaya
kibā anurāga kare, kibā duḥkha diyā māre,
mora prāṇeśvara kṛṣṇa——anya naya

SYNONYMS

sakhi he—O My dear friend; *śuna*—just hear; *mora*—My; *manera*—of the mind; *niścaya*—decision; *kibā*—whether; *anurāga*—affection; *kare*—shows; *kibā*—or; *duḥkha*—unhappiness; *diyā*—bestowing; *māre*—kills; *mora*—My; *prāṇa-īśvara*—the Lord of life; *kṛṣṇa*—Kṛṣṇa; *anya naya*—and no one else.

TRANSLATION

"My dear friend, just hear the decision of My mind. Kṛṣṇa is the Lord of My life in all conditions, whether He shows Me affection or kills Me by giving Me unhappiness.

TEXT 50

ছাড়ি' অন্য নারীগণ,   মোর বশ তনুমন,
মোর সৌভাগ্য প্রকট করিয়া ।
তা-সবারে দেয় পীড়া,   আমা-সনে করে ক্রীড়া,
সেই নারীগণে দেখাঞা ॥ ৫০ ॥

chāḍi' anya nārī-gaṇa, mora vaśa tanu-mana,
mora saubhāgya prakaṭa kariyā
tā-sabāre deya pīḍā, āmā-sane kare krīḍā,
sei nārī-gaṇe dekhāñā

SYNONYMS

chāḍi'—giving up; *anya*—other; *nārī-gaṇa*—women; *mora*—My; *vaśa*—control; *tanu-mana*—mind and body; *mora*—My; *saubhāgya*—fortune; *prakaṭa kariyā*—manifesting; *tā-sabāre*—unto all of them; *deya pīḍā*—gives distress; *āmā-*

sane—with Me; *kare krīḍā*—performs loving activities; *sei nārī-gaṇe*—unto these women; *dekhāñā*—showing.

TRANSLATION

"Sometimes Kṛṣṇa gives up the company of other gopīs and becomes controlled, mind and body, by Me. Thus He manifests My good fortune and gives others distress by performing His loving affairs with Me.

TEXT 51

কিবা তেঁহো লম্পট, শঠ, ধৃষ্ট, সকপট,
অন্য নারীগণ করি' সাথ ।
মোরে দিতে মনঃপীড়া, মোর আগে করে ক্রীড়া,
তবু তেঁহো—মোর প্রাণনাথ ॥ ৫১ ॥

kibā teṅho lampaṭa, śaṭha, dhṛṣṭa, sakapaṭa,
anya nārī-gaṇa kari' sātha
more dite manaḥ-pīḍā, mora āge kare krīḍā,
tabu teṅho——mora prāṇa-nātha

SYNONYMS

kibā—or; *teṅho*—He; *lampaṭa*—debauchee; *śaṭha*—deceitful; *dhṛṣṭa*—obstinate; *sakapaṭa*—with a cheating propensity; *anya*—other; *nārī-gaṇa*—women; *kari'*—accepting; *sātha*—as companions; *more*—unto Me; *dite*—to give; *manaḥ-pīḍā*—distress in the mind; *mora āge*—in front of Me; *kare krīḍā*—performs loving affairs; *tabu*—still; *teṅho*—He; *mora prāṇa-nātha*—the Lord of My life.

TRANSLATION

"Or, since after all He is a very cunning, obstinate debauchee with a propensity to cheat, He takes to the company of other women. He then indulges in loving affairs with them in front of Me to give distress to My mind. Nevertheless, He is still the Lord of My life.

TEXT 52

না গণি আপন-দুঃখ, সবে বাঞ্ছি তাঁর সুখ,
তাঁর সুখ—আমার তাৎপর্য ।
মোরে যদি দিয়া দুঃখ, তাঁর হৈল মহাসুখ,
সেই দুঃখ—মোর সুখবর্য ॥ ৫২ ॥

nā gaṇi āpana-duḥkha, sabe vāñchi tāṅra sukha,
tāṅra sukha——āmāra tātparya
more yadi diyā duḥkha, tāṅra haila mahā-sukha,
sei duḥkha——mora sukha-varya

SYNONYMS

nā—not; *gaṇi*—I count; *āpana-duḥkha*—own personal misery; *sabe*—only; *vāñchi*—I desire; *tāṅra sukha*—His happiness; *tāṅra sukha*—His happiness; *āmāra tātparya*—the aim of My life; *more*—unto Me; *yadi*—if; *diyā duḥkha*—giving distress; *tāṅra*—His; *haila*—there was; *mahā-sukha*—great happiness; *sei duḥkha*—that unhappiness; *mora sukha-varya*—the best of My happiness.

TRANSLATION

"I do not mind My personal distress. I only wish for the happiness of Kṛṣṇa, for His happiness is the goal of My life. However, if He feels great happiness in giving Me distress, that distress is the best of My happiness.

PURPORT

Śrīla Bhaktisiddhānta Sarasvatī Ṭhākura says that a devotee does not care about his own happiness and distress; he is simply interested in seeing that Kṛṣṇa is happy, and for that purpose he engages in various activities. A pure devotee has no way of sensing happiness except by seeing that Kṛṣṇa is happy in every respect. If Kṛṣṇa becomes happy by giving him distress, such a devotee accepts that unhappiness as the greatest of all happiness. Those who are materialistic, however, who are very proud of material wealth and have no spiritual knowledge, like the *prākṛta-sahajiyās,* regard their own happiness as the aim of life. Some of them aspire to enjoy themselves by sharing the happiness of Kṛṣṇa. This is the mentality of fruitive workers who want to enjoy sense gratification by making a show of service to Kṛṣṇa.

TEXT 53

যে নারীরে বাঞ্ছে কৃষ্ণ, তার রূপে সতৃষ্ণ,
তারে না পাঞা হয় দুঃখী ।
মুই তার পায় পড়ি', লঞা যাঙ হাতে ধরি',
ক্রীড়া করাঞা তাঁরে করোঁ সুখী ॥ ৫৩ ॥

ye nārīre vāñche kṛṣṇa, tāra rūpe satṛṣṇa,
tāre nā pāñā haya duḥkhī
mui tāra pāya paḍi', lañā yāṅa hāte dhari',
krīḍā karāñā tāṅre karoṅ sukhī

SYNONYMS

ye nārīre—the woman whom; *vāñche kṛṣṇa*—Kṛṣṇa desires to have in His company; *tāra rūpe satṛṣṇa*—attracted to her beauty; *tāre*—her; *nā pāñā*—not getting; *haya duḥkhī*—becomes unhappy; *mui*—I; *tāra pāya paḍi'*—falling down at her feet; *lañā yāṅa*—taking, go; *hāte dhari'*—catching the hand; *krīḍā*—pastimes; *karāñā*—bringing about; *tāṅre*—Lord Kṛṣṇa; *karoṅ sukhī*—I make happy.

TRANSLATION

"If Kṛṣṇa, attracted by the beauty of some other woman, wants to enjoy with her but is unhappy because He cannot get her, I fall down at her feet, catch her hand and bring her to Kṛṣṇa to engage her for His happiness.

TEXT 54

কান্তা কৃষ্ণে করে রোষ, কৃষ্ণ পায় সন্তোষ,
সুখ পায় তাড়ন-ভর্ৎসনে ।
যথাযোগ্য করে মান, কৃষ্ণ তাতে সুখ পান,
ছাড়ে মান অল্প-সাধনে ॥ ৫৪ ॥

kāntā kṛṣṇe kare roṣa, kṛṣṇa pāya santoṣa,
sukha pāya tāḍana-bhartsane
yathā-yogya kare māna, kṛṣṇa tāte sukha pāna,
chāḍe māna alpa-sādhane

SYNONYMS

kāntā—the beloved; *kṛṣṇe*—unto Lord Kṛṣṇa; *kare roṣa*—shows anger; *kṛṣṇa pāya santoṣa*—Kṛṣṇa becomes very happy; *sukha pāya*—obtains happiness; *tāḍana-bhartsane*—by chastisement; *yathā-yogya*—as it is suitable; *kare māna*—shows pride; *kṛṣṇa*—Lord Kṛṣṇa; *tāte*—in such activities; *sukha pāna*—obtains happiness; *chāḍe māna*—gives up pride; *alpa-sādhane*—by a little endeavor.

TRANSLATION

"When a beloved gopī shows symptoms of anger toward Kṛṣṇa, Kṛṣṇa is very satisfied. Indeed, He is pleased when chastised by such a gopī. She shows her pride suitably, and Kṛṣṇa enjoys that attitude. Then she gives up her pride with a little endeavor.

TEXT 55

সেই নারী জীয়ে কেনে, কৃষ্ণ-মর্ম ব্যথা জানে,
তবু কৃষ্ণে করে গাঢ় রোষ ।
নিজ-সুখে মানে কাজ, পড়ুক তার শিরে বাজ,
কৃষ্ণের মাত্র চাহিয়ে সন্তোষ ॥ ৫৫ ॥

sei nārī jīye kene, kṛṣṇa-marma vyathā jāne,
tabu kṛṣṇe kare gāḍha roṣa
nija-sukhe māne kāja, paḍuka tāra śire vāja,
kṛṣṇera mātra cāhiye santoṣa

SYNONYMS

sei nārī—that woman; *jīye*—lives; *kene*—why; *kṛṣṇa-marma*—Kṛṣṇa's heart; *vyathā*—unhappy; *jāne*—knows; *tabu*—still; *kṛṣṇe*—unto Kṛṣṇa; *kare*—does; *gāḍha roṣa*—deep anger; *nija-sukhe*—in her own happiness; *māne*—considers; *kāja*—the only business; *paḍuka*—let there fall; *tāre*—of her; *śire*—on the head; *vāja*—a thunderbolt; *kṛṣṇera*—of Kṛṣṇa; *mātra*—only; *cāhiye*—we want; *santoṣa*—the happiness.

TRANSLATION

"Why does a woman continue to live who knows that Kṛṣṇa's heart is unhappy but who still shows her deep anger toward Him? She is interested in her own happiness. I condemn such a woman to be struck on the head with a thunderbolt, for we simply want the happiness of Kṛṣṇa.

PURPORT

A devotee who is satisfied only with his own sense gratification certainly falls down from the service of Kṛṣṇa. Being attracted by material happiness, he later joins the *prākṛta-sahajiyās,* who are considered to be nondevotees.

TEXT 56

যে গোপী মোর করে দ্বেষে, কৃষ্ণের করে সন্তোষে,
কৃষ্ণ যারে করে অভিলাষ ।
মুই তার ঘরে যাঞা, তারে সেবোঁ দাসী হঞা,
তবে মোর সুখের উল্লাস ॥ ৫৬ ॥

ye gopī mora kare dveṣe, kṛṣṇera kare santoṣe,
kṛṣṇa yāre kare abhilāṣa
mui tāra ghare yāñā, tāre sevoṅ dāsī hañā,
tabe mora sukhera ullāsa

SYNONYMS

ye gopī—any *gopī* who; *mora*—unto Me; *kare dveṣe*—shows envy; *kṛṣṇera kare santoṣe*—but satisfies Kṛṣṇa; *kṛṣṇa*—unto Lord Kṛṣṇa; *yāre*—unto whom; *kare*—does; *abhilāṣa*—desiring; *mui*—I; *tāra*—her; *ghare yāñā*—going to the house; *tāre sevoṅ*—shall render service unto her; *dāsī hañā*—becoming a maidservant; *tabe*—then; *mora*—My; *sukhera ullāsa*—awakening of happiness.

TRANSLATION

"If a gopī envious of Me satisfies Kṛṣṇa and Kṛṣṇa desires her, I shall not hesitate to go to her house and become her maidservant, for then My happiness will be awakened.

TEXT 57

কুষ্ঠী-বিপ্রের রমণী, পতিব্রতা-শিরোমণি,
পতি লাগি' কৈলা বেশ্যার সেবা ।
স্তম্ভিল সূর্যের গতি, জীয়াইল মৃত পতি,
তুষ্ট কৈল মুখ্য তিন-দেবা ॥ ৫৭ ॥

kuṣṭhī-viprera ramaṇī, pativratā-śiromaṇi,
pati lāgi' kailā veśyāra sevā
stambhila sūryera gati, jīyāila mṛta pati,
tuṣṭa kaila mukhya tina-devā

SYNONYMS

kuṣṭhī-viprera—of the *brāhmaṇa* who suffered from leprosy; *ramaṇī*—the wife; *pati-vratā-śiromaṇi*—the topmost of chaste women; *pati lāgi'*—for the satisfaction of her husband; *kailā*—performed; *veśyāra sevā*—service to a prostitute; *stambhila*—stopped; *sūryera gati*—the movement of the sun; *jīyāila*—revived; *mṛta pati*—the dead husband; *tuṣṭa kaila*—satisfied; *mukhya*—the principal; *tina-devā*—three deities or demigods.

TRANSLATION

"The wife of a brāhmaṇa suffering from leprosy manifested herself as the topmost of all chaste women by serving a prostitute to satisfy her husband.

She thus stopped the movement of the sun, brought her dead husband back to life and satisfied the three principal demigods [Brahmā, Viṣṇu and Maheśvara].

PURPORT

The *Āditya Purāṇa, Mārkeṇḍeya Purāṇa* and *Padma Purāṇa* tell about a *brāhmaṇa* who was suffering from leprosy but had a very chaste and faithful wife. He desired to enjoy the company of a prostitute, and therefore his wife went to her and became her maidservant, just to draw her attention for his service. When the prostitute agreed to associate with him, the wife brought her the leprotic husband. When that leper, the sinful son of a *brāhmaṇa,* saw the chastity of his wife, he finally abandoned his sinful intentions. While coming home, however, he touched the body of Mārkeṇḍeya Ṛṣi, who thus cursed him to die at sunrise. Because of her chastity, the woman was very powerful. Therefore when she heard about the curse, she vowed to stop the sunrise. Because of her strong determination to serve her husband, the three deities—namely Brahmā, Viṣṇu and Maheśvara—were very happy, and they gave her the benediction that her husband would be cured and brought back to life. This example is given herein to emphasize that a devotee should engage himself exclusively for the satisfaction of Kṛṣṇa, without personal motives. That will make his life successful.

TEXT 58

"কৃষ্ণ—মোর জীবন, কৃষ্ণ—মোর প্রাণধন,
কৃষ্ণ – মোর প্রাণের পরাণ ।
হৃদয়-উপরে ধরোঁ, সেবা করি' সুখী করোঁ,
এই মোর সদা রহে ধ্যান ॥ ৫৮ ॥

"kṛṣṇa——mora jīvana, kṛṣṇa——mora prāṇa-dhana,
kṛṣṇa——mora prāṇera parāṇa
hṛdaya-upare dharoṅ, sevā kari' sukhī karoṅ,
ei mora sadā rahe dhyāna

SYNONYMS

kṛṣṇa—Lord Kṛṣṇa; *mora jīvana*—My life and soul; *kṛṣṇa*—Lord Kṛṣṇa; *mora prāṇa-dhana*—the wealth of My life; *kṛṣṇa*—Lord Kṛṣṇa; *mora prāṇera parāṇa*—the life of My life; *hṛdaya-upare*—on My heart; *dharoṅ*—I hold; *sevā kari'*—serving; *sukhī karoṅ*—I make happy; *ei*—this; *mora*—My; *sadā*—always; *rahe*—remains; *dhyāna*—meditation.

TRANSLATION

"Kṛṣṇa is My life and soul. Kṛṣṇa is the treasure of My life. Indeed, Kṛṣṇa is the very life of My life. I therefore keep Him always in My heart and try to please Him by rendering service. That is My constant meditation.

TEXT 59

মোর সুখ—সেবনে, কৃষ্ণের সুখ—সঙ্গমে,
অতএব দেহ দেঙ দান ।
কৃষ্ণ মোরে 'কান্তা' করি', কহে মোরে 'প্রাণেশ্বরি,'
মোর হয় 'দাসী'-অভিমান ॥ ৫৯ ॥

mora sukha——sevane, kṛṣṇera sukha——saṅgame,
ataeva deha deṅa dāna
kṛṣṇa more 'kāntā' kari', kahe more 'prāṇeśvari',
mora haya 'dāsī'-abhimāna

SYNONYMS

mora sukha—My happiness; *sevane*—in service; *kṛṣṇera sukha*—Kṛṣṇa's happiness; *saṅgame*—by union with Me; *ataeva*—therefore; *deha*—My body; *deṅa*—I offer; *dāna*—as charity; *kṛṣṇa*—Lord Kṛṣṇa; *more*—Me; *kāntā kari'*—accepting as beloved; *kahe*—says; *more*—to Me; *prāṇa-īśvari*—the most beloved; *mora*—My; *haya*—there is; *dāsī-abhimāna*—considering His maidservant.

TRANSLATION

"My happiness is in the service of Kṛṣṇa, and Kṛṣṇa's happiness is in union with Me. For this reason, I give My body in charity to the lotus feet of Kṛṣṇa, who accepts Me as His loved one and calls Me His most beloved. It is then that I consider Myself His maidservant.

TEXT 60

কান্ত-সেবা-সুখপূর, সঙ্গম হৈতে সুমধুর,
তাতে সাক্ষী—লক্ষ্মী ঠাকুরাণী ।
নারায়ণ-হৃদি স্থিতি, তবু পাদসেবায় মতি,
সেবা করে 'দাসী'-অভিমানী ॥ ৬০ ॥

kānta-sevā-sukha-pūra, saṅgama haite sumadhura,
tāte sākṣī——lakṣmī ṭhākurāṇī

nārāyaṇa-hṛdi sthiti, tabu pāda-sevāya mati,
sevā kare 'dāsī'-abhimānī

SYNONYMS

kānta-sevā-sukha-pūra—the service of the Lord is the home of happiness; *saṅgama haite su-madhura*—sweeter than direct union; *tāte*—in that; *sākṣī*—evidence; *lakṣmī ṭhākurāṇī*—the goddess of fortune; *nārāyaṇa-hṛdi*—on the heart of Nārāyaṇa; *sthiti*—situation; *tabu*—still; *pāda-sevāya mati*—her desire is to serve the lotus feet; *sevā kare*—renders service; *dāsī-abhimānī*—considering herself a maidservant.

TRANSLATION

"Service to My lover is the home of happiness and is more sweet than direct union with Him. The goddess of fortune is evidence of this, for although she constantly lives on the heart of Nārāyaṇa, she wants to render service to His lotus feet. She therefore considers herself a maidservant and serves Him constantly."

TEXT 61

এই রাধার বচন, বিশুদ্ধপ্রেম-লক্ষণ,
আস্বাদয়ে শ্রীগৌর-রায় ।
ভাবে মন নহে স্থির, সাত্ত্বিকে ব্যাপে শরীর,
মন-দেহ ধরণ না যায় ॥ ৬১ ॥

ei rādhāra vacana, viśuddha-prema-lakṣaṇa,
āsvādaye śrī-gaura-rāya
bhāve mana nahe sthira, sāttvike vyāpe śarīra,
mana-deha dharaṇa nā yāya

SYNONYMS

ei—this; *rādhāra vacana*—the statement of Śrīmatī Rādhārāṇī; *viśuddha-prema-lakṣaṇa*—the symptoms of pure love of Kṛṣṇa; *āsvādaye*—tastes; *śrī-gaura-rāya*—Lord Śrī Caitanya Mahāprabhu; *bhāve*—because of this ecstasy; *mana nahe sthira*—the mind is not steady; *sāttvike*—the symptoms of transcendental love; *vyāpe*—spread over; *śarīra*—the body; *mana-deha*—mind and body; *dharaṇa*—sustaining; *nā yāya*—is not possible.

TRANSLATION

These statements by Śrīmatī Rādhārāṇī show the symptoms of pure love for Kṛṣṇa tasted by Śrī Caitanya Mahāprabhu. In that ecstatic love, His mind was

unsteady. Transformations of transcendental love spread throughout His entire body, and He could not sustain His body and mind.

TEXT 62

ব্রজের বিশুদ্ধপ্রেম,— যেন জাম্বূনদ হেম,
আত্ম-সুখের যাহাঁ নাহি গন্ধ ।
সে প্রেম জানা'তে লোকে, প্রভু কৈলা এই শ্লোকে,
পদে কৈলা অর্থের নির্বন্ধ ॥ ৬২ ॥

vrajera viśuddha-prema,—— yena jāmbū-nada hema,
ātma-sukhera yāhāṅ nāhi gandha
se prema jānā'te loke, prabhu kailā ei śloke,
pade kailā arthera nirbandha

SYNONYMS

vrajera—of Vṛndāvana; *viśuddha-prema*—the pure love of Kṛṣṇa; *yena*—like; *jāmbū-nada hema*—the golden particles found in the Jāmbū River; *ātma-sukhera*—of personal sense gratification; *yāhāṅ*—where; *nāhi gandha*—there is not even a scent; *se prema*—that love of Godhead; *jānā'te loke*—to advertise among the people; *prabhu*—Śrī Caitanya Mahāprabhu; *kailā*—has written; *ei śloke*—this verse; *pade*—in different steps; *kailā arthera nirbandha*—has clarified the real meaning.

TRANSLATION

The pure devotional service in Vṛndāvana is like the golden particles in the River Jāmbū. In Vṛndāvana there is not a trace of personal sense gratification. It is to advertise such pure love in this material world that Śrī Caitanya Mahāprabhu has written the previous verse and explained its meaning.

TEXT 63

এইমত মহাপ্রভু ভাবাবিষ্ট হঞা ।
প্রলাপ করিলা তত্তৎ শ্লোক পড়িয়া ॥ ৬৩ ॥

ei-mata mahāprabhu bhāvāviṣṭa hañā
pralāpa karilā tat-tat śloka paḍiyā

SYNONYMS

ei-mata—in this way; *mahāprabhu*—Śrī Caitanya Mahāprabhu; *bhāva-āviṣṭa hañā*—being overwhelmed by ecstatic love; *pralāpa karilā*—said crazy words; *tat-tat*—appropriate; *śloka paḍiyā*—by reading the verse.

TRANSLATION

Thus overwhelmed by ecstatic love, Śrī Caitanya Mahāprabhu spoke like a madman and recited suitable verses.

TEXT 64

পূর্বে অষ্ট-শ্লোক করি' লোকে শিক্ষা দিলা।
সেই অষ্ট-শ্লোকের অর্থ আপনে আস্বাদিলা॥ ৬৪ ॥

pūrve aṣṭa-śloka kari' loke śikṣā dilā
sei aṣṭa-ślokera artha āpane āsvādilā

SYNONYMS

pūrve—formerly; *aṣṭa-śloka kari'*—composing eight verses; *loke śikṣā dilā*—gave instruction to the people in general; *sei*—those; *aṣṭa-ślokera*—of the eight stanzas; *artha*—the meaning; *āpane āsvādilā*—personally tasted.

TRANSLATION

The Lord had formerly composed these eight verses to teach people in general. Now He personally tasted the meaning of the verses, which are called the Śikṣāṣṭaka.

TEXT 65

প্রভুর 'শিক্ষাষ্টক'-শ্লোক যেই পড়ে, শুনে।
কৃষ্ণে প্রেমভক্তি তার বাড়ে দিনে-দিনে॥ ৬৫ ॥

prabhura 'śikṣāṣṭaka'-śloka yei paḍe, śune
kṛṣṇe prema-bhakti tāra bāḍe dine-dine

SYNONYMS

prabhura—of Śrī Caitanya Mahāprabhu; *śikṣā-aṣṭaka*—of the eight instructions; *śloka*—the verses; *yei*—anyone who; *paḍe*—recites; *śune*—or hears; *kṛṣṇe*—unto Lord Kṛṣṇa; *prema-bhakti*—ecstatic love and devotion; *tāra*—his; *bāḍe*—increases; *dine-dine*—day after day.

TRANSLATION

If anyone recites or hears these eight verses of instruction by Śrī Caitanya Mahāprabhu, his ecstatic love and devotion for Kṛṣṇa increase day by day.

TEXT 66

যদ্যপিহ প্রভু – কোটীসমুদ্র-গম্ভীর ।
নানা-ভাব-চন্দ্রোদয়ে হয়েন অস্থির ॥ ৬৬ ॥

yadyapiha prabhu——koṭī-samudra-gambhīra
nānā-bhāva-candrodaye hayena asthira

SYNONYMS

yadyapiha—although; *prabhu*—Śrī Caitanya Mahāprabhu; *koṭī-samudra-gambhīra*—as deep as millions of oceans; *nānā*—various; *bhāva*—of ecstatic emotions; *candrodaye*—because of the moonrise; *hayena*—sometimes becomes; *asthira*—restless.

TRANSLATION

Although Śrī Caitanya Mahāprabhu is as deep and grave as millions of oceans, when the moon of His various emotions rises, He becomes restless.

TEXTS 67-68

যেই যেই শ্লোক জয়দেব, ভাগবতে ।
রায়ের নাটকে, যেই আর কর্ণামৃতে ॥ ৬৭ ॥
সেই সেই ভাবে শ্লোক করিয়া পঠনে ।
সেই সেই ভাবাবেশে করেন আস্বাদনে ॥ ৬৮ ॥

yei yei śloka jayadeva, bhāgavate
rāyera nāṭake, yei āra karṇāmṛte

sei sei bhāve śloka kariyā paṭhane
sei sei bhāvāveśe karena āsvādane

SYNONYMS

yei yei—whatever; *śloka*—verses; *jayadeva*—Jayadeva Gosvāmī; *bhāgavate*—in *Śrīmad-Bhāgavatam; rāyera nāṭake*—in the drama made by Rāmānanda Rāya; *yei*—whatever; *āra*—also; *karṇāmṛte*—in the book named *Kṛṣṇa-karṇāmṛta,* written by Bilvamaṅgala Ṭhākura; *sei sei bhāve*—in those ecstatic emotions; *śloka*—verses; *kariyā paṭhane*—reading regularly; *sei sei*—in that particular; *bhāva-āveśe*—ecstatic love; *karena āsvādane*—He tastes.

TRANSLATION

When Śrī Caitanya Mahāprabhu read the verses of Jayadeva's Gīta-govinda, of Śrīmad-Bhāgavatam, of Rāmānanda Rāya's drama Jagannātha-vallabha-nāṭaka and of Bilvamaṅgala Ṭhākura's Kṛṣṇa-karṇāmṛta, He was overwhelmed by the various ecstatic emotions of those verses. Thus He tasted their purports.

TEXT 69

দ্বাদশ বৎসর ঐছে দশা—রাত্রি-দিনে ।
কৃষ্ণরস আস্বাদয়ে দুইবন্ধু-সনে ॥ ৬৯ ॥

dvādaśa vatsara aiche daśā——rātri-dine
kṛṣṇa-rasa āsvādaye dui-bandhu-sane

SYNONYMS

dvādaśa vatsara—for twelve years; *aiche daśā*—such a condition; *rātri-dine*—day and night; *kṛṣṇa-rasa*—transcendental bliss and mellows in connection with Kṛṣṇa; *āsvādaye*—He tastes; *dui-bandhu-sane*—with two friends, namely Rāmānanda Rāya and Svarūpa Dāmodara Gosvāmī.

TRANSLATION

For twelve years, Śrī Caitanya remained in that state day and night. With His two friends, He tasted the meaning of those verses, which consist of nothing but the transcendental bliss and mellows of Kṛṣṇa consciousness.

TEXT 70

সেই সব লীলারস আপনে অনন্ত ।
সহস্র-বদনে বর্ণি' নাহি পা'ন অন্ত ॥ ৭০ ॥

sei saba līlā-rasa āpane ananta
sahasra-vadane varṇi' nāhi pā'na anta

SYNONYMS

sei saba—all these; *līlā-rasa*—transcendental mellows of Śrī Caitanya Mahāprabhu's pastimes; *āpane*—personally; *ananta*—the Personality of Godhead Ananta; *sahasra-vadane*—with His thousands of faces; *varṇi'*—describing; *nāhi*—not; *pā'na*—gets; *anta*—the limit.

TRANSLATION

Even Anantadeva, who has thousands of faces, could not reach the end of describing the transcendental bliss of Śrī Caitanya Mahāprabhu's pastimes.

TEXT 71

জীব ক্ষুদ্রবুদ্ধি কোন্ তাহা পারে বর্ণিতে ?
তার এক কণা স্পর্শি আপনা শোধিতে ॥ ৭১ ॥

jīva kṣudra-buddhi kon tāhā pāre varṇite?
tāra eka kaṇā sparśi āpanā śodhite

SYNONYMS

jīva—living being; *kṣudra-buddhi*—limited intelligence; *kon*—who; *tāhā*—that; *pāre*—is able; *varṇite*—to write; *tāra*—of that; *eka kaṇā*—one particle; *sparśi*—I touch; *āpanā śodhite*—to correct myself.

TRANSLATION

How, then, could an ordinary living being with very little intelligence describe such pastimes? Nevertheless, I am trying to touch but a particle of them just to rectify my own self.

TEXT 72

যত চেষ্টা, যত প্রলাপ,—নাহি পারাবার।
সে সব বর্ণিতে গ্রন্থ হয় সুবিস্তার ॥ ৭২ ॥

yata ceṣṭā, yata pralāpa,——nāhi pārāvāra
sei saba varṇite grantha haya suvistāra

SYNONYMS

yata ceṣṭā—all activities; *yata pralāpa*—all crazy talking; *nāhi pārāvāra*—there was no limit; *sei saba*—all of them; *varṇite*—to describe; *grantha*—the book; *haya*—would be; *su-vistāra*—very voluminous.

TRANSLATION

There is no limit to Śrī Caitanya Mahāprabhu's activities and His words of madness. Therefore describing them all would greatly increase the size of this book.

TEXT 73

বৃন্দাবন-দাস প্রথম যে লীলা বর্ণিল।
সেইসব লীলার আমি সূত্রমাত্র কৈল ॥ ৭৩ ॥

vṛndāvana-dāsa prathama ye līlā varṇila
sei-saba līlāra āmi sūtra-mātra kaila

SYNONYMS

vṛndāvana-dāsa—Vṛndāvana dāsa Ṭhākura; *prathama*—at first; *ye*—whatever; *līlā*—pastimes; *varṇila*—described; *sei-saba*—all of those; *līlāra*—of the pastimes; *āmi*—I; *sūtra-mātra kaila*—prepared only the synopsis.

TRANSLATION

Whatever pastimes Śrīla Vṛndāvana dāsa Ṭhākura has first described I have merely summarized.

TEXT 74

তাঁর ত্যক্ত 'অবশেষ' সংক্ষেপে কহিল।
লীলার বাহুল্যে গ্রন্থ তথাপি বাড়িল ॥ ৭৪ ॥

tāṅra tyakta 'avaśeṣa' saṅkṣepe kahila
līlāra bāhulye grantha tathāpi bāḍila

SYNONYMS

tāṅra—his; *tyakta*—left out; *aveśeṣa*—remainders; *saṅkṣepe kahila*—I have described very briefly; *līlāra bāhulye*—because of the numerousness of the pastimes; *grantha*—this book; *tathāpi*—still; *bāḍila*—has increased.

TRANSLATION

I have only very briefly described the pastimes of Śrī Caitanya Mahāprabhu not described by Vṛndāvana dāsa Ṭhākura. Nevertheless, because those transcendental pastimes are so numerous, the size of this book has increased.

TEXT 75

অতএব সেইসব লীলা না পারি বর্ণিবারে।
সমাপ্তি করিলুঁ লীলাকে করি' নমস্কারে ॥ ৭৫ ॥

ataeva sei-saba līlā nā pāri varṇibāre
samāpti kariluṅ līlāke kari' namaskāre

SYNONYMS

ataeva—therefore; *sei-saba*—all those; *līlā*—pastimes; *nā pāri*—I am not able; *varṇibāre*—to narrate; *samāpti kariluṅ*—now I have finished; *līlāke*—to the pastimes; *kari' namaskāre*—offering my respectful obeisances.

TRANSLATION

It is impossible to describe all the pastimes elaborately. I shall therefore end this description and offer them my respectful obeisances.

TEXT 76

যে কিছু কহিলুঁ এই দিগ্‌দরশন ।
এই অনুসারে হবে তার আস্বাদন ॥ ৭৬ ॥

ye kichu kahiluṅ ei dig-daraśana
ei anusāre habe tāra āsvādana

SYNONYMS

ye kichu—whatever; *kahiluṅ*—I have said; *ei*—this; *dik-daraśana*—just to make an indication; *ei anusāre*—in this way; *habe*—there will be; *tāra*—of that; *āsvādana*—tasting.

TRANSLATION

What I have described gives merely an indication, but by following this indication one may obtain a taste of all the pastimes of Śrī Caitanya Mahāprabhu.

TEXT 77

প্রভুর গম্ভীর-লীলা না পারি বুঝিতে ।
বুদ্ধি-প্রবেশ নাহি তাতে, না পারি বর্ণিতে ॥ ৭৭ ॥

prabhura gambhīra-līlā nā pāri bujhite
buddhi-praveśa nāhi tāte, nā pāri varṇite

SYNONYMS

prabhura—of Śrī Caitanya Mahāprabhu; *gambhīra*—deep; *līlā*—the pastimes; *nā pāri*—I am not able; *bujhite*—to understand; *buddhi-praveśa nāhi*—my intelligence cannot penetrate; *tāte*—because of this; *nā pāri*—I am not able; *varṇite*—to describe properly.

TRANSLATION

I cannot understand the very deep, meaningful pastimes of Śrī Caitanya Mahāprabhu. My intelligence cannot penetrate them, and therefore I could not properly describe them.

TEXT 78

সব শ্রোতা বৈষ্ণবের বন্দিয়া চরণ ।
চৈতন্যচরিত্র-বর্ণন কৈলুঁ সমাপন ॥ ৭৮ ॥

saba śrotā vaiṣṇavera vandiyā caraṇa
caitanya-caritra-varṇana kailuṅ samāpana

SYNONYMS

saba śrotā—all readers; *vaiṣṇavera*—of the Vaiṣṇavas; *vandiyā caraṇa*—offering respectful obeisances unto the lotus feet; *caitanya-caritra*—of the characteristics of Śrī Caitanya Mahāprabhu; *varṇana*—description; *kailuṅ*—I have done; *samāpana*—finishing.

TRANSLATION

After offering my respectful obeisances to the lotus feet of all my Vaiṣṇava readers, I shall therefore end this description of the characteristics of Śrī Caitanya Mahāprabhu.

TEXT 79

আকাশ—অনন্ত, তাতে যৈছে পক্ষিগণ ।
যার যত শক্তি, তত করে আরোহণ ॥ ৭৯ ॥

ākāśa——ananta, tāte yaiche pakṣi-gaṇa
yāra yata śakti, tata kare ārohaṇa

SYNONYMS

ākāśa—the sky; *ananta*—unlimited; *tāte*—in that sky; *yaiche*—just as; *pakṣi-gaṇa*—all types of birds; *yāra*—of someone; *yata śakti*—whatever power; *tata*—that much; *kare ārohaṇa*—rises up and up.

TRANSLATION

The sky is unlimited, but many birds fly higher and higher according to their own abilities.

TEXT 80

ঐছে মহাপ্রভুর লীলা—নাহি ওর-পার।
'জীব' হঞা কেবা সম্যক্ পারে বর্ণিবার ? ৮০ ॥

aiche mahāprabhura līlā——nāhi ora-pāra
'jīva' hañā kebā samyak pāre varṇibāra?

SYNONYMS

aiche—similarly; *mahāprabhura līlā*—the pastimes of Śrī Caitanya Mahāprabhu; *nāhi ora-pāra*—there is no limit above or below; *jīva hañā*—being an ordinary living entity; *kebā*—who; *samyak*—fully; *pāre*—is able; *varṇibāra*—to describe.

TRANSLATION

The pastimes of Śrī Caitanya Mahāprabhu are like the unlimited sky. How, then, can an ordinary living being describe them all?

TEXT 81

যাবৎ বুদ্ধির গতি, ততেক বর্ণিলুঁ।
সমুদ্রের মধ্যে যেন এক কণ ছুঁইলুঁ ॥ ৮১ ॥

yāvat buddhira gati, tateka varṇiluṅ
samudrera madhye yena eka kaṇa chuṅiluṅ

SYNONYMS

yāvat—as far; *buddhira gati*—the limit of my intelligence; *tateka*—that far; *varṇiluṅ*—I have described; *samudrera madhye*—in the midst of the great ocean; *yena*—just like; *eka kaṇa*—one particle; *chuṅiluṅ*—I have touched.

TRANSLATION

I have tried to describe them as far as my intelligence allows, as if trying to touch a drop in the midst of a great ocean.

TEXT 82

নিত্যানন্দ-কৃপাপাত্র—বৃন্দাবন-দাস।
চৈতন্যলীলায় তেঁহো হয়েন 'আদিব্যাস' ॥ ৮২ ॥

nityānanda-kṛpā-pātra——vṛndāvana-dāsa
caitanya-līlāya teṅho hayena 'ādi-vyāsa'

SYNONYMS

nityānanda—of Lord Nityānanda Prabhu; *kṛpā-pātra*—the favorite devotee; *vṛndāvana-dāsa*—Vṛndāvana dāsa Ṭhākura; *caitanya-līlāya*—in the pastimes of Śrī Caitanya Mahāprabhu; *teṅho*—He; *hayena*—is; *ādi-vyāsa*—the original Vyāsadeva.

TRANSLATION

Vṛndāvana dāsa Ṭhākura is Lord Nityānanda's favorite devotee, and therefore he is the original Vyāsadeva in describing the pastimes of Śrī Caitanya Mahāprabhu.

PURPORT

Śrīla Bhaktisiddhānta Sarasvatī Ṭhākura says that all writers after Vṛndāvana dāsa Ṭhākura who are pure devotees of Śrī Caitanya Mahāprabhu and who have tried to describe the Lord's activities are to be considered like Vyāsa. Śrīla Vṛndāvana dāsa Ṭhākura is the original Vyāsadeva in describing *caitanya-līlā,* and all others who follow in his footsteps by describing Śrī Caitanya Mahāprabhu's pastimes are also to be called Vyāsadeva. The bona fide spiritual master is called Vyāsa because he is a representative of Vyāsa. Worshiping the birthday of such a spiritual master is called Vyāsa-pūjā.

TEXT 83

তাঁর আগে যদ্যপি সব লীলার ভাণ্ডার ।
তথাপি অল্প বর্ণিয়া ছাড়িলেন আর ॥ ৮৩ ॥

tāṅra āge yadyapi saba līlāra bhāṇḍāra
tathāpi alpa varṇiyā chāḍilena āra

SYNONYMS

tāṅra āge—before him; *yadyapi*—although; *saba*—all; *līlāra*—of the pastimes; *bhāṇḍāra*—full store; *tathāpi*—still; *alpa*—very little; *varṇiyā*—describing; *chāḍilena*—he left; *āra*—the others.

TRANSLATION

Although Vṛndāvana dāsa Ṭhākura has within his jurisdiction the full store of Śrī Caitanya Mahāprabhu's pastimes, he has left aside most of them and described but a small portion.

TEXT 84

যে কিছু বর্ণিলুঁ, সেহ সংক্ষেপ করিয়া ।
লিখিতে না পারেন, তবু রাখিয়াছেন লিখিয়া ॥ ৮৪॥

ye kichu varṇiluṅ, seha saṅkṣepa kariyā
likhite nā pārena, tabu rākhiyāchena likhiyā

SYNONYMS

ye kichu varṇiluṅ—whatever I have described; *seha*—them; *saṅkṣepa*—briefly; *kariyā*—doing; *likhite nā pārena*—Vṛndāvana dāsa Ṭhākura was not able to describe; *tabu*—still; *rākhiyāchena*—has kept; *likhiyā*—recording in writing.

TRANSLATION

What I have described was left aside by Vṛndāvana dāsa Ṭhākura, but although he could not describe these pastimes, he gave us a synopsis.

TEXT 85

চৈতন্যমঙ্গলে তেঁহো লিখিয়াছে স্থানে-স্থানে ।
সেই বচন শুন, সেই পরম-প্রমাণে ॥ ৮৫ ॥

caitanya-maṅgale teṅho likhiyāche sthāne-sthāne
sei vacana śuna, sei parama-pramāṇe

SYNONYMS

caitanya-maṅgale—in the book named *Caitanya-maṅgala; teṅho*—Vṛndāvana dāsa Ṭhākura; *likhiyāche*—has written; *sthāne-sthāne*—in several places; *sei vacana śuna*—please hear those statements; *sei parama-pramāṇe*—that is the foremost proof.

TRANSLATION

In his book named Caitanya-maṅgala [Caitanya-bhāgavata], he has described these pastimes in many places. I request my readers to hear that book, for that is the best evidence.

TEXT 86

সংক্ষেপে কহিলুঁ, বিস্তার না যায় কথনে ।
বিস্তারিয়া বেদব্যাস করিব বর্ণনে ॥ ৮৬ ॥

saṅkṣepe kahiluṅ, vistāra nā yāya kathane
vistāriyā veda-vyāsa kariba varṇane

SYNONYMS

saṅkṣepe kahiluṅ—I have described very briefly; *vistāra nā yāya kathane*—it is not possible to describe them in full; *vistāriyā*—elaborating; *veda-vyāsa*—a representative of Vyāsadeva; *kariba*—will do; *varṇane*—describing.

TRANSLATION

I have described the pastimes very briefly, for it is impossible for me to describe them in full. In the future, however, Vedavyāsa will describe them elaborately.

TEXT 87

চৈতন্যমঙ্গলে ইহা লিখিয়াছে স্থানে-স্থানে ।
সত্য কহেন,—'আগে ব্যাস করিব বর্ণনে' ॥ ৮৭ ॥

caitanya-maṅgale ihā likhiyāche sthāne-sthāne
satya kahena,——'āge vyāsa kariba varṇane'

SYNONYMS

caitanya-maṅgale—in the book named *Caitanya-maṅgala; ihā*—this statement; *likhiyāche*—has written; *sthāne-sthāne*—in many places; *satya*—the truth; *kahena*—he says; *āge*—in the future; *vyāsa kariba varṇane*—Vyāsadeva will describe them more elaborately.

TRANSLATION

In Caitanya-maṅgala, Śrīla Vṛndāvana dāsa Ṭhākura has stated in many places the factual truth that in the future Vyāsadeva will describe them elaborately.

PURPORT

The statement *āge vyāsa kariba varṇane* is similar to a text in the *Caitanya-bhāgavata* (First Chapter, text 180) in which Vṛndāvana dāsa Ṭhākura says:

śeṣa-khaṇḍe caitanyera ananta vilāsa
vistāriyā varṇite āchena veda-vyāsa

"The unlimited pastimes of Śrī Caitanya will be described by Vyāsadeva in the future." Śrīla Bhaktisiddhānta Sarasvatī Ṭhākura says that these statements indicate that in the future, other representatives of Vyāsadeva will elaborately describe Lord Caitanya's pastimes. The purport is that any pure devotee in the disciplic succession who describes the pastimes of Śrī Caitanya Mahāprabhu is confirmed to be a representative of Vyāsadeva.

TEXT 88

চৈতন্য-লীলামৃত-সিন্ধু—দুগ্ধাব্ধি-সমান ।
তৃষ্ণানুরূপ ঝারী ভরি' তেঁহো কৈলা পান ॥ ৮৮ ॥

caitanya-līlāmṛta-sindhu——dugdhābdhi-samāna
tṛṣṇānurūpa jhārī bhari' teṅho kailā pāna

SYNONYMS

caitanya-līlā-amṛta-sindhu—the ocean of nectarean pastimes of Śrī Caitanya Mahāprabhu; *dugdha-abdhi-samāna*—exactly like the ocean of milk; *tṛṣṇā-anurūpa*—according to one's thirst; *jhārī*—the pitcher; *bhari'*—filling; *teṅho*—he; *kailā pāna*—drank.

TRANSLATION

The ocean of nectarean pastimes of Śrī Caitanya Mahāprabhu is like the ocean of milk. According to his thirst, Vṛndāvana dāsa Ṭhākura filled his pitcher and drank from that ocean.

TEXT 89

তাঁর ঝারী-শেষামৃত কিছু মোরে দিলা ।
ততেকে ভরিল পেট, তৃষ্ণা মোর গেলা ॥ ৮৯ ॥

tāṅra jhārī-śeṣāmṛta kichu more dilā
tateke bharila peṭa, tṛṣṇā mora gelā

SYNONYMS

tāṅra jhārī-śeṣa-amṛta—the remnants of the milk of Vṛndāvana dāsa Ṭhākura's pitcher; *kichu*—some; *more dilā*—has given to me; *tateke*—by those remnants; *bharila peṭa*—my abdomen is filled; *tṛṣṇā mora gelā*—now my thirst has gone.

TRANSLATION

Whatever remnants of milk Vṛndāvana dāsa Ṭhākura has given me are sufficient to fill my belly. Now my thirst is completely satiated.

TEXTS 90-91

আমি—অতিক্ষুদ্র জীব, পক্ষী রাঙ্গাটুনি ।
সে যৈছে তৃষ্ণায় পিয়ে সমুদ্রের পানী ॥ ৯০ ॥
তৈছে আমি এক কণ ছুঁইলুঁ লীলার ।
এই দৃষ্টান্তে জানিহ প্রভুর লীলার বিস্তার ॥ ৯১ ॥

āmi——ati-kṣudra jīva, pakṣī rāṅgā-ṭuni
se yaiche tṛṣṇāya piye samudrera pānī

taiche āmi eka kaṇa chuṅiluṅ līlāra
ei dṛṣṭānte jāniha prabhura līlāra vistāra

SYNONYMS

āmi—I; *ati-kṣudra jīva*—a very insignificant living being; *pakṣī rāṅgā-ṭuni*—just like a little bird with a red beak; *se*—he; *yaiche*—just as; *tṛṣṇāya*—in thirst; *piye*—drinks; *samudrera pānī*—the water of the sea; *taiche*—in the same way; *āmi*—I; *eka kaṇa*—one small particle; *chuṅiluṅ*—touched; *līlāra*—of the pastimes of Śrī Caitanya Mahāprabhu; *ei dṛṣṭānte*—by this example; *jāniha*—all of you know; *prabhura*—of Śrī Caitanya Mahāprabhu; *līlāra vistāra*—expansion of the pastimes.

TRANSLATION

I am a very insignificant living being, like a small red-beaked bird. Just as such a bird drinks the water of the sea to quench its thirst, so I have touched only a drop of the ocean of Śrī Caitanya Mahāprabhu's pastimes. From this example, you may all understand how expansive are the pastimes of Śrī Caitanya Mahāprabhu.

TEXT 92

'আমি লিখি',—এহ মিথ্যা করি অনুমান ।
আমার শরীর কাষ্ঠপুতলী-সমান ॥ ৯২ ॥

'āmi likhi',——eha mithyā kari anumāna
āmāra śarīra kāṣṭha-putalī-samāna

SYNONYMS

āmi likhi—I write; *eha mithyā*—this is false; *kari anumāna*—I can infer; *āmāra śarīra*—my body; *kāṣṭha-putalī-samāna*—is exactly like a wooden doll.

TRANSLATION

I infer that "I have written" is a false understanding, for my body is like a wooden doll.

TEXT 93

বৃদ্ধ জরাতুর আমি অন্ধ, বধির ।
হস্ত হালে, মনোবুদ্ধি নহে মোর স্থির ॥ ৯৩ ॥

vṛddha jarātura āmi andha, badhira
hasta hāle, manobuddhi nahe mora sthira

SYNONYMS

vṛddha—an old man; *jarā-ātura*—troubled by invalidity; *āmi*—I; *andha*—blind; *badhira*—deaf; *hasta hāle*—my hands tremble; *manaḥ-buddhi*—mind and intelligence; *nahe*—not; *mora*—my; *sthira*—steady.

TRANSLATION

I am old and troubled by invalidity. I am almost blind and deaf, my hands tremble, and my mind and intelligence are unsteady.

TEXT 94

নানা-রোগগ্রস্ত,—চলিতে বসিতে না পারি ।
পঞ্চরোগ-পীড়া-ব্যাকুল, রাত্রি-দিনে মরি ॥ ৯৪ ॥

nānā-roga-grasta,——calite vasite nā pāri
pañca-roga-pīḍā-vyākula, rātri-dine mari

SYNONYMS

nānā-roga-grasta—affected by so many diseases; *calite*—to walk; *vasite*—to sit down; *nā pāri*—I am not properly able; *pañca-roga-pīḍā-vyākula*—always disturbed by five kinds of disease; *rātri-dine*—day or night; *mari*—I can die any time.

TRANSLATION

I am infected by so many diseases that I can neither properly walk nor properly sit. Indeed, I am always exhausted by five kinds of disease. I may die at any time of the day or night.

TEXT 95

পূর্বে গ্রন্থে ইহা করিয়াছি নিবেদন।
তথাপি লিখিয়ে, শুন ইহার কারণ ॥ ৯৫ ॥

pūrve granthe ihā kariyāchi nivedana
tathāpi likhiye, śuna ihāra kāraṇa

SYNONYMS

pūrve—previously; *granthe*—in the book; *ihā*—this; *kariyāchi nivedana*—I have submitted to the readers; *tathāpi*—still; *likhiye*—I write; *śuna*—please hear; *ihāra kāraṇa*—the reason for this.

TRANSLATION

I have previously given an account of my inabilities. Please hear the reason why I nevertheless still write.

TEXTS 96-98

শ্রীগোবিন্দ, শ্রীচৈতন্য, শ্রীনিত্যানন্দ।
শ্রীঅদ্বৈত, শ্রীভক্ত, আর শ্রীশ্রোতৃবৃন্দ ॥ ৯৬ ॥
শ্রীস্বরূপ, শ্রীরূপ, শ্রীসনাতন।
শ্রীরঘুনাথ-দাস শ্রীগুরু, শ্রীজীবচরণ ॥ ৯৭ ॥
ইঁহা-সবার চরণ-কৃপায় লেখায় আমারে।
আর এক হয় – তেঁহো অতিকৃপা করে ॥ ৯৮ ॥

śrī-govinda, śrī-caitanya, śrī-nityānanda
śrī-advaita, śrī-bhakta, āra śrī-śrotṛ-vṛnda

śrī-svarūpa, śrī-rūpa, śrī-sanātana
śrī-raghunātha-dāsa śrī-guru, śrī-jīva-caraṇa

iṅhā-sabāra caraṇa-kṛpāya lekhāya āmāre
āra eka haya,——teṅho ati-kṛpā kare

SYNONYMS

śrī-govinda—Śrī Govindadeva; *śrī-caitanya*—Śrī Caitanya Mahāprabhu; *śrī-nityānanda*—Lord Nityānanda; *śrī-advaita*—Advaita Ācārya; *śrī-bhakta*—other devotees; *āra*—also; *śrī-śrotṛ-vṛnda*—the readers of this book; *śrī-svarūpa*—

Svarūpa Dāmodara Gosvāmī; *śrī-rūpa*—Śrī Rūpa Gosvāmī; *śrī-sanātana*—Śrī Sanātana Gosvāmī; *śrī-raghunātha-dāsa*—Śrī Raghunātha dāsa Gosvāmī; *śrī-guru*—my spiritual master; *śrī-jīva-caraṇa*—the lotus feet of Śrī Jīva Gosvāmī; *iṅhā sabāra*—of all of them; *caraṇa-kṛpāya*—by the mercy of the lotus feet; *lekhāya*—causes to write; *āmāre*—me; *āra eka*—another one; *haya*—there is; *teṅho*—He; *ati-kṛpā kare*—shows me very great favor.

TRANSLATION

I am writing this book by the mercy of the lotus feet of Śrī Govindadeva, Śrī Caitanya Mahāprabhu, Lord Nityānanda, Advaita Ācārya, other devotees and the readers of this book, as well as Svarūpa Dāmodara Gosvāmī, Śrī Rūpa Gosvāmī, Śrī Sanātana Gosvāmī, Śrī Raghunātha dāsa Gosvāmī, who is my spiritual master, and Śrī Jīva Gosvāmī. I have also been specifically favored by another Supreme Personality.

TEXT 99

শ্রীমদনগোপাল মোরে লেখায় আজ্ঞা করি'।
কহিতে না যুয়ায়, তবু রহিতে না পারি ॥ ৯৯ ॥

śrī-madana-gopāla more lekhāya ājñā kari'
kahite nā yuyāya, tabu rahite nā pāri

SYNONYMS

śrī-madana-gopāla—the Madana-mohana Deity of Vṛndāvana; *more*—me; *lekhāya*—causes to write; *ājñā kari'*—by giving the order; *kahite*—to say; *nā yuyāya*—is not befitting; *tabu*—still; *rahite*—to remain silent; *nā pāri*—I am not able.

TRANSLATION

Śrī Madana-mohana Deity of Vṛndāvana has given the order that is making me write. Although this should not be disclosed, I disclose it because I am unable to remain silent.

TEXT 100

না কহিলে হয় মোর কৃতঘ্নতা-দোষ।
দম্ভ করি বলি' শ্রোতা, না করিহ রোষ ॥ ১০০ ॥

nā kahile haya mora kṛta-ghnatā-doṣa
dambha kari bali' śrotā, nā kariha roṣa

SYNONYMS

nā kahile—if I do not say; *haya*—there is; *mora*—my; *kṛta-ghnatā-doṣa*—fault of ingratitude; *dambha kari*—I am proud; *bali'*—taking as; *śrotā*—O readers; *nā kariha roṣa*—do not be angry.

TRANSLATION

If I did not disclose this fact, I would be guilty of ingratitude to the Lord. Therefore, my dear readers, please do not consider me too proud and be angry at me.

TEXT 101

তোমা-সবার চরণ-ধূলি করিনু বন্দন ।
তাতে চৈতন্য-লীলা হৈল যে কিছু লিখন ॥ ১০১ ॥

tomā-sabāra caraṇa-dhūli karinu vandana
tāte caitanya-līlā haila ye kichu likhana

SYNONYMS

tomā-sabāra—of all of you; *caraṇa-dhūli*—the dust of the feet; *karinu vandana*—I have prayed to; *tāte*—for that reason; *caitanya-līlā*—the pastimes of Lord Śrī Caitanya Mahāprabhu; *haila*—there was; *ye*—whatever; *kichu*—some; *likhana*—writing.

TRANSLATION

It is because I have offered my prayers unto the lotus feet of all of you that whatever I have written about Śrī Caitanya Mahāprabhu has been possible.

TEXT 102

এবে অন্ত্যলীলাগণের করি অনুবাদ ।
'অনুবাদ' কৈলে পাই লীলার 'আস্বাদ' ॥ ১০২ ॥

ebe antya-līlā-gaṇera kari anuvāda
'anuvāda' kaile pāi līlāra 'āsvāda'

SYNONYMS

ebe—now; *antya-līlā-gaṇera kari anuvāda*—I beg to repeat all the facts of this *Antya-līlā; anuvāda kaile*—if it is repeated; *pāi*—I get; *līlāra*—of the pastime; *āsvāda*—taste.

TRANSLATION

Now let me repeat all the pastimes of the Antya-līlā, for if I do so I shall taste the pastimes again.

TEXT 103

প্রথম পরিচ্ছেদে—রূপের দ্বিতীয়-মিলন ।
তার মধ্যে দুইনাটকের বিধান-শ্রবণ ॥ ১০৩ ॥

prathama paricchede——rūpera dvitīya-milana
tāra madhye dui-nāṭakera vidhāna-śravaṇa

SYNONYMS

prathama paricchede—in the First Chapter; *rūpera*—of Rūpa Gosvāmī; *dvitīya-milana*—the second meeting with Lord Caitanya; *tāra madhye*—within that chapter; *dui-nāṭakera*—of the two dramas; *vidhāna-śravaṇa*—hearing of the process of writing.

TRANSLATION

The First Chapter describes how Rūpa Gosvāmī met Śrī Caitanya Mahāprabhu for the second time and how the Lord heard his two dramas [Vidagdha-mādhava and Lalita-mādhava].

TEXT 104

তার মধ্যে শিবানন্দ-সঙ্গে কুক্কুর আইলা ।
প্রভু তারে কৃষ্ণ কহাঞা মুক্ত করিলা ॥ ১০৪ ॥

tāra madhye śivānanda-saṅge kukkura āilā
prabhu tāre kṛṣṇa kahāñā mukta karilā

SYNONYMS

tāra madhye—in that chapter; *śivānanda-saṅge*—with Śivānanda Sena; *kukkura*—the dog; *āilā*—came; *prabhu*—Śrī Caitanya Mahāprabhu; *tāre*—unto him (the dog); *kṛṣṇa kahāñā*—inducing to chant Kṛṣṇa; *mukta karilā*—liberated.

TRANSLATION

That chapter also describes the incident of Śivānanda Sena's dog, who was induced by Śrī Caitanya Mahāprabhu to chant the holy name of Kṛṣṇa and was thus liberated.

TEXT 105

দ্বিতীয়ে—ছোট-হরিদাসে করাইলা শিক্ষণ।
তার মধ্যে শিবানন্দের আশ্চর্য দর্শন ॥ ১০৫ ॥

dvitīye——choṭa-haridāse karāilā śikṣaṇa
tāra madhye śivānandera āścarya darśana

SYNONYMS

dvitīye—in the Second Chapter; *choṭa-haridāse*—Junior Haridāsa; *karāilā śikṣaṇa*—He taught very strictly; *tāra madhye*—within that chapter; *śivānandera*—of Śivānanda Sena; *āścarya darśana*—the wonderful vision.

TRANSLATION

In the Second Chapter the Lord instructively punished Junior Haridāsa. Also in that chapter is the wonderful vision of Śivānanda Sena.

TEXT 106

তৃতীয়ে—হরিদাসের মহিমা প্রচণ্ড।
দামোদর-পণ্ডিত কৈলা প্রভুরে বাক্যদণ্ড ॥ ১০৬ ॥

tṛtīye——haridāsera mahimā pracaṇḍa
dāmodara-paṇḍita kailā prabhure vākya-daṇḍa

SYNONYMS

tṛtīye—in the Third Chapter; *haridāsera*—of Ṭhākura Haridāsa; *mahimā pracaṇḍa*—very forceful glories; *dāmodara-paṇḍita*—Dāmodara Paṇḍita; *kailā*—made; *prabhure*—Śrī Caitanya Mahāprabhu; *vākya-daṇḍa*—impudence of chastising by words.

TRANSLATION

In the Third Chapter is a description of the forceful glories of Haridāsa Ṭhākura. That chapter also mentions how Dāmodara Paṇḍita spoke words of criticism to Śrī Caitanya Mahāprabhu.

TEXT 107

প্রভু 'নাম' দিয়া কৈলা ব্রহ্মাণ্ড-মোচন।
হরিদাস করিলা নামের মহিমা-স্থাপন ॥ ১০৭ ॥

prabhu 'nāma' diyā kailā brahmāṇḍa-mocana
haridāsa karilā nāmera mahimā-sthāpana

SYNONYMS

prabhu—Śrī Caitanya Mahāprabhu; *nāma diyā*—delivering the holy name; *kailā*—did; *brahmāṇḍa-mocana*—the liberation of the universe; *haridāsa*—Haridāsa; *karilā*—did; *nāmera*—of the holy name; *mahimā-sthāpana*—the establishment of the glories.

TRANSLATION

The Third Chapter also tells how Śrī Caitanya Mahāprabhu delivered everyone by bestowing upon the universe the holy name of the Lord, and it describes how Haridāsa Ṭhākura established the glories of the holy name by his practical example.

TEXT 108

চতুর্থে—শ্রীসনাতনের দ্বিতীয়-মিলন।
দেহত্যাগ হৈতে তাঁর করিলা রক্ষণ ॥ ১০৮ ॥

caturthe——śrī-sanātanera dvitīya-milana
deha-tyāga haite tāṅra karilā rakṣaṇa

SYNONYMS

caturthe—in the Fourth Chapter; *śrī-sanātanera*—of Sanātana Gosvāmī; *dvitīya-milana*—visiting for the second time; *deha-tyāga haite*—from committing suicide; *tāṅra karilā rakṣaṇa*—Śrī Caitanya Mahāprabhu protected him.

TRANSLATION

The Fourth Chapter describes Sanātana Gosvāmī's second visit with Śrī Caitanya Mahāprabhu and how the Lord saved him from committing suicide.

TEXT 109

জ্যৈষ্ঠ-মাসের ধূপে তাঁরে কৈলা পরীক্ষণ।
শক্তি সঞ্চারিয়া পুনঃ পাঠাইলা বৃন্দাবন ॥ ১০৯ ॥

jyaiṣṭha-māsera dhūpe tāṅre kailā parīkṣaṇa
śakti sañcāriyā punaḥ pāṭhāilā vṛndāvana

SYNONYMS

jyaiṣṭha-māsera—of the month of May-June; *dhūpe*—in the sunshine; *tāṅre*—him; *kailā*—did; *parīkṣaṇa*—examining; *śakti*—potency; *sañcāriyā*—giving him; *punaḥ*—again; *pāṭhāilā vṛndāvana*—sent back to Vṛndāvana.

TRANSLATION

The Fourth Chapter also tells how Sanātana Gosvāmī was tested in the sunshine of Jyaiṣṭha [May and June] and was then empowered and sent back to Vṛndāvana.

TEXT 110

পঞ্চমে—প্রদ্যুম্নমিশ্রে প্রভু কৃপা করিলা।
রায়-দ্বারা কৃষ্ণকথা তাঁরে শুনাইলা ॥ ১১০ ॥

pañcame——pradyumna-miśre prabhu kṛpā karilā
rāya-dvārā kṛṣṇa-kathā tāṅre śunāilā

SYNONYMS

pañcame—in the Fifth Chapter; *pradyumna-miśre*—unto Pradyumna Miśra; *prabhu*—Śrī Caitanya Mahāprabhu; *kṛpā karilā*—showed mercy; *rāya-dvārā*—with the help of Rāmānanda Rāya; *kṛṣṇa-kathā*—topics of Kṛṣṇa; *tāṅre śunāilā*—made him hear.

TRANSLATION

In the Fifth Chapter, the Lord showed His favor to Pradyumna Miśra and made him hear topics of Kṛṣṇa from Rāmānanda Rāya.

TEXT 111

তার মধ্যে 'বাঙ্গাল'-কবির নাটক-উপেক্ষণ।
স্বরূপ-গোসাঞি কৈলা বিগ্রহের মহিমা-স্থাপন ॥১১১

tāra madhye 'bāṅgāla'-kavira nāṭaka-upekṣaṇa
svarūpa-gosāñi kailā vigrahera mahimā-sthāpana

SYNONYMS

tāra madhye—within that chapter; *bāṅgāla-kavira*—of a poet from Bengal; *nāṭaka-upekṣaṇa*—the rejection of the drama; *svarūpa-gosāñi*—Svarūpa Dāmodara Gosvāmī; *kailā*—did; *vigrahera*—of the Deity; *mahimā-sthāpana*—the establishment of the glories.

TRANSLATION

Also in that chapter, Svarūpa Dāmodara Gosvāmī rejected the drama of a poet from Bengal and established the glories of the Deity.

TEXT 112

ষষ্ঠে—রঘুনাথ-দাস প্রভুরে মিলিলা।
নিত্যানন্দ-আজ্ঞায় চিড়া-মহোৎসব কৈলা ॥ ১১২ ॥

ṣaṣṭhe——raghunātha-dāsa prabhure mililā
nityānanda-ājñāya ciḍā-mahotsava kailā

SYNONYMS

ṣaṣṭhe—in the Sixth Chapter; *raghunātha-dāsa*—Raghunātha dāsa Gosvāmī; *prabhure mililā*—met Lord Śrī Caitanya Mahāprabhu; *nityānanda-ājñāya*—by the order of Nityānanda Prabhu; *ciḍā-mahotsava kailā*—performed the festival of chipped rice.

TRANSLATION

The Sixth Chapter describes how Raghunātha dāsa Gosvāmī met Śrī Caitanya Mahāprabhu and performed the chipped rice festival in accordance with Nityānanda Prabhu's order.

TEXT 113

দামোদর-স্বরূপ-ঠাঞি তাঁরে সমর্পিল।
'গোবর্ধন-শিলা', 'গুঞ্জামালা' তাঁরে দিল ॥ ১১৩ ॥

dāmodara-svarūpa-ṭhāñi tāṅre samarpila
'govardhana-śilā', 'guñjā-mālā' tāṅre dila

SYNONYMS

dāmodara-svarūpa-ṭhāñi—to the care of Svarūpa Dāmodara Gosvāmī; *tāṅre samarpila*—the Lord entrusted him; *govardhana-śilā*—the stone from Govardhana Hill; *guñjā-mālā*—the garland of small conchshells; *tāṅre dila*—delivered to him.

TRANSLATION

The Lord entrusted Raghunātha dāsa Gosvāmī to the care of Svarūpa Dāmodara Gosvāmī and gave Raghunātha dāsa the gift of a stone from Govardhana Hill and a garland of small conchshells.

TEXT 114

সপ্তম-পরিচ্ছেদে—বল্লভ ভট্টের মিলন।
নানা-মতে কৈলা তাঁর গর্ব খণ্ডন॥ ১১৪॥

saptama-paricchede——vallabha bhaṭṭera milana
nānā-mate kailā tāṅra garva khaṇḍana

SYNONYMS

saptama-paricchede—in the Seventh Chapter; *vallabha bhaṭṭera milana*—the meeting of Vallabha Bhaṭṭa with Śrī Caitanya Mahāprabhu; *nānā-mate*—in various ways; *kailā*—did; *tāṅra*—his; *garva*—pride; *khaṇḍana*—dismantling.

TRANSLATION

The Seventh Chapter tells how Śrī Caitanya met Vallabha Bhaṭṭa and dismantled his false pride in various ways.

TEXT 115

অষ্টমে—রামচন্দ্র-পুরীর আগমন।
তাঁর ভয়ে কৈলা প্রভু ভিক্ষা সঙ্কোচন॥ ১১৫॥

aṣṭame——rāmacandra-purīra āgamana
tāṅra bhaye kailā prabhu bhikṣā saṅkocana

SYNONYMS

aṣṭame—in the Eighth Chapter; *rāmacandra-purīra āgamana*—the arrival of Rāmacandra Purī; *tāṅra bhaye*—because of fear of him; *kailā*—did; *prabhu*—Śrī Caitanya Mahāprabhu; *bhikṣā saṅkocana*—minimizing His eating.

TRANSLATION

The Eighth Chapter describes the arrival of Rāmacandra Purī and how Śrī Caitanya Mahāprabhu minimized His eating due to fear of him.

TEXT 116

নবমে—গোপীনাথ-পট্টনায়ক-মোচন।
ত্রিজগতের লোক প্রভুর পাইল দরশন॥ ১১৬॥

navame——gopīnātha-paṭṭanāyaka-mocana
trijagatera loka prabhura pāila daraśana

SYNONYMS

navame—in the Ninth Chapter; *gopīnātha-paṭṭanāyaka-mocana*—the deliverance of Gopīnātha Paṭṭanāyaka, the brother of Rāmānanda Rāya; *tri-jagatera*—of the three worlds; *loka*—the people in general; *prabhura*—of Śrī Caitanya Mahāprabhu; *pāila daraśana*—got the audience.

TRANSLATION

In the Ninth Chapter is a description of how Gopīnātha Paṭṭanāyaka was delivered and how the people of the three worlds were able to see Śrī Caitanya Mahāprabhu.

TEXT 117

দশমে—কহিলুঁ ভক্তদত্ত-আস্বাদন ।
রাঘব-পণ্ডিতের তাহাঁ ঝালির সাজন ॥ ১১৭ ॥

daśame——kahiluṅ bhakta-datta-āsvādana
rāghava-paṇḍitera tāhāṅ jhālira sājana

SYNONYMS

daśame—in the Tenth Chapter; *kahiluṅ*—I have described; *bhakta-datta-āsvādana*—the tasting of the food given by the devotees; *rāghava-paṇḍitera*—of Rāghava Paṇḍita; *tāhāṅ*—therein; *jhālira sājana*—the assortment in the bags.

TRANSLATION

In the Tenth Chapter I have described how Śrī Caitanya Mahāprabhu tasted the food given by His devotees, and I have also described the assortments in the bags of Rāghava Paṇḍita.

TEXT 118

তার মধ্যে গোবিন্দের কৈলা পরীক্ষণ !
তার মধ্যে পরিমুণ্ডা-নৃত্যের বর্ণন ॥ ॥ ১১৮ ॥

tāra madhye govindera kailā parīkṣaṇa
tāra madhye parimuṇḍā-nṛtyera varṇana

SYNONYMS

tāra madhye—within that chapter; *govindera*—of Govinda, His personal assistant; *kailā*—did; *parīkṣaṇa*—testing; *tāra madhye*—in that chapter; *parimuṇḍā-nṛtyera varṇana*—description of Lord Caitanya Mahāprabhu's dancing in the temple.

TRANSLATION

Also in that chapter is a description of how the Lord examined Govinda and how He danced in the temple.

TEXT 119

একাদশে—হরিদাস-ঠাকুরের নির্যাণ ।
ভক্ত-বাৎসল্য যাহাঁ দেখাইলা গৌর ভগবান্ ॥ ১১৯

ekādaśe——haridāsa-ṭhākurera niryāṇa
bhakta-vātsalya yāhāṅ dekhāilā gaura bhagavān

SYNONYMS

ekādaśe—in the Eleventh Chapter; *haridāsa-ṭhākurera niryāṇa*—the disappearance of Śrīla Haridāsa Ṭhākura; *bhakta-vātsalya*—affection for the devotee; *yāhāṅ*—wherein; *dekhāilā*—exhibited; *gaura bhagavān*—Śrī Caitanya Mahāprabhu, the Supreme Personality of Godhead.

TRANSLATION

The Eleventh Chapter describes the disappearance of Haridāsa Ṭhākura and how Śrī Caitanya Mahāprabhu, the Supreme Personality of Godhead, showed His affection for His devotees.

TEXT 120

দ্বাদশে—জগদানন্দের তৈল-ভঞ্জন ।
নিত্যানন্দ কৈলা শিবানন্দেরে তাড়ন ॥ ১২০ ॥

dvādaśe——jagadānandera taila-bhañjana
nityānanda kailā śivānandere tāḍana

SYNONYMS

dvādaśe—in the Twelfth Chapter; *jagadānandera*—of Jagadānanda Paṇḍita; *taila-bhañjana*—breaking the oil pot; *nityānanda*—Lord Nityānanda; *kailā*—performed; *śivānandere tāḍana*—the chastisement of Śivānanda Sena.

TRANSLATION

In the Twelfth Chapter are descriptions of how Jagadānanda Paṇḍita broke a pot of oil and how Lord Nityānanda chastised Śivānanda Sena.

TEXT 121

ত্রয়োদশে—জগদানন্দ মথুরা যাই' আইলা ।
মহাপ্রভু দেবদাসীর গীত শুনিলা ॥ ১২১ ॥

trayodaśe——jagadānanda mathurā yāi' āilā
mahāprabhu deva-dāsīra gīta śunilā

SYNONYMS

trayodaśe—in the Thirteenth Chapter; *jagadānanda*—Jagadānanda Paṇḍita; *mathurā yāi'*—going to Mathurā; *āilā*—returned; *mahāprabhu*—Śrī Caitanya Mahāprabhu; *deva-dāsīra*—of the *deva-dāsī* dancing girl; *gīta śunilā*—heard the song.

TRANSLATION

In the Thirteenth Chapter, Jagadānanda Paṇḍita went to Mathurā and returned, and Śrī Caitanya Mahāprabhu by chance heard a song sung by a deva-dāsī dancing girl.

TEXT 122

রঘুনাথ-ভট্টাচার্যের তাহাঁই মিলন ।
প্রভু তাঁরে কৃপা করি' পাঠাইলা বৃন্দাবন ॥ ১২২ ॥

raghunātha-bhaṭṭācāryera tāhāṅi milana
prabhu tāṅre kṛpā kari' pāṭhāilā vṛndāvana

SYNONYMS

raghunātha-bhaṭṭācāryera—of Raghunātha Bhaṭṭa; *tāhāṅi*—there; *milana*—meeting; *prabhu*—Śrī Caitanya Mahāprabhu; *tāṅre*—to him; *kṛpā kari'*—showing causeless mercy; *pāṭhāilā vṛndāvana*—sent to Vṛndāvana.

TRANSLATION

Also in the Thirteenth Chapter, Raghunātha Bhaṭṭa met Śrī Caitanya Mahāprabhu, who by His causeless mercy sent him to Vṛndāvana.

TEXT 123

চতুর্দশে—দিব্যোন্মাদ-আরম্ভ বর্ণন ।
'শরীর' এথা প্রভুর, 'মন' গেলা বৃন্দাবন ॥ ১২৩ ॥

caturdaśe——divyonmāda-ārambha varṇana
'śarīra' ethā prabhura, 'mana' gelā vṛndāvana

SYNONYMS

caturdaśe—in the Fourteenth Chapter; *divya-unmāda-ārambha*—the beginning of the spiritual trance of Śrī Caitanya Mahāprabhu; *varṇana*—describing; *śarīra*—the body; *ethā*—here; *prabhura*—of Śrī Caitanya Mahāprabhu; *mana*—the mind; *gelā*—went; *vṛndāvana*—to Vṛndāvana.

TRANSLATION

The Fourteenth Chapter describes the beginning of the Lord's spiritual trance, in which His body was at Jagannātha Purī but His mind was in Vṛndāvana.

TEXT 124

তার মধ্যে প্রভুর সিংহদ্বারে পতন ।
অস্থি-সন্ধি-ত্যাগ, অনুভাবের উদ্গম ॥ ১২৪ ॥

tāra madhye prabhura siṁha-dvāre patana
asthi-sandhi-tyāga, anubhāvera udgama

SYNONYMS

tāra madhye—in that chapter; *prabhura*—of Śrī Caitanya Mahāprabhu; *siṁha-dvāre patana*—falling down by the Siṁha-dvāra gate; *asthi-sandhi*—of the joints of the bones; *tyāga*—release; *anubhāvera udgama*—the awakening of a trance and emotion.

TRANSLATION

Also in that chapter is a description of how Śrī Caitanya Mahāprabhu fell down in front of the Siṁha-dvāra gate of Jagannātha temple, His bones separated at the joints, and how various transcendental symptoms awakened.

TEXT 125

চটক-পর্বত দেখি' প্রভুর ধাবন ।
তার মধ্যে প্রভুর কিছু প্রলাপ-বর্ণন ॥ ১২৫ ॥

caṭaka-parvata dekhi' prabhura dhāvana
tāra madhye prabhura kichu pralāpa-varṇana

SYNONYMS

caṭaka-parvata—the hill known as Caṭaka-parvata; *dekhi'*—seeing; *prabhura dhāvana*—the running of Śrī Caitanya Mahāprabhu; *tāra madhye*—in that chapter; *prabhura*—of Śrī Caitanya Mahāprabhu; *kichu*—some; *pralāpa varṇana*—talking like a madman.

TRANSLATION

Also in that chapter there is a description of how Śrī Caitanya Mahāprabhu ran toward Caṭaka-parvata and spoke like a madman.

TEXT 126

পঞ্চদশ-পরিচ্ছেদে—উদ্যান-বিলাসে ।
বৃন্দাবনভ্রমে যাহাঁ করিলা প্রবেশে ॥ ১২৬ ॥

pañcadaśa-paricchede——udyāna-vilāse
vṛndāvana-bhrame yāhāṅ karilā praveśe

SYNONYMS

pañcadaśa-paricchede—in the Fifteenth Chapter; *udyāna-vilāse*—in His pastimes within the garden; *vṛndāvana-bhrame*—His taking the garden to be Vṛndāvana; *yāhāṅ*—where; *karilā praveśe*—He entered.

TRANSLATION

In the Fifteenth Chapter is a description of how Śrī Caitanya Mahāprabhu entered a garden on the shore of the sea, mistaking the garden for Vṛndāvana.

TEXT 127

তার মধ্যে প্রভুর পঞ্চেন্দ্রিয়-আকর্ষণ ।
তার মধ্যে করিলা রাসে কৃষ্ণ-অন্বেষণ ॥ ১২৭ ॥

tāra madhye prabhura pañcendriya-ākarṣaṇa
tāra madhye karilā rāse kṛṣṇa-anveṣaṇa

SYNONYMS

tāra madhye—within that; *prabhura*—of Śrī Caitanya Mahāprabhu; *pañca-indriya-ākarṣaṇa*—the attraction of the five senses; *tāra madhye*—within that chapter; *karilā*—did; *rāse*—in the *rāsa* dance; *kṛṣṇa-anveṣaṇa*—searching for Kṛṣṇa.

TRANSLATION

Also in that chapter is a description of the attraction of Lord Caitanya's five senses to Kṛṣṇa and how He searched for Kṛṣṇa in the rāsa dance.

TEXT 128

ষোড়শে—কালিদাসে প্রভু কৃপা করিলা ।
বৈষ্ণবোচ্ছিষ্ট খাইবার ফল দেখাইলা ॥ ১২৮ ॥

ṣoḍaśe——kālidāse prabhu kṛpā karilā
vaiṣṇavocchiṣṭa khāibāra phala dekhāilā

SYNONYMS

ṣoḍaśe—in the Sixteenth Chapter; *kāli-dāse*—unto Kālidāsa; *prabhu*—Śrī Caitanya Mahāprabhu; *kṛpā karilā*—showed favor; *vaiṣṇava-ucchiṣṭa khāibāra*—of eating the remnants of food left by Vaiṣṇavas; *phala dekhāilā*—showed the result.

TRANSLATION

The Sixteenth Chapter tells how Śrī Caitanya Mahāprabhu showed His mercy to Kālidāsa and thus demonstrated the result of eating the remnants of the food of Vaiṣṇavas.

TEXT 129

শিবানন্দের বালকে শ্লোক করাইলা ।
সিংহদ্বারে দ্বারী প্রভুরে কৃষ্ণ দেখাইলা ॥ ১২৯ ॥

śivānandera bālake śloka karāilā
siṁha-dvāre dvārī prabhure kṛṣṇa dekhāilā

SYNONYMS

śivānandera—of Śivānanda Sena; *bālake*—the son; *śloka karāilā*—made to compose a verse; *siṁha-dvāre*—at the Siṁha-dvāra gate of the Jagannātha temple; *dvārī*—the doorkeeper; *prabhure*—unto Śrī Caitanya Mahāprabhu; *kṛṣṇa dekhāilā*—showed Lord Kṛṣṇa.

TRANSLATION

It also describes how Śivānanda's son composed a verse and how the doorkeeper of the Siṁha-dvāra showed Kṛṣṇa to Śrī Caitanya Mahāprabhu.

TEXT 130

মহাপ্রসাদের তাহাঁ মহিমা বর্ণিলা ।
কৃষ্ণাধরামৃতের ফল-শ্লোক আস্বাদিলা ॥ ১৩০ ॥

mahā-prasādera tāhāṅ mahimā varṇilā
kṛṣṇādharāmṛtera phala-śloka āsvādilā

SYNONYMS

mahā-prasādera—of the remnants of the food of the Lord, *mahā-prasāda; tāhāṅ*—there; *mahimā*—the glories; *varṇilā*—described; *kṛṣṇa-adhara-amṛtera*—of the nectar from the lips of Kṛṣṇa; *phala-śloka*—the verse mentioning the result; *āsvādilā*—tasted.

TRANSLATION

Also in that chapter, the glories of mahā-prasāda are explained, and a verse is tasted describing the effect of nectar from the lips of Kṛṣṇa.

TEXT 131

সপ্তদশে—গাভী-মধ্যে প্রভুর পতন ।
কূর্মাকার-অনুভাবের তাহাঁই উদ্গম ॥ ১৩১ ॥

saptadaśe——gābhī-madhye prabhura patana
kūrmākāra-anubhāvera tāhāṅi udgama

SYNONYMS

saptadaśe—in the Seventeenth Chapter; *gābhī-madhye*—among the cows; *prabhura patana*—the falling down of Śrī Caitanya Mahāprabhu; *kūrma-ākāra-anubhāvera*—of ecstatic emotion in the form of a tortoise; *tāhāṅi*—there; *udgama*—awakening.

TRANSLATION

In the Seventeenth Chapter, Śrī Caitanya Mahāprabhu fell among the cows and assumed the form of a tortoise as His ecstatic emotions awakened.

TEXT 132

কৃষ্ণের শব্দ-গুণে প্রভুর মন আকর্ষিলা ।
""কাস্ত্র্যঙ্গ তে" শ্লোকের অর্থ আবেশে করিলা ॥১৩২॥

kṛṣṇera śabda-guṇe prabhura mana ākarṣilā
"kā stry aṅga te" ślokera artha āveśe karilā

SYNONYMS

kṛṣṇera—of Lord Kṛṣṇa; *śabda-guṇe*—by the qualities of the sound; *prabhura*—of Śrī Caitanya Mahāprabhu; *mana*—the mind; *ākarṣilā*—was attracted; *kā stry aṅga te ślokera*—of the verse beginning with the words *kā stry aṅga te; artha*—the meaning; *āveśe*—in ecstasy; *karilā*—described.

TRANSLATION

Also in the Seventeenth Chapter, the attributes of Kṛṣṇa's sound attracted the mind of Śrī Caitanya Mahāprabhu, who described in ecstasy the meaning of the "kā stry aṅga te" verse.

TEXT 133

ভাব-শাবল্যে পুনঃ কৈলা প্রলপন ।
কর্ণামৃত-শ্লোকের অর্থ কৈলা বিবরণ ॥ ১৩৩ ॥

bhāva-śābalye punaḥ kailā pralapana
karṇāmṛta-ślokera artha kailā vivaraṇa

SYNONYMS

bhāva-śābalye—from the aggregate of all ecstatic emotions; *punaḥ*—again; *kailā pralapana*—He talked like a madman; *karṇāmṛta-ślokera*—of a verse from *Kṛṣṇa-karṇāmṛta; artha*—the meaning; *kailā vivaraṇa*—described in detail.

TRANSLATION

Due to the conjunction of various ecstatic emotions, Śrī Caitanya Mahāprabhu again began speaking like a madman and described in detail the meaning of a verse from Kṛṣṇa-karṇāmṛta.

TEXT 134

অষ্টাদশ পরিচ্ছেদে – সমুদ্রে পতন ।
কৃষ্ণ-গোপী-জলকেলি তাহাঁ দরশন ॥ ১৩৪ ॥

aṣṭādaśa paricchede——samudre patana
kṛṣṇa-gopī-jala-keli tāhāṅ daraśana

SYNONYMS

aṣṭādaśa paricchede—in the Eighteenth Chapter; *samudre patana*—the Lord's falling into the ocean; *kṛṣṇa-gopī-jala-keli*—the water pastimes of Kṛṣṇa and the *gopīs; tāhāṅ daraśana*—seeing there.

TRANSLATION

In the Eighteenth Chapter, the Lord fell into the ocean, and in ecstasy He saw the pastimes of the water fight between Kṛṣṇa and the gopīs.

TEXT 135

তাহাঁই দেখিলা কৃষ্ণের বন্য-ভোজন ।
জালিয়া উঠাইল, প্রভু আইলা স্ব-ভবন ॥ ১৩৫ ॥

tāhāṅi dekhilā kṛṣṇera vanya-bhojana
jāliyā uṭhāila, prabhu āilā sva-bhavana

SYNONYMS

tāhāṅi—there; *dekhilā*—He saw; *kṛṣṇera*—of Kṛṣṇa; *vanya-bhojana*—a picnic in the forest; *jāliyā*—a fisherman; *uṭhāila*—caught Him; *prabhu*—the Lord; *āilā*—returned; *sva-bhavana*—to His own residence.

TRANSLATION

In that dream, Śrī Caitanya Mahāprabhu saw Kṛṣṇa's picnic in the forest. As Lord Caitanya floated in the sea, a fisherman caught Him, and then the Lord returned to His own residence.

TEXT 136

ঊনবিংশে—ভিত্ত্যে প্রভুর মুখসংঘর্ষণ ।
কৃষ্ণের বিরহ-স্ফূর্তি-প্রলাপ-বর্ণন ॥ ১৩৬ ॥

ūnaviṁśe——bhittye prabhura mukha-saṅgharṣaṇa
kṛṣṇera viraha-sphūrti-pralāpa-varṇana

SYNONYMS

ūnaviṁśe—in the Nineteenth Chapter; *bhittye*—on the walls; *prabhura mukha-saṅgharṣaṇa*—the rubbing of the face of the Lord; *kṛṣṇera viraha-sphūrti*—the awakening of separation from Kṛṣṇa; *pralāpa-varṇana*—and talking like a crazy person.

TRANSLATION

In the Nineteenth Chapter is a description of how Lord Śrī Caitanya Mahāprabhu rubbed His face against the walls and spoke like a madman because of separation from Kṛṣṇa.

TEXT 137

বসন্ত-রজনীতে পুষ্পোদ্যানে বিহরণ ।
কৃষ্ণের সৌরভ্য-শ্লোকের অর্থ-বিবরণ ॥ ১৩৭ ॥

vasanta-rajanīte puṣpodyāne viharaṇa
kṛṣṇera saurabhya-ślokera artha-vivaraṇa

SYNONYMS

vasanta-rajanīte—on a spring night; *puṣpa-udyāne*—in a flower garden; *viharaṇa*—the wandering; *kṛṣṇera*—of Lord Kṛṣṇa; *saurabhya-ślokera*—of a verse about the bodily fragrance; *artha-vivaraṇa*—describing the meaning.

TRANSLATION

That chapter also describes Kṛṣṇa's wandering in a garden on a spring night, and it fully describes the meaning of a verse about the scent of Kṛṣṇa's body.

TEXT 138

বিংশ-পরিচ্ছেদে—নিজ-'শিক্ষাষ্টক' পড়িয়া ।
তার অর্থ আস্বাদিলা প্রেমাবিষ্ট হঞা ॥ ১৩৮ ॥

viṁśa-paricchede——nija-'śikṣāṣṭaka' paḍiyā
tāra artha āsvādilā premāviṣṭa hañā

SYNONYMS

viṁśa-paricchede—in the Twentieth Chapter; *nija-śikṣāṣṭaka paḍiyā*—reciting His own *Śikṣāṣṭaka* verses; *tāra artha*—their meaning; *āsvādilā*—tasted; *prema-āviṣṭa hañā*—being absorbed in ecstatic love.

TRANSLATION

In the Twentieth Chapter, Lord Śrī Caitanya Mahāprabhu recited His own eight stanzas of instruction and tasted their meaning in ecstatic love.

TEXT 139

ভক্তে শিখাইতে যেই শিক্ষাষ্টক কহিলা।
সেই শ্লোকাষ্টকের অর্থ পুনঃ আস্বাদিলা ॥ ১৩৯ ॥

bhakte śikhāite yei śikṣāṣṭaka kahilā
sei ślokāṣṭakera artha punaḥ āsvādilā

SYNONYMS

bhakte—the devotees; *śikhāite*—to teach; *yei*—that which; *śikṣā-aṣṭaka*—eight instructions; *kahilā*—described; *sei śloka-aṣṭakera*—of the same eight verses; *artha*—the meaning; *punaḥ āsvādilā*—again He tasted.

TRANSLATION

Śrī Caitanya Mahāprabhu composed those eight stanzas to instruct the devotees, but He also personally tasted their meaning.

TEXT 140

মুখ্য-মুখ্য-লীলার অর্থ করিলুঁ কথন।
'অনুবাদ' হৈতে স্মরে গ্রন্থ-বিবরণ ॥ ১৪০ ॥

mukhya-mukhya-līlāra artha kariluṅ kathana
'anuvāda' haite smare grantha-vivaraṇa

SYNONYMS

mukhya-mukhya-līlāra—of the chief pastimes of Lord Śrī Caitanya Mahāprabhu; *artha*—the meaning; *kariluṅ*—have done; *kathana*—describing; *anuvāda haite*—by repeating them again; *smare*—one remembers; *grantha-vivaraṇa*—the description in the book.

TRANSLATION

I have thus described the principal pastimes and their meaning, for by such repetition one can remember the descriptions in the book.

TEXT 141

এক এক পরিচ্ছেদের কথা—অনেকপ্রকার।
মুখ্য-মুখ্য কহিলুঁ, কথা না যায় বিস্তার ॥ ১৪১ ॥

eka eka paricchedera kathā——aneka-prakāra
mukhya-mukhya kahiluṅ, kathā nā yāya vistāra

SYNONYMS

eka eka paricchedera—of every chapter; *kathā*—description; *aneka-prakāra*—different varieties; *mukhya-mukhya kahiluṅ*—I have repeated only the principal ones; *kathā*—discussions; *nā yāya*—not possible; *vistāra*—expansion.

TRANSLATION

In every chapter there are various topics, but I have selected only those that are principal, for not all of them could be described again.

TEXTS 142-143

শ্রীরাধা-সহ 'শ্রীমদনমোহন'।
শ্রীরাধা-সহ 'শ্রীগোবিন্দ'-চরণ ॥ ১৪২ ॥
শ্রীরাধা-সহ শ্রীল 'শ্রীগোপীনাথ'।
এই তিন ঠাকুর হয় 'গৌড়িয়ার নাথ' ॥ ১৪৩ ॥

śrī-rādhā-saha 'śrī-madana-mohana'
śrī-rādhā-saha 'śrī-govinda'-caraṇa

śrī-rādhā-saha śrīla 'śrī-gopīnātha'
ei tina ṭhākura haya 'gauḍiyāra nātha'

SYNONYMS

śrī-rādhā-saha—with Śrīmatī Rādhārāṇī; *śrī-madana-mohana*—the Deity Madana-mohanajī; *śrī-rādhā-saha*—with Śrīmatī Rādhārāṇī; *śrī-govinda-caraṇa*—the lotus feet of Śrī Govindajī; *śrī-rādhā-saha*—with Śrīmatī Rādhārāṇī; *śrīla śrī-gopīnātha*—the all-beautiful and opulent Gopīnāthajī; *ei tina*—all these three; *ṭhākura*—Deities; *haya*—are; *gauḍiyāra nātha*—worshipable by all the Gauḍīya Vaiṣṇavas.

TRANSLATION

The Vṛndāvana Deities of Madana-mohana with Śrīmatī Rādhārāṇī, Govinda with Śrīmatī Rādhārāṇī, and Gopīnātha with Śrīmatī Rādhārāṇī are the life and soul of the Gauḍīya Vaiṣṇavas.

TEXTS 144-146

শ্রীকৃষ্ণচৈতন্য, শ্রীযুত নিত্যানন্দ।
শ্রীঅদ্বৈত-আচার্য, শ্রীগৌরভক্তবৃন্দ ॥ ১৪৪ ॥

শ্রীস্বরূপ, শ্রীরূপ, শ্রীসনাতন ।
শ্রীগুরু শ্রীরঘুনাথ, শ্রীজীবচরণ ॥ ১৪৫ ॥
নিজ-শিরে ধরি' এই সবার চরণ ।
যাহা হৈতে হয় সব বাঞ্ছিত-পূরণ ॥ ১৪৬ ॥

śrī-kṛṣṇa-caitanya, śrī-yuta nityānanda
śrī-advaita-ācārya, śrī-gaura-bhakta-vṛnda

śrī-svarūpa, śrī-rūpa, śrī-sanātana
śrī-guru śrī-raghunātha, śrī-jīva-caraṇa

nija-śire dhari' ei sabāra caraṇa
yāhā haite haya saba vāñchita-pūraṇa

SYNONYMS

śrī-kṛṣṇa-caitanya—Lord Śrī Caitanya Mahāprabhu; *śrī-yuta nityānanda*—Lord Nityānanda; *śrī-advaita-ācārya*—Śrī Advaita Prabhu; *śrī-gaura-bhakta-vṛnda*—the devotees of Śrī Caitanya Mahāprabhu; *śrī-svarūpa*—Svarūpa Dāmodara Gosvāmī; *śrī-rūpa*—Śrī Rūpa Gosvāmī; *śrī-sanātana*—Śrīla Sanātana Gosvāmī; *śrī-guru*—the spiritual master; *śrī-raghunātha*—Raghunātha dāsa Gosvāmī; *śrī-jīva-caraṇa*—the lotus feet of Śrīla Jīva Gosvāmī; *nija-śire dhari'*—catching on my head; *ei sabāra caraṇa*—the lotus feet of all of them; *yāhā haite*—by which action; *haya*—there is; *saba*—all; *vāñchita-pūraṇa*—the fulfilling of desires.

TRANSLATION

So that my desires may be fulfilled, I place the lotus feet of these personalities on my head: Lord Śrī Caitanya Mahāprabhu, with Lord Nityānanda, Advaita Ācārya and Their devotees, as well as Śrī Svarūpa Dāmodara Gosvāmī, Śrī Rūpa Gosvāmī, Śrī Sanātana Gosvāmī, Śrī Raghunātha dāsa Gosvāmī, who is my spiritual master, and Śrīla Jīva Gosvāmī.

PURPORT

Śrīla Raghunātha dāsa Gosvāmī was the instructing spiritual master of Kṛṣṇadāsa Kavirāja Gosvāmī and has therefore been described as *śrī-guru.*

TEXT 147

সবার চরণ-কৃপা—'গুরু উপাধ্যায়ী' ।
মোর বাণী—শিষ্যা, তারে বহুত নাচাই ॥ ১৪৭ ॥

sabāra caraṇa-kṛpā——'guru upādhyāyī'
mora vāṇī——śiṣyā, tāre bahuta nācāi

SYNONYMS

sabāra—of all of them; *caraṇa-kṛpā*—the mercy of the lotus feet; *guru upādhyāyī*—my teacher of Vedic instruction; *mora vāṇī*—my words; *śiṣyā*—the disciples; *tāre*—them; *bahuta nācāi*—I made dance in various ways.

TRANSLATION

The mercy of their lotus feet is my spiritual master, and my words are my disciples that I have made dance in various ways.

PURPORT

Upādhyāyī, or *upādhyāya,* refers to one who teaches when approached (*upetya adhīyate asmāt*). In the *Manu-saṁhitā* it is said:

eka-deśaṁ tu vedasya
vedāṅgāny api vā punaḥ
yo 'dhyāpayati vṛtty-artham
upādhyāyaḥ sa ucyate

"One who teaches others a part of the *Vedas* or literatures supplementary to the *Vedas* may be called *upādhyāya." Upādhyāya* also refers to one who teaches art.

TEXT 148

শিষ্যার শ্রম দেখি' গুরু নাচান রাখিলা ।
'কৃপা' না নাচায়, 'বাণী' বসিয়া রহিলা ॥ ১৪৮ ॥

śiṣyāra śrama dekhi' guru nācāna rākhilā
'kṛpā' nā nācāya, 'vāṇī' vasiyā rahilā

SYNONYMS

śiṣyāra—of the disciples; *śrama*—the fatigue; *dekhi'*—seeing; *guru*—the spiritual master; *nācāna rākhilā*—stopped causing the dancing; *kṛpā*—mercy; *nā nācāya*—does not make dance; *vāṇī*—the words; *vasiyā*—sitting down; *rahilā*—remain silent.

TRANSLATION

Seeing the fatigue of the disciples, the spiritual master has stopped making them dance, and because that mercy no longer makes them dance, my words now sit silently.

TEXT 149

অনিপুণা বাণী আপনে নাচিতে না জানে ।
যত নাচাইলা, নাচি' করিলা বিশ্রামে ॥ ১৪৯ ॥

anipuṇā vāṇī āpane nācite nā jāne
yata nācāilā, nāci' karilā viśrāme

SYNONYMS

anipuṇā vāṇī—inexperienced words; *āpane*—by themselves; *nācite*—to dance; *nā*—not; *jāne*—know how; *yata*—whatever; *nācāilā*—caused to dance; *nāci'*—after dancing; *karilā viśrāme*—took rest.

TRANSLATION

My inexperienced words do not know how to dance by themselves. The mercy of the guru made them dance as much as possible, and now, after dancing, they have taken rest.

TEXT 150

সব শ্রোতাগণের করি চরণ বন্দন ।
যাঁ-সবার চরণ-কৃপা—শুভের কারণ ॥ ১৫০ ॥

saba śrotā-gaṇera kari caraṇa vandana
yāṅ-sabāra caraṇa-kṛpā——śubhera kāraṇa

SYNONYMS

saba—all; *śrotā-gaṇera*—of the readers; *kari*—I do; *caraṇa vandana*—worshiping the lotus feet; *yāṅ-sabāra*—of all of whom; *caraṇa-kṛpā*—the mercy of the lotus feet; *śubhera kāraṇa*—the cause of all good fortune.

TRANSLATION

I now worship the lotus feet of all my readers, for by the mercy of their lotus feet there is all good fortune.

TEXT 151

চৈতন্যচরিতামৃত যেই জন শুনে ।
তাঁর চরণ ধুঞা করোঁ মুঞি পানে ॥ ১৫১ ॥

caitanya-caritāmṛta yei jana śune
tāṅra caraṇa dhuñā karoṅ muñi pāne

SYNONYMS

caitanya-caritāmṛta—the description of Lord Śrī Caitanya's pastimes; *yei jana śune*—anyone who hears; *tāṅra caraṇa*—his lotus feet; *dhuñā*—washing; *karoṅ*—do; *muñi*—I; *pāne*—drinking.

TRANSLATION

If one hears the pastimes of Lord Śrī Caitanya Mahāprabhu as described in Śrī Caitanya-caritāmṛta, I wash his lotus feet and drink the water.

TEXT 152

শ্রোতার পদরেণু করোঁ মস্তক-ভূষণ ।
তোমরা এ-অমৃত পিলে সফল হৈল শ্রম ॥ ১৫২ ॥

śrotāra pada-reṇu karoṅ mastaka-bhūṣaṇa
tomarā e-amṛta pile saphala haila śrama

SYNONYMS

śrotāra—of the audience; *pada-reṇu*—the dust of the lotus feet; *karoṅ*—I make; *mastaka-bhūṣaṇa*—a decoration on my head; *tomarā*—all of you; *e-amṛta*—this nectar; *pile*—have drunk; *sa-phala*—successful; *haila*—has become; *śrama*—my labor.

TRANSLATION

I decorate my head with the dust of the lotus feet of my audience. Now you have all drunk this nectar, and therefore my labor is successful.

TEXT 153

শ্রীরূপ-রঘুনাথ-পদে যার আশ ।
চৈতন্যচরিতামৃত কহে কৃষ্ণদাস ॥ ১৫৩ ॥

śrī-rūpa-raghunātha-pade yāra āśa
caitanya-caritāmṛta kahe kṛṣṇadāsa

SYNONYMS

śrī-rūpa—Śrīla Rūpa Gosvāmī; *raghunātha*—Śrīla Raghunātha dāsa Gosvāmī; *pade*—at the lotus feet; *yāra*—whose; *āśa*—expectation; *caitanya-caritāmṛta*—the book named *Caitanya-caritāmṛta;* *kahe*—describes; *kṛṣṇadāsa*—Śrīla Kṛṣṇadāsa Kavirāja Gosvāmī.

TRANSLATION

Praying at the lotus feet of Śrī Rūpa and Śrī Raghunātha, always desiring their mercy, I, Kṛṣṇadāsa, narrate Śrī Caitanya-caritāmṛta, following in their footsteps.

TEXT 154

চরিতমমৃতমেতচ্ছ্রীলচৈতন্যবিষ্ণোঃ
শুভদমশুভনাশি শ্রদ্ধয়াস্বাদয়েদ্‌যঃ ।
তদমলপদপদ্মে ভৃঙ্গতামেত্য সোঽয়ং
রসয়তি রসমুচ্চৈঃ প্রেমমাধ্বীকপূরম্‌ ॥ ১৫৪ ॥

caritam amṛtam etac chrīla-caitanya-viṣṇoḥ
śubhadam aśubhanāśi śraddhayāsvādayed yaḥ
tad-amala-pada-padme bhṛṅgatām etya so 'yaṁ
rasayati rasam uccaiḥ prema-mādhvīka-pūram

SYNONYMS

caritam—the character; *amṛtam*—nectarean; *etat*—this; *śrīla*—most opulent; *caitanya*—Lord Caitanya Mahāprabhu; *viṣṇoḥ*—of He who is Lord Viṣṇu Himself, the Supreme Personality of Godhead; *śubhadam*—giving auspiciousness; *aśubha-nāśi*—destroying all inauspiciousness; *śraddhayā*—with faith and love; *āsvādayet*—should taste; *yaḥ*—anyone who; *tat-amala-pada-padme*—at the spotless lotus feet of the Supreme Personality of Godhead; *bhṛṅgatām etya*—becoming like a bumblebee; *saḥ*—that person; *ayam*—this; *rasayati*—tastes; *rasam*—transcendental mellow; *uccaiḥ*—a large quantity; *prema-mādhvīka*—of the wine of ecstatic love; *pūram*—full.

TRANSLATION

Caitanya-caritāmṛta is filled with the activities of Śrī Caitanya Mahāprabhu, who is the Supreme Personality of Godhead Himself. It invokes all good fortune and destroys everything inauspicious. If one tastes the nectar of Caitanya-caritāmṛta with faith and love, I become like a bumblebee tasting the honey of transcendental love from his lotus feet.

TEXT 155

শ্রীমন্মদনগোপাল-গোবিন্দদেব-তুষ্টয়ে ।
চৈতন্যার্পিতমস্ত্বেতচ্চৈতন্যচরিতামৃতম্‌ ॥ ১৫৫ ॥

śrīman-madana-gopāla-
govindadeva-tuṣṭaye
caitanyārpitam astv etac
caitanya-caritāmṛtam

SYNONYMS

śrīmat—all-beautiful; *madana-gopāla*—of the Deity Madana-mohana; *govinda-deva*—of the Deity Śrī Govindadeva in Vṛndāvana; *tuṣṭaye*—for the satisfaction; *caitanya-arpitam*—offered to Śrī Caitanya Mahāprabhu; *astu*—let it be; *etat*—this book; *caitanya-caritāmṛtam*—containing the nectarean activities of Lord Śrī Caitanya Mahāprabhu.

TRANSLATION

Since this book, Caitanya-caritāmṛta, is now complete, having been written for the satisfaction of the most opulent Deities Madana-mohanajī and Govindajī, let it be offered at the lotus feet of Śrī Kṛṣṇa Caitanyadeva.

TEXT 156

পরিমলবাসিতভুবনং
স্বরসোন্মাদিত-রসজ্ঞ-রোলম্বম্ ।
গিরিধরচরণাম্ভোজং
কঃ খলু রসিকঃ সমীহতে হাতুম্ ॥ ১৫৬ ॥

parimala-vāsita-bhuvanaṁ
svarasonmādita-rasajña-rolambam
giridhara-caraṇāmbhojaṁ
kaḥ khalu rasikaḥ samīhate hātum

SYNONYMS

parimala—with the scent; *vāsita*—perfumed; *bhuvanam*—the whole world; *sva-rasa-unmādita*—inspired by their own mellows; *rasa-jña*—devotees; *rolambam*—like bumblebees; *giridhara-caraṇa-ambhojam*—the lotus feet of Lord Giridhari; *kaḥ*—who; *khalu*—certainly; *rasikaḥ*—a realized soul; *samīhate hātum*—endeavors to give up.

TRANSLATION

Realized devotees are like bumblebees maddened by their own mellows at Kṛṣṇa's lotus feet. The scent of those lotus feet perfumes the entire world. Who is the realized soul that could give them up?

TEXT 157

শাকে সিন্ধ্বগ্নিবাণেন্দৌ জৈ্যষ্ঠে বৃন্দাবনান্তরে ।
সূর্যাহেঽসিতপঞ্চম্যাং গ্রন্থোঽয়ং পূর্ণতাং গতঃ ॥১৫৭ ॥

śāke sindhv-agni-vāṇendau
jyaiṣṭhe vṛndāvanāntare
sūryāhe 'sita-pañcamyāṁ
grantho 'yaṁ pūrṇatāṁ gataḥ

SYNONYMS

śāke—in the Śakābda Era; *sindhu-agni-vāṇendau*—in 1537; *jyaiṣṭhe*—in the month of Jyaiṣṭha (May-June); *vṛndāvana-antare*—in the forest of Vṛndāvana; *sūrya-ahe*—on the day of the sun (Sunday); *asita-pañcamyām*—on the fifth day of the dark fortnight; *granthaḥ*—book; *ayam*—this (*Caitanya-caritāmṛta*); *pūrṇatām*—completion; *gataḥ*—achieved.

TRANSLATION

In Vṛndāvana in the year 1537, Śakābda Era, in the month of Jyaiṣṭha [May-June], on Sunday, the fifth day of the waning moon, this Caitanya-caritāmṛta has been completed.

Thus end the Bhaktivedanta purports to the Śrī Caitanya-caritāmṛta, Antya-līlā, *Twentieth Chapter, describing the meaning of* Śikṣāṣṭaka *and how the Lord tasted it Himself.*

END OF THE ANTYA-LĪLĀ

Concluding Words

Today, Sunday, November 10, 1974—corresponding to the 10th of Kārttika, Caitanya Era 488, the eleventh day of the dark fortnight, the Rāma-ekādaśī—we have now finished the English translation of Śrī Kṛṣṇadāsa Kavirāja Gosvāmī's *Śrī Caitanya-caritāmṛta* in accordance with the authorized order of His Divine Grace Bhaktisiddhānta Sarasvatī Ṭhākura Gosvāmī Mahārāja, my beloved eternal spiritual master, guide and friend. Although according to material vision His Divine Grace Śrīla Bhaktisiddhānta Sarasvatī Ṭhākura Prabhupāda passed away from this material world on the last day of December, 1936, I still consider His Divine Grace to be always present with me by his *vāṇī,* his words. There are two ways of association—by *vāṇī* and by *vapu. Vāṇī* means words, and *vapu* means physical presence. Physical presence is sometimes appreciable and sometimes not, but *vāṇī* continues to exist eternally. Therefore we must take advantage of the *vāṇī,* not the physical presence. *Bhagavad-gītā,* for example, is the *vāṇī* of Lord Kṛṣṇa. Although Kṛṣṇa was personally present five thousand years ago and is no longer physically present from the materialistic point of view, *Bhagavad-gītā* continues.

In this connection we may call to memory the time when I was fortunate enough to meet His Divine Grace Śrīla Prabhupāda, sometime in the year 1922. Śrīla Prabhupāda had come to Calcutta from Śrīdhāma Māyāpur to start the missionary activities of the Gauḍīya Maṭha. He was sitting in a house at Ulta Danga when through the inducement of an intimate friend, the late Śrīman Narendranātha Mallika, I had the opportunity to meet His Divine Grace for the first time. I do not remember the actual date of the meeting, but at that time I was one of the managers of Dr. Bose's laboratory in Calcutta. I was a newly married young man, addicted to Gandhi's movement and dressed in khadi. Fortunately, even at our first meeting, His Divine Grace advised me to preach the cult of Śrī Caitanya Mahāprabhu in English in the Western countries. Because at that time I was a complete nationalist, a follower of Mahatma Gandhi's, I submitted to His Divine Grace that unless our country were freed from foreign subjugation, no one would hear the message of Śrī Caitanya Mahāprabhu seriously. Of course, we had some argument on this subject, but at last I was defeated and convinced that Śrī Caitanya Mahāprabhu's message is the only panacea for suffering humanity. I was also convinced that the message of Śrī Caitanya Mahāprabhu was then in the hands of a very expert devotee and that surely the message of Śrī Caitanya Mahāprabhu would spread all over the world. I could not, however, immediately take up his instructions to preach, but I took his words very seriously and was always thinking of how to execute his order, although I was quite unfit to do so.

In this way I passed my life as a householder until 1950, when I retired from family life as a *vānaprastha*. With no companion, I loitered here and there until 1958, when I took *sannyāsa*. Then I was completely ready to discharge the order of my spiritual master. Previously, in 1936, just before His Divine Grace passed away at Jagannātha Purī, I wrote him a letter asking what I could do to serve him. In reply, he wrote me a letter, dated 13 December 1936, ordering me, in the same way, to preach in English the cult of Śrī Caitanya Mahāprabhu as I had heard it from him.

After he passed away, I started the fortnightly magazine *Back to Godhead* sometime in 1944 and tried to spread the cult of Śrī Caitanya Mahāprabhu through this magazine. After I took *sannyāsa*, a well-wishing friend suggested that I write books instead of magazines. Magazines, he said, might be thrown away, but books remain perpetually. Then I attempted to write *Śrīmad-Bhāgavatam*. Before that, when I was a householder, I had written on *Śrīmad Bhagavad-gītā* and had completed about eleven hundred pages, but somehow or other the manuscript was stolen. In any case, when I had published *Śrīmad-Bhāgavatam*, First Canto, in three volumes in India, I thought of going to the U.S.A. By the mercy of His Divine Grace, I was able to come to New York on September 17, 1965. Since then, I have translated many books, including *Śrīmad-Bhāgavatam, Bhakti-rasāmṛta-sindhu, Teachings of Lord Caitanya* (a summary) and many others.

In the meantime, I was induced to translate *Śrī Caitanya-caritāmṛta* and publish it in an elaborate version. In his leisure time in later life, His Divine Grace Bhaktisiddhānta Sarasvatī Ṭhākura would simply read *Caitanya-caritāmṛta*. It was his favorite book. He used to say that there would be a time when foreigners would learn the Bengali language to read *Caitanya-caritāmṛta*. The work on this translation began about eighteen months ago. Now, by the grace of Śrī Caitanya Mahāprabhu and His Divine Grace Bhaktisiddhānta Sarasvatī Ṭhākura, it is finished. In this connection I have to thank my American disciples, especially Śrīman Pradyumna dāsa Adhikārī, Śrīman Nitāi dāsa Adhikārī, Śrīman Jayādvaita dāsa Brahmacārī and many other boys and girls who are sincerely helping me in writing, editing and publishing all these literatures.

I think that His Divine Grace Bhaktisiddhānta Sarasvatī Ṭhākura is always seeing my activities and guiding me within my heart by his words. As it is said in *Śrīmad-Bhāgavatam, tene brahma hṛdā ya ādi-kavaye*. Spiritual inspiration comes from within the heart, wherein the Supreme Personality of Godhead, in His Paramātmā feature, is always sitting with all His devotees and associates. It is to be admitted that whatever translation work I have done is through the inspiration of my spiritual master because personally I am most insignificant and incompetent to do this materially impossible work. I do not think myself a very learned scholar, but I have full faith in the service of my spiritual master, His Divine Grace Śrīla Bhaktisiddhānta Sarasvatī Ṭhākura. If there is any credit to my activities of translating, it is all due to His Divine Grace. Certainly if His Divine Grace were physically present at this time, it would have been a great occasion for jubilation, but even though he is not physically present, I am confident that he is very pleased by this work of translation. He was very fond of seeing many books published to spread the Kṛṣṇa consciousness movement. Therefore our society, the International Society for Krishna Consciousness, has formed to execute the order of Śrī Caitanya Mahāprabhu and His Divine Grace Śrīla Bhaktisiddhānta Sarasvatī Ṭhākura.

It is my wish that devotees of Lord Caitanya all over the world enjoy this translation, and I am glad to express my gratitude to the learned men in the Western countries who are so pleased with my work that they are ordering in advance all my books that will be published in the future. On this occasion, therefore, I request my disciples who are determined to help me in this work to continue their cooperation fully, so that philosophers, scholars, religionists and people in general all over the world will benefit by reading our transcendental literatures such as *Śrīmad-Bhāgavatam* and *Śrī Caitanya-caritāmṛta.*

Thus end the Bhaktivedanta purports to Śrī Caitanya-caritāmṛta, *dated November 10, 1974, at the Bhaktivedanta Book Trust, Hare Kṛṣṇa Land, Juhu, Bombay.*

References

The statements of *Śrī Caitanya-caritāmṛta* are all confirmed by standard Vedic authorities. The following authentic scriptures are quoted in this book on the pages listed. Numerals in bold type refer the reader to *Śrī Caitanya-caritāmṛta's* translations. Numerals in regular type are references to its purports.

Āditya Purāṇa, 273

Amṛta-pravāha-bhāṣya (Bhaktivinoda Ṭhākura), 1, 119, 179, 243

Bhakti-rasāmṛta-sindhu (Rūpa Gosvāmī), **232**

Caitanya-bhāgavata (Vṛndāvana dāsa Ṭhākura), 287

Caitanya-caritāmṛta (Kṛṣṇadāsa Kavirāja), 247, 248

Garuḍa Purāna, 18

Gaurāṅga-stava-kalpavṛkṣa (Raghunātha dāsa), **43-44, 216-217**

Govinda-līlāmṛta (Kṛṣṇadāsa Kavirāja), **58, 223-224**

Hari-bhakti-vilāsa (Sanātana Gosvāmī), 12

Lalita-mādhava (Rūpa Gosvāmī), 195

Mahābhārata, 15, 16, 48, 107

Manu-saṁhitā, 313

Mārkeṇḍeya Purāṇa, 273

Nṛsiṁha Purāṇa, **28-29**

Padma Purāṇa, 17, 18, 273

Skanda Purāṇa, 48

Śrīmad-Bhāgavatam, **13,** 17, **57,** 107, **130, 201, 233-237, 237-**240, **247-248,** 320

Tattva-sāgara, 18

Glossary

A

Ācārya—a spiritual master who teaches by his own example.

Acintya-bhedābheda-tattva—Lord Caitanya's "simultaneously one and different" doctrine, which establishes the inconceivable simultaneous existence of the Absolute Truth as both personal and impersonal.

Ārati—ceremony of worshiping the Lord by the offering of various auspicious articles such as incense, flowers, water, fans, ghee lamps, foodstuff, etc.

Ardha-bāhya—half-external consciousness.

Avaiṣṇava—a nondevotee.

Avatāra—(lit., one who descends) an incarnation of the Lord who descends from the spiritual sky to the material universe with a particular mission described in scriptures.

B

Bhagavān—(*bhaga*—opulence; *vān*—possessing) the possessor of all opulences, which are generally six—wealth, strength, fame, beauty, knowledge and renunciation; an epithet of the Supreme Person.

Brahman—(1) the infinitesimal spiritual soul; (2) the all-pervading impersonal aspect of Kṛṣṇa; (3) the Supreme Personality of Godhead; (4) the total material substance.

Brāhmaṇa—the intelligent class of men, according to the system of social and spiritual orders.

Bramajyoti—(*brahma*—spiritual; *jyoti*—light) the impersonal effulgence emanating from the body of Kṛṣṇa.

C

Cakravākī—the female counterpart of the *cakra* bird. When the male *cakra* bird and the female *cakravākī* bird are separated they make mournful sounds during the night.

Caṇḍālas—dog-eaters; the lowest class of human beings.

D

Dama—self-control.

Dāmodara—(*Dāma*—rope; *udara*—belly or waist) a name of Kṛṣṇa given to him when he was bound around the waist with a rope by mother Yaśodā.

Dharma—that which is the natural established order of things or that which is the natural established function of the living being.

G

Gauracandra—(*gaura*—golden; *candra*—moon) a name of Lord Caitanya Mahāprabhu denoting his appearance to be like that of a golden moon.

Gopīs—pure devotees of Kṛṣṇa who were related to Him as cowherd girl friends in the mood of conjugal love.
Govinda—the name of Kṛṣṇa which means "He who pleases the senses and the cows."

J

Jñānī—one who is engaged in the cultivation of knowledge (especially by philosophical speculation). Upon attaining perfection, a *jñānī* surrenders to Kṛṣṇa.

K

Khāḍi—cotton cloth.
Kṛṣṇa-kathā—narrations spoken by or about Kṛṣṇa.
Kṣatriya—the administrative or protective occupation according to the system of four social and spiritual orders.
Kuṅkuma—a sweetly-flavored reddish powder which is thrown on the bodies of worshipable persons.

M

Madana-mohana—the name of Kṛṣṇa which means "He who charms Cupid."
Mādhava—a name of Kṛṣṇa comparing him to the sweetness of springtime or the sweetness of honey.
Madhupati—name of Kṛṣṇa in Dvārakā.
Mahā-bhāgavata—a devotee in the highest stage of devotional life.
Mahā-mantra—the great chanting for deliverance: Hare Kṛṣṇa, Hare Kṛṣṇa, Kṛṣṇa Kṛṣṇa, Hare Hare/ Hare Rāma, Hare Rāma, Rāma Rāma, Hare Hare.
Mahā-prasāda—See: prasāda.
Mantra—(*manas*—mind; *tṝ*—to deliver) a pure sound vibration to deliver the mind from its material inclinations.
Māyā—(*mā*—not; *yā*—this) illusion; an energy of Kṛṣṇa's which deludes the living entity into forgetfulness of the Supreme Lord.
Mlecchas—class of men outside the four social and spiritual divisions of Vedic society whose standards of morality, religion, ways of living etc. are abominable.
Mukunda—the name of Kṛṣṇa which means "the giver of liberation."

N

Nārāyaṇa—the four-handed expansion of the Supreme Lord Kṛṣṇa.

P

Paṇḍita—a learned scholar.
Paramātmā—the Supersoul, the localized aspect of the Supreme Lord within the heart of all living entities.

Pika—the Indian cuckoo bird.

Prakṛti—material nature (lit., that which is predominated) There are two *prakṛtis—aparā-prakṛti,* the material nature, and *parā-prakṛti,* the spiritual nature (living entities)—which are both predominated over by the Supreme Lord.

Prasāda—(lit., mercy) food offered to Kṛṣṇa, which becomes spiritual when offered and which

Prasāda—(lit., mercy) food offered to Kṛṣṇa, which becomes spiritual when offered and which can purify the living entity.

S

Sac-cid-ānanda-vigraha—(*sat*—eternal existence; *cit*—knowledge; *ānanda*—bliss; *vigraha*—form) the eternal form of the Supreme Lord, which is full of bliss and knowledge; or, the eternal transcendental form of the living entity.

Śama—control of one's senses.

Saṅkīrtana-yajña—the sacrifice prescribed for the age of Kali; that is, congregational chanting of the name, fame and pastimes of the Supreme Lord.

Śāstra—revealed scripture.

Satya—truthfulness.

Siṁha-dvāra—the lion gate outside the Jagannātha temple in Purī.

Śrīvatsa—white hair on the chest of Lord Viṣṇu representing the goddess of fortune Lakṣmī.

Śuka—parrot.

Sukṛti—pious activities performed by the mercy of Kṛṣṇa.

U

Upādhyāya—a teacher who makes a living teaching Sanskrit grammar.

Uttamaśloka—the name of Kṛṣṇa which means "one who is praised by chosen words and verses."

V

Vaikuṇṭhas—(lit., without anxiety) the eternal planets of the spiritual sky.

Vaiṣṇava—a devotee of the Supreme Lord Viṣṇu, or Kṛṣṇa.

Vaiśya—the class of men involved in business and farming, according to the system of four social and spiritual orders.

Vāli—name of a monkey who was the son of Indra, the king of heaven, and elder brother of Sugrīva, the monkey king in the epic Rāmāyaṇa.

Vāṇī—the words of the spiritual master, which exist eternally.

Vapu—the physical presence of the spiritual master.

Vrajendra—Nanda Mahārāja, the foster father of Lord Kṛṣṇa.

Vṛndāvana—the site of Kṛṣṇa's transcendental village pastimes, exhibited when He was present on earth about five thousand years ago.

Vyāsa-pūjā—worship of the appearance day of the bona fide spiritual master, who represents Vyāsa, the compiler of Vedic literature.

Y

Yadupati—the name of Kṛṣṇa which means "King of the Yadu dynasty."

Yavanas—a class of untouchable men who are outside of the four spiritual and social divisions of Vedic society. A term usually referring to the Mohammedans.

Yoga-māyā—the internal potency of the Lord, which hides Him from nondevotees.

Bengali Pronunciation Guide

BENGALI DIACRITICAL EQUIVALENTS AND PRONUNCIATION

Vowels

অ a আ ā ই i ঈ ī উ u ঊ ū ঋ ṛ

ৠ ṝ এ e ঐ ai ও o ঔ au

ং ṁ *(anusvāra)* ঁ ṅ *(candra-bindu)* ঃ ḥ *(visarga)*

Consonants

Gutterals:	ক ka	খ kha	গ ga	ঘ gha	ঙ ṅa
Palatals:	চ ca	ছ cha	জ ja	ঝ jha	ঞ ña
Cerebrals:	ট ṭa	ঠ ṭha	ড ḍa	ঢ ḍha	ণ ṇa
Dentals:	ত ta	থ tha	দ da	ধ dha	ন na
Labials:	প pa	ফ pha	ব ba	ভ bha	ম ma
Semivowels:	য ya	র ra	ল la	ব va	
Sibilants:	শ śa	ষ ṣa	স sa	হ ha	

Vowel Symbols

The vowels are written as follows after a consonant:

া ā ি i ী ī ু u ূ ū ৃ ṛ ৄ ṝ ে e ৈ ai ো o ৌ au

For example: কা kā কি ki কী kī কু ku কূ kū কৃ kṛ

কৄ kṝ কে ke কৈ kai কো ko কৌ kau

The letter *a* is implied after a consonant with no vowel symbol.

The symbol *virāma* (्) indicates that there is no final vowel. क् k

The letters above should be pronounced as follows:

a –like the *o* in h*o*t; sometimes like the *o* in go; final *a* is usually silent.
ā –like the *a* in f*a*r.
i, ī –like the *ee* in m*ee*t.
u, ū –like the *u* in r*u*le.
ṛ –like the *ri* in *ri*m.
ṝ –like the *ree* in *ree*d.
e –like the *ai* in p*ai*n; rarely like *e* in b*e*t.
ai –like the *oi* in b*oi*l.
o –like the *o* in g*o*.
au –like the *ow* in *ow*l.
ṁ –*(anusvāra)* like the *ng* in so*ng*.
ḥ –*(visarga)* a final *h* sound like in Ah.
ṅ –*(candra-bindu)* a nasal *n* sound like in the French word *bon*.
k –like the *k* in *k*ite.
kh –like the *kh* in Ec*kh*art.
g –like the *g* in *g*ot.
gh –like the *gh* in bi*g-h*ouse.
ṅ –like the *n* in ba*n*k.
c –like the *ch* in *ch*alk.
ch –like the *chh* in mu*ch-h*aste.
j –like the *j* in *j*oy.
jh –like the *geh* in colle*ge-h*all.
ñ –like the *n* in bu*n*ch.
ṭ –like the *t* in *t*alk.
ṭh –like the *th* in ho*t-h*ouse.
ḍ –like the *d* in *d*awn.
ḍh –like the *dh* in goo*d-h*ouse.
ṇ –like the *n* in g*n*aw.
t–as in *t*alk but with the tongue against th the teeth.
th–as in ho*t-h*ouse but with the tongue agains the teeth.
d–as in *d*awn but with the tongue against the teeth.
dh–as in goo*d-h*ouse but with the tongue against the teeth.
n–as in *n*or but with the tongue against the teeth.
p –like the *p* in *p*ine.
ph –like the *ph* in *ph*ilosopher.
b –like the *b* in *b*ird.
bh –like the *bh* in ru*b-h*ard.
m –like the *m* in *m*other.
y –like the *j* in *j*aw. य
y –like the *y* in *y*ear. य़
r –like the *r* in *r*un.
l –like the *l* in *l*aw.
v –like the *b* in *b*ird or like the *w* in d*w*arf.
ś, ṣ –like the *sh* in *sh*op.
s –like the *s* in *s*un.
h–like the *h* in *h*ome.

This is a general guide to Bengali pronunciation. The Bengali transliterations in this book accurately show the original Bengali spelling of the text. One should note, however, that in Bengali, as in English, spelling is not always a true indication of how a word is pronounced. Tape recordings of His Divine Grace A. C. Bhaktivedanta Swami Prabhupāda chanting the original Bengali verses are available from the International Society for Krishna Consciousness, 3764 Watseka Ave., Los Angeles, California 90034.

Index of Bengali and Sanskrit Verses

This index constitutes a complete alphabetical listing of the first and third line of each four-line verse and both lines of each two-line verse in *Śrī Caitanya-caritāmṛta*. In the first column the transliteration is given, and in the second and third columns respectively the chapter-verse references and page number for each verse are to be found.

K

L

M

N

R

S

T

General Index

Numerals in bold type indicate references to *Śrī Caitanya-caritāmṛta's* verses. Numerals in regular type are references to its purports.

A

Abhijñāna-śakuntala-nāṭaka
quoted, **136**
A.C. Bhaktivedanta Swami
activities of, 320
meeting of Bhaktisiddhānta Sarasvatī and, 319
Activities
committing sinful on strength of chanting, 4
no limit to Caitanya's, **280**
of A.C. Bhaktivedanta Swami seen by Bhaktisiddhānta Sarasvatī, 320
of Caitanya as wild and insane, **192-193**
of Jagadānanda Paṇḍita pleased Caitanya, **181**
of Kṛṣṇa's flute, **69-70**
of Kṛṣṇa's lips as perplexing, **59-60**
of one in transcendental love, **231-232**
of pure devotee meant for Kṛṣṇa's happiness, 269
pure devotees have no motive for fruitive, **12**
Āditya Purāṇa
cited on chastity of *brāhmaṇa's* wife, 273
Advaita Ācārya
Caitanya's message to, **186**
Kṛṣṇadāsa Kavirāja writes by mercy of, **291-292**
Agitation
as ecstatic symptom of Caitanya, **243**
Āiṭoṭā
Caitanya wandered near temple of, **130**
Akrūra
Kṛṣṇa left Vṛndāvana with, 201
Amṛta-pravāha-bhāṣya
Eighteenth Chapter in summarized in, 119
Nineteenth Chapter summarized in, 179
Sixteenth Chapter summarized, 1
Amṛta-pravāha-bhāṣya
Twentieth Chapter summarized in, 243
Anantadeva
can't describe one day of Caitanya's ecstasies, **112-113**
unable to describe Caitanya's pastimes, **125, 279-280**
Anger
as ecstatic symptom of Caitanya, **245**
Kṛṣṇa satisfied when *gopī* displays, **270**
Anxiety
as ecstatic symptom of Caitanya, **103, 245**
of Caitanya in separation, **208-209**
Api bata madhu-puryām ārya-putro
verses quoted, 236-237
Art
Kṛṣṇa as reservoir of, **199-200**
Association
of Kṛṣṇa attained by chanting, **250**
vāṇī and *vapu* as two forms of, 319
Attachment
for chanting prevented by offenses, **251**
hearing about Kṛṣṇa frees one from material, 236
to household affairs as miserable, 236
Austerities
already performed by one who chants the holy name, **14**
nectar of Kṛṣṇa's lips obtained on strength of, **68-69**
performed by goddess of fortune, **102**
performed by Kṛṣṇa's flute, **71-72**

B

Back to Godhead
started by A.C. Bhaktivedanta Swami in 1944, 320
Balarāma
Kṛṣṇa left Vṛndāvana with, 201

Caitanya Mahāprabhu
as Supreme Lord, **26, 220, 316**
Caitanya-caritāmṛta offered to lotus feet of, **316-317**
felt like Rādhārāṇī, **265**
induced the whole world to chant the holy name, **35-36**
International Society for Krishna Consciousness formed to execute order of, 321
Kṛṣṇadāsa Kavirāja writes by mercy of, **291-292**
only most fortunate relish mad words of, **243**
three states of consciousness of, **152**
Caitanya-maṅgala
See: *Caitanya-bhāgavata*
Caṇḍāla
as devotee can deliver his family, **26**
Chanting
correct method of, **253-256**
ecstatic symptoms of, **261**
frees one from undesirable habits, **248**
of devotees roused Caitanya, **87**
offenses prevent attachment for, **251**
of 'Hari' while taking *prasāda,* **56**
of holy name by trees and immovable plants, **35-36**
power of, **14**
results and effects of, **248-250**
salvation attainable in Kali-yuga by, **246-247**
while gambling as offensive, 4
Charity
Rādhā gives Her body to Kṛṣṇa in, **274**
Conditioned soul
as eternal servant of Kṛṣṇa, **258-260**
Conjugal love
Kṛṣṇa's body as essence of, **198-199**
Kṛṣṇa can't give up, 236
Consciousness
three states of Caitanya's, **152**
Culture
Kṛṣṇa as reservoir of, **199-200**
Cupid
Govinda's glance awakens influence of, 238
Kṛṣṇa as enchanter of, **223-224**
Cupid
Rādhā thought of Kṛṣṇa as, **108-109**

D

Death
as inevitable in heavenly, middle and lower planets, 235
Deity
Caitanya-caritāmṛta written for satisfaction of, **316-317**
of Śrī Madana-gopāla worshiped by Jhaḍu Ṭhākura, 8
Demigods
can't estimate Caitanya's mercy, **38-39**
prasāda difficult to obtain for, **48, 65, 97, 131**
Determination
as ecstatic symptom of Caitanya, **103**
Devotees
advanced do not advertise themselves, 257
astonished at Caitanya, **191-192**
bumblebees at Kṛṣṇa's lotus feet, **317**
Caitanya maintained external consciousness in company of, **39**
chanted Hare Kṛṣṇa *mantra* loudly, **87**
don't care about their own happiness and distress, 269
drink nectar of Kṛṣṇa's lips, **72-73**
dust of feet of as powerful substance, **32**
entered Jagannātha-vallabha with Caitanya, **218**
entreated Caitanya to stay with Śaṅkara, **212-213**
instructed by Caitanya in tasting ecstatic love, **1-2**
Kṛṣṇadāsa Kavirāja writes by mercy of, **291-292**
obtained water that washed Caitanya's feet, **25**
seated in the heart along with Paramātmā, 320
should be recognized as *bhāgavatas,* 17
should serve Kṛṣṇa without personal motives, 273

H

Śeṣa-khaṇḍe caitanyera ananta vilāsa
verses quoted, 287
Śikṣāṣṭaka
anyone who recites or hears increases love for Kṛṣṇa, **277**
Caitanya as author of, 249
eighth verse of advertises pure love, **276**
eighth verse of quoted, **265-266**
fifth verse of quoted, **259**
first verse of quoted, **248-249**
fourth verse of quoted, **257-258**
second verse of quoted, **251**
sixth verse of quoted, 261
third verse of quoted, **253-254**
unhappiness and lamentation forgotten hearing second verse of, **250-251**
Simplicity
as brahminical quality, 16
Sītādevī
Ramacandra attached to, 235
Śiva
Gaṇeśa as son of, **125**
Śivānanda Sena
Purīdāsa as son of, **34**
Skanda Purāṇa
quoted on belief in *prasāda* by pious, 48
Spiritual master
representative of bona fide is Vyāsa, 285
faith of A.C. Bhaktivedanta Swami in service of his, 320
Śrīmad-Bhāgavatam
A.C. Bhaktivedanta Swami published First Canto of in India, 320
Caitanya overwhelmed by reading, **278-279**
cited on story of Piṅgalā, 107
quoted on chanting by incarnation of Kṛṣṇa, **247-248**
quoted on *gopīs'* chastisement of providence, **201**
quoted on insane speech of Rādhā, **233**-237
quoted on Kṛṣṇa's lips, **57**
quoted on Kṛṣṇa's water sports, **130**
Śrīmad-Bhāgavatam
quoted on qualifications of a devotee, **13**
quoted on songs of queens of Dvārakā, **237**-240
quoted on spiritual inspiration from the heart, 320
quoted on symptoms of castes in *śāstras,* 17
Svarūpa Dāmodara recited from, **91-92**
Sthito brāhmaṇa-dharmeṇa
verses quoted, 16
Submissiveness
as ecstatic symptom of Caitanya, **243**
Śūdra
characteristics of found in *brāhmaṇa,* 16
Śūdra-yonau hi jātasya
verses quoted, 16
Śūdra tu yad bhavel
verses quoted, 16
Śukadeva Gosvāmī
described Vidura, **213-214**
Supplication
as ecstatic symptom of Rādhā, **264**
Supreme Lord
Caitanya as, **220, 316**
expands Himself by holy names, **251**
explains who is His devotee, **12**
sits in the heart with all His devotees and associates, 320
Śūrpaṇakha
Rāmacandra cut off nose of, 235
Suṣyad-ghradāḥ karśitā bata
verses quoted, 239
Śva-pākam iva nekṣeta
verses quoted, 17
Svarūpa Dāmodara
acts as exorcist for fisherman, **145-146**
Caitanya tasted songs and verses with, **244-245**
explains intention of Purīdāsa, **36**
knew secret of Advaita's message, **189-190**
Kṛṣṇadāsa Kavirāja writes by mercy of, **291-292**
made Caitanya lie down, **207**
received *prasāda* of Lord Jagannātha, **52**

Visṛja śirasi pādaṁ vedmy ahaṁ
verses quoted, 235
Vraja
See: Vṛndāvana
Vrajendra-nandana
Kṛṣṇa known as, **71**
decorated Kṛṣṇa and *gopīs,* **167**
Caitanya's friends in like His own life, **216-217**
compared to garden of Jagannātha-vallabha, **218**
eyes of residents of like *cakora* birds, **195**
fruits availbale in, **168-169**
inhabitants of pursue sound of Kṛṣṇa's flute, **199**
Kṛṣṇa left, 201
women of like lilies, **196-197**
wonderful trees and creepers in, **167**
Vṛndāvana dāsa Ṭhākura
as favorite devotee of Nityānanda, **284-285**
Vyāsadeva
of Caitanya's pastimes is Vṛndāvana dāsa Ṭhākura, **284-285**
will describe Caitanya's pastimes in the future, **287**

W

Women
body of Kṛṣṇa remains fixed in minds of, **197-198**
complete annihilation of by Kṛṣṇa's jokes, **95-96**
easily available to Kṛṣṇa, 235
effects of Kṛṣṇa's flute on, **101-102**
effects on of scent of Kṛṣṇa's body, **223-229**
Kṛṣṇa has no fear of killing, **205**
Kṛṣṇa's lips disturb minds of, **60**
Kṛṣṇa responsible for killing of, **66-67**
of Mathurā got nectar of Kṛṣṇa's lips, 234
of Vṛndāvana like lilies, **196-197**
World, material
as void because of separation from Kṛṣṇa, **262**
Caitanya's verse advertises pure love in, **276**
nectar of Kṛṣṇa's lips diminishes lamentation in, **57**
Worship
in age of Kali chanting is process of, **247**
of lotus feet of readers by Kṛṣṇadāsa Kavirāja, **314-315**
of the Deity by Advaita, **190**

Y

Yad-anucarita-līlā-karṇa-piyuṣa-
verses quoted, 236
Yadu dynasty
Kṛṣṇa as king of, 235
Yadupati
as name of Kṛṣṇa, 235
Yamunā
Kṛṣṇa and *gopīs* enter, **130**
mistaken for sea by Caitanya, **131**
pastimes of Kṛṣṇa and *gopīs* in, **154-166**
water of was crystal clear, **159**
as universally purifying, **73**
Yasya yal lakṣaṇaṁ proktaṁ
quoted, 17
Yathā kāñcanatāṁ yati
verses quoted, 18

Z

Zeal
as ecstatic symptom of Rādhārāṇī, **264**

The Author

His Divine Grace A. C. Bhaktivedanta Swami Prabhupāda appeared in this world in 1896 in Calcutta, India. He first met his spiritual master, Śrīla Bhaktisiddhānta Sarasvatī Gosvāmī, in Calcutta in 1922. Bhaktisiddhānta Sarasvatī, a prominent devotional scholar and the founder of sixty-four Gauḍīya Maṭhas (Vedic Institutes), liked this educated young man and convinced him to dedicate his life to teaching Vedic knowledge. Śrīla Prabhupāda became his student, and eleven years later (1933) at Allahabad he became his formally initiated disciple.

At their first meeting, in 1922, Śrīla Bhaktisiddhānta Sarasvatī Ṭhākura requested Śrīla Prabhupāda to broadcast Vedic knowledge through the English language. In the years that followed, Śrīla Prabhupāda wrote a commentary on the *Bhagavad-gītā,* assisted the Gauḍīya Maṭha in its work and, in 1944, without assistance, started an English fortnightly magazine, edited it, typed the manuscripts and checked the galley proofs. He even distributed the individual copies freely and struggled to maintain the publication. Once begun, the magazine never stopped; it is now being continued by his disciples in the West.

Recognizing Śrīla Prabhupāda's philosophical learning and devotion, the Gauḍīya Vaiṣṇava Society honored him in 1947 with the title "Bhaktivedanta." In 1950, at the age of fifty-four, Śrīla Prabhupāda retired from married life, and four years later he adopted the *vānaprastha* (retired) order to devote more time to his studies and writing. Śrīla Prabhupāda traveled to the holy city of Vṛndāvana, where he lived in very humble circumstances in the historic medieval temple of Rādhā-Dāmodara. There he engaged for several years in deep study and writing. He accepted the renounced order of life (*sannyāsa*) in 1959. At Rādhā-Dāmodara, Śrīla Prabhupāda began work on his life's masterpiece: a multivolume translation and commentary on the eighteen thousand verse *Śrīmad-Bhāgavatam* (*Bhāgavata Purāṇa*). He also wrote *Easy Journey to Other Planets.*

After publishing three volumes of *Bhāgavatam,* Śrīla Prabhupāda came to the United States, in 1965, to fulfill the mission of his spiritual master. Since that time, His Divine Grace has written over forty volumes of authoritative translations, commentaries and summary studies of the philosophical and religious classics of India.

In 1965, when he first arrived by freighter in New York City, Śrīla Prabhupāda was practically penniless. It was after almost a year of great difficulty that he established the International Society for Krishna Consciousness in July of 1966. Under his careful guidance, the Society has grown within a decade to a worldwide confederation of almost one hundred *āśramas,* schools, temples, institutes and farm communities.

In 1968, Śrīla Prabhupāda created New Vṛndāvana, an experimental Vedic community in the hills of West Virginia. Inspired by the success of New Vṛndāvana, now a thriving farm community of more than one thousand acres, his students have since founded several similar communities in the United States and abroad.

In 1972, His Divine Grace introduced the Vedic system of primary and secondary education in the West by founding the *Gurukula* school in Dallas, Texas. The school began with 3 children in 1972, and by the beginning of 1975 the enrollment had grown to 150.

Śrīla Prabhupāda has also inspired the construction of a large international center at Śrīdhāma Māyāpur in West Bengal, India, which is also the site for a planned Institute of Vedic Studies. A similar project is the magnificent Kṛṣṇa-Balarāma Temple and International Guest House in Vṛndāvana, India. These are centers where Westerners can live to gain firsthand experience of Vedic culture.

Śrīla Prabhupāda's most significant contribution, however, is his books. Highly respected by the academic community for their authoritativeness, depth and clarity, they are used as standard textbooks in numerous college courses. His writings have been translated into eleven languages. The Bhaktivedanta Book Trust, established in 1972 exclusively to publish the works of His Divine Grace, has thus become the world's largest publisher of books in the field of Indian religion and philosophy. Its latest project is the publishing of Śrīla Prabhupāda's most recent work: a seventeen-volume translation and commentary—completed by Śrīla Prabhupāda in only eighteen months—on the Bengali religious classic *Śrī Caitanya-caritāmṛta.*

In the past ten years, in spite of his advanced age, Śrīla Prabhupāda has circled the globe twelve times on lecture tours that have taken him to six continents. In spite of such a vigorous schedule, Śrīla Prabhupāda continues to write prolifically. His writings constitute a veritable library of Vedic philosophy, religion, literature and culture.

DATE DUE

5-3-76			